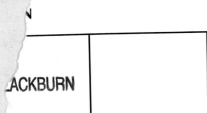

ACKBURN

'A u ... ws apart our patronizing attitude ... Victorian family' Jane Ridley, *Spectator*

'... ous and relevant' *Times Literary Supplement*

'... luminating stories culled from the detective courts, ad ... ces and institutes for the mentally impaired. A find' Judith Flanders, *Sunday Telegraph*

'An e ... illuminating book . . . [It is] in the fastidious detail that her book comes alive' *Observer*

'A "book ... rvels". What marks out *Family Secrets* as an important book is not so much its breadth as its depth . . . the result is a clear-sighted investigation into what our forebears felt was private, and what they kept secret' Kathryn Hughes, *Guardian*

'A well-researched, timely and absorbing book. [It] invites us to enquire more closely into how and when and why families keep secrets and guard their privacy' Hilary Mantel

'Riveting' *The Times*

'Fascinating reading' *Scotsman*

'An engrossing retelling of modern British social history from the inside out' Amanda Foreman

'A rich and rewarding study. Cohen reconstructs the lives she uncovers in the archives with empathy and imagination' *Literary Review*

'Everyone who reads this lucid book – a memorable sentence on every page – will understand their world more clearly' *History Today*

'An impressive piece of history' *Independent*

'In her landmark book, Deborah Cohen provides a history of shame, secrecy and privacy since Victorian times' *Your Family Tree*

ABOUT THE AUTHOR

Born into a family with its own fair share of secrets, Deborah Cohen was educated at Harvard and Berkeley. She teaches British history at Northwestern University, where she holds the Ritzma Professorship of the Humanities. Her last book was the award-winning *Household Gods*, a history of the British love-affair with the home.

Family Secrets

The Things We Tried to Hide

DEBORAH COHEN

PENGUIN BOOKS

PENGUIN BOOKS

Published by the Penguin Group
Penguin Books Ltd, 80 Strand, London WC2R 0RL, England
Penguin Group (USA) Inc., 375 Hudson Street, New York, New York 10014, USA
Penguin Group (Canada), 90 Eglinton Avenue East, Suite 700, Toronto, Ontario, Canada M4P 2Y3
(a division of Pearson Penguin Canada Inc.)
Penguin Ireland, 25 St Stephen's Green, Dublin 2, Ireland (a division of Penguin Books Ltd)
Penguin Group (Australia), 707 Collins Street, Melbourne, Victoria 3008, Australia
(a division of Pearson Australia Group Pty Ltd)
Penguin Books India Pvt Ltd, 11 Community Centre, Panchsheel Park, New Delhi – 110 017, India
Penguin Group (NZ), 67 Apollo Drive, Rosedale, Auckland 0632, New Zealand
(a division of Pearson New Zealand Ltd)
Penguin Books (South Africa) (Pty) Ltd, Block D, Rosebank Office Park,
181 Jan Smuts Avenue, Parktown North, Gauteng 2193, South Africa

Penguin Books Ltd, Registered Offices: 80 Strand, London WC2R 0RL, England

www.penguin.com

First published by Viking 2013
Published in Penguin Books 2014
001

Copyright © Deborah Cohen, 2013
All rights reserved

The moral right of the author has been asserted

Typeset by Palimpsest Book Production Limited, Falkirk, Stirlingshire
Printed in Great Britain by Clays Ltd, St Ives plc

ISBN: 978-0-141-04857-4

www.greenpenguin.co.uk

To Tom Silfen and Alice Kasdan

'Of my father, my mother, myself, I know in the end practically nothing.'

J. R. Ackerley, *My Father and Myself*

Contents

Illustrations

Photographic credits

1 National Trust for Scotland; 2 Edinburgh University Museums and Collections; 3 Newberry Library; 4, 6–9, 31 Northwestern University Library; 5, 21–2, 24–7, 35, 37 private collections; 10, 11, London Metropolitan Archives; 12–15, reproduced by kind permission of the Langdon Down Museum of Learning Disability, www.langdondownmuseum.org.uk; 16–20, 23 Croydon Local Studies Library and Archives Service; 28 from Rupert Croft-Cooke, *The Life for Me*; 29 Kroch Library, Rare and Manuscripts Collection, Cornell University; 30 from *The Isis*, 1956, by kind permission of the Editors; 32 Cardiff University Library: Special Collections and Archives; 33 Mirrorpix; 34 copyright © National Portrait Gallery, London; 36 John Haynes/Lebrecht Music and Arts; 38 from Margaret Wilkins, *A Family Affair*; 39 © Wall to Wall Media Limited

Introduction

Celia Ward was resourceful and she was desperate. Thirty-seven years old, the well-heeled wife of a director of English Steel, she wanted the baby that neither God nor nature had provided. To Ward's aid in the winter of 1920 came Miss Edith Hart, a capable spinster keenly attuned to the virtues of secrecy. Since the start of the war, Miss Hart had arranged the illicit adoptions of hundreds of illegitimate children. There were plenty of babies to be had, for illegitimacy rates had soared over the course of the war, and Britain's mother and baby homes were packed full of disappointed would-be war brides. 'I intend to do everything in my power to introduce the child as my own to everyone (except of course my husband),' Ward confided to Miss Hart. She would take the youngest female infant Miss Hart had available. She would proceed to a nursing home for a month in order to complete the ruse. None of her friends or neighbours would ever know what she had done. When her daughter was ten, Celia Ward reported to Miss Hart with pleasure that the girl was turning out 'splendidly', but reminded her co-conspirator of one fundamental condition. Miss Hart should never call again.

This is a book about what families attempted to hide in the past and why. It journeys from the secrets British men made on the frontier of empire in late eighteenth-century India to the confessional vanguard of modern genealogy more than two centuries later. Both a history of secrets and of how they were revealed, it tells of agonized discussions behind closed doors and traverses, too, the crowded, perfume-suffused chamber of the Divorce Court, where a family's most intimate disgrace was filleted for public view. It is a book about personal, apparently idiosyncratic decisions: taking a disabled son to a garden party, hiding an adopted daughter's origins, talking ceaselessly (or not at all) about a homosexual uncle. In delving into the familial dynamics of shame and guilt, it investigates the part that families, so often regarded as the agents of repression, have played in the transformation of social mores from the Victorian era to the present day.

Today the closely guarded skeleton in the closet can seem as quaint an item as the antimacassar. A substantial segment of the population is eager to share with strangers even the most humiliating of life's trials; the rest of us are more than willing to listen. That Americans, caricatured the world over as undiscriminating blabbermouths, display little deference to familial shame is perhaps not surprising. But what of the British, whose reputation for gentlemanly reticence once helped to define a national stereotype? From the House of Windsor, whose dirty linen has been aired so minutely that hardly a seam remains unscrutinized, to the ordinary house next door, skeletons have been mercilessly routed from Albion's cupboards. Confessional culture has become a fixture in a country where, it was once said, Englishmen when sober do not 'give themselves away'. It was in the UK that the so-called 'misery memoir' dominated the bestseller lists, racking up in 2006 eleven of the country's top-selling hundred paperback titles. To the British, too, belongs the feat of transforming genealogy from a leisure-time occupation of retirees into international prime-time television. *Who Do You Think You Are?*, which exposes the ancestral secrets of the nation's celebrities for a domestic viewing audience of five to seven million, is the thinking person's reality TV, with spin-off versions in twelve other countries, including the United States.

Shame has not been banished of course. But secrecy as a familial strategy for reckoning with disgrace or misfortune is now viewed as destructive, a malign practice that erodes trust, especially between family members. Its burdens are handed down through the generations in the form of mysterious silences and subjects best avoided. Family secrets interrupt truth, deforming identity. To restore to the family tree the bastard or the suicide pruned out by a judgemental ancestor is thus to know oneself better. And yet, for all of the attention that has been devoted to unmasking the family secrets of the past, we understand very little about the functions they once served.

To encounter Celia Ward and her husband in their elegant sitting room, laying the groundwork for the concealment of their newly arrived baby, is to enter a world whose emotional habits, though in many respects very different from our own, were neither as irrational nor as benighted as they are often portrayed.

This is a story in which basic premises are in constant motion. What counted as a dread secret in one era hardly raised eyebrows in another. 'Nothing changes more than the notion of what is shocking,' observed the writer Elizabeth Bowen in 1959, on the cusp of a decade that would vividly bear out her pronouncement. While much that was previously shameful (especially in the realm of sexuality) was normalized in the 1960s and 1970s, secrecy tends to run in circles rather than straight lines. In the mid twentieth century, families sought to hide away for a lifetime mentally disabled children whom their Victorian grandparents had cherished at home. Enlightenment generates as many family secrets as ignorance. Incest, the most shocking of modern secrets, was viewed by many middle-class Victorians as the deplorable but also unexceptional consequence of life in a one-room tenement. Similarly, domestic violence is today more secretive than it was in the late nineteenth century, when many, especially in working-class neighbourhoods, tended to view it as inevitable.

Running through this book are the entangled histories of secrecy and privacy. Privacy and secrecy share a common past, which has been obscured by the fact that privacy is today a hallowed right while secrets are perceived as damaging. And yet, the distinction between privacy and secrecy has not always been so bright. For Samuel Johnson, writing his famous *Dictionary* (1755), the two terms were nearly interchangeable. Privacy was the 'state of being secret; secrecy', while secrecy was 'privacy; state of being hidden'. While the ideal of privacy was well established by the late eighteenth century, protecting oneself and one's family from incursions was ever a struggle, all the more so as the tide of evangelical revival – and the pervasive moralism left in its wake – toppled the wall between private character and public conduct that the Georgians had sought to erect. 'In this country,' acknowledged the *Spectator* in the 1860s, 'privacy is almost

impossible.' Between a legal system that insisted upon transparency
and a burgeoning and relentless press, 'Somehow or other everything
gets divulged . . .'

For the Victorians, then, privacy meant keeping people out of
your business; the domestic fortress was privacy's stronghold, and
Dickens's Mr Wemmick, with his suburban cottage guarded by a
moat and drawbridge, its comic embodiment. Secrecy was privacy's
indispensable handmaiden, for the various sorts of shame that could
be visited upon families – an illegitimate birth, a son with a propen-
sity for 'unnatural crimes', suicide, insanity, adultery, bankruptcy
– were catastrophic, subject both to legal disability and to social scorn
if they were known. Not only were the stakes high, but the threat of
exposure lurked everywhere. The opportunities to gather information about the affairs of complete strangers proliferated in the
nineteenth century, whether on the crowded streets of anonymous
big cities (the lair of blackmailers) or in the pages of a ruthless penny
press. The fantasy of removing the roofs from other people's houses
and peeping in, as Sherlock Holmes said, 'at the queer things which
are going on', vied with the sense of being watched by countless pairs
of eyes. So often regarded as a Victorian birthright, privacy was in
fact a hard-won prize, achieved, as the radical campaigner G. J. Holyoake explained in 1868, only by 'necessary and justifiable secrecy'.

When William Makepeace Thackeray declared in *The History of
Pendennis* (1848–50) that 'Every house has its skeleton in it somewhere', he expressed a Victorian commonplace, as well as the
first-hand knowledge of a man haunted by two secrets of his own: a
half-Indian sister, born to his father's mistress in Bengal, and a wife
who had suffered a nervous collapse and had to be placed in confinement. Secrets were a strategy of defence and protection, a means of
guarding a black sheep as well as the family's reputation. What had to
be concealed was as integral a part of the family bond as the open
pleasures of hearth and home. The family was supposed to be transparent within – husbands and wives were not to harbour secrets from
each other, nor daughters from their mothers – and opaque from
without. As a bestselling Victorian conduct manual advised, 'There

are private histories belonging to every family, which, though they operate powerfully upon individual happiness, ought never to be named beyond the home-circle.' It was not only expected that the family would conceal its affairs from outsiders. As a testament to familial solidarity, secret-keeping was also praiseworthy. Well into the twentieth century, secrecy forged the bonds of trust.

How secrecy served as the unlikely bulwark of privacy and why secrecy and privacy have come apart are twin problems this book seeks to explain. From the vantage point of today's confessional culture, the family secret figures as the dead end, the obstacle in the path of progress towards the more enlightened and tolerant societies we have built. The grim-faced ancestors who excised evidence of an illegitimate birth or a 'feeble-minded' relation are cast as personally repressive but also helpless in the face of overwhelming societal dictates. 'That's the way things were then' is the shrugging refrain of genealogical chat-rooms, a portrait endorsed by the many histories in which families appear as reactive, even inert. In the stories we tell ourselves about the liberalization of social norms, whether the softening of the stigma of illegitimacy or the coming of gay rights, families are hardly granted a speaking part. Our explanations of why mores change focus instead upon public events: the formation of pressure-groups and social movements, protest marches and letter-writing campaigns, Parliamentary inquiries and new laws.

But what about the sea-changes that took place behind closed doors? After all, it was in families, equipped with the ambiguous prerogatives of intimacy, that most people confronted illicit behaviours and dread stigmas they had never before contemplated. Their responses cannot be plotted on a neat grid, and they varied dramatically over time. And yet, if families were not invariably accepting, neither were they as uniformly repressive as popular lore would suggest. At either extreme, and certainly in the grey areas in between, families helped to shape social mores. Family secrets could carry significant psychic costs, but they could also stretch the boundaries of acceptable conduct. In some cases, as in the history of adoption, family secrets helped to create the intellectual and social bedrock upon which new legal distinctions would be built.

This is a history, told from within families, of how society changed. So that the family could escape censure, behaviour that was condemned as wicked would be covered up. Necessity shaded into justification. The notion that your son's queerness was nobody's business – not the law's nor your next-door neighbour's – did not erase your shame about the wrongdoing. But it lent legitimacy to the effort to shield an errant relation (and the family as a whole) from nosey outsiders. In this way, family secrets accustomed those who took part to a moral relativism about behaviour. They set a cornerstone for the edifice of privacy constructed around human difference in the mid twentieth century. What started as a means of protecting a family's reputation would eventually help to pave the way for a much more capacious definition of privacy, defined as the right to live as you wish, at home of course but in public as well. Privacy had become intertwined with personal freedom. As privacy was written into law in Britain between the 1930s and the 1990s, secrecy was ever more vilified, chiefly because it was no longer necessary.

A history of secrecy may at first seem an implausible endeavour, for it is a 'self-evident proposition', the Oxford metaphysician Henry Mansel once noted, that 'a secret, so long as it is a secret, is a secret.' But family secrets were shared secrets, whether by a pair of relatives or a populous clan, and hence required the constant management of information, both inside and outside the family. Who should be told what, who could and could not be trusted, who deserved to know. Family secrets are sustained as much by talk as by silence, and hence have left traces that if at points stubbornly elusive are also instructive. Shot through the papers of many a genteel imperial family, for instance, was the frantic effort to conceal the parentage of children who appeared in Britain, motherless, off the East India ships. The files of a Christian adoption agency chronicle the carefully laid plans of upstanding couples to present bastards as their own babies, secrets that anxiously announced themselves in the adopters' pleas for guarantees of the strictest confidentiality. In an institution where so-called 'idiots' disappeared into a lifetime of non-existence, the need for secrecy, by contrast, was assumed: still, there was the firm of London solicitors engaged by the father of one inmate to ensure that his wife never again had to hear the child's name.

Research for this book depended upon exceptional access to confidential files. In the records of a defunct mother and baby home, carried up from the basement of the local council's Post-Adoption Counselling Service, I had the bird's eye view of the erstwhile Adoption Secretary, matching up unmarried women desperate to keep their pregnancies a secret with church-going would-be adopters who intended to make the child their own. In Edinburgh, staff had to cut the plastic bands strapped tightly around marriage-counselling files from the 1940s and 1950s before I could begin my research. At the London Metropolitan Archives, where I had unprecedented access to the Tavistock Clinic's case files, I sat at a separate table to ensure that no other reader could see the names on the folders. While the records of the Divorce Court, that engine of relentless disclosure, are open to anyone who wishes to see them, the other twentieth-century archives I have consulted are still closed; I was granted permission to read these records on the condition that I anonymize all individuals, changing names and identifying details. The situations that I explore will be familiar, but none of the specific cases will be recognizable, even to a family's intimates.

Although duchesses as well as dustmen appear in this book, it is mostly about those in between, the broad swathe of so-called 'respectable' Britons ranging from the comfortably situated upper middle class, sheltered behind their high garden walls, to the much larger number of tradesmen, schoolteachers and clerks whose security from the outside world was marked only by a lace curtain. The ability to hush up a scandal was a privilege distributed unequally. The Brighton greengrocers who could afford to install their unmarried daughter at a mother and baby home had a chance of concealing what had happened, unlike their maid, whose oversized housecoat could not hide her shame from the discerning eyes of the street. Crowded four and five to a room, in lodgings with paper-thin walls, the poor had, as one sympathetic Victorian reporter phrased it, 'no domestic secrets – no private affairs!' Barely shielded from the curiosity of their neighbours, they had in addition to contend with the prying investigations of 'friendly visitors' from church and charity who from the late nineteenth century fanned out across Britain's slums under the banner of moral reform. For the familial disgraces of their well-to-do friends, the friendly visitor might maintain some grudging respect, but the secrets of the poor were there to be discovered. Questions about the family budget became inquiries into how much its adult members drank; an inspection of a slatternly bed launched a probe into the sleeping arrangements of the household. When the slum-dweller proved uncooperative, it was often more fruitful, friendly visitors discovered, to ask the inevitably well-informed neighbours.

Keeping a secret, like keeping a servant, was one way, then, to define the middle class. It was not just a matter of ability but of inclination. Reticence, an attribute claimed by the Victorian middle class, had by the early twentieth century – contemporaries thought – spread more broadly through the ranks of aspiring working people. Talking in public about one's problems, by contrast, betrayed a certain lack of interest in social advancement, at least through the 1950s. His mother's downwardly mobile publican family, remembered the playwright John Osborne, seemed unconscious of the dictates of reserve that regulated her husband's middle-class, though impecunious, relatives. His mother's family 'talked about their troubles' (Osborne enclosed the phrase in quotes), a characteristic that until the defiant counter-cultural self-exposés of the succeeding decades marked them as the rough rather than the respectable.

There are an infinite number of stories to tell about families, for they are all famously unhappy (and perhaps also happy) in their own ways. Mine takes as its plot-line the interplay between families and changing social mores over the past two centuries; its chapters explore how the intimate knowledge accumulated within families did or did not translate beyond their confines. Writing about the families of the past is an enterprise that necessarily balances the universal and the particular, for the emotions that families call forth (love as well as hate, the warmth of protection and the struggle against dependence) are uncannily familiar even as the context in which people live out their family lives – whether considered from the standpoint of legal frameworks, social structures or the brute facts of demography – has often changed utterly. Because the specific dynamics of families stubbornly frustrate generalization, both the microscope and the wide-angle lens are required. The broad outlines of why family members responded as they did to a disabled child or a queer uncle are more easily compared than are the intricacies of their particular reactions, but without exploring the latter we have snuffed out the humanity of the subject. Detailed sketches of individual families serve in this book as the basis for comparisons across different sorts of social stigma.

This book proceeds in three parts. The first, framed by the duelling Victorian imperatives of secrecy and disclosure, charts the fragility of privacy in an era in which it was supposedly sacrosanct. I start with the secrets that followed British adventurers home from empire. As British men built the foundations of world hegemony in far-away places, they also acquired new mixed-race relations alongside their riches. Would these 'connexions' be stashed away, like Rochester's deranged Jamaican wife, Bertha, or discreetly integrated into the family line? Either way, imperial families became freighted with each other's secrets, a particularly vexing burden since what had to be hidden in Britain had been only too visible in India. From India the book heads, like many imperial couples themselves, to the Divorce Court. Beginning in the mid nineteenth century, middle-class Englishmen and Englishwomen could, essentially for the first time in history, get a divorce, but only at the price of exposing the tawdry details of a failed marriage before the public. Outfitted with its own corps of snoopers, the Divorce Court was both the most intrusive and, in its consequences, the most ironic of Victorian institutions. As the Victorians exalted familial privacy, they also set in motion the machinery that would help to lay it bare.

The central part of the book – a set of chapters about mental disability, adoption and homosexuality – considers how families came to terms with relatives who fell short of society's standards, and explores, too, what it meant to live as a family secret. As debates about nature versus nurture came to a boil between the late nineteenth century and the 1950s, what people felt guilty about and what they sought to conceal changed dramatically. Where shame for the Victorians largely accumulated around bad choices and moral failures, their descendants would confront new forms of disgrace. The science of heredity implicated the family, but so, too, did the dawn of psychological (especially Freudian) interpretations of human development. Increasingly suspect and prone to blame, the families of the mid twentieth century – smaller, homogeneous and keenly attuned to deviance – may have hid even more than the secretive Victorians they excoriated. There was, though, an important distinction between the stigmas families truly feared and those that they attributed chiefly to the prejudice of others. Some things mattered only if the neighbours knew about them. Easily mistaken for hypocrisy, this reaction just as often signalled the willingness of relatives to overlook an age-old bias accompanied by a fear that others would not; this is the switch-point between families and their social worlds. Buried in the countless familial exchanges about highly stigmatized subjects is a key to how new rights to privacy were carved from family secrets.

The final section of the book traces the rise of modern confessional culture from the 1930s through the 1970s. From the Divorce Court, which devised excruciating new ways of extracting the truth from its petitioners, to the tabloids which courted readers by plying them with each other's confessions, to the efflorescence of marriage counselling, that outpost of social work among the middle class, British reserve seemed newly threatened: 'in the name of pity', one woman exhorted her fellow tabloid readers in 1936, 'end this "confession" nonsense.' Until the late 1960s, the cherished privacy of the family would discourage public exposure; what confessions there were came cloaked in anonymity. It seemed that secrets, recognized as corrosive, could be purged from the private realm. But as the focus shifted from the fragile sanctity of the family to its repressive effects upon the individual, so, too, did the chorus of disclosures swell, incited by attacks on 'suffocating' familial privacy. To out family secrets became the first step on the road to liberation; transparency was a watchword for relationships. How openness could be reconciled with privacy and whether families could survive without their secrets became the legacies for our time.

PART I

Telling Secrets

1. The Nabob's Secrets

For more than three years, in letters that took eleven months to cross the globe, Robert Bruce and his brother John argued about a dead girl. Robert, a captain in the Bengal Artillery, was headstrong and heedless, John, a professor of logic at Edinburgh University, was painfully cautious. The girl was Robert Bruce's half-Indian daughter. She had a fair complexion and light brown hair; in her father's description, 'You never beheld a prettier or finer Child in your life.' Robert Bruce intended to send her to England to be educated. But by the early 1780s, when the first letter containing his brother's objections to the plan arrived, the girl was already dead, aged seven. The argument, now a matter of principle and injured fraternal feelings, continued. To John Bruce's agonized demurrals of guardianship – and his insistence on the impossibility of introducing such a child into genteel Edinburgh society – Robert tartly retorted that he never meant she should 'be unfortunate enough to go near Scotland'. Had death in battle not stared him in the face every day, he would not even have informed his brother about his child in the first place. And he had no intention of embarrassing the Bruce family with 'his little <u>black</u> connections'. If it had been necessary to his daughter's happiness 'to have kept her birth a secret, it should have even been done from herself'.

In all the indignant correspondence that passed between the brothers, Robert Bruce never once hinted that he had a second Eurasian daughter, born shortly after the death of his beloved first-born. Spurned once by his family, Bruce would not make the same mistake twice. Neither would he abandon his plans to bring his daughter home. In 1786, he boarded a ship for England, bringing with him a five-year-old girl whom he introduced as Margaret Stewart. To all who inquired, Bruce explained that she was the daughter of a friend who had no choice but to remain in India, a plausible tale since children, both white and Eurasian, were often assigned to the care of returning comrades. This was also what he told little Margaret Stewart. Robert Bruce intended to honour his angry vow to his brother John. He would not further embarrass the Bruce family with his black connections. Rather, he would keep the truth about Margaret's birth a secret, even from herself.

India in the late eighteenth century was a place where young men went to get rich. The nabob was a controversial new species of grandee who made his fortune in India and returned home to enjoy his treasure. The nabob's wealth was fabled. A ferret belonging to Robert Clive, the governor of Bengal, wore a diamond-encrusted collar. But if a nabob could catapult his family into rarefied social circles, a stint in the colonies left many relatives with a great deal to explain – or to hide. Empire was a hothouse for secrets of all kinds. India was famously the place where families banished their black sheep, hoping to keep their mischief far from home. But India loosened the morals of even otherwise reputable Britons, or so it seemed to scandalized contemporaries. There were over 20,000 British men in India at the turn of the nineteenth century, the vast majority of them unmarried. They left a rich human legacy: more than half of the children baptized in Calcutta's St John's Church in the late eighteenth century were illegitimate Eurasians. The nabob's treasure would come home. But what about the children of empire? Were they to be acknowledged or hidden away?

The trouble with keeping colonial secrets was that, in the colonies, they were hardly secrets at all. In India, wrote one mid-nineteenth-century observer, 'there are no secrets about anything, for every one knows his neighbour's affairs quite as well as he does himself – we all inhabit glass houses in that country'. The liaisons that the family back home wanted most desperately to keep in London's shadows were paraded in the bright sun in Cawnpore and Calcutta. Indian mistresses lived openly in the homes of British men and took their names. Their mixed-race children did the same. A man's friends knew about his intimate relationships – indeed, might visit him in the company of his *bibi* (or native companion), witness the baptisms of his Eurasian children, even act as their guardians. The mistresses often knew one another and formed their own well-connected networks. If not exactly legitimate, the nabob's household was familiar and unremarkable. In a colonial society that accepted their behaviour as ordinary, British men had no need for secrecy until they wanted to go home. Then a family secret that had never been secret became both hard to keep and hard to live with. Riches came from India, but so, too, did shame and guilt.

If Robert Bruce's first choice was to hide the shame of Margaret's birth, he was careful to provide a back-up plan. Before departing from India, Bruce entered into an arrangement intended to assure her a measure of financial security and, perhaps more importantly, a possibility of marriage. Bruce and a fellow artillery officer, William Denby, the father of a mixed-race son, entered into a tontine. A popular form of eighteenth-century investment, tontines combined elements of life insurance and the lottery. In this case, the tontine stipulated that, if the two children married, the proceeds would provide a substantial marriage settlement. If not, the children would come into their separate shares on their eighteenth birthdays. If either did not survive to collect, the other would take the entire sum. In 1786, the two fathers embarked for England with their incognito offspring in tow, Margaret Bruce travelling as Margaret Stewart and William Denby Jr as William Jackson. Their secrets were tenuous at best, but their tontine, as it turned out, was a safe bet: in 1804, it would pay out £2000, a small fortune.

Seventeen years before, when Robert Bruce went off to India, he had no fortune and little prospect of ever gaining one. The Bruces of Earlshall were an old Scottish family. But the early death of Robert's father had left his mother with only a small income, and three young children to support. Robert and his two siblings, Peggie and John, grew up in straitened circumstances. They were devoted to each other and to their self-sacrificing mother, but also resentful of those well-off relatives who ignored the family's plight. Robert's elder brother John, who was clever at school, won powerful patrons and eventually also an education at the University of Edinburgh. But Robert was not a promising scholar, so his grief-stricken mother placed the fifteen-year-old boy in the service of the East India Company as a lowly midshipman. As he prepared to depart for the colonies, Robert wrote her brave letters about how happy he was, pleading with her to 'now be easy as I have been so lucky'.

In India, Robert Bruce became, as he put it, 'somebody'. While still a young man, he led the Native Artillery in Colonel Goddard's expedition against the Maratha empire, marching across the Indian peninsula from Culpee to Surat. Warren Hastings, the corrupt Governor-General of Bengal, selected him to lead one of his corps. As a consequence of the emoluments that flowed to all in Hastings's service, Bruce grew rich, rich enough to provide his mother with a comfortable old age and his unmarried sister, Peggie, with a modest income of her own. He bought a new, three-storey town house in Edinburgh's stylish New Town for his family, and helped John, long at the mercy of Henry Dundas, Scotland's political manager and virtual overlord, to wrench himself free from some of Dundas's schemes. When he arrived in Britain after nearly two decades in India, Robert Bruce could look with satisfaction on all he had achieved: 'I have fought my way through the World to what I am, and to where I am, without the assistance of any friends but those of my own making.' All that he had he wished his 'Dearest & best of mothers' and his two siblings to have.

But as Robert Bruce established his family among the New Town's gentry, he kept secret from them the true identity of the little girl he brought home from India. Once in England, little Margaret was boarded out to school. On holidays, Bruce took her travelling to Harrogate and Leeds. As Robert reported to his sister, Margaret had an amiable disposition: 'She is not like other children for she never minds strangers. Is intimate with anybody in the course of an hour. And never cries or is troublesome.' For two years, Bruce maintained the deception. But by 1788, he had decided to return to India without

Margaret. In need of a home for his daughter and struck perhaps by the genuine fondness his mother and sister displayed for her, Bruce finally confessed the truth to his family. Aged seven, Margaret was installed in Robert's New Town house. To the world at large, she was still Margaret Stewart, daughter of Bruce's army friend; she called her father 'Captain Bruce'.

If all British houses, as William Thackeray observed, contained skeletons, imperial families such as his own had more than their fair share. That was not just because of the infamous 'connexions' that men acquired abroad. It was also a product of the intimacy that empire demanded of families. Success in India depended upon one's relations, even more so than in comparable business enterprises at home. At a time when money was difficult to transfer from India to Britain, it was family members who managed remittances. So far preferable were relatives considered in business dealings that an uncle who was a compulsive gambler could be viewed as a safer bet than a commercial agent. Single men in India beseeched family members at home to find them suitable brides, just as young men in Britain who hoped to make a career in the East India Company counted upon patronage from older relations who were already established there. Those who remained in the empire called upon relatives in Britain to raise their children; at such moments, the physical distance that allowed secrets to be kept also forced them out within the family circle. For families, the wealth amassed by a brother or cousin in India or the West Indies could be transformative; it could even lay the foundation for a dynasty. But precisely because of this entanglement, this familial closeness, everyone was also saddled with their relatives' secrets.

Although he had once sworn never to burden his family with his indiscretions, Robert Bruce now passed his subterfuge on to them completely. It was Robert's spinster sister and ailing mother who nursed Margaret through fevers and comforted her when well-born schoolmates refused to speak to her, regarding the parentless child as 'below their station'. They doted on their new charge so avidly that Robert Bruce, on a jaunt to Calais, ordered them not to spoil her.

Peggie, in return, objected to her brother John that Robert lacked the appropriate paternal feeling: 'he is rather more cool, than any parent ought to be to so fine a child as she is. He alone is to blame for the disadvantages of birth she labours under.' John Bruce, too, was soon devoted to his brother's child, despite his original objections. Peggie stoked John's affection for the little girl: 'my Mother thinks she resembles your constitution and smartness' and 'much does she chatter about you, what a fine creature you are'. His mother's love for her grandchild sealed John's attachment. Her deathbed injunction, 'be kind to her when I am gone', both John and Peggie took as a sacred command. John took Margaret's education in hand, selecting her tutors from the best masters in Edinburgh. The child, he told Robert, is more 'like our Mother than any of us'. 'I am as much attached to her, as if she were my own. I am sure I see her as such.' Peggie, ever hopeful that she could inculcate proper paternal sentiments in Robert, meanwhile assured him that Margaret was his 'very picture, and never was a child so like a parent in dispositions', while also pledging 'she never shall want a Mother while I can do this duty for her'.

However proud John and Peggie were of their niece's virtues, keeping the secret of her origins was a constant trial. When Margaret was ten, Peggie wrote to John in a panic: 'Margaret Stuart I am frightened is getting a black downiness on her lip.' She exhorted John to find a remedy for a hairy upper lip, 'but don't let Bob know'. Preserving the secret was vital for Robert's reputation as an eligible bachelor about Edinburgh. For John, who had spent nearly his entire life seeking to recapture his family's honour, anything that besmirched the lineage of the Bruces, of Earlshall, was anathema. Most importantly, Margaret's chances in society depended upon it. Whatever tolerance Edinburgh had once extended to Eurasians, prejudice in the late eighteenth century was on the rise. In the hyperbolic imaginings of the Scottish army officer Innes Munro it seemed that nearly one boy in ten at school in Britain was coloured, arrived from either the West or East Indies – an influx that Munro urged the government to ban, on the grounds that they 'may so sensibly degenerate the race, and give a sallow tinge to the complexion of Britons'. Writing to his son in India, one Scottish father in 1801 rehearsed what was increasingly the conventional wisdom. It was 'the duty of every man to provide for what <u>yellow</u> sons & daughters they might have in India'. However, children sired in India ought to stay there, 'as they always feel but awkward here'.

To his siblings' distress, however, Robert Bruce did not appear to recognize the quandary in which he had placed his family. In form, Robert kept up the fiction of his role as distant guardian, asking after Margaret's welfare when he was away and sending her the occasional present. However, among his Edinburgh coterie of India friends, who met for a curry and a night of drinking, the girl's story was out. As Robert prepared to return to India – fed up with the pretensions of Scottish society and apparently unable to secure a bride – he drunkenly taunted his sister. She might hear rumours around town that Robert had two native mistresses in India: one was Margaret's mother; the other her wet nurse. As Peggie wrote to John in outrage the next morning, 'think what a terrible thing it was to tell us, that our promising child was nursed by a strumpet, and to say I might hear of it hearafter without any explanation'. The worst of it was that the Bruces could not be sure who already knew the truth.

Wholly apart from the family's reputation, John and Peggie wished to shield Margaret Stuart's feelings. Her 'little heart', Peggie was certain, would break when 'she knows what she is'. But by the time Robert Bruce returned to India, in 1791, Margaret already suspected more than her aunt imagined. To her first dance, aged eleven, Margaret wanted to wear a brooch with Robert's portrait, a wish Peggie refused, she reported to John, 'as it will set people a talking'. John Bruce exhorted his brother to write to Margaret from India 'as she begins to be (I am afraid) very sensible of her situation, and feels strongly every attention that is paid to her by you'. Although Robert conducted himself with reserve in Britain, his letters from India were more benevolent. He instructed Margaret about manners, advised her to correct her temper, suggested that she be attentive to dress – and directed her never to trust anybody with her secrets. In Margaret's letters to 'my Dear Colonel', her eagerness to please was evident, as was her claim upon his affections: 'I have nothing but my little heart to send you, in return I hope you will not refuse to accept of it.' It would be her 'constant study', she wrote, to merit his friendship and protection. Reporting on her progress in writing and dance, she told him that she sought to imitate 'the virtuous example of our dear Mother'. In addition, she agreed with him that it would be 'perfectly improper' to tell anyone other than Peggie her secrets. This letter had just reached Robert Bruce when he died, aged forty-two, of an ulcerated liver, in 1796 near Patna. Margaret's letters were among the effects discovered in his bureau.

Robert's death presented Peggie and John with a new problem. His final will was murky about Margaret's share. In order to assure Margaret's inheritance, they would have to reveal that she was Robert's illegitimate daughter. Faced with the prospect of confessing their family's disgrace – and in the process depriving themselves of a larger share of Robert's fortune – Peggie and John did not hesitate. John Bruce quickly sought the best legal advice to bolster his niece's position. He was 'anxious', he wrote to the lawyer, 'to secure to her <u>absolutely</u> what was intended for her'. The archives of the Chancery Court indicate just how unusual the Bruce siblings were. The merchant Samuel Beachcroft sent his five half-caste children to England in the care of his two brothers, along with a clear bequest to each child of £5000. The Beachcroft children had to sue their uncles – and spend twenty years in Chancery Court – to get the inheritance that their father had obviously intended for them.

In Robert Bruce's family, by contrast, there came together every factor that could lead a man's siblings to embrace a half-caste child and protect her secret. Robert Bruce had neither legitimate children nor a British wife to alter the dynamic of the Bruces' original family unit. Margaret's position in the family had been cemented by her grandmother's love. Robert's death in India converted the parental roles John and Peggie had long assumed into a tribute to his memory.

Because their own childhood had been marked by loss and isolation, John and Peggie identified with Margaret's vulnerability. Their determination to secure her rights was a means of remedying the wrong they had suffered as children. It helped that their niece was a vivacious and quick-witted child, who proved a solace to the fretful spinster and her often despondent bachelor brother. And then there was the fact that she looked white.

Did Margaret actually pass for European in Edinburgh society? The pallor and black hair of a mixed-race child could be explained by a Portuguese mother or even Jewish intermarriage; Henry Dundas's Eurasian niece, christened Mary in Bombay, became Maria in Scotland, perhaps to cloak her parentage. But in the two portraits painted of Margaret – the first (ill. 1), when she was a young woman, by the renowned Henry Raeburn; the second (ill. 2), decades later, by Sir Francis Grant, portraitist to Queen Victoria – there is no trace of the 'dusky' pallor her contemporaries would have expected of a half-caste. In Raeburn's portrait, Margaret's complexion is fair with girlish pink cheeks. That could, of course, reflect the wishes of the sitter and her family, an imaginative whitening to match her surroundings. Still, the portraits are consistent with Robert Bruce's initial descriptions of his daughter and make sense of John and Peggie's elaborate efforts to guard the secret of Margaret's mixed parentage, which continued long after her illegitimacy had been officially disclosed.

John's campaign to conceal Margaret's past reached back to India, where her native mother was carefully scrubbed out of the record. At the time of Robert's death, Margaret's mother was living in Calcutta on a small pension he had paid her. However, Robert did not leave her anything in his will. On the advice of a cousin in India, John arranged to pay his brother's 'old Servant' an annuity of twenty-five rupees a month for the rest of her life. He also took care to ensure that no record of the transaction appeared in the files; employed since 1792 as Keeper of State Papers, the nation's chief archivist, John knew how to bury a secret. As John explained to his cousin, such secrecy was required in order to spare

Margaret's feelings. 'In a case of so much delicacy towards a young person, who, as you know, has been treated, not with all the delicacy you or myself could have expected, we must act, for her sake, in the way we are doing.' Margaret's mother would be untraceable, not just to outsiders, but to Margaret herself. In the thousands of letters and documents contained in the Bruce family papers, these fragments are the only evidence of her. She does not even have a name; John's cousin in India identified her only as Beebie Begum, the equivalent of 'Mrs Mrs'. When Margaret used the word 'mother' it was to refer to her grandmother or, later, to Peggie. Perhaps Margaret had been told that her mother was dead; either way, for the purposes of the record, and for Margaret's life, she had vanished.

Robert Bruce's siblings had done their best to cover his trail from India. But in a small society such as Edinburgh, where old India men were numerous, it was unrealistic to imagine that the truth could be hidden for ever, especially given Robert's own indiscretions. A letter sent in the 1820s suggests that, at least in some quarters of Edinburgh society, Margaret's mixed-race background was common knowledge. In a long, chatty dispatch to her son in India, Mrs Robert Low, wife of a retired army captain, reported about the doings in their Fife neighbourhood, where John Bruce had purchased the ruins of the royal palace of Falkland. Upon Margaret Bruce's marriageability, Mrs Low cast a gimlet eye: 'she is lively and agreeable, but is of colour and her age above forty'.

Margaret's dubious parentage perhaps helps to explain why neither Edinburgh nor Scotland furnished a husband for her. She ought to have had good marriage prospects. As a consequence of her father's legacy, she had nearly £20,000 of her own at the age of twenty-six, with the possibility of much more to come. In 1809, John Bruce had acquired the post of King's Stationer, which carried the lucrative monopoly over printing rights to the Bible in Scotland. Given John Bruce's obvious fondness for his niece, any suitor could have expected that Margaret would also inherit at least part of her uncle's estate, rumoured to be in the hundreds of thousands of pounds. But even in

London, where Margaret, then in her thirties, kept house for John Bruce, she appears to have been spurned socially. From Edinburgh, Peggie sought to console her: 'nothing but being unknown has prevented you from proper receptions'.

So it was that Onesiphorus Tyndall's courtship of Margaret struck most observers as a matter of money, not love. The Bristol lawyer was a decade younger than Margaret, tall and fine-looking with, as one of his friends put it, 'a most <u>provoking air of success</u>'. One of a brood of nine children, he had little family money of his own and expensive tastes. He outfitted his Lincoln's Inn chambers with porcelainware by Spode, travelled in luxurious style on the Continent, became the confidant of the Marquess of Bute, and, by the time he proposed to Margaret, was reportedly £50,000 in debt. Even Margaret seems to have had her doubts about his motivations, and John Bruce was opposed to the union, on the grounds that his niece ought to marry a businessman. Onesiphorus pursued her for six years, but on the eve of accepting him – a year after John Bruce's death had indeed made her one of Scotland's richest women – she backed away. When Margaret eventually agreed to the union, in 1828, it was on the condition of a pre-marital settlement that protected her property. Onesiphorus would also take the name of Bruce.

Despite the sceptics, the Tyndall-Bruces were a well-matched, loving pair. They had no children of their own, but spent their time touring Europe and building a magnificent new estate in the town of Falkland, where they played host to hordes of Tyndall nieces and nephews. In London, Margaret had lived in a secluded fashion – her pious aunt Peggie urged her not to act like a 'Methodest' – but with Onesiphorus at her side, she occupied her days choosing ebony armoires, marquetry cabinets and closets full of fashionable dresses, as well as dispensing charity. In the year that Sir Francis Grant painted her portrait, she regretted only that her uncle and aunt, who died in 1833, were not alive to witness her happiness. It would have been such a 'solace' to them, she wrote to Onesiphorus, had they 'allowed themselves to rest on the hope that a kind and affectionate protector would be raised, to comfort the only being in whom they were interested'. Margaret Bruce lived to the age of eighty-eight, surviving Onesiphorus by fourteen years. Her estate, valued at over £300,000, passed to her cousins, the Hamiltons, whom she obliged to assume the surname Tyndall-Bruce. The woman who came to Britain under an alias managed to impose her own hard-won name on two separate gentry families.

What of the tontine that Robert Bruce had created to secure Margaret's future and the mixed-race boy who was her co-beneficiary? Like Robert Bruce, William Denby sought to keep his son's true identity a secret 'even from himself'. Under the name William Jackson, the five-year-old boy was boarded in a Yorkshire school, where his brown skin – he had a 'dark complexion like that of a mixt blood' – could hardly have escaped attention. Denby told the truth to his own brother, but never revealed to young Jackson that he was anything more than a guardian. When the boy was seventeen, they quarrelled and Jackson ran off to sea as a lowly deckhand aboard a slaving ship. In desperate need, Jackson wrote to Denby's brother asking for help. He had learned, somehow, that Denby was his father and about the existence of the tontine. 'I am shocking barbarously & cruelly hurt in this world by those who call themselves my guardian friends both in my Rights & Propertys.' When he returned to Britain, Jackson intended to claim his property. In the meantime, he asked his uncle to 'write to a poor unfortunate Orphan (or rather a Cast off)', noting in a postscript, 'I am only a poor Cleanser of Decks on Board this ship.' The plea was too late. In 1801, aged twenty, William Jackson died in the Port Royal Hospital in Jamaica.

If Margaret's life was the stuff of fairy tales, William Jackson's was firmly pinned down by the social realities of the time. Without family support, there were few avenues open to an obviously dark-skinned boy in Georgian England. A loyal and well-connected family had secured a fortune for Margaret Bruce. But William Jackson was 'cast off'. His father even tried to keep the news of Jackson's death quiet so that he could collect his son's share of the tontine. That the story came out was due to the diligent efforts of John Bruce, already a wealthy man, but determined to obtain for Margaret everything that was rightfully hers. As a consequence of her uncle's efforts, another £2000 was added to Margaret's account in 1805. Not much, as it turned out, for Margaret Bruce, but a fortune and a future that William Jackson would never see.

Francis Fowke was the most accommodating of uncles. A retired East India Company servant, he had opened his modest house in the Cotswold hilltop town of Malmesbury to a host of nieces and nephews, legitimate and illegitimate, whose parents were still on the Subcontinent. He adopted as his own the bastard daughter of his oldest brother. He took charge of the white illegitimate sons that his nephews, Frank Fowke and Will Hollond, sent home from India. But when Will wrote to his Uncle Francis to request that he add to the brood two more boys – Will's Eurasian sons – there the old man drew the line. Citing the 'inconveniences attending such an Offspring', he refused to act as the boys' guardian. 'I would be glad to cherish them but am so circumstanced that I cannot.' Uncle Francis then proceeded to admonish his namesake Frank, the Resident in Benares, to steer clear of his cousin Will's example. 'On this subject I am sorry for Will but I am not angry with him.'

Will Hollond and his cousin Frank Fowke were the latest representatives of two families, much intermarried, who had plied the India trade since the early eighteenth century. East India Company servants, they dealt, on the side, in diamonds and later opium. The first two generations of Fowkes, related by marriage both to the phenomenally wealthy Clives and the quintessential imperial administrators, the Stracheys, made careers in India that were, by comparison, unspectacular. Francis Fowke – Uncle Francis to both Frank and Will – retired from a stint with the Company with a small sufficiency. Frank's father gambled away one fortune made in India and had to return to Benares, an old man, to try to accumulate another. The Hollonds, similarly, made enough in India to buy a handsome country house, but had to send out the next generation of sons, of whom Will was the youngest, to secure the family's fortunes. The aim, as Uncle Francis put it in a letter to his nephew Frank, was a 'comfortable independancy'. He closed with the exhortation: 'May you get rich, may you return soon, may you have an Offspring from a fair virtuous British wife – and be happy.'

But for Frank Fowke and Will Hollond, as for Robert Bruce and many other imperial men, Uncle Francis's prescription was not so easily followed. The prospect of finding a virtuous British wife in late-eighteenth-century India was dim: there were vastly more white men than women, and what white women there were – by lore, debauched milliners' apprentices, superannuated prostitutes – hardly made promising marriage material. In his letters home to his brother John, Robert Bruce explained his native liaison as more an Indian exigency than a true lapse of judgement. Youth had combined with opportunity and loneliness in a 'Country where such acts are not look'd on as Crimes by its inhabitants'. He had been on command with native troops in a remote part of the country without a 'soul whom I could make a companion of. Or converse with. A young beautifull Girl in that situation Jack was too great a temptation.' Similarly, the trader Samuel Beachcroft, writing to his brother in London, justified his relationship with a native woman – and the five resulting half-caste children – as a 'necessity' in order not to have sacrificed his health.

For most British men, liaisons with native women were passing fancies, affairs of convenience. In Britain, a young buck unable or unwilling to marry might patronize prostitutes, perhaps cultivate a mistress, where in India he readily took a *bibi* instead. Only in the exceptional case did romance, an ever more prominent consideration in late-eighteenth-century marriage, figure in a man's sentiments. When he departed for England in 1786, Frank Fowke unsentimentally transferred responsibility for his 'female friend' to a compatriot, who gladly accepted the charge, 'as I have so good an Opinnion of your last, that I do not doubt liking her'. While loyal concubinage over a number of years could earn an Indian woman a financial settlement, even a place in her consort's will, the euphemisms men used to describe these relationships attest to the embarrassment, even disgrace, they felt about them. Robert Bruce's nameless mistress was identified as his 'old servant'. Other men made provisions for their 'ancient housekeepers', their 'companions' or their 'girls'. Very few acknowledged affairs with native women in the absence of children to explain. Confessing to their relatives, otherwise blustery men wrote as penitents. His 'imprudent connection', Samuel Beachcroft assured his brother, was a 'subject that I am sure cannot give you more real pain than it has me'.

In the late eighteenth century, race was not yet the overweening, biologically determined category it would become fifty years later. In the minds of many observers, what distinguished India and Britain was as much climate and culture as it was skin colour. It seemed, for instance, entirely possible that British men exposed to the reputedly enervating Subcontinent would behave like Indians, their mores no less susceptible than their fair complexions – now turned 'Asiatic tawny' in Robert Bruce's description – to the influence of their new environment. The civilizational hierarchies that the Victorians would spend so much time adumbrating were still tentative. Will Hollond's comparison of the Indians to the French, both of whom did everything in such an 'awkward' way, but got on 'passably well', did not appear far-fetched.

Still, even before racial categories hardened, colour loomed large. Keeping a white mistress was one thing, a 'black' one something very different. For eighteen years, Will Hollond lived in the remote outpost of Dhaka. There he grew rich in the diamond and opium trades, and commanded the East India Company's Council of Revenue. But as he prepared to leave Dhaka for good, taking his two sons – but not their Indian mother – home with him, he pondered the consequences of his 'connexions'. The 'Girl's situation afflicts me exceedingly', Hollond confessed to his cousin Frank, so much so that he had even considered a subterfuge. 'I have many times determined to grant a request she has often made to me to go home with the children as their Aya.' The boys' mother would be passed off in England as their native nursemaid. The deception broached, Hollond quickly set the idea aside. His letter to Frank continued as if he were writing directly to his mistress: 'All that I can do for you is to do every thing in my power to make your life as tolerable to you as possible in this country and that I will do to the utmost point.'

For the vast majority of India men, as for Frank Fowke and Will Hollond, bringing home a black bride, or even a black concubine, was unthinkable. Arrangements that were customary in British India would be, they knew, ruinous in Britain. The only marriage that they contemplated was to a white woman, a subject that pre-occupied them even as they lived with their *bibi*s. Thus even tender-hearted Will Hollond, who acknowledged that he 'could not help dropping a tear' when he thought about the misery his mistress would suffer in losing her two boys, knew that she could not accompany him home even as a servant. He was, he reassured his cousin, 'sensible of the impropriety of it . . . poor girl it cannot be done'.

And yet, Will thought about his Eurasian children differently from how he did their native mother. That the boys were his chattels, severable at will from their mother's guardianship, was a matter of British law. The surprise is that so many British men did so. Bringing a Eurasian child home was almost exclusively the prerogative of those with means, as common soldiers had neither the funds to pay their passage nor official dispensation. Nonetheless, in the late eighteenth and early nineteenth centuries, half-caste children were a common enough sight upon homeward-bound ships from the East as well as the West Indies. While fathers may have sent home more readily children with lighter complexions (like Margaret Bruce), those with darker skin were not excluded. In 1799, Samuel Beachcroft dispatched his son and namesake to his brother with the warning that the boy's colour inclined to mahogany 'and his seat of honour is as black as cole'.

Some men had in mind that their offspring would return to India after a few years of schooling in Britain, bound either for service in the East India Company or a suitable marriage. But just as many fathers apparently saw Britain as their children's real home. Separating them permanently from their Indian mothers was a means of erasing mixed heritage. It was also a wager about their future. In India, there was already too much prejudice against the half-caste. Beginning in the 1780s, Eurasian orphans were barred from returning to Britain. The new Governor-General, Lord Cornwallis, enacted legislation to shut mixed-race people out of the higher reaches of Company civil and military service, leaving an increasingly large and impoverished Eurasian population – prevented by law from landholding and often also excluded from their mothers' families – dependent upon Company clerical posts or lesser jobs, such as fifers or drummers, reserved for them in the army. In Britain, or so many fathers hoped, their children's horizons would be brighter.

Aboard the ship *Barwell*, which set sail for England in January 1784, were Will Hollond and his two Eurasian sons, Henry and Charles. The Hollonds returned to England tremendously rich. Will settled his family in Mayfair. He sent Henry and Charles to Cheam, the public school that he had himself attended. At the Mayfair mansion, Hollond's two youngest boys were joined on school holidays by a party of India-born, white illegitimate sons – Hollond's own boy and his cousin Frank Fowke's as well – the ménage that Uncle Francis had previously superintended. Frank Fowke had followed his cousin Will home, just after Pitt's India Bill put an end to the corruption that had made nabobs' fortunes. Boys 'White and Brown', as Frank put it, accompanied the rich young bachelors as they restlessly jaunted from London to watering holes and racing towns across Britain. At Malmesbury, the two cousins visited Uncle Francis, who had become more jocular about Will's progeny. 'My love to the young brownies,' he wrote upon hearing that Henry and Charles were ill, 'the measles perhaps may blanch them a little.'

For a few years, Will and Frank thought of no subject more often than marriage. They became each other's confidants, exchanging long intimate letters about the virtues of this or that lady. Will Hollond was the more eligible of the two: he had brought more than

£100,000 home from India. In 1788, it seemed that he was finally hooked. The lady was a 'prize', in Frank's description, 'modest, handsome, well educated and well connected'. But she also apparently laid down certain conditions, chief among which was that he had to renounce his Eurasian sons. Hollond refused, his 'pride revolting at shutting my doors against two boys whom I have acknowledged & allowed to come home'. Under the circumstances, he wrote to Frank, marriage for him might well be impossible.

Despite the anxious pleas of their relations, neither Will Hollond nor Frank Fowke showed any sign of parlaying their Indian riches into a good marriage. Within a few years of his near-engagement, Will's family wrote him off as hopeless, 'a blundering lover' one female cousin called him. Frank followed in Will's footsteps. Even as the pair trawled London's marriage market for eligible brides, they acquired English mistresses. Frank took up with Mary Lowe, a London actress, for whom he rented a house in Mayfair. The pair went on to have fifteen illegitimate children together. Will Hollond's nineteen-year-old lover, Harriet Pope, made herself indispensable by mothering the houseful of boys he brought with him from India, to which the couple added eleven more children of their own. Uncle Francis's verdict on his two favourite nephews was clear-eyed: 'I see you are both doomed to concubinage.'

But the behaviour that had been relatively open in British India became the stuff of secrets at home. In India, even Frank Fowke's younger sister, Margaret, had been familiar with his illegitimate son. At home, however, Frank was forced to adapt his household patterns to suit a society characterized by an increasingly rigorous morality. He and Mary Lowe – and their huge crowd of bastard children – lived together in seclusion first in Wimbledon, then in a house he built in rural Wales. Twenty-four years into his relationship, his aunt Strachey apparently had no inkling of Fowke's large household. Frank's nephew met Mary Lowe only once, a chance encounter, after which his uncle hurried him out of the drawing room. The children of Frank Fowke and Mary Lowe grew to adulthood in complete ignorance of their illegitimacy.

For Will and Frank, scandal was the price of doing business, immensely profitable business at that. For Frank's much-adored little sister, Margaret, the notoriety that accompanied a family full of India men was far more burdensome. A beneficiary of the family's India money and connections – she married her brother's assistant in the Benares Residency – she wished, once she returned home to England, to travel in finer circles. But hardly had Margaret and her husband settled at home when a torrent of illegitimacy threatened to extinguish their social aspirations. First there was the humiliation of her father's British-born illegitimate daughter Sophy, who insisted upon identifying herself as Margaret's sister. Travelling in France in September 1789, Margaret and her husband chose to brave the chaos of the revolution rather than face the ignominy of Sophy's presence in London. Then there was the arrival home of Will's brother, her cousin Edward Hollond, in irons, arrested in Madras on charges of treason and corruption and transported home a prisoner. And then, of course, there were Frank and Will with their coterie of brown and white bastards and their stubborn refusals to marry. Margaret was the last of her family to give up hope that Frank would make an advantageous match. In India, the siblings had been devoted to each other, and Margaret cherished the thought that they would raise their children as companions. When she finally accepted that Frank's 'indulgence for irregular pleasures' was incorrigible, however, she distanced herself from him. Their correspondence trailed off, and she and her husband refused to receive Frank's children as their nieces and nephews.

In a handwritten memoir, Margaret's son, elevated to the peerage as the first Lord Ormathwaite, set out to explain the divergence in the fortunes of his mother and her brother. According to Ormathwaite, the Fowkes declined because of the bad habits that his uncle Frank – like 'W. Hollond, Sir Henry Strachey . . . & many others' – had contracted in empire. Those men who had indulged in concubinage in India had, Ormathwaite thought, become addicted to it. As a consequence, they sought the same sort of 'connexions' in England as they had enjoyed with native women in India. They had not understood that at home, however, unlike in India, illicit relationships were not so easily discarded or hushed up: 'The flaunting grasping kept mistress is a very different animal to the mild retired Hindoo girl.' Margaret had no choice but estrangement from her once beloved brother, in order to save her new family's reputation. She would keep his secrets as her own, but there was little she could or would do to keep his family from sinking into obscurity. During the two generations in which the Ormathwaites vaulted from minor gentry to a peerage, the Fowkes tumbled off the social ladder: two of Frank Fowke's grandchildren would live as servants on the estate he had built.

Empire was the shadow that haunted Ormathwaite's history of his family. For a generation raised on the instructive value of paradox, the moral of the Fowkes and other families like them was irresistible: India could wreck a man and his family even as it made them. Half-caste children, then, were only the most visible signs of a much more profound legacy. Ormathwaite's own manuscript memoir was private, intended only for the edification of his descendants. But in identifying India as a source both of immorality and of family secrets, he expressed a common Victorian sentiment. Those who published for a wider audience carefully pruned out the darker branches of their family trees. Alice Meadows Taylor apparently edited the memoir of her father, an army officer and novelist, to eliminate nearly all reference to her mother, the Eurasian daughter (by a Muslim lady) of the Eurasian banker William Palmer. Anna Leonowens, whose life-story furnished the plot line for *The King and I*, entirely fabricated her childhood in order to hide the fact that her mother, Mary Anne Glascott, was Eurasian; Leonowens was born not in Wales, as she claimed, but in Ahmadnagar, India. Only William Thackeray's intimates knew of his father's Eurasian family; until the mid twentieth century, his biographers delicately avoided the subject.

A taste for concubinage did not, of course, doom every nabob to downward mobility. Will Hollond's enormous wealth secured his family a place in the ruling elite for many generations to come. Yet it was not just money that protected the Hollonds. After a few years at home, Will, unlike his cousin Frank, began to make quiet concessions to decorum. He married Harriet Pope in a discreet ceremony, legitimizing his last three sons without exposing the lesser status of his earlier brood. Although he treated all of his boys equally for purposes of inheritance, Will nonetheless drew distinctions between them. Harriet's two oldest sons, both illegitimate, were sent away to India as young men: Francis as a servant of the Company and Richard as an army officer. Harriet's two younger sons, Edmund and Robert, both legitimate, proceeded to Cambridge to be educated as gentlemen. They would command vast country estates and live very much in the public eye: Edmund as a clergyman with eight livings; Robert as a lawyer, member of Parliament, socialite and famous early balloonist. Will Hollond did not so much prune his family tree as rearrange its branches. His manoeuvres paid off. By 1875, all of Will and Harriet's eleven children were ensconced in the pages of *Burke's Landed Gentry*, and this despite the fact that *Burke's*, as a rule, debarred illegitimate offspring. The family's entry, it is true, was oddly lacking in dates, either for the parents' marriage or their children's births. Unmoored in time, the Hollonds – at least the white ones – were firmly fixed in Britain's landed gentry.

Will Hollond's Eurasian sons did not make it into *Burke's*. Of the two boys who accompanied Will home from India in 1784, Henry left no trace, apparently dying very young. Charles was raised by Harriet Pope, very much a part of the family and beloved of his younger siblings. Like the white illegitimate boys, Charles was sent away as a young man, but not to India. Charles went west to America, entering the port of Philadelphia in 1798. Within a relatively few years, he reappeared as a successful merchant with a wife and family, an important benefactor of the Presbyterian Church, in the description of his pastor, 'an English gentleman of honorable descent'. Charles's brothers and cousins would remember him with significant gifts in their wills. The eldest, dying aboard ship on the way home from India, added a codicil to his will, leaving a bequest to Charles 'in remembrance of his kindness to me when a boy'.

When his Eurasian sons were boys, Will Hollond had decided to recognize them as his own, surrendering in the bargain his own chance at a respectable marriage. But whatever future Will may have imagined for young Charles when they sailed for home, his son would not make his life in England. Nor would he follow his illegitimate brothers into the imperial establishment. Charles was transported off stage, well bankrolled no doubt, but unlikely to bump into his relatives either at home in Hyde Park or abroad in the service of the Company. Even those fathers who proudly claimed their mixed-race children in India nevertheless found Britain more inhospitable than they had imagined, the lives they had once led abroad difficult to fathom and even more difficult to defend. Whatever ambivalence they felt about their Eurasian progeny was magnified. Long before new scientific ideas about race entered the picture, many fathers remorselessly distanced themselves from the children they had brought from India.

The principals of Colvin, Bazett & Co., a leading Calcutta mercantile house, were accustomed to pleading letters from the native companions and half-caste children their British clients had collected abroad. But the missive received in 1847 presented a problem of a different order. It came from Raheim Bibi, the long-time mistress of Peter Cochrane, one of Colvin's wealthiest clients. What the Indian lady wanted was a fair share of Cochrane's vast estate for herself and her daughter. That Raheim Bibi had lived openly with Cochrane for twenty-eight years was not in dispute. But the claim she made was far more explosive. According to Raheim Bibi, she was not just Cochrane's mistress, but his lawfully wedded wife.

As Raheim Bibi told the story, Peter Cochrane, an East India Company surgeon, had in 1790 donned native attire and taken a bride in a lavish wedding ceremony in the town of Farrukhabad. There were fireworks, music and days of feasting to celebrate the newlyweds. Raheim Bibi was fourteen years old. Cochrane was thirty-five. Though Raheim's father was dead, the girl's mother negotiated prudently. When Cochrane presented himself as a suitor, she insisted upon the Muslim marriage ceremony of *nikah* and a large dowry. She also demanded that the mullah who performed the original *nikah* repeat it, after Cochrane took her daughter to live eighty miles away, at the British camp in Cawnpore. At Farrukhabad, Cochrane signed the Muslim deed of marriage, the *kabin nama*, across the front; at Cawnpore, he signed it once again, on the back. On this marriage deed hinged a colossal inheritance. Cochrane's estate was worth more than £200,000.

That was the problem that Raheim Bibi, now seventy-one years old, presented in her 1847 letter to the Colvin firm. Her *kabin nama* no longer existed. The remaining scraps of the document she enclosed in her letter to show how 'Bengalee papers are attacked and eat up by insects'. In the absence of legal proof, she pleaded for justice: 'I can only say that I am the lawful widow of the late Dr Peter Cochrane am still alive and reside in the house built for me by the deceased . . . The living monument left by him in proof of his union with me as man and wife is my daughter Susan.' Raheim Bibi and her daughter had begun pressing their case in 1831, directly after Cochrane's death. It would take another thirty years for the House of Lords, in a long and strained decision, to reach a verdict as to whether Susan Cochrane was the legal heir to her father's fortune.

The eldest son of an old but impoverished Renfrewshire family, Peter Cochrane was twenty-five when he arrived at the British military station in Cawnpore in 1780. For a young man accustomed to habits of stringent economy, the sumptuous life that he could lead in India was a revelation. Every evening Peter dined in parties of '14 or 20 or more', had 'everything that my imagination places in the Catalogue of Comforts', and enjoyed, as he reported to his younger sister Joanna, marooned on the heavily mortgaged family estate of Clippens, 'luxuries without pain or trouble'. Joanna's pleas that he should return home and marry, Cochrane deflected: 'Can you procure me more in your Country or can you promise me so much?' 'Habits of much indulgence,' he admitted, had overtaken him in India. A man who had served the Company in Bengal was 'ill-calculated to subsist on porridge'. Once he had made enough money to live in Scotland as he could in India, he assured his sister, he would 'hasten home with all the ardour of a lover to his Mistress'.

Living in India reinforced Cochrane's sense of himself as a cosmopolitan, impatient with the prejudices and inhibitions he associated with Britain. To his sister he confessed – trusting her 'good sense' and 'experience with the world' – not just that he had fathered children in Cawnpore, but his very deep regret that they had not survived. 'My father was right in his conjecture I might have sent him home some black bairns but I cannot now god almighty having provided for them.' He embraced the illegitimate children his brother Hugh had sired in Scotland, and exhorted Joanna to 'despise' the 'very great prejudice' against illegitimates. For his own part, he promised to support Hugh's children, for they 'are not the less nearly allied to us in blood for being illegitimate'. And in 1808, he wrote to her about the birth of his own mixed-race daughter, Susan, now four months old. Ideally, of course, the Cochranes would have had legitimate children, for despite his own broad-mindedness Cochrane could not deny that the genuine article was better. In their absence, however, he would make the 'substitutes', as he called them, his heirs.

When Susan was less than a year old, Peter Cochrane wed a British woman. Cochrane's bride was the daughter of Colonel (later General) Fearon, and related through her sister to the prominent East India Company family the Ahmutys; she was thirty-four years younger than Peter and a very good match, which he secured through a munificent marriage settlement. He had married, he told his sister, to 'afford a chance of preserving the legitimate name of the family'. But he was also taken by lively, young Margaret Fearon, confiding to his journal, 'my heart had nothing left to wish for'. Margaret delighted her husband by producing two heirs, Peter and John, in quick succession. But Susan – whom Peter always acknowledged and treated as his daughter – was not forgotten. 'Pleasing' accounts of his little girl wove through Peter's letters home to Joanna. After the marriage, Joanna offered to take Susan to live with her in Scotland. Peter, ever gratified by his sister's 'liberality and sentiment' given the 'prejudice entertained against this class of children by many very worthy people in your Country', nonetheless declined her offer. 'We shall bring her home with us'.

Unembarrassed to admit his 'black' bairn, there was nonetheless much that Peter Cochrane withheld from his sister. His long letters never once mentioned Raheim Bibi, much less revealed that by 1808 he had been living with Susan's mother for eighteen years. Nor was there any reference to domestic arrangements that would have appalled even the most tolerant of sisters. After their wedding, Peter Cochrane brought Margaret Fearon back to the house in Cawnpore that he shared with Raheim Bibi, and there the trio lived together, with Susan. When Cochrane moved to Calcutta, where he had been appointed senior member of the East India Company's Medical Board, the two women accompanied him. In Calcutta, again, Peter Cochrane lived for more than a year in the same house with both Raheim Bibi and Margaret Fearon, in the fashionable white stucco and neo-classical neighbourhood of Chowringhee (ill. 3). When Peter and Margaret moved into a new house across the street, Cochrane renovated their original dwelling for Raheim Bibi. According to Susan, Cochrane visited Raheim Bibi daily, and Margaret Fearon and the couple's two young sons, John and Peter, too, paid frequent calls upon Susan and her mother.

The arrangement that Cochrane could not admit to his sister in Scotland was known to everyone in Cawnpore and Calcutta. Friends came to call on the Cochrane household, including Alexander Colvin, later senior partner in the Colvin firm and an intimate of Peter's. As Colvin would later attest, Peter Cochrane had always recognized Susan as his daughter, and treated her as such. Similarly, Raheim Bibi was known as 'Bebee Cochrane', the equivalent of Mrs Cochrane, or 'Madame Cochrane'. In Peter Cochrane's tightly knit Calcutta community, Raheim Bibi's friends were the mistresses of Cochrane's friends. As for friends and family back in Britain, Peter's reluctance to acknowledge

Raheim did not extend to his Eurasian daughter. Like the white children of wealthy India men, Susan was sent off to an expensive London boarding school at the age of six to be educated in the fashion of a proper British girl.

But as Cochrane himself prepared to return to Britain, his attitude towards Susan began a slow slide towards ambivalence. The will he drafted in 1818 provided generous bequests to both Susan and her mother: a *lakh* of rupees for Susan (the equivalent of £12,500) and, for Raheim Bibi, the use for life of her Calcutta house, along with a substantial monthly stipend. Further, Cochrane delegated to his wife Margaret Fearon the task of Susan's proper upbringing, including not only the finer arts of music and dance but a first-rate education in letters as well, so that 'grace and eloquence might accompany her fortune'. Yet at the same time, Cochrane sought to sanitize his mixed-race household. Raheim Bibi was identified as Cochrane's 'ancient housekeeper', practically a code word for concubine. And Susan was demoted from Cochrane's daughter to 'a child born at Cawnpore in the East Indies'. Mixing equal portions of dismissal and affection, Cochrane committed to his trustees the care of 'the little girl Susan Cochrane for whose safety welfare and protection I am no less anxious than for those of my sons Peter and John'. Paternal concern he could still admit; but paternity he sought to hide.

But if Cochrane had imagined a triumphal return to his ancestral homeland, what awaited the family in Scotland was decidedly inglorious. The fortune he made in India permitted him to rescue from his father's creditors the family estate of Clippens in Renfrewshire, and to build a new, larger house on the property. Almost as soon as the Cochranes settled at Clippens, however, they chafed at the restrictions upon their prerogatives. Peter argued bitterly with his neighbours about high taxes and toll-gates on roads. Meanwhile, Margaret Fearon began to dally openly with a handsome groom in her husband's employ. Unwilling to disguise her affair (any more than Peter had in Calcutta), Margaret was soon pursued through the Renfrewshire streets by young boys shouting insults.

The local gentry ceased calling on the family, who were left virtually ostracized. In the midst of this turmoil, Susan came home from school, completing the picture of colonial depravity. After less than five years back in Scotland, Peter and Margaret Cochrane had enough. They were not about to suffer the scorn of Scottish provincials. The family decamped in 1825: Susan back to India; Peter, Margaret and the boys to the Continent. None of them would ever spend another night at Clippens.

At first, Cochrane's redeployment of his family appeared a success. Susan, aged seventeen, was sent to Calcutta with a view to her 'settlement in life', taking with her Cochrane's explicit promise of £2000 as a marriage portion and the tantalizing hint of much more to come: 'nor will that be all: she is and shall be noticed in my will'. While the employment prospects of mixed-race men were more and more limited in British India, comely Eurasian women, especially those outfitted with sizeable dowries, could still find white husbands in the country. Within a year, Cochrane's bait had been taken; Susan married Henry Moorhouse, a lieutenant in His Majesty's 13th Regiment, and returned to live with him in Ireland. In the meantime, Peter and Margaret established themselves in all luxury in Paris, first on the Boulevard des Capucines and then at the Place Vendôme, decorating their apartments with the richest appointments, waited on by eight or nine servants and hosting lavish dinner parties. The Cochranes also took Margaret's groom with them. During the five years they lived in Paris, he was a constant visitor to the house, often accompanying Mrs Cochrane, and sometimes Peter as well, when they drove out of the city.

In Cawnpore and Calcutta, Peter Cochrane had lived as he wished, accustomed to neighbours who either did not care or averted their eyes. When he removed his household to Paris, he needed no secrets because his private life was private once again. But within a few years, the family he had precariously maintained self-destructed anyway. Half a world away in India, but still privy to reports from her network of India men and native mistresses, Raheim Bibi got the bad news before Susan. In 1830, she wrote to her daughter in 'extreme sorrow and grief' to report that Peter was much reduced and Margaret Fearon 'now controls his affairs and exercises much restraint over his person in his present helpless and unhappy situation'. Susan should look after her own interest, Raheim warned, as 'I apprehend Mrs Cochrane will not be disposed to part with any property to be appropriated to your benefit.' Raheim Bibi had the story right, but her warning was too late by a matter of months. In December 1829, Cochrane had amended his will. Gone was Susan's original bequest of a *lakh* of rupees. Gone, too, was the marriage settlement of £2000 her father had promised. The only notice Cochrane took of his daughter was back-handed. Her children, if any, would become Peter's residual legatees, inheriting if Cochrane's two sons both predeceased her and left no children of their own. When Cochrane died in 1831, Susan and her husband learned what would have seemed impossible a few years earlier. She took nothing from her father's massive estate, not even her dowry.

What had happened to alter Susan's fortunes so drastically? In India, Margaret Fearon had been forced to accept Susan and her mother, to share a name and a house with them, even to oversee Susan's education as a fine English lady. Now she could erase them both. When she returned to London after Cochrane's death, she sought to wrest herself free of the family's Indian encumbrances. Besides, Fearon had her own legacy to protect. The two sons for whom Peter Cochrane held out so much hope proved wastrels and drunkards, kicked out of one school after another. Young Peter, Cochrane's elder son and namesake, infuriated his father by marrying his aunt's lady's maid while still under age. Cochrane was on his way back to Scotland, reportedly to revise his will, perhaps to resurrect Susan as an heir, when he died, aged seventy-six.

Almost immediately the Cochrane estate was tied up in the Court of Chancery. The argument that Susan and Henry Moorhouse initially advanced was straightforward. Peter Cochrane could change his will, but the promises he made as part of Susan's marriage settlement could not be broken. Margaret Fearon and her sons, as Raheim Bibi had predicted, conceded nothing, refusing to share with Susan even a shilling of their massive inheritance. It took four years for the Chancery Court to decide that Susan was entitled to her £2000 dowry. It took another seventeen years for the Lord Justices of Appeal to rule that Cochrane's open-ended promise in his marriage settlement letter – 'nor will that be all; she is and shall be noticed in my will' – did not encompass the original *lakh* of rupees or anything else. So manifestly harsh was the verdict, given the magnitude of Cochrane's fortune, that Lord Cranworth offered from the bench an extraordinary confession of regret: 'with all his heart, he wished the Court could come to another conclusion than it was bound to do'.

Twenty-five years into the litigation, with little to show for her efforts, Susan changed course. She had always assumed that she was Cochrane's 'natural' daughter, a bastard. Cochrane himself certainly thought so. But that was because neither had recognized the legal implications of that long-ago ceremony when Peter Cochrane and Raheim Bibi celebrated their *nikah*. As Britain expanded its dominion over India, British law gradually became the governing standard for the entire continent. But, in 1790, the Kingdom of Oudh, where the marriage took place, was still a sovereign state; a wedding there, valid under Muslim law, was just as binding as a wedding in France or America. In 1857, the year that the Mutiny shook the foundations of British rule in India, Susan filed a new suit alleging that she was a legitimate heir, entitled to share in her father's estate. As a matter of law, her point was never seriously challenged. But everything now turned on proving that sixty-seven years earlier Peter Cochrane had taken Raheim Bibi as his legal wife.

When Raheim Bibi wrote to the Colvin firm in 1847, she did not believe there was any such proof. Her material evidence, the *kabin nama*, had fallen prey to Bengali ants. In a series of distressed letters, she advised her daughter that establishing the marriage was 'a very hopeless job'. 'When sixty years have elapsed since its occurrence, it is quite out of my power to produce any documentary evidence, or point out any one then present.' A year later, Raheim Bibi died, aged seventy-two, still resident in the home that Peter Cochrane built for her. Now on her own for the first time, Susan applied to the Chancery Court for an official fact-finding commission to India. But from the moment Susan hinged her claim to the estate on her father's marriage, the Court's sympathy ran dry. It wasn't just that she declared herself Cochrane's legal heir; it was also that there were no other heirs in sight to contest her claim. Margaret Fearon was dead and so were her two sons, having industriously drunk themselves to death. Susan stood to take everything. The Vice-Chancellor, Sir R. T. Kindersley, himself born in 1792 in Madras to an East India Company family, refused to take even the first step of authorizing an investigation: 'nothing but native testimony could be obtained – and even that was too stale a date'.

Rebuffed by the Court, Henry and Susan Moorhouse dispatched their own investigators. To their aid came an English lady named Mrs Meer Hassan Ali, author of several widely cited books on Indian culture, and her former husband, a Lucknow noble who taught at the East India Company's military academy. They were joined by Major (later Lieutenant General) William Crommelin, chief engineer of public works in Oudh. Like Mrs Hassan Ali and her husband, Crommelin had reason to believe Susan's story. His uncle had wed an Indian princess a few years earlier. Working around the turmoil of the Mutiny, Susan's team assembled a volume of written statements attesting to the 1790 *nikah*. Their prize exhibit was the affidavit of a 'very respectable' ninety-year-old Indian lady, 'body shaking with palsy', who had been a guest at the ceremony. A child at the time, she still remembered the *nikah*. It had been celebrated, as was customary, with lavish dinners and a fireworks display. Farrukhabad's *qazi*, the district's chief Muslim religious officer, had read the nuptials.

But native testimony was not going to win the case for Susan, probably not ever and certainly not in the wake of the Mutiny. She needed a European witness and believed that she had one. In her briefs to the Court, Susan confidently asserted that Alexander

Colvin would confirm everything. Colvin did, in fact, corroborate much of Susan's story. But with respect to the critical admission that Susan expected and needed, Colvin offered a devastating denial. He knew nothing about the *nikah*. Nor had he ever heard Cochrane refer to Raheim Bibi as his native wife. She was his mistress, nothing more. Colvin's rebuff was joined by the rest of the European community, a decisive failure of proof so far as Kindersley was concerned. 'Could it be believed that a ceremony taking place with such festivities should not have attracted general notice, particularly when Dr Cochrane was said to have appeared in native garb?' The old lady's recollections of fireworks and feasting Kindersley viewed as beneath contempt. The 'whole case', he concluded, was 'so contradictory and improbable' that there could be no point in continuing with it.

Deeming the case 'of very great interest and importance', the House of Lords heard the whole matter of Susan Cochrane's inheritance reargued for four days. But the outcome was the same. The fact that Susan had waited twenty-five years to make a case for her own legitimacy was, in the view of the English judges, an irredeemable blow to her credibility. The affidavits that Meer Hassan Ali and Major Crommelin had so painstakingly gathered were again disregarded. By the 1860s, Indian (and especially Hindu) marriage practices – described as barbarous and backward – served as a justification of British rule, making it seem all the more implausible that a British man had once participated in the native rite. Echoing Kindersley's judgment, Lord Chelmsford concluded that it was 'almost impossible for any rational mind to believe either that any marriage existed, or that, if such a marriage ever took place, any reliable evidence can possibly be procured which could substantiate satisfactorily the fact of such a marriage having taken place'. Lord Cranworth, who a decade earlier had regretted with all his heart ruling against Susan, now decreed that she should pay the costs of her failed appeal.

By asserting the legality of her parents' marriage, Susan had made her case about the legitimacy of an entire class of unions. If a half-caste child could appear without any official documents and carry off an inheritance – based solely on the evidence of a native mother and friends – every imperial man's legacy was in jeopardy. Anticipating this reaction, Susan's lawyer had attempted to assure the House of Lords that her case was exceptional. There was 'no doubt', he acknowledged, that East India Company men 'constantly formed connexions' with native women. But while the vast majority of such liaisons was 'generally void and of no effect', Susan's claim was different: Peter Cochrane had undergone a 'Mahommedan' marriage in an independent Mahommedan state. A narrow door, perhaps, but still too wide for either the European community in India or the House of Lords to countenance.

Still, it was not just the bias of British judges and colonials that doomed Susan's case: it was rather Peter Cochrane's shame. He had no reservation about announcing Susan's birth to his sister, he was at first proud to claim her. Native 'connexions' he could admit as well, as an abstraction. But as a real person, perhaps also a native wife, Raheim Bibi vanished from Cochrane's account of his life; had it not been for Susan's legal case, she would have largely disappeared from the historical record as well. Cochrane's 1818 will was worse than an omission; Cochrane expressly repudiated Raheim Bibi, dismissing her as his 'ancient housekeeper'. Here Susan ran afoul of her own argument. Raheim Bibi was supposed to be different, a native wife, yet on the written record that Cochrane created Raheim Bibi was nothing more than a mistress. So when Alexander Colvin described her in the same way, his testimony was virtually impossible to challenge. Raheim Bibi saw how the story would end when she wrote to the Colvin firm in 1847. All she had to offer to support her marriage to Peter Cochrane was their daughter Susan: 'the living monument left by him in proof of his union with me as man and wife'. That was not going to be enough.

Susan spent virtually all of her adult life pursuing a piece of her inheritance. She died in 1863, a year after the House of Lords dismissed her claim. The contest over her father's massive estate rolled on. With Peter Cochrane's sons both dead, Susan's offspring would finally have been next in line. But Susan died childless. The lady's maid that young Peter wed over his father's furious objections was also dead and also childless. She had married a second and then a third time. It was her third husband who led the opposition to Susan for over twenty years. He ended up taking a major share of Cochrane's estate, the rest going to an assortment of distant kinfolk, all unintended beneficiaries of one nabob's shame.

In India, British men made secrets, but didn't need to keep them – at least, not so long as they remained in India. Protected by a societal consensus that their behaviour, unimaginable back home, was ordinary in the colonies, their mixed-race households were unapologetically open to view. Once they returned to Britain, whatever privacy they enjoyed depended upon secrecy. For the families of returning India men, however, the problem was that half-caste children were secrets that could not be hidden. Because of the way British men lived in India, a man's relations could not know who was already privy to their disgrace. Nor could they count on a nabob to guard the truth. Fathers were proud and ashamed, evasive as well as open. In their wills and their letters, in the confidences they divulged over an Edinburgh curry, they left a trail of evidence. Their ambivalence grew in Britain, but, by bringing their children home, they had already committed the ultimate revelatory act. Their families were saddled with a secret over which they had no control.

From the 1820s and 1830s, the stream of half-caste children sent to Britain slowed to a trickle. Although early in the eighteenth century the East India Company had encouraged marriages between its officials and native women, by the time that Peter Cochrane made his will in 1818, Indian mistresses were frowned upon and intermarriage strictly prohibited. It became apparent, too, that Britain was even less welcoming than India to those of mixed race. The idea that Britain would succour Eurasian offspring had always been something of a fantasy, indulged by men who also recognized that the news of a half-caste bastard would hardly please their relatives. Long before the Victorians invented modern, scientific ideas of race, there was a nearly unbridgeable gulf between what British men did in India and what they were willing to acknowledge at home.

In mid-Victorian Britain, as racial mixture was ever more vilified, the kinds of relationships that India men had carried on in the late eighteenth century became shocking, their openness almost unfathomable. Even in British India, tales such as Cochrane's belonged to an exotic past. The presence of significant numbers of white women, together with Company disapproval and heightened missionary activity, combined to drive concubinage underground. By the 1830s, just one of every six British men's wills noticed a native companion, while the numbers of mixed-race children who were baptized had plummeted. At the same time, six times as many Eurasians were born in Madras, Bombay and Calcutta as 'pure' Europeans. In the Victorian empire, British men still had sex with native women and fathered Eurasian children, but now they sought to conceal these relationships entirely.

As native wives vanished from the historical record, Victorian novelists — with their unerring instinct for the culture's nerve ends — delved into the phenomenon of interracial liaisons. From the mid nineteenth century, a spate of novels spelled out the calamitous consequences of these earlier unions. They were tragic and hopeless, often acts of male selfishness, and auguries of familial disaster. There was, Victorian novelists assured their readers, a racial divide that could not be traversed. The half-caste Leonora of John Lang's two-shilling potboiler, *Will He Marry Her?*, published in 1858, the year after the Indian Mutiny, had translucent skin, 'white as marble'. Her fiancé, the instructively named Augustus Reckless, sought to conceal her parentage, but neither the secret nor their marriage was possible. Immediately after their wedding, Leonora dies of an apoplectic fit. Within a few hours, her skin begins to darken until, that evening, 'it was as black as the blackest night'. On her body was written the ineradicable truth of race.

The most foreboding fictional character of all, however, was the figure who in real life was expunged from the record: the native mother. In her 1847 'A Legend of Forfarshire', the Irish novelist Selina Bunbury summoned up for the readers of *Fraser's Magazine* the heart-rending moment when a native woman has to relinquish her children. Bunbury's was a scene of violence, straight out of an abolitionist's tale. The man no longer wants his Indian consort, but he insists upon keeping their children. Four men are required to contain her: 'the mother's heart was rent in twain, she raved, she implored, she execrated by turns'. Eventually all that is left to her is revenge. Retribution comes not just to the British man who has discarded her, but to his new white family as well. Her brothers order his murder, his baby son is killed, and his young wife broken.

The desolation of native mothers, if noticed at all by their British companions, was put firmly out of mind. Will Hollond's grief over the 'poor girl' whose children he took to England rated an entry in a letter to his cousin Frank, but he carried away her sons all the same. Near the end of his life, Peter Cochrane explained his decision to send Susan to England as inevitable, a matter outside his control: 'her mother Poor Soul did not like the separation, but we always do it'. Payments to an 'ancient housekeeper' helped to appease pangs of conscience where they made themselves felt. Once the native woman's children were in Britain, her obliteration was nearly complete; she was a shadowy memory even to her sons and daughters. Still, the tragedy of the Indian mother haunted some Victorians. She stood for all of the secrets men made in empire and all of the shadows that threatened imperial families from afar.

2. Revelation in the Divorce Court

Annie Cheese lived her short life in the shadow of the Divorce Court. The only child of a Herefordshire magistrate, Annie – tall, graceful, with a profusion of golden hair cascading down her back – was the envy of Rotten Row. Married at the age of nineteen, she was barely twenty-four when her husband sued for divorce. In the newspapers, for all the world to read, were the facts that Annie's heartbroken father could barely bring himself to acknowledge. While her husband, the dissolute Captain Thomas Lloyd, was imprisoned in a debtors' jail, Annie, the mother of a little boy and girl, had eloped to Paris with her lover, and there given birth to an illegitimate child. Worse still was to follow. When the newspapers found Annie Cheese again, two years after her family's dissection in the Divorce Court, she was an exile from polite society, living in Gloucester under an assumed name with another notorious veteran of the Divorce Court, whose own trial had laid bare his cruelty and drunkenness. Barred from remarrying by their failed divorces, the couple passed as Captain and Mrs Drummond, driving out in a pony basket carriage, for which Annie held the reins.

In 1853, the year that Annie married, divorce was virtually impossible, a prerogative reserved for the very rich. For 300 years, calls to legalize divorce had foundered. The vast majority of English households abominated the 'very name of divorce', explained *The Times*, because their own marriages were so content. When the Divorce Court was finally established in 1857, its mandate was to safeguard the sanctity of marriage. The Court would release from the marital bond an innocent yoked to a sinner, provided of course that the victim who brought the charges in fact had no blemishes of his or her own. If these few aberrant unions could be dissolved, the institution of marriage would be strengthened. Because the Court, like every other English tribunal, was to conduct its business openly, the disgrace of publicity would deter all but the most desperate. In the future, too, the threat of a full airing in the papers would have a salutary effect upon family life. Before taking a paramour or beating his wife, a man would think twice about the opprobrium he was courting. Public humiliation would be both the punishment and the cure for marital misconduct.

But by the end of the Divorce Court's second year, when Annie's case was heard, it was clear how disastrously misguided the original conception had been. Far from reducing the numbers of divorces, the Court was immediately besieged by petitioners. In its first two sessions, the Court granted more divorces than had been allowed in the entirety of the previous century. Moreover, publicity did not prove the bar originally intended. Over the course of 1858 and 1859, most of the Seven Deadly Sins made a daily appearance, replete with flamboyantly lurid details, in the British press. Not even the dirtiest French romances, Queen Victoria complained to her Lord Chancellor, were 'as bad as what is daily brought and laid upon the breakfast-table of every educated family in England'. There were, it turned out, many more unhappy marriages than anyone had imagined – and many more English husbands and wives willing to air their private misery in order to break the marriage bond.

In the uproar that followed the Divorce Court's first two tumultuous years, Annie Cheese's divorce case, *Lloyd v. Lloyd and Chichester*, marked a turning-point. It was the first instance of collusion detected by the Court. In cases of collusion, spouses could agree in advance to confect or sanitize charges and to eliminate counter-charges, finger-pointing and name-calling, thus short-circuiting the exposure that the law intended to inflict. One would play the role of innocent petitioner; the other would accept guilt without even showing up for trial. Such an arrangement struck at the heart of the Court's mission, raising the harrowing possibility that unhappy couples could divorce simply because they wanted to. Rather than a punitive exercise in fault-finding, divorce would become effectively consensual. Collusion was the family secret that made possible the end of the family.

What made collusion such an intractable challenge for the new court was that it was difficult, if not impossible, to discover. So long as the family kept its silence, who was to say which party was the malefactor and which the unbesmirched? Even apparently warring spouses would join in a lie in order to be free of each other. What the Court needed, it became clear, was the ability to reach into the bedroom and parlour, to take the roofs off private houses, to make use of all the watching eyes. Enter the Queen's Proctor, a public prosecutor whose sole charge was to ferret out the secrets that petitioners and their families sought to hide.

Given the Victorian investment in domestic privacy, the Divorce Court, bolstered by the prying Queen's Proctor, was a spectacularly invasive innovation. There had always been humiliating Chancery cases that dredged up illegitimate children and insane relatives. And the 'criminal conversation' suits that preceded the establishment of the Divorce Court exposed to view the hanky-panky among the well-born. Nosey parkers, too, were nothing new; India men such as Peter Cochrane and Robert Bruce felt all too keenly what Jane Austen termed 'a neighbourhood of voluntary spies'. But the Divorce Court went a fundamental step further. Now the conduct of marriage was an official public concern. After the Divorce Court's first few startling years, the number of petitions rose only slowly. But, like all social experiments, the Divorce Court risked a cascade of unintended consequences. Did the public outing of marital misconduct strengthen or undermine the institution of marriage? Did the threat of investigations into collusive behaviour dissuade unhappy spouses from entering the Court or did it just make them into savvier and more determined liars?

It was always apparent when the Divorce Court was in session. Outside the Gothic buildings of the Royal Courts of Justice was a throng clamouring for admittance. Loafers, so-called 'law students' and smartly attired ladies lined up two-deep to witness the proceedings. As soon as the doors opened, they crowded the passage-ways, swarming into boxes reserved for jurors and witnesses. It was the only court in Britain where wooden barriers were required to regulate spectators. The Court itself was small, nearly square, with poor acoustics that required judges continually to admonish emotional witnesses, 'Speak out!' Had the ceilings not been so high, though, the room would have been suffocating. The Divorce Court was drenched in perfume – white rose, heliotrope, patchouli; one judge famously complained of a headache brought on by warring scents. Unpolished panelled oak ran halfway up the walls, above which was a stretch of grey stone, punctuated by windows. Facing the witness stand suspended like a theatre box above the oak panelling was a cramped public gallery with seating for thirty-three members of the public (ill. 4). For those lucky enough to gain front-row seats, opera glasses allowed scrutiny of the witnesses' countenances.

What most struck observers was the presence of well-dressed ladies. Whether rubbing shoulders with plebeians outside in the crowd of spectators, cool and collected or flushed and trembling on the stand, and everywhere the perfumed cambric handkerchief, the novelty of women made itself felt. Before the Divorce Court opened its doors in 1858, only four women in the history of England had obtained a divorce. Divorce was a rich man's luxury, requiring an arduous tour through the Ecclesiastical Courts, an action in the court of common law to recover damages against a wife's lover, and, finally, an Act of Parliament that permitted a man to remarry. The new Matrimonial Causes Act of 1857 put divorce in the hands of the law courts, bringing it within the means of drapers and clerks – and, most revolutionarily, their wives. For the first time, women could petition for divorce, though they required more stringent grounds than men. Husbands could divorce adulterous wives; wives needed to prove adultery plus one of a number of grievous injuries: incest, bigamy, sodomy, extreme cruelty or desertion for longer than three years.

Though the Divorce Court ruled her life, Annie Cheese never entered it. Thomas Lloyd's case – as it first appeared – was open-and-shut, an administrative matter so straightforward that neither husband nor wife appeared in court the November day in 1859 that Lloyd's lawyer presented the divorce petition. Like the vast majority of cases that year, *Lloyd v. Lloyd and Chichester* was undefended. The facts were as simple as they were shameful. Three years after his marriage, Captain Lloyd had ended up in prison for his debts. While he was confined in the Queen's Bench, his young wife had formed an attachment with George August Hamilton Chichester, a friend of Lloyd's whom she met when visiting her husband in jail. When Lloyd was imprisoned a second and third time, Annie had eloped with Chichester to Paris. The evidence was all the more compelling, or so it must have seemed, because it came from Annie's own household: Mrs Morgan, a servant of Annie's father, appeared in court to testify that Annie was living with Chichester in France and that the couple had an illegitimate child. Her evidence was corroborated by Jane Earlam, Annie's own maid.

That evidence should have been the end of it. But just after Jane Earlam's testimony, something unprecedented happened. The presiding judge, Sir Cresswell Cresswell, demanded to question a gentleman in the audience, a Mr Isaacson, whom neither party had called to testify. Cresswell – tall and slender, supercilious in his manner – was the Divorce Court's first judge ordinary. A curmudgeonly bachelor sixty-five years old, he was, as the wags of the day noted, a curious choice to command the fate of Britain's five million married women. Cresswell had been disappointed early in love, an experience that left him, or so his critics believed, 'soured and cynical'. What he lacked in personal experience of marriage he made up for in industry. In the six years he presided over the Court, Cresswell decided more than 1000 cases, working at a superhuman pace in a term that stretched from November to August. As Cresswell laid down the foundations of Britain's family law, he just as vigorously rooted out the lies and deceptions that threatened the Court's credibility. The role of autocrat came easily. Cresswell commanded Isaacson to the stand.

Captain Lloyd's divorce case began to unravel as soon as Isaacson told his story. A friend of both Lloyd's and Chichester's, Isaacson had served the divorce papers on Annie in Paris. Though he was ostensibly an agent of Captain Lloyd, it soon transpired that Isaacson was actually bankrolled by Annie Cheese's father. James Cheese had opposed his daughter's marriage to Lloyd, had refused even to receive him after the couple was wed. Now he was working behind the scenes to broker an arrangement by which Lloyd would agree to a divorce. He not only provided family retainers as witnesses, but agreed, after heated negotiation, to pay his ne'er-do-well son-in-law several hundred pounds to file a divorce petition. But James Cheese's attempt to spare his daughter further disgrace backfired spectacularly when an errant letter found its way into the hands of the Court's clerk, tipping off Judge Cresswell to the plan. A chortling crowd of Divorce Court spectators heard how Isaacson had made merry with Mrs Lloyd and Chichester over the course of his three weeks in Paris: dining out in restaurants night after night, paying for Chichester's lodgings, even calling upon the couple when they were in bed. The bare outlines of Annie's behaviour were damning enough. She who should have conducted herself as a penitent, mourning the wreckage she had made of her life, was instead cavorting like a courtesan. Her father, who ought to have cast her off, was instead financing her depravity. The evidence of adultery was undeniable, but so, too, was the fact of collusion, which under the terms of the Divorce Act was an absolute bar to divorce. Captain Lloyd's petition was dismissed.

For the magistrate James Cheese, until this moment a man of standing, his daughter's shame would now be compounded by his own dishonour. Excoriated for his part in the 'conspiracy', he was assailed in the press: 'We cannot conceive a more utterly profligate and disgraceful case.' For critics of the Divorce Court, the lesson was obvious. The Court was a 'playground of perjurers', upon which Sir Cresswell Cresswell, despite his best intentions, was unable to impose order. Had not Cresswell, in his official Parliamentary report the year before, noted with satisfaction that the Divorce Court had seen no case of collusion? And yet, as Annie's case demonstrated, fraud and collusion were rife, a conclusion reinforced by the fact that over 80 per cent of divorce cases were undefended. Without an apparatus to conduct its own investigation into the most intimate realms of family life, the Court was at the mercy of its petitioners.

Before the Divorce Court started work, the notion of a government officer charged with the duty of prying into connubial affairs was almost unthinkable. In the original debates around the new marriage law, the idea was mooted, only to be summarily dismissed as an intolerable intrusion. But after two years' scrutiny in the harsh light of the Divorce Court, family life no longer appeared an inviolable bastion of harmony – or morality. The revelations of the Divorce Court stripped away easy notions of conjugal felicity, causing even romantics 'to doubt the reality of our eyesight'. Nothing was what it seemed. Did the solicitously tender husband of yesterday's dinner party commence to abuse his wife once they entered their carriage? Was the demure young wife a secret drunkard? In 1857, the year that the Divorce Court was written into law, *The Times* had proclaimed the vast majority of English marriages contented, even happy; by 1859, the paper's editors acknowledged the 'misery which was silently suffered under the old system'. An apparently jovial family party glimpsed through a window would never look the same again.

At stake was nothing less than the middle classes' vaunted reputation for virtue. From the late eighteenth century, Britain's middling orders had insisted that they, of all classes of the land, were uniquely moral; it was on this basis that they had laid claim to the vote in 1832. That aristocrats still fell prey to the old Regency vices of whoring and tippling was to be expected. No one could be surprised that illegitimacy, bigamy and cruelty were rampant among the lower classes. Entirely unanticipated, however, was the fatal blow that the Divorce Court so quickly dealt to the cherished self-conception of the middle classes. Two weeks after Annie Cheese's debauchery was paraded through the papers, *The Times* declared that Judge Cresswell was 'holding up a mirror to the age'. Reflected in Cresswell's looking-glass was 'a strange revelation of the secret doings of the middle classes in this country'.

What the 1859 cases revealed, in fact, was a staggering catalogue of vice, all the more shattering – and enthralling – because of the ordinariness of the lives involved. Mr Samuel Alexander, son of an Ipswich banker, had been married twenty years, when his wife, the mother of four children, committed adultery with a groom in his employ. The confectioner Mr Wilton's wife ran away with a sailor to Jersey. After seven years of marriage, the engraver Alfred Bacon was cuckolded by his own brother, whom his wife 'frequently' concealed in cupboards when he came home unexpectedly. Mr Allen, a military outfitter with premises in the Strand, sued his wife for adultery with a Captain D'Arcy, only to have it revealed in the course of the trial that he had conspired in his wife's ruin. Critical to what the jury denounced as a 'base conspiracy' was the fact that both 'Captain' and 'D'Arcy' were fictions, concocted by Mr Allen to turn a crony of his, the unromantically named Mr Milburn, into an irresistibly dashing hero. According to the *Morning Chronicle*, the demonic home-wrecker Asmodeus, prying the roofs off houses, was 'as nothing to Baron Cresswell in the Divorce Court'.

Small wonder that many Britons started the day by turning first to the 'spicy' pages of the newspaper. In the serious papers like *The Times*, reporting from the Divorce Court was discreetly located on the third or fourth page, but for those less decorous publications, such as the *Pall Mall Gazette*, it was front-page news. Here, in the nexus between the 'hideous' Divorce Court and press, fulminated Matthew Arnold, had the 'gross unregenerate British Philistine . . . stamped an image of himself'. Born at the same moment, the Divorce Court and the mass-circulation press were made for each other. The Divorce Court got the publicity to humiliate moral reprobates. The newspapers got the fodder they needed to power a gigantic leap into the mass market. The mid-century explosion of the newspaper industry – fuelled by the repeal of the stamp tax in 1855, together with the invention of cheaper printing – soon boosted British circulation figures to the highest in the world. The *Daily Telegraph* printed a staggering 141,700 copies in 1860, an increase of more than 500 per cent over its circulation just four years before. Scandal sold papers at the moment when there were more papers than ever before to sell.

Even the most sanguine of the Divorce Court's original advocates had to acknowledge that its effects had been almost precisely the opposite of what was intended. Lord Campbell, an architect of the original bill, confessed to his journal that he felt like Frankenstein, 'afraid of the monster I have called into existence'. The tide of filth in the papers, the ever-increasing backlog of cases, the unchecked opportunities for collusion: in the aftermath of the 1859 session, there were few who believed that the Court could continue as originally constituted. Two proposals occupied Parliament. The first was a measure to empower a new public official, the Queen's Proctor, to investigate cases of suspected collusion. The second was to close the Court whenever the claims of decency required it.

Creating an office of the Queen's Proctor proved uncontroversial. Collusion was no longer merely a theoretical menace; after Annie's case, it was real and had to be stamped out. Closing the Court, however, was another matter. The proposal debated in Parliament was modest: it gave the presiding judge the power to exclude the public and press from those trials either injurious to public morality or likely to cause great pain to the families involved. But the motion ignited a storm of protest. If the Divorce Court could be shut, what would become of the general principle that English justice was conducted openly? Those MPs who defended tradition opposed the measure, but so, too, did liberal champions of working men, who feared that the well-to-do would be shielded while the poor were exposed. Was it right, demanded the radical MP J. A. Roebuck, that the middle class 'should continue to appear as models of angelic purity when they were as earthly and immoral as any other class?' Against the critics of the Court who despaired of the corrupting influence of publicity were arrayed those who continued to believe in its deterrent power. Secrecy encouraged domestic vice; openness promoted virtue. In a Parliamentary vote, virtue triumphed handily. The Court remained open.

What the fate of the two proposals showed was that petitioners to the Divorce Court could not hope to escape the ordeal with their skeletons undisturbed. Even as Parliament refused to shield the most depraved revelations from public scrutiny, it also created in the

Queen's Proctor a mechanism for forcing out anything else that might still be hidden. From 1860 onwards, all divorce decrees would be provisional. The Queen's Proctor had three (later six) months to file a motion to intervene in cases of suspected collusion, forcing a second trial before the Court. Proving collusion required the assistance of people with information about the couple's private lives. It was originally envisioned that the Queen's Proctor would gather information by posting notices in the neighbourhood where the divorcing couple lived. However, between anonymous letters, nosey tradesmen, and the omnipresent solicitors, the Queen's Proctor soon found that there was enough work to do without advertising for additional leads. Relatives, the Queen's Proctor imagined, would be the best informants of all.

George Drummond, the young Viscount Forth, was a monster. No one who heard his wife's testimony – or read the reports splashed across the nation's papers – could have doubted it. From the moment Forth married the nineteen-year-old Harriett Capel in 1855, he terrorized her. He hit her when his coat was missing a button or the meat was cooked too long. When she was pregnant, Forth threatened to blind her. When the Forths' son was a year and a half old, he beat the little boy so badly that he was covered in bruises. Drunk most of the day, Forth depended upon Harriett's family for an income. However, that did not stop him from preying upon the rest of the Capels. He attacked Harriett's younger brother and tried to strangle her sister. The only member of the family who escaped his violence was Mrs Charlotte Capel, Harriett's formidable mother.

If the Capels had hoped to extricate themselves from Viscount Forth quietly, the events of one winter night in 1858 made it clear that Harriett had to go, whatever the publicity. At nine o'clock, the time that her daughter normally retired for the evening, Mrs Capel heard screams from an upstairs bedroom. There was Forth, maniacal, brandishing a pistol at his wife and her two siblings. Mrs Capel told the Court: 'I was the only person that dared go near him and I pushed it aside.' Harriett – half undressed, her hair hanging down her back

– ran to the house of a neighbouring magistrate for protection. Never again would she live with Forth. Two years after that evening, Lady Forth filed a divorce petition, charging her husband with extreme cruelty and adultery with 'various' women.

Drummond v. Drummond was the sort of trial that invariably drew a crowd. Both parties clung to the fringes of the aristocracy. Harriett was the niece of the Earl of Essex and a granddaughter of Viscount Maynard; her father, a dandy, was an intimate of the Count d'Orsay. She was a young lady of 'prepossessing' appearance, and her refined manner made a painful contrast to the testimony she offered about the barbarities of the Forths' domestic life (ill. 5). Forth was the first-born son of the Earl of Perth. His father, possessor of six Scottish and three French titles, had scarcely two shillings to rub together; he spent a lifetime trying to recover the family's hereditary estates lost as a consequence of their loyalty to the Jacobite cause. And Viscount Forth himself was already notorious. As a young man of twenty, he had carried the regimental colours at the Crimean battle of the Alma. An argument with his commanding officer at Sebastopol had caused Forth to resign his commission. Whether he was merely grossly insubordinate or, as the story circulated, had 'bolted' in fear from the trenches was never settled, but for three decades Forth became the favoured symbol of aristocratic cowardice in the radical press. He returned home from the Crimea to be flayed by the papers. Harriett Capel married him a few months later.

Even for readers accustomed to Divorce Court revelations, the morning papers on 18 April 1861 announced a startling development. The Queen's Proctor had made his first public appearance, intervening in the *Drummond* case. Lady Forth, the Proctor charged, was not an innocent victim, but herself an adulteress. Since leaving her husband, she had been living with a man named Edward Dering, indeed had travelled to the United States with him. The Proctor went still further. He alleged that Lady Forth, who purportedly sought relief from her husband's cruelty, was in fact acting in collusion with him. As in Annie Cheese's case, if the collusion charge were proven, Harriett would be barred from ever obtaining a divorce.

The power of the Queen's Proctor was immediately evident. To watch Harriett manoeuvre is like seeing a reckless mouse come for the first time upon a very determined cat. Early in April, the Queen's Proctor demanded that Lady Forth submit to examination in the Divorce Court. Twice his clerk called upon Harriett, who was living with her mother in Hampstead, to serve a subpoena. Twice Mrs Capel's servants had denied that she was there, and disavowed all knowledge of where she was to be found. In exasperation the Attorney General – the ruthless Sir Richard Bethell – went to the Divorce Court to get an order to force Harriett to show up. He also offered Harriett's lawyer a deal: if Harriett dropped the adultery charges and abandoned her divorce petition, the Court would grant her a judicial separation. She would not be able to marry again, but she would be free from Forth's tyranny.

Harriett's lawyer, Kenneth Macaulay, thought he could do better than a judicial separation. Widely reckoned a brilliant advocate, Macaulay, a member of the famously brainy society of Cambridge Apostles, was a star of the Midland Circuit. This was the first case to be tried under the new Act and Macaulay believed he had strong grounds to oust the Proctor entirely and to keep Harriett off the stand. Appearing for the Queen's Proctor was the eminent jurist Serjeant Pigott, alongside the Attorney General, a duo that attested to the government's stake in the success of this new endeavour. To open his case, Macaulay argued that the Queen's Proctor was empowered only to show collusion. Adultery – he claimed – was a private matter between husband and wife, not a concern of the public prosecutor. But Sir Cresswell Cresswell rebuffed Macaulay. According to Cresswell, the public had a legitimate interest in seeing adultery exposed, whether by the Proctor or by anyone with relevant information. Harriett Capel came to the Court a victim of gross brutality. Now she would be prosecuted for immorality.

Having lost his opening gambit, Macaulay reversed course. Lady Forth would withdraw her divorce petition, seeking only a separation on grounds of cruelty. It was not what Harriett had wanted, but it was the only alternative to prevent excruciating testimony about her own adultery from being spun out in the papers. Macaulay called his first witness, Mrs Capel, to tell the story of Forth's cruelty. Mrs Capel had barely been sworn when Serjeant Pigott rose to cross-examine. Macaulay objected again: the Proctor's mandate was to police divorce; he had no standing where the petitioner sought only a separation. Cresswell again brushed aside Macaulay's attempt to limit the Proctor's reach. The public interest in exposing collusion could not be foreclosed by so simple a ploy as switching pleas. Before the trial began, Harriett could have had this bargain from the Attorney General. Now it was too late. As Pigott began his interrogation, it became clear that Harriett's mother, whose assigned role had been to expose her daughter's tormentor, was unprepared for the very different part she would play. All that the family had sought to conceal would be on display. 'What am I to be examined on now?' asked Mrs Capel.

Charlotte Capel was agitated, at points tearful. In an upstairs bedroom two years earlier, she had pushed aside a madman's gun to save her children. Now the noose was tightening and strong nerves could save no one. Pigott was painstaking and courteous, a perfect choice to cross-examine a lady. Yes, she had accompanied her daughter to secure lodgings in Grosvenor Square, but no, she did not remember whom Harriett had said they were for. 'I have a very bad memory and will not answer what I do not remember.' A gentleman 'occasionally' visited Harriett there, breakfasted with her at one o'clock and stayed in the evening past nine. Asked his name, Mrs Capel at first declined to answer. Cresswell commanded her reply. 'Must I? It was Mr Dering.' Pigott sharpened his inquiries, confirming what the Queen's Proctor had alleged. Harriett had accompanied Mr Dering to America the previous spring, a year after she separated from Forth. She had gone, so Mrs Capel claimed, without her mother's knowledge. Upon her return Harriett had lived with Dering at various addresses in London. Now she resided at home. But yes, Dering came to visit her there too, in her mother's own house.

Harriett's adultery was exposed, but Macaulay still had one ploy left. Because Harriett would have to take the stand, his third argument was his least favourite, but it was by far his strongest. In several hours of gruelling testimony, Harriett catalogued the horror of her marriage. When she was finished, Macaulay offered his final plea. Only collusion, he insisted, was an automatic bar to divorce. But the Attorney General had failed completely to show collusion. True, Harriett had committed adultery. But Parliament expressly gave judges the power to grant a divorce even where both spouses had sinned – even in cases of mutual misconduct. If ever a case warranted the exercise of that discretion, it was this one. Indeed, Forth's conduct was so odious that it was inconceivable that Cresswell would not free Harriett from a life of misery.

The Attorney General's reaction was thunderous: there was collusion here, he just couldn't prove it. Had the evidence been available he would have had 'this lady' up on criminal charges at the Old Bailey. In the interests of public morality, Harriett Capel, an admitted adulteress, had to be denied the Court's protection. Cresswell announced that he would take some time to consider, given that this was the first case under the new Act. A week later, he issued a decision that would haunt the Divorce Court well into the twentieth century: 'I think a wife guilty of adultery cannot be a petitioner in this Court on the ground of any matrimonial offence of the husband, and I dismiss the petition.'

What so outraged the Attorney General was the obviousness of an unlawful arrangement that he could not show in court. Surely Forth knew of Harriett's adultery, yet filed no counter-charges. In the parlance of the Divorce Act, he failed to 'recriminate'. Harriett, of course, knew that Forth would not defend the case. As Cresswell saw it, if this was not collusion in the strict legal sense, it amounted to the same thing. For doubling the immorality – and keeping their secret from the Court – the couple would be rewarded with a free pass out of marriage. Cresswell's ruling supplied a simple solution. Where the Queen's Proctor exposed a petitioner's adultery, divorce would be barred. Though his order was couched in terms of a guilty wife, in practice the precedent applied equally to men. The discretion that Parliament had expressly granted to permit divorce in cases of mutual misconduct would not be exercised. All Macaulay's manoeuvres had come to this: the most miserable of marriage bonds, where both parties had found other lovers, would henceforth be unbreakable.

Where, as what little remained of his reputation was razed in the Divorce Court, was Viscount Forth? In her original complaint, Harriet had alleged that her husband had been unfaithful with a number of women after he left her in the winter of 1858. But though much was heard about Forth, nothing was heard from him. Without Charlotte Capel to pay his bills, Forth had narrowly escaped imprisonment for bankruptcy in 1860. As Harriett's divorce suit played out through the spring of 1861, Forth was on the run. By July, he had retreated to Gloucester, a once-fashionable spa town that was, by mid-century, full of louche characters and invalids, where he went under the name of Captain Drummond. In the Spa Hotel, a large but dingy Regency-era establishment, Forth lived with the woman whose own divorce trial had helped to summon the Queen's Proctor into existence: Annie Cheese.

Even on the run, the young Viscount and his paramour were the sort of people who could not help but to attract attention to themselves. He was tall and handsome, a distinguished-looking man; Annie Cheese was a celebrated beauty, who in defiance of the conventions of the day wore her wavy, blonde hair loose like a girl's. Though they rode out every day in the pony carriage, Annie at the reins, Captain and Mrs Drummond apparently had no acquaintances in Gloucester. They visited nowhere nor were they visited by anybody; 'an air of mystery hung over their movements'. They were, however, entirely devoted to each other. In Forth's behaviour to Annie Cheese there was no sign of the viciousness that had wrecked his marriage to Harriett Capel. To Annie he was solicitous and tender. He still drank large quantities of spirits every day, but so, too, apparently did she. In the summer of 1861, she was nearly seven months pregnant with his child.

Annie delivered a daughter in mid-September, but almost immediately afterwards fell gravely ill. For three weeks, Forth tended her day and night; because she called out for him constantly, he refused to leave her side. Never in his life, commented Annie Cheese's doctor, had he ever seen 'so much attention lavished upon a lady by a gentleman'. When Annie finally died, early on the morning of 8 October, Forth seemed almost out of his mind. Annie's doctor prevented him from cutting his throat, but when he reproached Forth for his cowardice, the young Viscount cried: 'What am I to do? I am perfectly alone and friendless; my father has deserted me, and now the only friend I had left is dead.' Weeping, in a drunken frenzy, Forth began to pack his and Annie's clothes. He told the nurse that Annie's father would pay for the hotel room, that he was travelling to London, and then to Brussels, with the baby. But whatever plans Forth had in mind hardly withstood the hopelessness of his situation. In the afternoon of the day Annie died, Forth grabbed a bottle of laudanum and drank half of it before the landlady wrested it out of his hands. Efforts to revive him failed.

For the papers, Forth's suicide was an opportunity to dredge up the revelations of the Divorce Court, his ignominious military career, even the second Earl of Perth's disastrous support for the Pretender. It served, predictably, as a morality tale: 'that mysterious and awful retribution which, even in this life, appears to track the footsteps of the guilty'. However fitting the story's end, for the Victorian reading public, its details required adjustment. Annie's acts – her elopement with Chichester, her debauchery in Paris – were almost too incredible to be believed. The papers endowed her with a sad history. At the age of twenty, they reported, Annie Cheese had been seduced by a nobleman, with whom she had two children. She had subsequently become penitent and married Captain Lloyd. She was, in other words, more sinned against than sinning. It was left to Captain Lloyd to write to the papers to reassert the humiliating details of his own divorce.

Annie's body was taken by railway to Herefordshire, where she was interred in the family crypt. Mr and Mrs Cheese adopted Annie's infant. They had stalwartly stood by their errant daughter – paying even the hotel bill in Gloucester – as she disgraced the family's name. Now they made the baby Annie's namesake, christening the little girl Ann Cowper Lloyd. Forth's funeral in Gloucester was a desolate affair, attended only by a handful of relatives, who followed the hearse in a single mourning coach. That the deceased was a nobleman would not have been evident to a passer-by: the horses wore no plumes, the drivers no cloaks. The Earl of Perth, Forth's father, stayed away. But Charlotte Capel arrived in Gloucester the day before the funeral. Mrs Capel had no intention of paying homage to her son-in-law. She came to Gloucester solely to take care of business. She needed a copy of Forth's death certificate in order that Harriett could marry Dering immediately.

A month after Forth's suicide, Harriett and Edward Cholmeley Dering, eldest son of the Conservative MP of the same name, married quietly at St John's Church in Paddington. After eloping to America and residing under aliases in London, after having their adulterous relationship exposed in all the papers by the Queen's Proctor, they went to live together in all propriety at Dering's country-seat in Herefordshire. To all appearances, the Derings were a most affectionate couple. But the ordeal of the Divorce Court was not so easily left behind.

For Harriett, life was irrevocably changed. Shunned by the local ladies, she was confined to the society of her husband's male friends and relatives. One of her husband's fellow club-men, Captain Theophilus Alexander Blakeley, became an especially frequent visitor to Dering's London house in Bolton Street, near Green Park. As Dering spent more time at the Army and Navy Club, Blakeley – an armaments inventor whose company supplied the Confederacy – entertained Harriett. He dined with her and took her riding, sometimes with her husband along, sometimes alone. By 1865, Blakeley, himself a married man, was visiting Harriett three times a day: at noon, at five o'clock, and again from ten to twelve at night. The following year, Harriett fled from Dering's house in the country and met her mother at the Great Western Hotel adjoining Paddington Station. Her marriage to Dering was over. She and Blakeley spent the next two weeks masquerading as a Colonel and Mrs Fellowes, living together in rooms at the Italianate Great Northern Hotel.

For a second time – incredibly – Harriett Capel landed in the Divorce Court. Unlike her case against Forth, however, *Dering v. Dering and Blakeley* was a straightforward matter of adultery. Although Blakeley and Harriett denied the charge, neither showed up in Court and their lawyers offered no defence. The presiding judge was no longer Sir Cresswell Cresswell, who had died in 1864, but Sir James Wilde. Where Cresswell was icy and snappish, Wilde, happily and advantageously married to a daughter of the Earl of Radnor, was a man of the world. Handsome and amiable, Wilde was inclined to take the sympathetic view of human foibles (ill. 6). It took him only a single afternoon to grant Dering's divorce petition. Captain Fearon, a close friend of Dering's, provided all of the testimony needed. As Fearon told the story, Edward and Harriett Dering had seemed very happy until recently. At Edward's request, Fearon himself had gone to the Great Western Hotel to plead with Harriett to return home. She refused and became hysterical, and left in a cab bound for Blakeley's house. Considering the scandalous facts, Fearon cast the principals in the most redemptive light possible. Harriett was distraught and frantic, Dering was devastated but willing to forgive, and Blakeley, even, had vowed to break off the affair before Harriett threw herself on his mercy. So routine was the case that it rated barely a paragraph in *The Times*.

Harriett's divorce from Forth had been derailed by the intervention of the Queen's Proctor. This time it was her own parents who intervened. On 1 November 1867, Adolphus and Charlotte Capel entered their petition in the Divorce Court, alleging that Harriett had carried on an adulterous affair with Captain Blakeley for six months before she left her husband. Either Dering had connived in the affair or he had been so negligent about his wife's conduct that he had no right to complain of her infidelity; in either case, he did not deserve a divorce. Presented with the Capels' accusations, the Queen's Proctor opened his own investigation. It would become one of the most expensive interventions of the nineteenth century. The Queen's Proctor confirmed the Capels' charges and went a step further: the affair between Harriett and Blakeley had actually begun much earlier than even the Capels alleged. By the winter of 1865, Mrs Dering and Captain Blakeley were 'habitually' committing adultery, a fact of which Dering must have been aware but had withheld from the Court.

Where the Derings' first trial was a model of restraint, the second, beginning in June 1868, ripped the veil off the couple's private life. For the Queen's Proctor, the star witness was Jane Thake, Harriett's lady's maid. It was she who revealed to the Court that Blakeley visited Harriett three times a day, staying late into the night. That fact would have been damning enough, but there was more. Thake testified that after Blakeley visited, Harriett's hair was sometimes disordered and her manner excited. Harriett wore a crinoline when she went out or had company, but she took it off when she was at home alone with Blakeley. Thake had carried letters between Harriett and Blakeley. She had also seen how Harriett cried and had hysterics when Mrs Blakeley sought, unsuccessfully, to prohibit her from seeing the Captain. On the month-long Mediterranean yacht trip that the Derings took with Captain Blakeley, the Derings occupied separate cabins, with Blakeley's in between. Mrs Dering and Captain Blakeley spent all of their time together, while Dering, often drunk, whiled away the hours on board with the sailors. Mrs Blakeley left her cabin door open at night.

Servants had always been the best informants as to the secret doings of their masters, but the Divorce Court left no doubt about just how much they knew – and were willing to say. Lined up in the witness box to turn the tables on their erstwhile superiors was a horde of domestic tattle-tales, 'with vengeance clearly written on their features'. If ladies' maids were so often peeping through the keyhole at the exact moment of an embrace, observed the *London Review*, how much time did they spend tracking completely innocent prey? 'How do the people pass their days who invariably notice the pulling down or the drawing up of a blind?' After the revelations of the Divorce Court, every would-be adulteress ought to be aware of the 'greedy watchfulness' with which her servants inspected her every move. There was no family secret that the servants did not know.

If the servants, Argus-like, saw everything, the second Dering trial hinged on the question of how much Harriett's husband had known. After her lady's maid took the stand, it seemed at the very least improbable that Dering was blind to the goings-on in his household. Dering, Jane Thake told the Court, was aware that Blakeley spent the evenings with his wife, for she had often heard Harriett tell him so. The testimony of Dering's butler was more ambiguous. Mrs Dering's conduct was a subject of conversation among the servants. However, the butler did not believe that his master harboured any suspicions. Indeed, when the butler informed Dering that his wife had run away with Captain Blakeley, Dering had dismissed the story as 'all a romance'. The Queen's Proctor called the yacht-master, who attested to the 'gradually increasing familiarity' between Blakeley and Mrs Dering aboard ship. Called upon to explain what he meant, the yacht-master offered, to the amusement of the Court's spectators, the Victorian husband's plain common sense. Though he was by no means a jealous man, he would not let his wife sit 'hugged up' to another man, as Mrs Dering had often been to Blakeley.

Against the retinue of servants offered up by the Queen's Proctor, Dering's lawyer summoned his client's relatives and friends to the stand. Captain Fearon returned to add meat to the bones of his former statement. When he entreated Harriett to reconcile with her husband, she had rushed about the Great Western Hotel 'like a maniac' and banged her head upon the table: 'she should go mad if she was bullied any more'. Dering's brother and uncle painted a portrait of a once devoted married couple, of a husband who trusted his wife in all regards, and was in addition habitually temperate. Perhaps, his lawyer acknowledged, Edward Dering had not been as vigilant as he ought to have been with a wife such as Harriett. But the case for connivance had entirely broken down. As powerful support for that view, Dering's lawyer read to the Court a letter that Harriett's father, Adolphus Capel, had written to his son-in-law after Harriett's elopement. It was a screed against Harriett, which expressed in the 'bitterest' terms his outrage at her wrongdoing and ingratitude while acknowledging Dering's 'unvarying kindness and indulgence'.

In summing up the evidence for the jury, Sir James Wilde demolished the Queen's Proctor's case. There was no evidence to support the accusation of collusion. Dering's distress at Harriett's elopement, moreover, hardly fitted the image of a man so eager to get rid of his wife that he connived in her adultery. What remained, then, was the charge of 'willful neglect or misconduct conducing to the adultery'. How was that portion of the Divorce Act, as yet untested, to be defined? Wilde urged the jury to take a broad view of the question, rejecting the conventional wisdom that the yacht-master had offered about the proper behaviour of a husband. What offended some men hardly gained the notice of others. Some husbands brooded over every little incident of married life, while others, less observant and jealous, took no umbrage. Wilde reminded the jury that while they had heard about episodes that ought to have alarmed Edward Dering, they knew nothing at all about the exchanges that might have assuaged his worries: the tender assurances that Harriett may have given her husband, the lies she may have told. Dering ought not to be yoked for the rest of his life to his adulterous wife simply because he was insufficiently suspicious.

Wilde's instructions to the jury in *Dering* reflected the sort of worldly understanding that earned him plaudits from Sir Cresswell Cresswell's detractors. In rejecting cramped notions of proper behaviour, he sought to show how unfathomable were the mysteries of private life, how variable human nature. Establishing fault – the leitmotif of the Divorce Act and Cresswell's Court – was a far more perilous enterprise than had been recognized. Reconciliation was, for Wilde, vastly preferable to divorce. However, he also envisioned a time when the Divorce Court would not mark the end of a person's reputation, but an episode in a life. In one widely reported case, Wilde urged a husband who had taken back his wife after a first episode of adultery to do it again. There would be a time in old age, he rhapsodized, when the couple would look back at this trying moment in their marriage with rueful fondness. The Divorce Court, rather than exercising a deterrent effect on misbehaving couples, might simply become a normal dimension of family life.

After deliberating only a short time, the jury's foreman apprised Wilde of their progress. They had set aside collusion and connivance, but were deadlocked on the question of Dering's negligence. Wilde's own broad-minded view of appropriate marital behaviour had apparently failed to sway the jurymen. He sent them back to continue their discussions, warning them that they had to reach a decision. An hour and a half later, the jury returned with a verdict. They decided against the Queen's Proctor and the Capels on all charges. Although Dering had shown a 'great want of caution', he was not guilty of misconduct. In clearing Dering's name, the jury had – Wilde pronounced – come to the right conclusion. At the same time, however, he refused to award Dering his costs. The Capels had good reasons for filing their petition and would not be penalized further.

What had led the Capels to seek to block their daughter's divorce from Dering? They, of all people, knew the risks of inciting the Queen's Proctor, and must have recognized the distress the family would suffer as a consequence of their petition. Had Harriett's utter immorality caused them finally to forsake her? That family members would turn against their own, after all, had been a founding hope of the Queen's Proctor. Adolphus Capel's letter certainly suggests that he was fed up with Harriett, and exempted Dering from blame. But Charlotte Capel's actions point to a different explanation. In the months after Dering's original divorce decree, Harriett and Blakeley had been living with Mrs Capel in her house in Deal, on the Kent coast. It was there that the Capels' intervention papers were prepared – by Harriett's lawyers. What is more, a month after the Capels filed their petition both Harriett and Blakeley added their own affidavits in support of the connivance claim. Far from repudiating their daughter, the Capels were once again doing Harriett's bidding.

Harriett's choice to bring in the Queen's Proctor, so perplexing in the moment, would become in time a familiar pattern in the Divorce Court. The vast majority of divorce cases were undefended, reflecting a common view that staying away was the least painful alternative. Once the verdict came down, however, parties who had acted prudently in the original trial, and suffered the punishing publicity,

sought redemption and revenge. A discreet tip to the Queen's Proctor, delivered in person or through a family member or solicitor,
could achieve both purposes. For Harriett Capel, the strategy was a
uniquely good bet. She had no reputation left to lose and no investment in keeping the divorce decree. Blakeley was a married man, so
she could not remarry anyway. This time, Dering would be on trial.
Even if the case failed, his fecklessness would be thoroughly aired.
He would for ever be the man who looked the other way while his
wife 'hugged up' with his friend. Besides, Harriett had no intention
of remaining in England while her crinolines were once again examined. By the time the trial began, she and Blakeley had sailed for
South America. His munitions business had failed; her life in England was wrecked; Harriett would have yet another fresh start.

Harriett got her revenge on Dering. He emerged from the second
trial looking a fool and, in the bargain, she kept her divorce. But
there would be no third act for Harriet Capel in the New World. As
the trial drew to a close in the summer of 1868, a steamship made its
slow way back from Peru, arriving in England less than a week after
the verdict. The news it carried was already more than a month old.
Harriett and Blakeley had died together in Lima in April 1868, victims of a yellow-fever epidemic that ravaged the city. For the papers,
the news was yet another opportunity to review the entire story and
to draw an appropriate lesson. The four leading players – Annie
Cheese, Viscount Forth, Harriett Capel and Alexander Blakeley –
bound together by their misadventures in the Divorce Court, were
all dead, struck down, as the *Liverpool Mercury* picturesquely observed,
in 'the full vigour of manhood or the full beauty of womanhood'. So
ended, judged the *Aberdeen Journal*, 'one of the greatest scandals of
modern times, by means of a retribution hurled on the heads of the
chief offenders'.

Of all of the shocking revelations in the *Drummond* and *Dering* cases,
Charlotte Capel's unblinking support for her refractory daughter
counted among the most scandalous. Intimately involved in the quotidian details of Harriett's affairs, even going along to rent the guilty

apartment, she had repeatedly hosted Harriett's lovers in her own house – the 'aggravating feature' of the entire saga, or so opined the *Sporting Gazette*. If newspaper readers concluded that Mrs Capel cared little for morality, they were right. Charlotte had her own secrets which inevitably shaped her loyalty to Harriett. Her husband, Adolphus Capel, had a famous name but was already twice bankrupt and penniless. Like Viscount Forth, he lived off Charlotte's income. The same year that Harriett married Forth, Charlotte Capel planned her own elopement. Her lover was the politician and lady's man George Smythe, later Viscount Strangford. Their passports had been procured, the date set, when Smythe's father fell seriously ill and the plan was abandoned, never to be revived. As Charlotte's love-affair ended, Harriett's terrifying marriage began.

Harriett's trials in the Divorce Court cost Charlotte Capel much more than a season of bad press. Charlotte was the eldest child and favourite daughter of Viscount Maynard. After her brother's early death, it was assumed that Charlotte and her sons would inherit her father's fortune. For a family that had relied for decades solely upon Charlotte's allowance to make ends meet, the Maynard estates, which produced more than £20,000 a year in rents alone, meant wealth beyond imagining. Lord Maynard died in 1865, four years after Harriett's disastrous appearance in the Divorce Court in the Forth case. As his will was read – all forty-seven pages including six codicils, the final one dated a month after the verdict in *Forth v. Forth* – it became clear that Charlotte's father had instead left his fortune to his late son's baby daughter. By the end of the will-reading, Canevari's portrait of Lord Maynard, which hung over the dining-room mantelpiece, was covered in pats of butter, which indignant Capel family members had flung at the judgemental old Viscount. Like Harriett, Charlotte Capel had little left to lose.

In the *Ladies' Companion* for the summer of 1853, nestled between patterns for smoking caps and poems about the sunrise, is an engraved plate of an exquisite girl (ill. 7): a perfect bow of a mouth, curly tresses and a graceful, composed countenance; she looks off into the distance with anticipation, a dove hugged to her chest. This is the

Honourable Mrs Adolphus Capel, not as she appeared the year the drawing was published, but as she had been two decades earlier, before her marriage. The plate is accompanied on the opposite page by a poem of three short stanzas by Julia Maynard, Charlotte's sister. The first tells of the 'golden bloom of youth' that 'matron cares had overshaded', of a 'laughing eye' that had assumed 'graver ray'. In her daughter, the second stanza continues, the 'mother's charms of girl-hood's days oft rosebud-like revive'. But the daughter – 'In part the Parent's second self' – was, as the poem's last lines suggest, not simply her mother's youthful mirror image: 'With darker locks than what were seen before, / And deeper shadows in the shining eyes'.

In twelve lines Julia Maynard infuses a standard Victorian senti-mental form – the bond between mother and daughter – with foreboding. When her aunt's poem appeared in the *Ladies' Companion*, Harriett was seventeen. Her father was already bankrupt. Her mother was a year away from the aborted elopement with Strangford. Har-riett's own engagement to the vilified Forth was in train. From Julia Maynard's vantage point inside the family, it was the entanglement between mother and daughter that had set Harriett's course. The daughter is her mother's 'second self'. She is to redeem her mother's youthful promise. But the imagery of the poem's first stanza haunts its final lines. The mother's 'graver ray' had cast 'deeper shadows' in the daughter's shining eyes.

To read the newspapers' attacks on Charlotte Capel and James Cheese is to imagine a Divorce Court undergirded by a social con-sensus that demanded painful exposure for families that sought to preserve their secrets. But there was another body of writing that also bore the impress of the Divorce Court – the so-called 'sensation novels' of the 1860s – and these authors drew a different set of les-sons. Produced in cheap editions to while away a railway journey or an afternoon at home, epitomized by blockbusters such as Wilkie Collins's *The Woman in White* (1860) or Mary Elizabeth Braddon's *Lady Audley's Secret* (1862), the sensation novel took as its chilling premise what the Divorce Court had so lavishly demonstrated: that behind the unruffled brows and pleasing comportment of 'people we

are in the habit of meeting' were concealed terrible secrets. The novelist Charles Reade acknowledged that his best plots and characters
were written directly from the pages of *The Times*. For masters of the
art, like Wilkie Collins, the trick was to concoct secrets beyond the
reader's imagining: Collins crowed that none of those who entered
bets about the plot of *The Woman in White* had succeeded in uncovering Sir Percival's secret.

The ventilation of secrets provided the sensation novel with its
dynamic narrative force, keeping readers compulsively turning the
pages in pursuit of revelations promised within. However, the ending that these novelists arrived at was not the public dissection of the
Divorce Court, but the affirmation of the family secret. After the
depravity of Sir Michael Audley's charming young wife has been laid
bare – her bigamy, her attempt to kill her first husband, her hidden
child, her insanity – the only course for the rest of the Audleys if
they wish to save their own good name is to turn her into a family
secret. The family's decision to hide her away in a 'home' abroad (and
thus to circumvent the law and its exposure) Braddon presents not
just as unavoidable, but a sensible, even meritorious conclusion to the
affair. In the world of novels, individual secrets such as Lady Audley's
are succeeded by family secrets, family secrets (as in Collins's 1871 *The
Dead Secret*) are replaced by other family secrets. What was a convention of the novel of sensation becomes, too, a leitmotif of later
Victorian masterpieces, such as George Eliot's *Middlemarch* and *Daniel
Deronda*, which reveal the truth to the reader only to defend the virtues of familial concealment from society's prying eyes.

For novelists, the desire of families such as the Cheeses or the
Capels to hide the sins of their reprobate members hardly needed
explaining. 'I only wish I could write something that would contribute to heighten men's reverence before the secrets of each other's
souls,' wrote George Eliot in the fateful year 1859, as English marriages were laid bare and her own irregular life hung on the edge of
exposure. It was perhaps no coincidence that the family secret was
the fictional solution arrived at by writers whose personal conduct
could not withstand the scrutiny of moralists. Wilkie Collins was a

bachelor possessed of both a 'housekeeper' companion, who entertained his friends at home but did not accompany him to dinner
parties, and a secret, morganatic household, which he conducted
under the name of 'William Dawson'. Braddon, like Eliot, lived with
a married man. While newspapers defended their scandalous reporting from the Divorce Court on the ground that they were performing
'public duties', the novelists retorted by endorsing family secrets.

But the manoeuvring by which dread transgressions were rendered secure family secrets was not just a fictional device. As the
Divorce Court's officials knew only too well, the attempt to root out
liars had, in the logic of an evolutionary adaptation, succeeded chiefly
in generating a hardier breed of family secrets.

The star witness of the 1910 hearings of the Royal Commission on
Divorce was an elderly gentleman with mutton-chop whiskers,
seventy-seven years old but still robust and dressed in his trademark
fur coat no matter the weather. Sir George Henry Lewis was the
most famous lawyer of his day. A 'man of many secrets', Lewis – or
so the *Strand Magazine* reported – knew 'enough to hang half-a-
dozen of the biggest men in the City'. His cases included all of the
causes célèbres of the era. Lewis counselled the Prince of Wales when
an outraged Sir Charles Mordaunt threatened to call him as a co-
respondent in his divorce case, and defended the cross-dressers Ernest
Boulton and Frederick Park, whose acquittal he obtained by portray-
ing the two men as overly enthusiastic amateur dramatists. A master
of cross-examination and a canny strategist, Lewis was as successful
in defending murderers as he was in preparing the well-heeled for
the Divorce Court. His work was his recreation, to which he added
a passionate zeal for art-collecting, especially Burne-Jones, Alma-
Tadema and Whistler.

Lewis was the sixth witness called and the only one of the Commission's interlocutors (including the Lord Chief Justice and the
managing director of *The Times*) so well known to its members that
he needed no introduction. Over the course of seventy-one sittings
through 1910 and 1911, the Commission would interview 246 wit-

nesses, from the country's most senior judges to police court missionaries, from professors of divinity to the representatives of the Mothers' Union. It wound up conducting a wholesale survey of the condition of matrimony in England and Wales in the half-century since divorce had become more readily available (ill. 8). The Commissioners inquired into the administration of the divorce laws, the utility and problems of newspaper reports, the effects of divorce upon children and relationships between husbands and wives, the morality of the people, the interests of society and the state in marriage, and 'generally the regard in which the marriage tie is held'. Of particular interest to the Commission was the situation of the 'poorer classes'. Since 1895, magistrates in the County Court system had been permitted to grant judicial separations and maintenance orders in cases of persistent cruelty. The numbers of orders granted – more than 7000 a year as opposed to 600 divorce decrees annually – indicated that relief in the Divorce Court was largely unavailable to the poor, and especially women.

To appear before the Royal Commission was, for Lewis, an opportunity to rehearse long-held beliefs before a more sympathetic audience. Twenty-five years earlier, in the *Fortnightly Review* for 1885, he had castigated the Divorce Court as 'savage and barbarous', as wicked an institution, ethically speaking, as planting criminals' heads on spikes had once been. By establishing different criteria for divorce for husbands and wives, the law subjected English women to 'the vilest oppression, such as the worst days of the Spanish Inquisition never invented'. Equally outrageous was the publication of 'family horrors' in the papers, which had a 'demoralising' effect upon the populace. All that the Divorce Court, in other words, claimed as promoting morality Lewis criticized as ignorant, damaging, or worse. That included the 'whole paraphernalia' of the Queen's Proctor, which served 'to create family gulfs, and to expose domestic horrors to the shame of at least two families, without providing any solution of the difficulties'.

Before the Royal Commission, the 'Jewish Voltaire' made what would be his last public appearance. He was as deliberate and shrewd as ever. Over the course of two days of testimony, Lewis reiterated the points he had made a quarter of a century before, now embellished with the authoritative nonchalance of the retiree. Publication of the details of divorce cases served no purpose, other than to stoke the blackmailer's courage. To deter suits, he had, he acknowledged, paid large sums of money on behalf of terrified (and sometimes innocent) clients. At the centre of Lewis's testimony was the old bugbear of collusion. It did not – he stated baldly – exist. What judges now termed collusion was caused by the Divorce Court itself, which wrongly treated a petitioner's adultery as a reason to deny divorce. By awarding divorces only to those with 'clean hands', the Court virtually assured that the majority of petitioners sought to hide evidence of their own conduct. Then when the respondent failed to file counter-charges, the Court saw a collusive arrangement and bound the couple together in perpetuity. The result, as Lewis concluded, is 'the spectacle that these two people will probably live a life of immorality afterwards because they cannot get married'. Mutual misconduct was all the more reason to grant a divorce.

After dutifully noting 'the greatest admiration for the way in which the King's Proctor has performed his duties always', Lewis went on to demonstrate that this worthy official served no useful purpose. He thought that the waiting period for a divorce, the decree *nisi*, ought to be abolished. If the King's Proctor had evidence, he should intervene before the case was tried. Further, such 'interference' by the King's Proctor would not be required at all if jurisdiction over divorce was transferred, as Lewis thought it ought to be, to local officials in the County Courts. For Lord Gorell, the chairman of the Royal Commission and himself a former President of the Divorce Court, the direction of Lewis's proposed changes was plain enough. Wouldn't the office of the King's Proctor be rendered unnecessary? 'Quite,' Lewis responded.

Was the Divorce Court a 'playground of perjurers' or – as Lewis suggested – did the Court's obsession with 'clean hands' force petitioners to lie? Was collusion rampant or had the Divorce Court itself transformed unhappy couples into conspirators? On this subject the

Commission heard radically divergent testimony. Where Lewis thought collusion, if it happened at all, took place 'once in a blue moon', Lord Alverstone, Lord Chief Justice and between 1885 and 1900 Attorney General, believed that it plagued the Court's operations. Under Alverstone, the Queen's Proctor had stepped up his interventions, filing twice as many cases per year as in the first two decades. Still, Alverstone insisted, collusion was so intractable, so widespread and so difficult to detect that up to 90 per cent of the guilty parties got away scot-free. The mutual misconduct rule, far from the source of the problem, was the bulwark of English morality. To honour divorce petitions by adulterers would open the door to dissolving unions simply because couples were incompatible. The office of the King's Proctor needed to be strengthened, not abolished.

The stalemate between Lewis and Alverstone was broken by the Commission's most surprising witness. Lord Desart had retired from the job of King's Proctor just a year before, having served under Alverstone for much of his fifteen-year tenure. Alverstone counted on his prosecutor's support, citing him repeatedly. What Alverstone had not counted on was Desart's conscience. Cases of true collusion, Desart testified, were 'very few', perhaps one or two a year out of as many as 600 investigated. The typical case was mutual misconduct and here Desart made a remarkable confession: 'I have felt over and over again, at any rate in a considerable number of cases, that my intervention has done more harm than good.' His reason was the same as George Lewis's – these were 'cases where it was hopeless that people would come together, where both would probably continue to live in irregular unions with persons with whom they had committed adultery'. Given the present state of public opinion, Desart could not see abolishing the clean-hands principle altogether. Rather, the Court should have discretion to grant divorces in such cases based on the 'circumstances as a whole'. Even that middle ground, however, he hedged around with serious misgivings. 'I confess feeling the greatest doubt as I do of the soundness of my opinion.'

By the time that the Commission reported, in 1912, Sir George Lewis was dead. But it was his arguments – bolstered by Lord Desart's regret – that carried the day. Fear of collusion, the Commission acknowledged, existed 'largely in the minds of many witnesses' and had been subject to a 'great deal of exaggeration'. As Lewis urged, it was the Court's mutual misconduct rule that compelled petitioners to conceal their behaviour, creating a 'very unsatisfactory state of things which is often confused with collusion'. The Commission's recommendation, following Lord Desart, was that the 'excessive restriction' placed on the Court's discretion be removed and 'the true reading of the statute restored'. The early decisions, of course, were Cresswell's, dating back to Harriett Capel's failed divorce. The 'true reading' of the statute was the same one that Kenneth Macaulay invoked on Harriett's behalf and Cresswell definitively rejected fifty years before. As Judge Wilde predicted, attitudes towards infidelity eventually softened, not least because the Divorce Court had proved how much of it there was.

In the 1880s, George Lewis had been a lonely voice in the Victorian wilderness, but by the early twentieth century he spoke for a substantial segment of the English Establishment. Much of what Lewis had criticized in his *Fortnightly* article the Commission attempted to address in its 1912 report. It urged equality for the sexes in divorce, greater access for the poor, and a wider set of grounds upon which a divorce could be obtained. In response to concerns about the corrosive effects of publicity – here, though on nothing else, Lewis and Alverstone were in agreement – the Commission pressed for substantial changes. Emphatically rejecting the mid-Victorian idea that exposure served to deter immorality, the Commission advised that no case be reported until a verdict had been reached and that judges be given wide latitude to forbid publication of any details. If Lewis was twenty-five years ahead of the Commission, he was forty or fifty ahead of the law. Most of these changes would ultimately be enacted, but not until after the First World War had drastically changed the English landscape, making divorce a much more commonplace occurrence.

The King's Proctor survived the Commission unscathed. A target of rising outrage after the war – denounced by one critic as an office 'conceived by men with dirty minds who revelled in the discovery of secret scandals' – the Proctor soldiered on through the 1970s, long after the other vestiges of Victorian divorce law had been swept away. Although 'intervening, like the Queen's Proctor', became a comic catch-phrase of the late-Victorian period, the fear of collusion that justified the office was as serious as ever, as was the conviction that only the Proctor stood between unhappy couples and the promise of divorce on demand. Indeed, by the 1880s, the Proctor's informal discovery techniques had been augmented by an army of state-sponsored investigators, a development that Desart, their erstwhile general, viewed in retrospect with serious misgivings. Still, independent investigation had become necessary because family members did not behave as the Queen's Proctor had expected they would. Although some, like the Capels, were willing to use the office of the Proctor to punish their former relatives by marriage, they did not willingly send their own black sheep to slaughter. James Cheese and Charlotte Capel proved far more typical Victorian parents than the outraged newspaper articles about their conduct would suggest.

The original justification for the Proctor had been to unmask liars. What its interventions ended up proving was that secret-keeping was endemic to a Divorce Court whose inquiry was confined to an exercise in gross fault-finding. All of the ambiguities of a marriage, the hidden injuries and secret histories had to be whittled down to a determination that one party was a sinner and the other an innocent. In 1892, Desart's predecessor, Augustus Keppel Stephenson, submitted his annual Parliamentary report. It had been an unusually successful year for the Proctor, for in addition to the thirty cases he had prosecuted in the Divorce Court, he had also obtained a perjury conviction in the Old Bailey. False testimony, Stephenson acknowledged, in most cases amounting to perjury, was 'constantly given and committed' in suits for the dissolution of marriage. 'Considering the nature of the issues,' Keppel continued, 'it can hardly be otherwise', particularly where the Proctor has intervened. Someone was always lying. No greater indictment of the Court's raison d'être could have been written. Summoned into existence to stamp out liars, the Queen's Proctor had in fact created a new generation of family secrets.

As its framers envisioned it, the Divorce Court was to produce, within its own heavily perfumed chambers, more truth in marriage and, beyond its walls, through the agents of the press, more morality in society. In 1859, *The Times* had likened Sir Cresswell Cresswell to the 'Confessor-General of England', before whose steely blue eyes were daily recited 'unsavoury' transgressions. However, the expiation that Cresswell offered came with a price: 'the confessions of his penitents are daily given to the world'. Broadcasting the confessions of penitents was supposed to make everyone else behave themselves out of the fear of publicity. But if the shame of exposure kept some people out of the Divorce Court, it did not do anything to prevent immorality more generally. In the half-century between the Act of 1857 and the Royal Commission, adultery seemed to have proliferated, rather than declined. The Divorce Court, observed the poet and barrister Alfred Austin in 1875, had 'familiarized the public mind' with conjugal infidelity. Rather than elevating the populace, the thousands of columns devoted every year to the obscene revelations of the Divorce Court – so concluded the vast majority of the Royal Commission's witnesses, even the newspapermen – had blighted English mores. Hearing other people's confessions did not inhibit Victorian readers. It set them free.

For believers in divine retribution, the fates of Annie Cheese, Viscount Forth, Harriett Capel and Alexander Blakeley offered proof that adulterers had more to fear than the censure of their neighbours. Members of the same fast social set – denizens of the Queen's Bench, parading down Rotten Row, cavorting in Paris – they had played, with ruinous consequences, a hand of rakish Regency cards in a punishing Victorian game. The families that stood so loyally by their children hardly fared better. Annie's mother died the summer after her daughter, aged sixty-six. The Hereford magistrate James Cheese, whose inept plotting helped call the Queen's Proctor into existence, followed his wife to the grave two years later. The baby born to

Annie and Forth in Gloucester died a month after her parents. Annie's six-year-old son by Captain Lloyd, who had been living with the Cheeses since his mother ran away to Paris, survived his grandmother by only a month. Within four years of the verdict, the entire Cheese family – save one girl – was gone.

When James Cheese died in 1864, he had a single heir: Ann Geraldine Lloyd, the daughter of Annie Cheese and Thomas Lloyd. Well-fixed if not outright wealthy, Ann Geraldine seemed to be headed down the same road as her mother. Married at sixteen to a lieutenant in the Royal Marines, she landed in the Divorce Court twelve years later, charging her husband with adultery and great cruelty in communicating to her a venereal disease. Two years later, however, Ann Geraldine stepped decisively out of her mother's shoes, taking as her second husband Captain (later General) Adolphus Brett Crosbie. Widely reckoned the most handsome man in the British army, Crosbie had been chosen by Queen Victoria in 1897 to lead the Diamond Jubilee parade, exemplifying for the benefit of foreign visitors England's best physical specimen. They were married for thirty-two years. In 1920, when Edward Walford made his survey of the Herefordshire gentry, Mrs Ann Crosbie, by then a widow of sixty-six, was living at Huntington Court, the graceful early-Georgian white stucco house, approached down a long driveway, where her mother had been born eighty-five years earlier.

Harriet Capel and Viscount Forth also left one child. Their son inherited his father's name, George, Lord Drummond, and his birthright as well. He was sole heir of the Earl of Perth, Duc de Melfort. This was the boy whom Forth had, while still a baby, beaten. Since his early childhood, George Drummond had lived with his grandmother, Charlotte Capel. He had grown up amid his father's tyrannical rages; his mother had left him behind when she married Edward Dering. At Deal, on the Kent coast, where Charlotte Capel spent the last few years of her life an invalid, George Drummond ran wild. The boon companion of the town's fishermen, a daring and handsome boy, he dressed in the fisherman's high boots and broad-brimmed cloth cap, and frequented the public houses where he was renowned both for his generosity and for his disdain of title and rank. When Charlotte Capel died, in 1871, he eloped with her nurse, Eliza Harrison, a married woman. He was fourteen, she twenty or so, and they engaged a steerage passage to New York.

From Scotland, an outraged Earl of Perth issued ultimatums. If George would leave Eliza Harrison and return home, the Earl's title – the lands were still in litigation – would be his. In America, Drummond held a succession of odd jobs, while Eliza worked as a domestic. He gathered clams and shot ducks in Long Island. Later, he worked as a porter in a Broadway clothing firm and, when that business failed, took a position in the press room of a newspaper, where he oiled machinery. He and his wife had a son who died and a little girl, Mary, who lived. The New World's hardships took their toll and Drummond, like so many other immigrants to the city, contracted tuberculosis, the disease of New York's poor. Admitted to the charity hospital St Luke's, he besought the Earl, now eighty, for assistance, but the stubborn old man, concerned more with his lineage in the abstract than his real-life descendants, was as willing to abandon his grandson as he had been his son. The Earl refused Drummond a farthing unless the young man consented to break off relations with his wife. To a friend of his grandson's he wrote: 'I cannot understand his mad infatuation for a person of so little worth as the woman he is living with.' Lady Edith Drummond, George Drummond's tender-hearted maiden aunt, sent a quarterly remittance of five pounds.

For the last Viscount Forth, however, the Victorian myth of an indissoluble marriage tie was a binding reality. Despite the relentless pressure to give up his wife for a life of privilege, George Drummond stuck with Eliza Harrison. When he died, at the age of thirty-one, in 1887, his wife was no longer the beauty she once had been. The newspapermen who showed up at Drummond's funeral to catch a glimpse of the tall and fair lady for whom an earldom had been sacrificed found instead a middle-aged seamstress, ruddy in complexion, with a 'dull, inexpressive' face, dressed in a cheap black jersey and a thick woollen skirt. The pair, as the Earl's relatives discovered to their relief, had never even been legally married, for Eliza's first husband had not divorced her. At the Earl of Perth's death, in 1902, his Scottish titles passed to a distant cousin. Interviewed by the papers, Eliza Harrison expected nothing at all: 'The old Earl did not recognize us, but I am sure we didn't care much about that.' Though for years afterwards, Miss Mary Drummond – an ice-cream waitress, then telephone girl in Brooklyn (ill. 9) – occasionally grabbed a headline in the New York papers with her romantic tale of a lost title, it was only in jest that her friends called her 'Lady Drummond'.

PART 2

Shame and Guilt, Nature and Nurture

3. Children Who Disappeared

Lucy Gardner and Elizabeth Scott-Sanderson arrived at the Normansfield Training Institution with the same diagnosis: both were deemed 'imbeciles from birth'. Five-year-old Lucy brought with her trunks full of pretty clothes, a wardrobe that her anxious mother regularly replenished with deliveries of frocks, bonnets, stockings, sachets, brushes, comb-bags and sashes. On her visits home, Lucy attended garden parties and teas. When she was away, neighbours and acquaintances inquired about her progress. Well known in her Scottish town, Lucy was, in her mother's description, a 'bright lovable little creature' who won the affection of everyone who encountered her. After four years of training, Lucy Gardner returned to a family that delightedly pronounced her much improved.

Elizabeth Scott-Sanderson never came home, not even for holidays. Institutionalized from the age of one, she spent the next thirty-plus years at Normansfield. Elizabeth also arrived at Normansfield with clothes, but aside from a set of drawers and petticoats when she was two, and a turquoise blue taffeta dress when she was twelve, she received no garments from home. Her mother visited once or twice a year during the first decade she was at Normansfield and sporadically thereafter. Her father came only twice. After Elizabeth reached her eighteenth year, she received no visitors – ever again. Her birth announcement is the only public acknowledgement of Elizabeth's life. To come upon it in *The Times* is jarring, a concrete footprint where everything else has been washed away. Elizabeth Scott-Sanderson was a family secret.

The most important difference in the fates of Elizabeth and Lucy was not their progress at Normansfield, but the moments in which they lived. Elizabeth was born in 1920, amid a wave of institutionalization that, by the mid-1960s, would deposit 64,000 mentally deficient children and adults in institutions across Britain. Like Elizabeth, they came disproportionately from the upper echelons of British society. The vast majority were sent away for the greater part of their lives. Lucy was born in 1878 at the height of the Victorian age. For the Victorians, an imbecile child was certainly an affliction, but not one that would be hidden away from friends and neighbours. Unlike an adulterous liaison or an illegitimate baby, the backward child reflected no wicked choice in life and no moral failing – the categories of transgressions that for the Victorians incurred the largest burdens of shame. Not until the interwar period did large numbers of mentally disabled children disappear into a lifetime of confinement.

The histories of Elizabeth Scott-Sanderson and Lucy Gardner are among the thousands preserved in the Normansfield archive. Founded for the feeble-minded children of the well-to-do, Normansfield was never an ordinary institution. However, its trajectory is nonetheless deeply symbolic. A beacon of the mid-Victorian faith in progress, the hospital became, by the 1970s, a Dickensian apparition in the London suburbs, emblematic of everything that could go wrong in institutions. Within the Normansfield archive, row upon row of mould-ridden, mottled black boxes, all meticulously alphabetized, contain the institution's correspondence with the outside world. The letters stacked so neatly in the decaying boxes offer a glimpse of how family secrets were made of backward children and expose to view the price paid in individual lives for a code of silence.

Normansfield was born in a spirit of optimism, the brainchild of Dr John Langdon Down and his wife Mary, ardent liberals and devout evangelicals. John Langdon Down's promise – 'to open out fresh realms of happiness for a class who have the strongest claims on our sympathy' – soon brought trainloads of worried parents to Normansfield's high iron gates. The institution, founded in 1868 in a Second Empire-style mansion on the outskirts of London, within a decade doubled and then tripled in size. By 1883, the year that Lucy Gardner arrived, Normansfield comprised a park of forty artfully manicured acres and a massive red-brick and Portland stone complex of buildings (ill. 10). Evident in the stately reception rooms and newly built Gothic theatre, observed the *Christian World*'s reporter, was 'the resolution to have the best of everything' (ill. 11).

The idea that idiots could be educated, even cured, was Victorian medical science's equivalent of the telegraph – proof that the limits of human achievement had hardly been tapped. No longer, vowed a new generation of reformers, would the weak in intellect, if poor, be abandoned to the mercies of the workhouse or, if rich, exiled to the care of servants. Pupils who came to Normansfield unable to say more than a few words, the newspapers reported, had learned to multiply seventeen and twenty-four, to sing hymns and to decline Latin nouns. On the lawn, fashionably dressed young ladies, all 'afflicted with idiocy in varying degrees', played croquet, while in the theatre younger children performed in musical recitals. Imposing from the outside, light and airy in its interior, Normansfield called to mind a well-endowed school, not a hospital. Although 'painful sights' of course abounded, Normansfield was a place where, as one reporter observed, 'idiots had been found to have a future'.

The vast majority of John Langdon Down's patients came to the institution directly from their homes and the expectation was that they would return there. Although the Langdon Downs accepted children as young as two, most of their Victorian patients ranged between the ages of eight and sixteen – and hence were well known in their neighbourhoods by the time they departed for Normansfield. Protected by their families' wealth and position from the fate of the village idiot, middle-class children who were unable to attend school (special state elementary schools for slow learners opened first in the 1890s) led lives that were tightly circumscribed, but hardly invisible. They spent their days accompanying mothers or nursemaids on their errands or, like Freddie Bailey, son of a spirit merchant, stacking shelves in his father's warehouse. Virginia Woolf's half-sister, Laura, joined the Stephen family at the dinner table every evening though, as Woolf later disparagingly observed, her 'idiocy was becoming daily more obvious'. Even children like four-year-old Edward Fanshawe, whose paralysis made outings difficult and whose sole means of communication was crying, were not excluded from social life. His mother had commissioned for him a padded 'contrivance' trimmed in moreen, which moved on castors so that the boy could join in the family's entertainments.

While parents sought to limit the public exposure of children, such as the epileptic or floridly insane, whose behaviour might attract a crowd, the merely backward participated openly in the life of the family. For the Victorians, the extraordinary advances reported in the training of mentally disabled children made them a matter of great interest, akin to the other scientific marvels of the age. It was the very uncertainty of their prognosis – together with a sense that it was the Christian's duty to love and tend the most vulnerable of God's children – that shaped how they were treated. Until the early twentieth century, Normansfield's inmates made regular trips home for their holidays. When at home, they attended pageants and church services, Sunday school openings and military drills. They accompanied parents and siblings to garden parties. At Normansfield, they had visitors – parents of course, but also aunts and uncles, old nurse-maids and family friends – who took them to London for an afternoon of shopping at Whiteley's department store or to the theatre. Neighbours asked after absent children and recommended new forms of treatment. Parents, in turn, seem to have solicited the opinions of friends about their children's development. After her son Georgie's three weeks at home in August 1891, Mrs Mary Baker proudly related the verdict of Canterbury's garden parties: 'All our friends think him wonderfully improved.' Normansfield parents requested prospectuses for the institution, which they dispatched to acquaintances whose offspring, they thought, might profit from Langdon Down's supervision.

Because Normansfield children were not sequestered in their institution, they had to be as presentable as their brothers and sisters – which helps explain the painstaking attention paid to their appearance (ill. 12). Although the Langdon Downs offered to procure clothes for their patients, few parents seemed willing to delegate that responsibility. Separated from her little daughter by 400 miles, Lucy Gardner's mother nonetheless sought to put together fetching ensembles, suggesting that the red ribbon sash be paired with the embroidered dress and promising to send new stockings to accompany her white dress 'as those she has will not look well with it'. Mrs Gardner was typical. Through an avalanche of letters about golf cloaks and petticoats, evening gowns and silk handkerchiefs, Agnes Grant wished to ensure that her sixteen-year-old daughter Cecilia remained ever in fashion: 'I like Cecilia always to look nice for every season.' Despite her other duties at home, Edward Fanshawe's mother – a widow with five young children – took care to find buttons to match his serge frock. Though fathers less frequently corresponded about matters of grooming, men such as Charles Wentworth, a Hampshire minister, had strong opinions. Objecting to the way in which his son Bernard's hair was brushed at Normansfield, Wentworth noted that when 'it is just a little bit waved and ruffled he looks best'. He 'longed' to see little Bernard in his new velveteen evening suit.

For Normansfield parents, more than stylish attire was at stake in dressing their children fashionably. As clothes made the man, some parents hoped through the garments they bought or the grooming they prescribed to effect an inner transformation. To erase the unsettling traces of arrested development, they ordered umbrellas with 'strong <u>manly</u>' handles or requested the cultivation of a son's moustache. Specifying the cut of her son's suit, Cuthbert Bentley's mother wanted him to 'look a bit more manly in the fit of his clothes when in town'. Even if clothing could not transform their children, it was a way of holding close a son or daughter who, for the most part, could not write letters or communicate with far-off parents. Lucy Gardner's mother dispatched another new bonnet for her daughter with the regret: 'we all wish so much we could see her dear wee sweet face in her new hat'.

For Victorian parents and mothers in particular, out of sight was emphatically not out of mind. Mrs Gardner wanted a picture of Normansfield so that she could look on the scenery of Lucy's daily life. Maurice Wheeler's mother asked Mrs Langdon Down to describe a 'little stretch' of her son's routine as she and her husband wished 'just to be able to think about what he is doing at certain times in the day'. Others requested a small token from the grounds, a pressed flower or an autumn leaf; as one mother wrote, 'I would prize from Normansfield just a tiny morsel of anything.' After her eighth letter in as many weeks, Louis Adler's mother apologetically explained: 'I am sorry to give so much trouble but we parted so reluctantly with our boy and my anxiety on his behalf must plead my excuse.' Mothers, it seems from the voluminous Victorian correspondence, worried constantly. Many advised Mrs Langdon Down about their child's particular susceptibility to chills and fretted when they heard that London had experienced a spell of damp weather. In preparation for ten-year-old Maurice's journey home, Mrs Ethel Wheeler asked Mrs Langdon Down to warn him not to put his fingers too near the train doors 'as they may be smashed in shutting'.

Even by the standards of Victorian sentimentality, Mrs Langdon Down's correspondents described their children with notable affection and longing. 'You can imagine,' wrote Mrs Julia Ticehurst of her son Harry, 'how often I wish I could just get one or two minutes to see him, poor little fellow.' Living apart from small children was not an uncommon experience for the Victorian upper middle class; parents sent toddlers home from the empire and five-year-old boys to boarding schools. However, the helplessness of backward children made the separation more painful and their parents' apprehensions all the keener. Begging Mrs Langdon Down to promise kindness, Mrs Wheeler wrote that her son 'has never been accustomed to harsh words or unkind treatment of any sort and it would drive me out of my senses if I thought he would get it now'. In letters written urgently, sometimes after 'strange dreams', they sought to emphasize qualities their children possessed that might not be apparent to the casual onlooker. Above all, their children felt more than it would seem. Freddie Bailey, characterized by his doctors as a 'drivelling idiot', was, in his parents' description, 'a child who enjoys life and takes a great interest in everything and is *most sensitive*'.

To send a child to Normansfield was, for most Victorian parents, a sacrifice redeemed only by the hope of improvement. Parents peppered Mary Langdon Down with anxious inquiries about their children's development, asking whether fingers had been coaxed into holding pens and minds trained to tell the time. They trusted, in God's will, that nothing was impossible; some counted even upon a cure. Although it was a 'dreadful trial' to part with their only son, the Baileys did it for Freddie's benefit; 'I shall miss him very much,' wrote his mother, 'but I hope it may please god to restore him.' According to the conventional wisdom of the time, it was the sensible mother who, recognizing the limits of her own abilities, consented to send her child for expert training. Mothers of large families especially accepted the need for outside help. Although it was a 'bitter grief' to send her eldest son Charlie to Normansfield, Henrietta Tresham knew that she could not adequately educate him with four other young children at home: 'I should give him my undivided attention and I could not, but deprive so many others of pleasure and attention.' Nonetheless, Mrs Langdon Down's correspondence demonstrates just how wrenching this decision could be. Reassured constantly about her youngest son Maurice's progress, Ethel Wheeler counted the days until he returned home: 'I felt when I left him behind and indeed ever since that all the light and brightness of my life had gone.'

At that time most children came to Normansfield, then, not because their parents wished to be rid of them, but because they were willing to wager significant sums on the chance for a better life. At 150 guineas a year, Normansfield cost nearly twice as much as the services of a trained nurse and was comparable to the price of Britain's best public schools. Victorian parents, following the guidance of the Langdon Downs, envisioned a stay of five to seven years. There were, of course, exceptions. Even to the most sanguine observer, it was clear that a child such as Edward Fanshawe, profoundly disabled in both movement and speech, could not benefit from Normansfield's training regimen. Torn between 'so many conflicting duties with so many children and particularly when one is the only parent', his mother – overwhelmed by the care of her other four, often sickly, offspring and widowed the previous year – sent her youngest son to

Normansfield because she could not cope. Still, she visited Edward every few weeks, brought him home for Christmas and other holidays and outfitted him with a special chair so he could remain a part of the family. The reporters who flocked to Normansfield reflected the optimism of the parents, recording heartening scenes, stories of 'minds freed from caskets', which the Langdon Downs in turn relayed to prospective clients.

By the end of the nineteenth century, Normansfield's admission and discharge registers told quite a different story: despite the ballyhooed successes, the improvement for which many parents longed was out of reach. Just 40 per cent of Normansfield's Victorian patients were discharged as 'relieved' or 'recovered', among them Georgie Baker, whose progress had so impressed his Canterbury neighbours. Twenty per cent left the institution without having made significant progress. While Lucy Gardner's mother was pleased with her daughter's training and brought her 'wee fret' home after four years, the Langdon Downs did not view her development as sufficiently significant to merit the designation 'relieved'. Seven per cent of the Langdon Downs' patients showed absolutely no improvement. Cecilia Grant, whose mother took such pains over her clothes, never went home. While at Normansfield her condition worsened. When she began after her mother's death to suffer delusions, she was transferred to the Birmingham City Asylum.

With the original vision of a five- to seven-year stay fast fading, Normansfield confronted the same situation as other idiot asylums across the country: their rooms were filling up with patients whose condition was less amenable to training, many of whom would never go home. Thirty per cent of Normansfield's Victorian patients remained in the institution for more than a decade. Some of these, such as Charlie Tresham, were discharged after twenty years as 'relieved', but many others – eighty of the 430 admitted in the nineteenth century – died in the institution after more than ten years. Among the long-stay patients were children such as Edward Fanshawe who were difficult to care for at home, either because of the severity of their disabilities or because one parent (usually their mother) had died. In other cases, parents seem, over time, to have become reconciled to the notion of Normansfield as a permanent home. John Barclay, a 'Mongol' child nearly ten years old, arrived at Normansfield in 1879. Though he learned to speak under the Langdon Downs' tuition, his parents never seem to have seriously considered bringing him home. After one of John's frequent visits home, his mother commented on her son's eagerness to return to Normansfield. 'He knew exactly when the week came to an end and it was time for him to go back to you, got out his bag the night before and half packed it, grinning with delight all the time and in the morning hardly took time to bid us goodbye he was in such a hurry to be off.' This was a story that the Langdon Downs heard often. Mrs Barclay continued: 'Not knowing anything of it yourself I don't think you <u>can</u> realize what it is to us, the comfort and satisfaction to see him going back to "school" with such joy . . .' At that point, John had been at Normansfield for twenty-three years: 'Our dear boy . . . is the happiest of our family, having no cares himself and being so well cared for.'

Mrs Barclay's letter, though heartfelt and gracious, would have been received by John Langdon Down as a distinctly equivocal endorsement. The happiness of long-stay patients was not the marker of success he had originally envisioned. But by the time John Barclay's mother wrote in 1902, John Langdon Down had been dead for six years. Normansfield remained a family enterprise, but a new era had begun, signalled as much by the Barclays' resigned satisfaction as the founder's passing.

For more than a century, from its opening in 1868 through to 1970, the story of Normansfield was intertwined with that of the Langdon Down family. John Langdon Down, its most famous member, identified the syndrome he called 'Mongolian idiocy', which today bears his name (ill. 13). During the Victorian period, his wife Mary was the public face of Normansfield. An attractive woman with a forthright gaze, 'Little Mother', as she was known, greeted new patients and their parents upon arrival. In detailed interviews, she took note of children's bedtime rituals, fears and favourite toys; she spent hours every day corresponding with patients' families (ill. 14). The Langdon Downs liked to say that Normansfield was run as a home. They delivered upon this promise by living, as a family, at the centre of the institution. In the original mansion, a suite of adjoining rooms served as the Langdon Downs' quarters. There, they raised three sons. Their second son, Reginald, who succeeded his father as medical director, brought up his own young family in the institution as well.

John Langdon Down and his wife were a Victorian success story, a real-life example of the rags-to-riches tale that so captivated nineteenth-century audiences. Born John Down, the son of a small-town grocer with a tendency to drink, he became one of the richest and most celebrated medical men of his day. At the age of thirty he had catapulted to the medical superintendency of the newly founded Royal Earlswood Asylum on the strength of a distinguished performance at the London Hospital. Under Down's leadership, Earlswood – the first institution in the English-speaking world for 'idiots' – sought to transform the feeble-minded into productive members of society. His training regimen strengthened limbs and minds and emphasized the concrete over the abstract. He set up a shop on the Earlswood premises so students could practise counting and reading in the context of giving change. He instilled discipline through a regimen of emotional rewards and punishments, chief among which was the withdrawal of the teacher's love.

Handsome and charming, with a facility for impressing well-connected patrons, John Langdon Down made a success of the Earlswood post. However, his sights were set higher. Earlswood was intended for those of modest means, but the Langdon Downs recognized the need for an establishment that would serve the well-heeled. While her husband concentrated on building up a London consulting practice, Mary, described by the *Christian World* as 'pre-eminently a lady of Miss Florence Nightingale's type', commandeered an army of attendants, nurses, gardeners and tradesmen at Normansfield. By the time that the new establishment opened its doors, its proprietors had by deed poll acquired a double-barrelled name to suit their new station in life; the Downs had become the Langdon Downs. Within a decade they had 120 souls under their care. From the three original acres Normansfield grew to more than forty, including three free-standing villas reserved for 'higher-grade' cases, workshops, a functioning farm and a boathouse on the Thames. When Mary Langdon Down died in 1900 (just four years after her husband), the family was worth more than £48,656 – nearly £3,000,000 today.

For the Langdon Downs, feeble-minded children were a calling, to which they brought the twin convictions of evangelical religion and advanced liberalism. The weak in intellect were the least finished of the Creator's work, which made their claim on their fellow creatures all the more pressing. To educate the idiot was to labour in the Lord's fields, planting moral sense in an inhospitable soil. If religious fervour provided the impetus, liberalism supplied the conviction it could be done. That even the dullest intellects could be awakened served to demonstrate the triumph of ideas about the improvability of mankind. Early and staunch advocates of women's suffrage, the Langdon Downs aligned themselves with the most daring fringe of liberal opinion. They were not, however, bohemians. They saw their lives in terms of 'providential' moments, combining a commitment to hard work with the sense of God's favour. On their youngest son's twenty-first birthday, his parents presented him with that most earnest-minded of Victorian presents: a pocket watch to ensure that he made good use of the moments the Lord granted him.

To all appearances, the Langdon Downs seemed a family singularly blessed. Yet their lives were shrouded by the same code of silence that would soon consume their patients. In 1883, their oldest son, Everleigh, bled to death in the Normansfield workshops after an altercation with his younger brother, Reginald. The young men tussled after Everleigh destroyed a piece of brass Reginald was turning. Reginald kicked his older brother in the shin and called him a fool. How a heavy paring chisel came to be lodged in Everleigh's groin – whether Reginald threw it or stabbed his brother – remains a mystery. The sole witness, the Normansfield carpenter, could not say one way or another. The inquest jury, convened in the Normansfield dining room, returned a verdict of accidental death in ten minutes. Though the inquest was reported in the local papers, in the face the Langdon Downs presented to the world the story was erased. All correspondence relating to the incident was destroyed and Everleigh's death was never spoken of again.

Twenty-two years later, after Reginald had assumed the role of director, his own eldest son was born in 1905. John Cleveland Langdon-Down, named for his eminent grandfather, was – it soon became apparent – a 'mongol'. What that meant Reginald was uniquely qualified to know. When his son was eight months old, Reginald Langdon-Down hosted a gathering of asylum physicians for a presentation based on his own case study of fourteen 'Mongoloids' in which he discussed their short life expectancy and limited mental capacity, and speculated as to causation. Reginald spent the rest of his life caring for people with Down's syndrome, discovering along the way the tell-tale palm crease that remains today a key marker of the condition. Yet it appears that he never revealed his intimate connection to the subject, not at that first Normansfield meeting nor ever in his long professional career. His correspondence with Normansfield parents never mentions John Cleveland, not even when they lamented that Reginald did not understand their concerns. Similarly, his daughter's account of life at Normansfield entirely omits her brother (ill. 15).

John Cleveland did attend the local school for a time, largely because his mother Jane refused to admit that there was anything at all different about him – a position she never relinquished despite the fact that she was a trained nurse who inherited Mary's duties at Normansfield and daily confronted the reality of her son's condition. Not until her death, in 1917, was John Cleveland schooled at Normansfield, where he lived with a care-giver for most of his life. When his father retired in 1951, John was finally admitted as a patient. His commitment papers, signed by one of Reginald's long-time associates, declared that he 'has never been able to hold his own in society and needs the constant care and attention of a companion'. His voice was 'gruff', his speech difficult to understand; when out for a walk, he stared at strangers and stood with his mouth open. He liked music and books on geography. Although John lived to the age of sixty-five and was photographed as a child, there are no pictures of him as an adult.

For half a century after his son's birth, Reginald Langdon-Down continued to run Normansfield, bringing to the institution the sensibility of a generation very different from his parents – one that increasingly came to view mental disability (or deficiency, as it was more often known) as a condition for which little improvement could be expected. While John Langdon Down had advocated the construction of purpose-built idiot asylums, his focus was training and rehabilitation. By the turn of the twentieth century, this was an ambition viewed as foolhardy, even dangerous. Writing in the *Economic Review* in 1903, the social reformer Mary Dendy lambasted those who misguidedly sought to return the idiot to the family circle. 'It was,' she wrote, 'to be deplored that idiots should be discharged after a period of training, no matter how admirable that training might be.' Dendy sought instead permanent confinement in purpose-built institutions, arguing that the hereditary nature of mental defect made it imperative that idiots, imbeciles and the merely feeble-minded be barred from producing families of their own. Reginald Langdon-Down went one step further. A prominent member of the Eugenics Society, he became one of Britain's leading advocates of the sterilization of the mentally unfit.

More than simply a man of his time, Reginald Langdon-Down was also a more pessimistic and aloof personality than either his parents or his genial younger brother, Percival. The devotion to Christianity and liberalism that motivated his parents was replaced, in Reginald, by a commitment to the medical profession and a passion for Oriental porcelain, pottery and furniture. When he moved into Normansfield after his mother's death, he redecorated in magnificent style, showcasing his superb collections of antiques. A wealthy man, Reginald was generous in extending credit to families who could not pay their bills; he took on the annual seaside holiday children such as Elizabeth Scott-Sanderson whose parents could not afford the trip. However, his abrupt manner offended those who were accustomed to the warm demeanour of the senior Langdon Downs. The constant reassurance that Mary Langdon Down provided grieving parents was, in her son's era, replaced by the stock response – 'No news is no news' – offered those who badgered for updates. His descriptions of his patients could be harsh. Consoling the aunt of a child who died at Normansfield, Reginald wrote: 'I am sure it must be a great relief to you to know that Winifred is at rest, especially as her life would never be a very great boon to her.'

Reginald may have been brusque, but his pessimism about Normansfield's patients was increasingly widely shared. Where Victorian parents believed that 'with God nothing is impossible', their Edwardian successors were coming to terms with what they reluctantly understood as a life-long condition. Leslie Stephen hoped that under his guidance, his daughter Laura's prospects would brighten. But after two fruitless decades of training – Laura, wrote Virginia Woolf, was 'really the most tragic thing' in her father's life – Stephen decided the case was hopeless and sent Laura off to Earlswood; in the words of his biographer, 'he could hardly bear to see her, let alone show affection'. At Normansfield, education was still part of the programme, but the emphasis was now on needlework, basket making and weaving, not Latin declension and mathematics. No longer did parents confidently look forward to a joyous homecoming. Fourteen-year-old Richard Taylor had been a patient at Normansfield for eight years when his father, a Cambridge professor, closed the savings account in his son's name because 'there is nothing served by going on with it'.

Parents such as the Taylors were reacting principally to their children's lack of improvement. But Reginald did little to relieve their concerns. The optimism that the elder Langdon Downs had encouraged was frowned upon, taken as evidence that a parent did not appreciate the extent of a child's handicap. The case of Bernard Wentworth, who arrived at Normansfield in 1900 at the age of four, captures the changing mood. The beloved only son of an elderly minister, Bernard was, as his father first wrote to Reginald Langdon-

Down, 'a limited rather than a slow boy'. The Reverend Wentworth first took Bernard for a course of hypnotic treatment in London, but when it failed, he reluctantly came to the conclusion that his little son required more specialized training. Initially encouraged by the Normansfield programme, Wentworth proudly reported that Bernard had said 'Boy' when he was playing with him on the stairs, and 'Don't' when he was being tickled. He imagined that Bernard would 'talk fairly well before long'. But Bernard's early progress proved ephemeral: on one trip home, he could say his name, on another, his powers of concentration seemed actually to have diminished. The Reverend Wentworth grew dismayed, interpreting his son's silence as a failure of will rather than capacity: 'I wish he would talk, lazy boy!' Bewildered, he pressed Reginald for an explanation. But the doctor's reply 'neither seemed to approve of the little fellow nor to hold out any hopes as to ultimate development'. Wentworth still anxiously solicited the Langdon-Downs' assessments, but his entreaties were strained, faint hope holding out against despair.

If Reginald and the Reverend Wentworth failed to communicate, it was because, in a very real sense, they were speaking different languages. For Reginald and many of his physician colleagues, the vision espoused by Bernard's father was long obsolete. The Wentworth boy's case was straightforward: little Bernard was fundamentally uneducable. For the Reverend Wentworth, Bernard's prospects – 'all such a struggle to me' – could not be dismissed because it seemed impossible that science held no remedy. Normansfield, Wentworth suspected, was not doing enough. Still, the Reverend Wentworth's final letters reveal the devastation of a parent for whom the Victorian promise of all-conquering progress was finally ebbing away. After his son had spent seven years at Normansfield, Wentworth confessed that his own expectations, if not as low as Reginald's, had become more a matter of paternal reflex than genuine conviction: 'I cannot help hoping that his intelligence may in time improve to some extent, though I try not to expect too much in that way.' Five years later, in 1912, the Reverend Wentworth at last removed Bernard from Normansfield. He recognized that mental progress was unlikely but

wanted to give his son 'a better chance of developing in other ways
– not that I feel very hopeful about that'.

The Reverend Wentworth's faith was in retreat, but he was still
determined to search for some 'better chance'. Bernard Wentworth,
like John Barclay a decade earlier, was not abandoned, not hidden
away. Long-stay institutions eventually created the conditions for
secret-keeping, but not quite yet. In the years before the First World
War, most Normansfield patients still visited their families at home,
at least once a year if not more frequently. But here, too, there were
signs of change. In most regards, Henrietta Weldon, the wife of a
country parson, resembled Normansfield's Victorian mothers. She
worried constantly about Percie, a 'higher-grade' imbecile resident at
the institution since 1893. She sent him clothes and pots of his favourite jam, and barraged the Langdon-Downs with questions about his
health. Percie visited his Dorset home regularly. Even after her son
had been at Normansfield seventeen years, Mrs Weldon still missed
him intensely. In 1907, she asked permission to bring 25-year-old
Percie home for a visit: 'such a longing came over me to see Percie I
am wanting him home <u>tomorrow</u>'.

Unlike her Victorian counterparts, however, Henrietta Weldon
found Percie deeply embarrassing. She wanted to see her son but she
did not wish him to accompany the family on their social rounds.
The same year that she brought Percie for a spontaneous visit, she
also asked Reginald Langdon-Down to explain to her son the boundaries of his social life at home. He would not be invited to the same
festivities as his siblings; nor, for that matter, would he be permitted
to attend the parties that the Weldons hosted for their friends. It was,
she said, a matter of appearances, citing Percie's false teeth and his
baldness: 'You see his wig may come off or his teeth come out and it
would be so awkward. I feel so sorry to give you this disagreeable
task to do but I feel you will know well how to do it.' Percie absorbed
the message. At the end of a fortnight at home, Mrs Weldon reported
a 'touching' incident to Reginald Langdon-Down. One day, when
the family had friends to tennis, she had sent Percie out to tea with an
old servant. Instead of returning home the short way across the lawn,

he came back by the road. When she asked him why, 'the dear fellow replied "because I thought perhaps you would rather your friends did not see me"'.

Not yet a family secret, Percie Weldon was a source of shame. He was allowed home, but hidden from view. In two decades of correspondence thick with details of home and parish life Henrietta Weldon rarely if ever reported a conversation she had had with anyone outside the family about Percie. Percie had a place in his mother's heart, but not her public persona. The change through the Edwardian period – in the Weldons as among other Normansfield families – was gradual, but perceptible. Disabled children attended garden parties less often than before, they were not discussed as openly, and Normansfield's parents, for the first time, complained about the cost of fancy attire. Evident, too, was a new conventional wisdom that the needs of healthy children had to be put above those of the disabled. 'Poor' Percie, as his mother put it, 'had to be the one thought of last'.

Why was Henrietta Weldon ashamed of her son? Was it that Percie's condition reflected badly on the family's genetic stock? Since the mid nineteenth century, leading physicians had speculated about the hereditary origins of feeble-mindedness. John Langdon Down believed that a feeble-minded child in the family cast suspicion on its ostensibly normal-seeming members. He devoted much of his prestigious series of Lettsomian lectures, in 1887, to a meditation on causation. Some weakness of mind, he acknowledged, was accidental, a product of a prolonged delivery or trauma at birth. Other cases demonstrated failures of development, usually in the fetal stage. But the largest number, he argued, were congenital and a product of heredity. Rejecting simplistic causes, such as consanguineous marriages, Langdon Down instead claimed that a subtle interplay between hereditary factors – such as a mother's constitutional excitability together with a father's tubercular history – was to blame. Langdon Down advised practitioners to interview parents separately, as each naturally wished to suppress details which might implicate his or her own line. Interrogated in turn, however, parents supplied 'all the facts which would appear to point to something in the opposite family as the potential cause of the affliction'.

But if heredity was the cause parents most feared, it was largely conspicuous by its absence in the Normansfield correspondence. Parents identified a host of other factors to explain their children's condition. Some were explicitly rejected by the Langdon Downs. The Reverend Wentworth, for instance, was certain that Bernard's slowness was due to masturbation; he blamed the development of the habit on the inattention of an elderly nursemaid: 'had he been under a different nurse at home from the beginning he would have been quite another child'. Henrietta Weldon thought that there must have been something in the Dorset climate to 'predispose' people to feeble-mindedness. For the most part, however, Victorian parents pointed to specific incidents that the Langdon Downs themselves accepted as causal: a fall from a carriage after which a child stopped speaking; an episode of teething that had produced seizures; a shock to the mother during pregnancy. Although the notion that an otherwise healthy fetus could be made an idiot by emotional disturbances is today discredited, it seemed both to the Langdon Downs and to Normansfield's parents an entirely sufficient explanation. The siege of Lucknow, wrote John Langdon Down, had been responsible for scores of feeble-minded children.

Given the supposed dominance of hereditarian modes of thought, it is striking how relatively limited their influence seems to have been outside medical and policy-making circles until the turn of the twentieth century. Thumb-sucking, John Langdon Down noted with disgust in the 1860s, was widely viewed as a cause of idiocy. Nearly forty years later, little had changed. In 1903, Mary Dendy criticized the public's reluctance to embrace the lessons of heredity – a state of affairs which was, to her mind, only 'slowly, very slowly' changing. Even at Normansfield, John Langdon Down's professional interest in the complex interactions of heredity did not necessarily translate into diagnoses. He judged heredity the culprit in just 5 per cent of all cases. In the vast majority, the causes of idiocy were unknown.

By the Edwardian period, however, heredity was on the agenda in a much more insistent fashion. The introduction of compulsory elementary education in the 1870s had revealed a large number of weak-minded children who could not be taught in normal schools. To reformers such as Mary Dendy, their problems were evidence of a hereditary 'neurotic taint', which threatened to swamp the healthy population. Imbeciles, surveys discovered, were to be found in every rescue home for prostitutes and every jail, signs of a population of sub-normals breeding out of control and an epidemic of recidivist criminality. Worst of all, to Dendy's mind, were those feeble-minded such as Percie Weldon, whose training might allow them to pass undetected in society, even to marry and have children more mentally defective than themselves.

By 1901, when the new category of feeble-minded was included in the census, statisticians discovered 133,000 mental defectives in Britain, a figure that bore out the most dire predictions. Writing in the *British Medical Journal* that same year, the physician W. H. Dickinson warned that Britain's future 'depended largely on the stamping out of feeble-mindedness'. The majority of witnesses who testified before the 1907 Parliamentary Committee on the Care and Control of the Feeble-Minded agreed not just that the problem of mental deficiency was passed down through the generations but that it was on the rise. In less than two decades, the notion of segregating the mentally disabled permanently was transformed from the fantasy of a few into social policy. The 1913 Mental Deficiency Act gave the authorities unprecedented powers to detain and segregate the weak in intellect; they, alone among all segments of the community, could be deprived of individual liberties that – it was argued – had never rightfully been theirs to enjoy.

Where the mid-Victorians tended to conceive of idiots as poor, doddering fools to be pitied, not feared, the weak in intellect had, by the turn of the century, become a danger – even *the* danger facing the nation. Henrietta Weldon did not need to believe the more extreme of Mary Dendy's propositions to feel shame about her son; even the hint of hereditary stigma was probably sufficient. At the age of twenty-six, after two stints of training at Normansfield, Percie could read and write well. However, his parents did not contemplate bringing him home to live. 'It is so sad,' wrote Henrietta Weldon, 'that even with his growing intelligence he is such a hopeless way off <u>ever</u> being able to earn his own living or be thoroughly dependable.' To be dependable meant not gawking or standing with one's mouth open – behaviour that might once have been ignored or even tolerated. The borderland of normal, the land that Percie inhabited, had become definitively abnormal. Patients discharged to their families as relieved or recovered in the institution's first half-century would scarcely have qualified for release in the fifty years that followed. Between 1900, when Reginald Langdon-Down took over the institution, and the First World War, Normansfield's patients were three times as likely to die in the institution as they were to leave it 'relieved'. The vision of permanent incarceration espoused by Mary Dendy was becoming a reality.

The Scott-Sandersons were the sort of family who announced their births, engagements, marriages and deaths in *The Times*. The news of a sixth daughter, Elizabeth, born in 1920, was no exception. Blessed with a peachy complexion and beautiful features, Elizabeth was an unusually placid baby, so much so that her mother soon began to worry. She showed no interest in her bottle and though she sat up and laughed when expected, after the fits started at seven months she could hardly hold up her head, and rarely smiled any more. Although the family doctor could find nothing physically wrong with the child, he thought it a hopeless case of mental impairment. For Lieutenant-Colonel Scott-Sanderson and his wife Edith, the prospect of raising Elizabeth at home with her five sisters, all on a military retirement pension, seemed an overwhelming hardship. By the time Edith Scott-Sanderson wrote to Reginald Langdon-Down, she was desperate to find a place for her baby to go.

Admitted to Normansfield at the age of one year, Elizabeth Scott-Sanderson was the youngest patient the institution had ever taken in. She was also the harbinger of a new phenomenon. Beginning in the 1920s, mentally disabled children of the middle and upper classes were dispatched from their homes at earlier and earlier ages, some even from birth. They were raised in isolated coastal towns or deep in the countryside with nurses such as a Miss Ault of the Priory or Miss MacDonald, who made a specialty of caring for young children. Reginald Langdon-Down knew of several dozen such establishments within a few hours of London, though each took only a handful of patients at a time. Private attendants were not new; in the eighteenth and nineteenth centuries, they had played an important role in caring for the mentally unstable, especially as parents aged or died. But in the interwar period, they came to form a crucial part of the underground economy of provision for mentally deficient children – a place to put babies directly from the nursing homes or hospitals where they had been born. Typical was the story of Thomas Palmer. An only child, he was injured by instruments in a difficult birth and took two hours to resuscitate; he did not cry until he was ten days old. His doctors declared him seriously damaged; his parents never took him home. Instead, they sent him to Miss MacDonald's, where he lived for seven years on the Sussex coast until serious fits compelled his transfer to Normansfield.

From the desperate letters of parents such as Edith Scott-Sanderson, it appears that demand for such private placement, at least in the 1920s, outstripped supply. In part, that was because mental deficiency was diagnosed earlier than it had been in the past. Doctors and midwives could often recognize 'mongolism' at birth, especially after Reginald Langdon-Down's discovery of the tell-tale palmar crease in 1908. The codification of developmental stages, too, meant that doctors were called in when a child failed to sit up or to roll over on time. Unlike in John Langdon Down's day, when specialists saw hope for improvement in most cases, interwar physicians gave parents little reason for optimism. By the time that Elizabeth Scott-Sanderson was eleven months old, her doctors had already recommended institutionalization. She would never be more than a vegetable and it was not 'wise', they counselled, to keep Elizabeth at home with the other five girls.

Mentally deficient children, especially of the middle and upper classes, disappeared with increasing frequency from the interwar period through to the early 1960s. The Registrar General's survey of 1949 discovered that those of the professional classes were more likely than all of the other occupational groups to institutionalize their seriously retarded children. While institutionalization need not have meant secret-keeping, the younger ages at which children were sent away made it possible to hide them from view. Henrietta Weldon could not, even if she had wanted to, have kept Percie a secret; he was already eleven when he went to Normansfield. But after the First World War doctors more and more advised parents to cut their losses. It was a 'hardship' for siblings to share the family home with a mentally deficient child. Early institutionalization became the remedy of choice. After their first daughter, Shelley, was born a 'mongol' in 1951, the Resident Paediatrician advised the actors Elspet Gray and Brian Rix to 'put her in a home and forget all about her. You're both young, you'll have other children, and there's no chance of it happening again.' '[Y]oung, disturbed, ashamed, frightened', in Rix's words, they sent Shelley to a private home and 'went miserably back to our empty flat'.

Edith Scott-Sanderson left no memoir to tell us what she was thinking on the morning she delivered Elizabeth to Normansfield. In a letter she sent Reginald Langdon-Down that evening, she expressed relief and gratitude that the baby was finally settled: 'One cannot but feel happy about the child, when one hears she is warmly received.' The remote stoicism of that sentence was tempered by the request that followed. Explaining that it would be many months before she could come to London again, she asked to see Elizabeth again the next day 'for even a few minutes'. If, in those final moments, Edith Scott-Sanderson was feeling the same misery and shame as the Rixes, her course was firmly set. Although the child 'notices nothing and feels nothing as far as we can judge', she and her husband wanted Elizabeth to be 'comfortable' and 'well looked after'. They did not expect her ever to return home.

The Normansfield where Mrs Scott-Sanderson left her daughter looked much the same as it had in Victorian times, but its mission was very different. Long-term custodial care had become the institution's basic orientation. Normansfield's patients would not come home, not even for holidays. Parents' visits, too, became fewer and further between. Guilt at having put sons and daughters away – in one mother's words, 'I felt like a murderess' – most likely made visits painful, as, too, did the sight of their children's deterioration. In Elizabeth's first two years at Normansfield, Mrs Scott-Sanderson saw her daughter four times. Afterwards she came once a year and once Elizabeth turned eighteen, not at all. By the standards of the time, she was a reasonably attentive parent, especially by comparison to her own husband, who came to see Elizabeth just twice. There were, of course, those patients whose families visited monthly or even weekly, though they became a small minority over the course of the 1920s and 1930s.

If parents visited less frequently, many institutions sought, for their own part, to limit familial involvement. Normansfield remained a privileged place: a parent or any other authorized relative or friend could, with a week's notice, visit almost any time, except Sundays. By contrast, at the Stoke Park Colony, founded in 1909 for the life-long segregation of the mentally defective, only parents or near relatives over sixteen years of age could visit. Patients could have no more than two visitors on one day; a visit could not exceed two hours. Requests to visit had to be made a week in advance and were not permitted on Saturdays or public holidays, meaning that parents who worked during the week were effectively barred from seeing their children regularly. Those parents who lived at a distance, as many of Stoke Park's families did, could apply to see their children on a Sunday, but no more than four times a year. Correspondence was similarly regulated. If relatives furnished them with stamps, patients who could write (always a small number) were permitted to send letters to their families once a month; however, parents were only allowed to request reports on their children from the Colony's authorities twice a year. With 1700 patients in residence, Stoke was the largest of Britain's hospitals for the mentally defective but not the most regimented.

The rules at the Botley Park Hospital for Mental Defectives were even more draconian: visiting days were, without exception, on Sundays and Wednesdays between the hours of 2 and 4 p.m.

Hospitals were jealous of their authority, but many parents, too, were willing to delegate their responsibilities to the institution. At Normansfield, nothing illustrated that change more vividly than clothing. Few interwar parents behaved as the Victorians had, sending outfits and worrying about flattering hairstyles. Edith Scott-Sanderson, like most others, requested that the Langdon-Downs procure whatever her daughter needed, with the reminder that she could not afford any expensive things. In advance of their children's birthdays, most Victorian parents, even those far away, ordered cakes and sent boxes of treats. By the interwar period, there were few such festivities. Mrs Potter had not seen her twelve-year-old son in a year when Reginald Langdon-Down wrote to her, in 1934: 'it is possible you may soon be coming to see him as today is his birthday'. Present-giving at Christmas, too, became a collective affair engineered by Normansfield's administration. Each year, Reginald made a trip to Hovenden warehouse to buy toys in bulk for the hospital's inmates.

Along with smart frocks, Christmas gifts and regular visits, interwar parents relinquished a much more momentous Victorian attribute: serious hope that their children would ever return. Three years into Elizabeth's stay at Normansfield, Edith Scott-Sanderson was delighted with her improvement and grateful, too, for the photographs Reginald Langdon-Down had sent of her little daughter. However, the way in which she expressed her admiration indicated the distance she intended to maintain: 'I thought she had come on really <u>wonderfully</u>, in fact I think she is a marvel and you must indeed be very proud of her and of how she has improved.' It was Reginald Langdon-Down who was to be proud of Elizabeth, not her mother. That Elizabeth was, as Edith Scott-Sanderson put it, 'a great credit' to the institution vindicated the decision to put her there in the first place. A year after arriving at Normansfield, Elizabeth had – Reginald Langdon-Down noted in his case book – made 'extraordinary progress'. The year before, she 'lay as a log', but now the toddler, 'keenly interested in whatever she sees', could sit up by herself, drink milk from a cup, and play with a sponge in the bath. Nonetheless, her parents never asked to take her home.

Short of her complete restoration to normality, the Scott-Sandersons had no intention of reclaiming their daughter. Harder to pinpoint is the moment when Elizabeth became a family secret. Because Elizabeth entered Normansfield when she was one year old, her existence would have been known to family intimates and neighbours. In such cases, if secrecy was impossible, sympathy and mutual embarrassment achieved much the same result. The disabled child was effectively purged from polite conversation, banned by an implicit code of silence. That was the case with Richard Atherton, who had been at Normansfield for thirty years when his mother died in the early 1920s. Mrs Atherton's solicitor, H. R. Toland, was the executor of her will. Though fully aware that Richard was a patient at Normansfield, the solicitor confessed to Reginald Langdon-Down that he had no idea why the young man had spent his life in an institution. 'I have not felt able to discuss his condition with Mrs Atherton or Miss Atherton.' It was not uncommon for grandparents never again to mention a child who had been sent away. Brian Rix recalled that his father wept on the day he heard about his granddaughter's condition, and then to the day he died never referred to her again.

Even parents could lower a curtain of denial that effectively banished the subject of disability. In 1937, Dr Arthur Jones, a Swansea doctor, wrote to Reginald Langdon-Down about his thirteen-year-old 'Mongol' son, whom he wished to place in an appropriate institution. He requested that Reginald not use the word 'Mongol' in his reply, as his wife 'so far, regards him as "backward" while she does not know the ultimate prognosis'. She was already 'most upset', and her husband did not wish her further grieved. The little boy was their only child; his father had for thirteen years kept the gravity of his son's condition to himself. Reginald could scarcely have been surprised. His own wife, despite the clear proof she confronted every day at Normansfield, refused to accept the reality of her son John Cleveland's condition. As one mother of a backward child put it, reflecting on the experiences of other parents she had known: 'There were people for whom it was such a blow; they just curled up inside and closed the door to the world.'

Walling off siblings from the truth was a more difficult task. Elizabeth's older sisters would have known of her birth, of course. A younger sister, the Scott-Sandersons' seventh and final daughter, was brought to see Elizabeth at Normansfield when she was ten. But that was the only time any of the sisters ever saw Elizabeth. She would have remained a dim memory at best, a painful subject best avoided. That is how David Towell remembers his older sibling. Because of a few stray photographs, Towell knew about his sister Pat, disabled by whooping cough at the age of two and institutionalized six years later, when he was born. He recalls, too, his mother knitting her bed jackets before Christmas; on one visit to Pat he was brought along, but told to wait in the car. His sister remained a shadowy presence, never discussed by his parents even as he grew older, neither entirely absent nor truly present.

To erase entirely a child's existence required a different level of organization and probably also desperation. But it could be done. In December 1941, just after the Japanese bombed Pearl Harbor, a year-old 'Mongol' baby was admitted to Normansfield. Willie Tunsdall came to the institution accompanied by his doctor and all of his things. The boy's mother had apparently had a nervous breakdown. As Reginald Langdon-Down noted for the record, she was 'not to hear any more about the child. Communication with father to be through solicitors or Doctor.' Willie's father had arranged for the family's housekeeper to visit the child once a month; no one else was permitted to see him. His father did not once visit Willie. For his son's second and third birthdays, Tunsdall sent expensive presents, a wooden engine and riding horse, from Hamley's. After Willie's younger brother was born, his father never again communicated with Normansfield. When Mr Tunsdall died, Willie was omitted from his obituary.

For Elizabeth Scott-Sanderson's parents, their peripatetic life made silence an obvious course. Perpetually strapped for money, Lieutenant-Colonel Scott-Sanderson travelled for a year to New Zealand with the thought of moving his family where a retired military pension might accommodate a middle-class life. When his plans in New Zealand did not work out, the Scott-Sandersons rented their Norfolk farm for several years, and moved to smaller houses in the countryside and, for a time, to France, where they put up in hotels. Somewhere in the course of their travels, whatever tenuous branch still connected Elizabeth to the family tree was finally severed. When Lieutenant-Colonel Scott-Sanderson died in 1932, his obituary listed six daughters. Elizabeth, then twelve – able to tell her nurses to 'go away' but little else – had been erased. For the public record, Elizabeth's life, like Willie Tunsdall's, had never been lived.

Two decades earlier, Henrietta Weldon was embarrassed by Percie – but not enough to outweigh her desire to see him regularly and even bring him home to visit. But as the eugenics movement reached its apogee in the 1920s and 1930s, the charge of a hereditary taint took on a more precise and devastating implication. The problem was no longer simply, as it had been for the Edwardians, that the feeble-minded, turned loose to propagate, would beget idiots. Now, the science of heredity had revealed that even those seemingly of normal intelligence could be 'carriers' for imbecility; one idiot in the family was an indictment of all. Against the backdrop of a plague of mental deficiency run nearly out of control – in 1929 the government's own committee reported that one in every one hundred Britons was mentally defective, for a total of more than 300,000 – the silence and secrecy that surrounded the feeble in mind intensified.

Why, after more than half a century, did hereditarian beliefs finally prevail? The new power accorded genes, we will see, did not translate to all situations. The notion that homosexual proclivities could be passed down in a family was never more than a fringe belief. The idea that idiocy could be transmitted between the generations, by contrast, gained currency because it fitted into the grooves already well worn by lunacy. Since at least the eighteenth century, madness had been widely viewed as a predisposition that inhered in families. Given the prevalent conflation of diseases of the mind, it was but a small step to imagine that imbecility ran in families the same way that derangement did. The poet Louis MacNeice discovered as much when, a young man and much in love in 1929, he told his fiancée about his 'mongol' brother, William. Unlike the rest of his family, who – in line with older Victorian attitudes – cheerfully embraced William as their Christian duty, MacNeice had often felt disgusted by his brother's condition. But nothing prepared him for the reaction of his would-be bride. Before she could consider marriage, she told him, her family would require a physician's certificate to prove that William's condition was not hereditary. Consider in this light the plight of the Scott-Sandersons: with six daughters to marry off, Elizabeth's disability was catastrophic. Secrecy seemed the only alternative.

More was at stake, of course, than eligibility for marriage. In an increasingly democratic society that valued intellectual achievement and stigmatized its absence, to have a mentally deficient child was to face personal and professional humiliation. When the only child of the pharmaceutical giant Henry Wellcome proved a slow learner, his father sent him to live in the countryside rather than expose him to scrutiny in London. The fact that his son was below average threatened Wellcome's own reputation as a man of genius and, he feared, might even imperil the fortunes of his company. Concealing mental deficiency had become a matter not just of personal pride but of class status. For two decades, eugenic propagandists had insisted upon the prevalence of imbecility among the lower orders. For those of the middle and upper classes, an imbecile in the family weakened claims to social superiority. Alice Merritt did not want to meet her son's new attendant 'because I mind people like that knowing it even more than those belonging to one's own class, very foolish and perhaps wrong, but so it is'.

Fathers, it would seem, felt even more keenly than mothers the ignominy of mental disability. Like Henry Wellcome, they may have seen themselves as more exposed to intellectual disgrace. Or, perhaps they simply lacked the emotional bond engendered by everyday care-giving. Fathers had always been secondary figures in the Normansfield correspondence, but after the First World War they receded still fur-ther into the distance. And where mothers died or, as in the case of Willie Tunsdall, broke down, disabled children were particularly vulnerable – in Willie's case, relegated to the care of a father who never visited and terminated all communication after the birth of another son. Long before she was excluded from her father's obitu-ary, Elizabeth Scott-Sanderson had effectively vanished from his life. In addition to his two visits, one paid when Elizabeth was five, the other when she was eleven, he wrote only one letter to Normans-field, in which – misspelling her name 'Elisabeth' – he informed Reginald Langdon-Down that he could not afford the regular seaside trip. He thought it unlikely that Elizabeth could enjoy it and, given his finances, could not afford to give her, as he put it, 'the benefit of the doubt'.

Hiding children in institutions was largely the prerogative of the well-to-do. Given the shortage of institutional places, most families had to wait years, even in desperate circumstances, for assistance. Moreover, working-class families were, it appears, less eager to resort to institutions than their social betters. Working-class fathers, in particular, seem to have viewed both mental disability and insti-tutionalization as a personal disgrace. Suspicious of the authorities, they were often unwilling to surrender control of their children. They, too, hid children, only at home. Those who sought institu-tional care frequently envisioned a temporary solution to help them over a difficult patch, not a lifetime. But, once certified, their abil-ities to bring children home were often limited. Even visiting, because of institutions' restrictive policies, was difficult. The longer children stayed in an institution, the less likely they were to have contact with their parents. Gradually the visits ceased, and the chil-dren, like Willie Tunsdall and Elizabeth Scott-Sanderson, became 'closed chapters' in their parents' lives.

What did it mean for Elizabeth – and the thousands of children like her – to spend the better part of a lifetime in an institution? The papers that chronicle Elizabeth Scott-Sanderson's life at Normansfield comprise a very thin sheaf. The early signs of progress that Reginald Langdon-Down detected – responding to nursery rhymes, drinking milk from a cup – did not yield lasting gains. While Elizabeth grew 'brighter and more cheerful', and made efforts to talk, her speech never progressed very far and she began to rock herself to and fro, 'an ominous sign' as Reginald reported to her mother. At the age of six, she slipped further backwards: more fits, more screaming, trouble walking. When she was eight, she fell and broke her two front teeth, 'a great pity', her mother observed, 'as it will just spoil her she was so pretty'. Although she could play with simple toys at the age of twenty, she did not have any other occupations. By 1955, the last recorded entry in the case books, Elizabeth had grown obese and was 'difficult and heavy to manage and cannot move about without assistance . . . She can do nothing for herself and at times she has periods of screaming.' Elizabeth was thirty-four years old and had lived in Normansfield virtually her entire life.

Empty as her life may have been, Elizabeth's confinement at Normansfield was relatively privileged. Beginning in the 1960s, Maureen Oswin, a teacher in a cerebral palsy unit, spent her weekends in so-called 'subnormality' hospitals across England. She observed hour after hour in the wards, pitching in to help when necessary. She counted, among other things, the number of times nurses interacted with children; she analysed how lunch was served and mail distributed; she eavesdropped as nurses and doctors discussed their charges; she watched as parents visited. She came, at first, with no credentials or funding – as she told *The Times*, 'it is a bit like the Victorian type of research, just me, poking around on my own'. The most upsetting sights she saw she did not publish in her two books, *The Empty Hours* and *Children Living in Long-Stay Hospitals*, for fear of the charge of sensationalism. Nevertheless, what she did say was sufficiently damning to impel a government memorandum on the abandonment of handicapped children and to turn Oswin into a pariah among mental health professionals.

Children in long-stay institutions, Oswin argued, lived the most deprived and isolated existence imaginable. In the typical ward, nurses played with, cuddled or spoke to the children just five minutes in a ten-hour period. The rest of the nurses' time was spent managing the ward's routine, sorting laundry, readying meals, and chatting with each other. Children were conveyed, as on an assembly line, through their meals and toilet, often stripped, bathed and finally readied for bed by different people. In between, especially on the weekends, there were long periods of isolation and boredom. Children spent entire afternoons staring at walls. They did not play with toys, but held them in their hands, a consequence, Oswin hypothesized, of the lack of stimulation by the staff and the shortage of playthings in crowded wards. So desperate were children for notice, reported Oswin, that they grabbed at her clothing and hands when she first entered the ward: 'Come *here*, lady', 'Come here to *me*, lady', 'Are you my mama?' To want attention on a long-stay ward was to be 'naughty'. Nurses talked about the children as if they were not present: 'Think,' said one, 'how a child like this could ruin your family, ruin your life.' Or: 'He'll be right ugly when he's older.'

Long-stay institutions, Oswin concluded, crushed any capacity a mentally handicapped child might have possessed. The earlier the institutionalization, the more devastating the consequences. Children who spent their early years at home came to the hospital with a rudimentary sense of play and language and were better able to gain the nurses' favour. Those who had lived there since they were babies or toddlers tended to be withdrawn and apathetic. The nurses nicknamed Graham 'corpse', because he sat stiff and quiet in his wheelchair and never sought eye contact. The longer the stay the more likely the children were to develop repetitive habits, such as sucking their hands or clothes, tearing up paper, or hitting themselves – compensation, Oswin believed, for the lack of mothering by the staff. One afternoon Oswin observed fourteen-year-old Sally, in hospital from the age of three, spend seven hours in her wheelchair chewing the end of the strap that held her in. None of the nurses touched her or talked to her the entire time.

Worst off were the children – as many as two thirds in some wards – whose families visited them infrequently or not at all. Not only were they deprived of the attention and affection of their parents, but they also received less notice from the staff. To be left in hospital without an advocate was nothing short of catastrophic. Admitted to the hospital at the age of two with cerebral palsy and epilepsy, Dennis could not talk and his legs, because of badly dislocated hips, stuck out at right angles. The orthopaedic surgeon decided that the boy was not worth operating on, even though Dennis's prospects without surgery were dismal: in a few years he would be impossible to bathe or manoeuvre through a door. A parent's intervention might have averted such a result. But too often, Oswin observed, hospitals were content to allow familial contact to dwindle. Nurses had ambivalent or even hostile attitudes to parents who had 'dumped' their children and did nothing to encourage their visits. At the same time, they did not want to be bothered with families whose expectations they deemed unrealistic. Oswin watched as parents who came to see their children once or twice a year stood to one side, not knowing the names of the staff and then 'creeping' away after only an hour: 'Nobody can guess what an ordeal such a visit must be.'

By the time Oswin was making her visits, the situation at Normansfield was not significantly different. Many of Reginald Langdon-Down's patients, like Elizabeth Scott-Sanderson, had lived in the institution for several decades. The regular reports Reginald sent home revealed little about particular patients – 'There is nothing special to say about XXX. He/she has been keeping in his/her usual health and going on steadily.' But the medical case books documented episodes of head-banging and screaming, and the need for sedation. By 1951, the year that Reginald Langdon-Down retired, the institution once viewed internationally as the epitome of enlightened treatment for the mentally disabled faced the same problems as the rest of Britain's sub-normal hospitals: decaying buildings, a shortage of staff, and large numbers of elderly and disabled patients. Although the Langdon-Down family maintained a connection to Normansfield, the hospital, at Reginald's retirement, was sold to the NHS.

The end to the Normansfield story was written early on a May morning, in 1976, when the institution's nurses walked out on strike, leaving 200 severely mentally disabled patients unattended for the better part of a day. An unprecedented event in the history of the National Health Service, the nurses' walk-out forced a government inquiry. Over the course of 124 days, the NHS's Committee of Inquiry heard from 145 witnesses who testified about drugged patients, 'nauseatingly soiled' toilets, rotten furniture, spoiled food, grounds littered with glass, and children lying naked in bed. It was, said one hospital volunteer, 'just as if Dickens had come alive again in the mid 1970s'. The regional health authority's administrator, a man who presumably knew his way around decrepit Victorian facilities and understaffed NHS hospitals, gave the most damning testimony: 'I was shocked by the situation at Normansfield and I am not easily shocked.'

The sequence of events that led to the horrific conditions at Normansfield was, in one sense, particular to the place – a result of the tyrannical and inept management of the institution's head physician. But it was also the product of a regime of secrecy that had developed over the course of the twentieth century. There had always been a paradox at the heart of John Langdon Down's vision of the institution: to be trained, the mentally disabled needed to be segregated. Institutions such as Normansfield created the conditions for secret-keeping, at the outset, inadvertently. But as hereditarian ideas strengthened and the definition of normality narrowed, the mentally disabled suffered a slow social death. At first, like Percie Weldon, they were kept out of the sight of neighbours and family friends. Then, as for Elizabeth Scott-Sanderson, they were never brought home and rarely visited. Finally, like Willie Tunsdall, they were imprisoned their entire lives in wards that became squalid and hopeless precisely because few visited or noticed.

The children of the Victorians viewed their parents as the most formidable secret-keepers. Literature and legend support that view, filling Victorian attics with lunatics of every stripe. The history of the mentally disabled, as reflected in Normansfield's rise and fall, tells a story that is almost precisely the opposite. Victorians of the middle and upper classes discussed learning difficulties more openly than did their parents and dramatically more frankly than would their children and grandchildren, who proved willing to conceal the mentally handicapped altogether.

Victorian openness proceeded, in large measure, from the new hope of improvement, and against a backdrop less coloured by hereditarian beliefs than has often been assumed. In an era in which the well-to-do had larger families than ever before, there may, too, have been a higher tolerance both for variation and for dependence. In the 1870s, one quarter of all British children lived in families with at least eleven siblings, assuring a diversity of life trajectories within a single family. What counted as normal in family size, too, was widely divergent, for it was as common to have no children as it was to have three, six or eight. By the 1920s and 1930s, the two-child family was becoming the norm, and for most women child-bearing was concentrated rather narrowly in the first decade of a marriage. From the late 1930s, the once substantial ranks of bachelors and spinsters were fast depleting, as marriage was becoming nearly universal; by the 1950s, people married around the same age, within an eight-year band. As families themselves became more homogeneous, deviations from the norm were increasingly difficult to accept.

An 'idiot' in the family had always been a misfortune and a source of sorrow. Since the beginning of time, families, too, had sought to rid themselves of inconvenient members. What changed in the early twentieth century was the scale of the problem and the scope of the solution. Failed efforts to redeem the weak in intellect during the era of optimism served as the proof that the task was itself impossible. Institutions such as Normansfield, founded to promote the integration of the mentally disabled, became the means by which they could be segregated for a lifetime. When the pendulum swung back to secrecy, it did so with the ferocity of repudiation. Not only were the mentally disabled ineducable, but they furnished the ranks of degenerates of all types. Feeble-minded children cast doubt on their parents' health and mental soundness, and endangered their siblings' prospects in marriage. Families that had been pitied became families to fear.

If societal attitudes were instrumental in the shift, it was parental shame that ultimately became the engine of secrecy, a phenomenon that accelerated after the First World War. When Edith Scott-Sanderson first wrote to Reginald Langdon-Down, she wanted Elizabeth removed from the house as soon as possible. Willie Tunsdall's parents wished to expunge any evidence that the child had existed. The idea that feeble-mindedness was transmissible struck fear in the heart of families, especially, it would seem, those of the middle and upper classes. So several generations of otherwise privileged children disappeared into the emptiness of Normansfield and its sister institutions.

Yet even at the height of institutionalization in the 1960s, less than one third of the mentally handicapped populace was institutionalized. Why did some families opt to keep a disabled child at home? Some children, obviously, were more easily cared for than others: behavioural problems precipitated many admissions to hospital. Family stability played an important role. The death or breakdown of one parent (especially the mother) accounted for many decisions to institutionalize, as did the arrival of younger siblings. Class made a difference, most obviously with regard to cost but also with respect to ingrained attitudes. If working-class parents saw institutions as temporary relief from the burdens of care, middle-class families often sought permanent confinement to conceal the disgrace of a tainted blood line. Here there was little difference between wealthy and titled families and the downwardly mobile Scott-Sandersons, who barely clung to the edges of the middle class. They were united by shame.

By the 1940s, parents who sought to keep their children at home had begun to push back, becoming the vanguard of a campaign for better services and schools, most successfully through the National Association for the Parents of Backward Children. To counteract a half-century's worth of propaganda about the deviant imbecile, they returned to the Victorian trope of the pitiable and eternal child. To combat the stigma that surrounded the issue of learning disability, they insisted that their children accompany them in public and solicited newspaper coverage for the Association's group outings. The National Association for the Parents of Backward Children became one of the largest grass-roots voluntary movements in post-war Britain.

As the first cracks appeared in the wall of silence that surrounded mental disability, Elizabeth Scott-Sanderson was still alive, though where exactly she was and even how long she lived are the final secrets in a life defined by secrecy. The last few reports that Reginald Langdon-Down sent Edith Scott-Sanderson about Elizabeth went unanswered; there is no correspondence after 1951 in the file, though Elizabeth's mother lived for thirteen years more. Elizabeth herself disappears from Normansfield's records after 1955, so it is possible that she died there or even that she was transferred to another institution. In a very real sense, her death had occurred years before. Her mother's last visit – the last time anyone visited – was in 1938. Perhaps her mother had already mourned for Elizabeth and committed her to a different keeper. The letter she wrote after that final visit suggests as much: 'Poor child, I am very sorry, I think it is all very sad and I know that you do all that can be done for her, which is a relief to my mind.'

4. Other People's Bastards

When the Litchfields wrote to Mrs Ransome Wallis, proprietress of the Mission of Hope, they knew exactly what they wanted. They wanted a little girl – not a servant, but a real daughter, a member of the family who would be their heir. Married ten years, they had been unable to have children of their own. Thomas Litchfield was fifty-six years old, his wife Gertrude sixteen years younger. Litchfield hoped to live to see the baby girl through to maturity, but 'if he should be taken first', he and his wife 'wished the child for company for her'. They preferred a girl with 'a fair amount of good looks', and they hoped she would be 'free from physical defects'. But with respect to one prized quality, the Litchfields were willing to be flexible: they would take the child 'even if her parents were not what they should be'. In 1919, their meaning could not be mistaken. But just to be sure, they made it explicit: 'an illegitimate child would do'.

For the unmarried mothers who travelled to Mrs Wallis's maternity home in south London, pregnancy was a life-wrecking disaster. Illegitimacy was the most common of family secrets. While illegitimacy rates had declined steadily through the Victorian period, at the turn of the twentieth century an estimated 65,000 children were still born out of wedlock each year. Among respectable folk in early-twentieth-century Britain, illegitimacy was imagined as a heritable moral weakness, passed down through the blood like a tendency to drink or thievery. Sexual immorality in a parent predicted depravity in a child. But so powerful a stigma was illegitimacy that it could corrupt by proximity as well. 'I am very anxious that it should not be known in the neighbourhood,' wrote one philanthropic lady to Mrs Wallis of an out-of-wedlock birth, 'I have always found it does some harm to all the young girls about.' A solicitor charged with managing the adoption of an illegitimate child requested: 'Please mark any reply PRIVATE as I have girls in my employ.' Illegitimacy was a taint that could destroy a woman's life, for ever damage her child, wreck her siblings' prospects in marriage, even harm the family business. 'If it would ease mother's and father's burden, I would do away with myself at once, only the shame would come to light,' grieved one young woman.

Why were the Litchfields willing to adopt a bastard? At a time when illegitimacy was widely construed as evidence of 'bad blood' and a symbol of degeneracy, adoptive parents regarded it as a defect that did not matter so long as it could be hidden. The interwar years marked the start of mass adoption, the first time that significant numbers of Britons took as their own the children of strangers. Although eugenicists inveighed against the practice, tens of thousands of children were adopted in the 1920s and 1930s, most by parents who knew absolutely nothing about the child other than the fact of illegitimacy. Other people, they recognized, would surely hold out-of-wedlock birth against the child if they knew. But the adopters' own desire for a child far outweighed any significance they accorded either eugenic arguments or the age-old stigma that had attached to illegitimacy. Even as parents such as the Scott-Sandersons hid mentally disabled children away in institutions for fear of the familial taint they advertised, thousands of other Britons like the Litchfields, or the resourceful Celia Ward and her husband, adopted bastards without apparent consternation. All that it required was the ability to keep a secret — or two.

Keeping a secret was what the Litchfields intended from the moment they picked up their new child. Dark-haired and winsome, the little girl was three and a half when the couple took her home in the summer of 1919. Her name had been Vera Rose Harris then; now she was Marjorie Litchfield. 'She seemed to take to her new position right away . . . and she takes the heart of everyone that sees her by storm,' wrote her new father with pride. Six months later, her parents could not imagine life without Marjorie and her funny little jumping-jack dances. If their daughter had not yet quite forgotten her past, neither did she wish to return to it. 'She speaks sometimes of her London friends and there is one in particular she speaks often about her Aunt Daisy, but when we ask her if she wants to go back she gives us a very emphatic no.' Aunt Daisy was a fast-fading memory, baby Vera Rose had been erased, only Marjorie Litchfield remained. And that was exactly how the Litchfields and Mrs Ransome Wallis wanted it.

When Mrs Wallis founded the Haven of Hope for Homeless Little Ones in 1893, Britain was still more than three decades away from legal adoption. But for Mrs Wallis, matching illegitimate children with loving families was a moral imperative that required no explanation and no enabling law. The daughter of the founder of the Paysander OxTongue empire, Mrs Wallis had, as a girl of twelve, been brought to the Lord her Saviour. When she was a young married woman, 'Saint Joan', as her brothers teasingly called her, took in illegitimate babies whose mothers could not care for them (ill. 16). Ever conscious that '"clothes make the man" even at the age of three weeks', she arranged her first adoption (to a minister's wife) by dressing the baby in her own daughter's pristine white robes, and presenting him in her child's crib. With that first adoption, Mrs Wallis joined a handful of charitably minded entrepreneurs who brokered the placement of 'friendless' children. By the First World War, she had added a network of discreetly located maternity homes to her children's rescue work, and enlisted her two unmarried daughters, husband and son in the Mission of Hope, as her concern was now called.

What seemed to Mrs Wallis and her fellow adoption workers an obvious solution to the problem of illegitimacy was much more controversial. Adoption was not legalized in Britain until 1926, and then only after a vigorous campaign by the new adoption societies founded at the war's end. Although children had been informally adopted for centuries, usually by their mother's kin, the natural parent could, at least in theory, reclaim the child at any point. The official-looking adoption agreements that Mrs Wallis drew up on stiff sky-blue paper had no force in law; the ties between children and their biological parents could never be severed. Not only were parental rights inalienable, but the stain of illegitimacy was supposed to be permanent. The intent of England's harsh bastardy laws was to inflict the sins of the parents upon their children; the stigma of illegitimacy was to follow a child through life. Illegitimate children did not automatically inherit from their natural parents. Even if their mothers and fathers later married, they remained life-long 'parentless at law'. Although the position of some illegitimates would be improved by interwar legislation, the public disgrace of their status was to persist. The distinction between legitimate and illegitimate was one of the most fundamental dividing lines of English law.

Mrs Ransome Wallis, remembered the journalist Harold Begbie fondly, had a nature that 'simplified so many problems of life'. Equipped with the smile of a 'spiritual Mona Lisa' and a talent for operating at the margins of legality, she presided over 2000 adoptions before 1926, and even hired a full-time children's secretary, Miss Edith Hart, for the purpose (ill. 17). In so doing, she ran contrary not just to the national child rescue organizations, but the country's moral welfare authorities as well. The established children's charities, such as Dr Barnardo's and the National Society for the Prevention of Cruelty to Children, did not permit adoptions; those who inquired at Dr Barnardo's were sent a form letter, which set forth 'important considerations' such as the fact that adoption was not legal, the likelihood of illegitimacy and mental taint, as well as 'the possibility of the child eventually turning out unsatisfactorily, in spite of the care bestowed upon it'. The proprietors of Britain's mother and baby homes were also vehemently opposed. Many unmarried mothers, they acknowledged, wished nothing more than to get rid of their babies. However, both for their own sake and that of their children, they had to be forced to face their responsibilities. Mother and baby homes required women to remain in the institution for a minimum of six months after the birth, so that they could learn to love their bastards.

In her own maternity homes, Mrs Wallis dispensed with many of the shibboleths of mother and baby work. She permitted women to leave the home after six weeks, the earliest point at which, according to the Mission's rules, they could give their babies up for adoption. Particularly vexing to her fellow moral welfare workers was Mrs Wallis's attitude to 'repeat offenders'. Most homes for unmarried mothers refused to admit women who had already had a child out of wedlock on the grounds that they threatened the work of moral regeneration. One illegitimate child was a grievous mistake; two placed a woman outside the pale. In workhouses, women who had fallen twice were forced to wear special uniforms to denote their crime. To Mrs Wallis, however, 'second cases' were, as her daughter Adeline observed, 'as reachable and salvable through the power of the Gospel as the first case'. Her guide was the Lord, whose words, painted on the walls of the delivery room, directed compassion: 'I the Lord Thy God will hold thy right hand, singing unto thee, Fear not. I will help thee.'

Marjorie Litchfield's mother – her dimly remembered Aunt Daisy – was 'a second case'. When Daisy Harris arrived at the Mission of Hope, Vera Rose was barely three, and Daisy was expecting her second child. Both children were war babies, both illegitimate. Vera Rose's father had died in the second year of the war, just before the girl was born. Of the whereabouts of her second child's father, Harris, a canteen worker, knew nothing. Her plight could hardly have been worse. Her parents were dead and she had no family upon whom she could call. 'Rokeby', the old-fashioned secluded brick mansion that served as the Mission's main maternity home, was in 1919 overloaded with inmates, and living conditions there, uncomfortable in the best of times, were spartan (ill. 18). To accommodate the flood of new cases (500 from one munitions plant alone), Mrs Wallis was running twelve maternity homes and was deeply in debt. Daisy's rations were short and she, like the other heavily pregnant inmates, was expected to scrub floors and work in the kitchen.

For women who wanted to keep their children and promised to pay for room and board, the Mission sought to make provisions, either through their own network of children's homes or with foster mothers. Mrs Wallis had already agreed to care for Daisy's new baby, a son named Peter, in the Mission's nursery in exchange for payments that amounted to more than a quarter of Daisy's weekly income. Even before the baby arrived, it was apparent that Daisy could hardly afford to maintain one child, let alone two. 'It grieves me very much to have to part with my child, but that seems the only thing. If you can get her adopted I will let her go, but I only pray she will get somewhere, where she will be treated kind.' Surrendering the daughter who knew her, rather than the new baby, was devastating, but three times as many adopters wanted girls as wanted boys (ills. 19 and 20). Within a month, little Vera Rose was gone.

From the perspective of the Mission of Hope, the Litchfields were an ideal adoptive couple. Thomas Litchfield was a bank clerk and, even better, a Sunday school teacher. As per Mrs Wallis's rules, Marjorie would be raised a Protestant, in a church-going household. Best of all, the Litchfields intended to keep the adoption a secret. For Miss Hart, the Mission of Hope's children's secretary, it was so much nicer for children never to know they were adopted. In the thick, blue leather-bound volumes where she kept track of the Mission's adoptions, Miss Hart noted with approval the ruses adoptive parents had engineered to carry out their deception. Mr Burr and his adoptive daughter were living with his mother, 'who loves the child and thinks it is his own!' Edwin Jones successfully passed off the boy he took from the Mission of Hope as his grand-nephew. A successful adoption, as Miss Hart saw it, was one in which neither the child nor the neighbours could discern anything unusual. After visiting Nina Stackhouse, adopted as a three-month-old in 1914, Miss Hart wrote: 'The child was well cared for in every way. She has music lessons and does not know she is adopted!' To conceal was to show love: James Fox's parents were 'terrified in case James should know he is not their own son! James has all a boy could want and is obviously adored!'

Few of the parents with whom Miss Hart corresponded needed any encouragement to keep the adoption a secret. Like the Litchfields, most assumed that the child's true origins would never be revealed. The Mission of Hope required that prospective adopters provide two confidential references (one of whom had to be their minister), but they – very often the only people who knew about the adoption – could be pledged to secrecy. Based upon the numbers of adopters who moved without, as was mandatory, informing the Mission of their forwarding addresses, there may have been many who transplanted to a new town to ensure that no one knew their children's origins. Miss Hart was sympathetic. When adoptive families petitioned her, especially when they were well-to-do, she often bent the Mission's requirements about annual visits and twice-yearly reports. Rather than sending one of the Mission's workers to check up on the child, she visited herself or, as in the case of Celia Ward, the wife of the English Steel executive, closed the file altogether. As she promised one adoptive mother: 'You may always rest assured I shall always keep your secret.'

Miss Hart's promise reflected a policy of secrecy that was vigorously defended by all the adoption societies founded after the First World War. The spectre of the natural parents' return, they argued, compelled adopters to conceal their child's origins. While very few biological parents in fact made any attempt to reclaim their children (according to one study, only in three of 1200 adoptions had the mother 'subsequently made a nuisance of herself'), those who had adopted feared that the birth mother or her relations might blackmail them or, as in *Pygmalion*, threaten to retrieve their progeny. Although Mrs Wallis's adoption agreements sought to guard against that possibility by making the birth mother liable for all costs the new parents had incurred, adopters nonetheless lived with the knowledge that the family they had made could be disrupted, even destroyed, by a knock on the door.

Even apart from legal insecurities, adoptive parents needed secrecy in order to make their families normal. The majority were childless couples drawn from the 'respectable' classes of society for whom infertility was increasingly a source of shame. In an era in which Marie Stopes's sex manual, *Married Love* (1918), became a bestseller, married folk such as the Litchfields who could not produce children were objects of pity, even derision. Infertility reeked of failure, of sexual and emotional incompatibility, all the more painful against a backdrop in which the nuclear family with its two children was becoming the norm. The very last thing that adoptive parents wanted was anything that made them stand out from their neighbours, a peculiarity that required explanation. On her deathbed, Alice Burr made her husband promise that he would never tell their daughter, Olive, that she was adopted. Mrs Burr had kept the secret not just from her husband's parents but from her own as well and she wanted it to stay that way even after she was gone. Similarly, Mrs P. J. Grantham kept her adoptive daughter Lucy's illegitimacy a secret even from her own mother, 'one of the sweetest women I ever knew'. She herself claimed to have forgotten Lucy's origins.

Then there were the feelings of the child to consider. To most adoptive parents, it seemed self-evident that children were better off not knowing the facts about their birth. 'Of course she knows nothing,' wrote one adoptive mother about her nineteen-year-old daughter, 'it would break her heart.' Adopters did not want their new children to feel that they had been abandoned, unloved, by their real parents. They especially dreaded the revelation of illegitimacy. Edith Marshall, who adopted three-month-old Elsie Harper from Mrs Wallis in 1908, intended to keep the secret so that her new daughter's 'feelings should never be hurt by knowing the stain of her birth'. Single men and women who adopted from the Mission of Hope concocted blood ties to deflect questions about the child's history. Maiden aunts acquired newly orphaned nieces. Elderly uncles manufactured young wards.

Many adoptive parents feared, as well, that their children would not love them as much if they knew the truth. Mrs Kirkwood never wanted to tell her son that he was adopted because 'it might make all the difference in love'. Love, a dimension of family life that most took for granted in the early twentieth century, seemed a much more fragile proposition in an adoptive family – an entity that most, including those who adopted, regarded as a 'second-best' alternative to the real thing. Adopters were surprised that they could love so avidly children who were not their own flesh and blood. After a vigil by her infant daughter's hospital bed, one adoptive mother wrote to

Miss Hart that she and her husband were 'as anxious as if she were our own offspring'. Model adopters were those, like Mrs Grantham, who had 'practically forgotten' that the child was not their own. Cementing the bonds of the adoptive family meant forgetting as well as denying.

Yet try as they might to forget their children's origins, heredity lurked as an intriguing mystery that adoptive parents could not entirely put aside. 'Was Charlotte's mother by any chance an actress,' wondered Winifred Bowers about her newly adopted daughter. 'I came across a picture of an actress as strikingly like Charlotte that we wondered if she was the mother. It would be interesting to know whether Charlotte is likely to inherit any artistic gift. It is a help in training a child to have some idea of what she may inherit. Can you give us any help?' Like Mrs Bowers, parents who were pleased with their adoptive children detected signs of 'refinement', for which they eagerly sought confirmation from Miss Hart. To Thomas Litchfield, his daughter Marjorie, 'both by her ways and appearances', seemed cut of a finer cloth. Although the Mission of Hope provided adoptive parents with little in the way of concrete information, Miss Hart gladly confirmed any impression of good breeding. She had every reason to believe, she told Litchfield, that Marjorie came from 'very superior people', though Daisy Harris would never have appeared to the bank clerk in that light.

But if heredity offered a promise of innate talents, it was also an excuse if the adoption soured. Seven-year-old Phyllis Bowden took things from her adoptive mother's house to give to other children. Fed up with the girl's petty thievery, her new mother decided in 1919 to send her back: 'I have tried every means to stop her and have now concluded it must be a taint she has inherited and that it is incurable.' Mrs Bowden had the weight of expert opinion on her side. To adopt a child, concluded an unofficial 'Select Committee' in 1920, was to transfer a being 'with a certain heredity' into an environment 'for which that heredity has in no wise prepared it'. There were few adoptive parents who would have seen the matter so darkly. Most adopters were willing to take on faith the scant information that Miss Hart provided, and if they cared about such things, to find gentility in their children's countenances.

Given the predominance accorded to inherited traits in the inter-war period and the rising tide of the eugenic movement, the determination displayed by the Litchfields and their fellow adopters is nothing short of astounding. Adoptive parents believed in the power of nurture. The leap of faith required to bring an unknown child into the home depended upon the expectation that the child could be moulded by her new environment. The widespread preference for girls probably reflected, among other things, the assumption that daughters were more malleable. Still, in an era in which everything about adoption was improvised, the key was secrecy, both inside and outside the family. When Ethel Prince's adoptive parents reported to the Mission that 'no one knows she is not our own' and, in the next letter, 'she is just the same to us as if she was born to us', they made plain the ways in which secrets bolstered the new family's legitimacy, not just in the eyes of the world, but for adopters themselves. Secrecy guaranteed both security and authenticity, all the more vital where legal protections were lacking.

The vast majority of adopters, like Thomas and Gertrude Litchfield, changed the child's surname to their own. Cooperative ministers baptized adoptive children privately and entered them in the church book under their new parents' names. Concealing an adoption once and for all was, Miss Hart reassured prospective adopters, a very simple matter. All that was required was for the new parent to take the child's so-called 'small' birth certificate to a lawyer, who would then 'tack' their own name on to the end. Issued when the child's birth was registered, the small birth certificate listed only the child's name, birth place and date, and so was easily altered (ill. 21). The cost was 'very trifling', the solution nearly foolproof. It was also utterly illegal, as one of Miss Hart's correspondents learned from his solicitor, when he attempted to follow the children's secretary's advice. No change could be made to a British birth certificate – ever. Undeterred, Miss Hart coun-

1. Margaret Tyndall-Bruce, painted by Henry Raeburn, before her marriage

2. Margaret Tyndall-Bruce of Falkland, painted by Sir Francis Grant

3. The district of Chowringhee, Calcutta, where Peter Cochrane lived with his family

4. The Divorce Court at the Royal Courts of Justice, an Edwardian-era sketch by Stanger Pritchard

5. Harriett Capel, by John Hayter

6. Sir James Wilde, 1863. He was the Judge Ordinary of the Divorce Court

7. Charlotte Capel as a young woman, in the *Ladies' Companion*, 1853

9. Miss Mary Drummond, ice-cream waitress. She was the granddaughter of the Earl of Perth

8. The Royal Commission on Divorce, 1910

10. Entrance to Normansfield, late nineteenth century

11. Normansfield's Gothic theatre and chapel

12. A Normansfield patient, *c.*1885. She is dressed in the latest style, with no expense spared

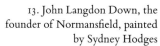

13. John Langdon Down, the founder of Normansfield, painted by Sydney Hodges

14. Mary Langdon Down at her writing desk

15. Reginald Langdon-Down with his children: Stella, Elspie and John

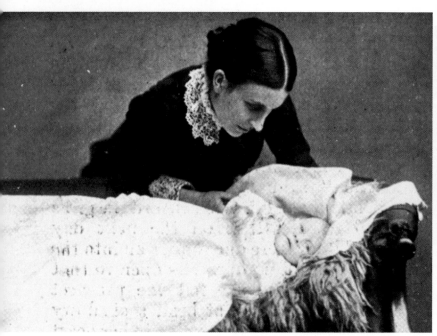

16. Mrs Ransome Wallis as a young woman

17. Mrs Wallis at work at Birdhurst Lodge, Croydon

18. Rokeby, one of the Mission's maternity homes

19. One of the girls that
the Mission placed for
adoption in the 1920s

20. The Mission of Hope's babies at tea

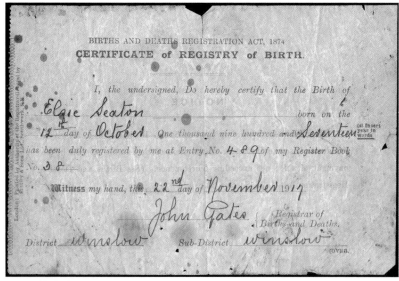

21. Certificate of registration of birth

selled perseverance: 'This is what a great many of my people do,' she wrote: 'try another lawyer.'

Little Marjorie's 'Aunt Daisy' could not stop thinking about her. Three months after parting with her daughter, Daisy Harris wrote in desperation to the Mission of Hope. Bypassing Miss Hart, Daisy addressed her letter to the person she hoped would be most sympathetic to her plight: Miss Adeline Wallis, Mrs Ransome Wallis's eldest daughter. A tall, energetic woman who impressed even sceptics with her religious ardour and 'extreme' friendliness, Miss Wallis had at the age of twenty-four taken over much of the day-to-day business of the Mission of Hope. Daisy apologized to Miss Wallis for being in arrears in her payments for baby Peter and expressed gratitude for the kind treatment she had received from the Wallises. Still, she was haunted by thoughts of her eldest child. 'I so wanted to ask you if there is any chance of me getting my darling child back . . . I do want her so. I feel that I cannot live without her.' Recognizing, perhaps, the futility of her cause, she continued: 'How I wish I had not let her go even if I cannot have her I wonder if the lady would have a photograph of her taken and sent me and do let me know how she is going on miss.' Three months later, Daisy wrote to Miss Hart directly. 'I have been waiting and hoping to receive a photograph of her from you. I would be so much happier if I could only see a photograph of her to see how she looks I have still a mother's love for her and shall never forget her. How I regret the day I parted with her. Of course I know that is no use now but I would very much like to know how she is sometimes.'

Daisy Harris was begging for a photograph. What she did not understand was that she was entitled to get her daughter back, for in 1919 adoption was outside the law, and, despite the forbidding appearance of Mrs Wallis's form, a mother's rights could not be terminated by her signature on its sky-blue page. But for women who bore children out of wedlock, the inalienability of parental rights was mostly a dead letter. Despite a consensus in both governmental and charitable circles that, as one official put it in 1920, 'every means should be taken to encourage the mothers of illegitimate children to bring them up and face the shame', there was little help forthcoming. An unmarried mother needed work so that she could support her baby, but keeping a job often required concealing her child. Very few employers would knowingly hire a woman with a bastard at home. Foster mothers were the solution of choice; they were discreet and a woman could see her baby with few restrictions. However, foster mothers were also expensive. Boarding her daughter with a foster mother during the war cost Daisy Harris nearly half of her weekly earnings. Barely able to pay her rent, she had little left for food, nothing at all for clothing or medical care – and no realistic option to keep Vera Rose.

In one respect, Daisy Harris's lack of alternatives was unusual. She had no relations to whom she could appeal for help. The vast majority of the Mission's unmarried mothers had family to whom they confessed their troubles. Most often they told their mothers, but frequently fathers, brothers and married sisters as well. An out-of-wedlock pregnancy became an emergency that mobilized an entire family. In the middle of the First World War, the Turners, greengrocers and 'very respectable people' in Canterbury, spirited away their newborn granddaughter in the middle of the night for fear that 'their business will be ruined'. By the time they contacted Mrs Wallis, the baby girl was hidden at their married daughter's house in London. Still, they had no intention of keeping the child. They wanted to arrange for her immediate adoption.

In working-class communities, families were much less willing to surrender an illegitimate child to a stranger. They feared (with some justification) that adopted children would be used as household drudges. To consign their own flesh and blood to the workhouse, a traditional dumping ground for unwanted children, was so abhorrent that any who could sought other solutions. The most common answer was simply to absorb the illegitimate son or daughter into the mother's family. Grandmothers pretended to be mothers and mothers acted like aunts. Florence Mayne took in her sister's illegitimate child because she and her husband could not have children of their own. Mrs Shaw agreed to raise her daughter's child as her own. There was, she confided to Miss Wallis, a possibility that her daughter would ultimately marry the baby's father. Even so, the deed would be done and Mrs Shaw would continue to act as the child's mother.

Such informal arrangements virtually assured that a family's disgrace would become common knowledge. The child might be kept in the dark for a while, but friends and neighbours were a different matter. Crowded housing and thin walls made secrecy next to impossible. Besides, lacking the resources to send erring daughters away for the term of their pregnancy, the drama of illegitimate birth was often played out in plain view anyway. Secrecy became a project that reached well beyond the family. Entire working-class neighbourhoods, the memoirs of illegitimate children make clear, conspired in the conversion of grandmother to mother, preserving fictional identities that, like Mrs Shaw's, would endure for a lifetime. When illegitimate children learned their origins, it was often because a schoolmate, in a vindictive moment, blurted out the truth.

Middle-class families proved much more willing to expunge completely an illegitimate child. Indeed, the higher class the family, the more pressure there was on the unmarried mother to give her baby up for adoption. After their 21-year-old daughter 'flatly refused' to part with her child, Edith Perrin's parents simply took the week-old baby away. Entirely dependent upon their families, the Mission of Hope's middle-class inmates hardly register their presence in the case files that disposed of their children. Other than her signature on the sky-blue form, there was no sign of 26-year-old Helen Williams in the thick bundle of papers that dealt with her son Harold's adoption. Everything was arranged by her mother, Nora Williams, on stationery embossed with the name of her house – 'The Lodge', in the middle-class town of Epsom. 'I am so happy and relieved in my mind,' Mrs Williams wrote to Mrs Ransome Wallis when baby Harold was finally adopted at the age of sixteen months. 'Last night I slept through the whole of the night! a thing I have not done for a year past.' Of Frances Nicholl, thirty-eight and unmarried in 1926 when her son Edward was born, there is even less evidence. Her mother, through the family solicitors, carried on all negotiations with the Mission of Hope; she signed the paperwork to surrender her grandson. All that we know of Frances is that she asked for a snapshot of Edward when he was three months old.

'Very superior families,' observed Miss Wallis, often find it 'impossible to face the disgrace of publicity.' It was in these families that the secret was most systematically hidden, even from siblings. Elizabeth Summers' parents knew about her baby son, but they insisted that the shameful news be kept from her brothers, both public school and university men. They sent Elizabeth away to a Yorkshire boarding house in November 1911, to have the baby. She returned home a month after the birth; her son Henry went to a foster mother, where he remained even after Elizabeth married a man who knew about her 'unfortunate past'. When Henry's foster mother closed her home during the turmoil of the First World War, Elizabeth and her new husband had no choice but to take the boy to live with them. But as soon as the war was over, Henry had to go. Not only did her husband refuse to shelter under his roof another man's child, but Elizabeth was 'exceedingly anxious' lest her relatives discover a transgression that was now nearly a decade past. Elizabeth arranged to hand her eight-year-old son to one of the Mission of Hope's workers on the platform of Liverpool's Lime Street railway station. She had dressed him in a sailor suit and hat.

To persuade unmarried daughters to part with their children, middle-class parents told their wayward offspring the same thing that Miss Hart did. To give up an illegitimate child was 'the best possible thing' for the little one, an act of maternal love. The new parents would give the child everything that the mother could not: a father's name, a home, a happy childhood. A mother who insisted upon keeping her baby ruined not just her own life, but her child's as well. It was, of course, a hardship to surrender a child, a great hardship, but one that had to be borne. As Miss Hart reminded one anguished mother: 'No one is more sorry for you than I am, and I can enter into what you are feeling, but at the same time, one has to be sensible, and when we have made a mistake, it is the penalty we have to pay, I am afraid.' With time, they advised, the pain would become easier to endure. When a woman married and had children with her husband, the entire episode – Miss Hart promised – would recede into the distance.

But as Miss Hart knew only too well, for many, and perhaps most, of the Mission's mothers, relinquishing a baby was a life-long regret. A middle-class spinster living at home, Caroline Hildesheim thought about the son she had surrendered in 1923 every day of her life. She petitioned Miss Hart each year for a photograph of her son, seventeen letters in all: 'no one can realize what it means to me to go day by day . . . if it had not been for shielding my parents I could have had my darling with me even now, but I must keep silent, but still where there is love there is sacrifice.' Rearing an illegitimate child could ruin a woman's life, but giving a baby up for adoption could shatter it in another way. Philip Rowman's mother went on to have two other sons, but she never overcame her guilt about abandoning her eldest. Three decades after relinquishing Philip, her youngest son was diagnosed with multiple sclerosis: 'It is very rare, and of unknown origin so you will understand how I cannot help thinking it is my punishment.' Guilt was compounded by silence. Some told new husbands about the baby in their past, but others kept the entire ordeal a secret.

Three years after adoption was legalized in England and Wales, Thomas Litchfield wrote to Miss Hart to clarify the rules. He and his wife Gertrude wanted to make Marjorie, now thirteen years old, their own by law. However, to do so, he feared, would require disclosing what they had always planned to keep secret. Miss Hart confirmed Litchfield's suspicion. If the Litchfields went in for legal adoption, Marjorie's new birth certificate would be stamped 'adopted' right across the face of it. As soon as Marjorie required proof of identity – if she trained as a teacher, as they hoped, or when she eventually married – she would learn that the Litchfields were not her natural parents.

Britain's first adoption law required that adoptive parents trade secrecy for legality. Adoption was to be open – an acknowledged fact both to the child herself and to the public at large – and transparent. Mothers who gave children up for adoption had the right to know to whom their child would go; on the form that they signed to surrender their parental rights, the adopters' name and address were listed. To legalize the arrangement, adoptive parents had to attend their local courts. Adoption hearings were conducted *in camera*, but there was always the possibility of encountering the natural mother, who could be called upon to appear. Once an adoption order was finalized, the child's new name, birth date and adoptive parents would be entered into the Adopted Children's Register, a certified copy of which would serve as the child's new birth certificate. Adoption records, like birth records, were completely open. A curious member of the public could consult the Register at any time.

The civil servants who crafted the 1926 law aimed to do away with the obsessive secrecy that had long enshrouded operations such as the Mission of Hope. Unsympathetic to the adopters' desire to pass children off as their own, they joined a distaste for 'hiding up things' with the common law's age-old concern for the natural parents' prerogatives. Zealously guarding the state's 'official' secrets, Whitehall prescribed transparency for British citizens. Once the adoptive parents' rights were secured, officials reasoned, there would be no need for secrets. Efforts to obscure a child's history were not only 'wholly unnecessary' but 'objectionable'. The 1926 law made only one concession to secrecy: no one would be able to trace a child's original birth certificate on the basis of her entry in the Adopted Children's Register. So Marjorie Litchfield would be publicly branded as adopted, but Daisy Harris and baby Vera Rose would remain hidden. In theory, Marjorie got a fresh start with the evidence of her illegitimacy expunged. In practice, the situation was not nearly so favourable. Adoption, to most people, signalled illegitimacy. The new birth certificate effectively exposed the one piece of information it was intended to hide.

For those, like the Litchfields, who had taken children from the Mission of Hope before 1926, the new adoption law posed two immediate problems. There was first of all the devastating fact that the child – and everyone else who had also been kept in the dark – would eventually have to be told about the adoption. Then there was the provision that the natural mother had to provide her consent. Either would have been sufficient to dissuade many parents from complying with the new law's requirements. For Mrs Gurney the decision was easy. Her adopted son, Frederick, she wrote to Miss Hart, 'is so much my boy that I forget that anyone else ever had him . . . The only thing I dread is that he will ever find out that we are not his real parents.' Legalizing Frederick's adoption was not worth the risk of losing her son's love or exposing his true position to the world. The new adoption law, lamented one mother, far from solidifying her parental claims, stood in her way: 'in our hearts he is our boy, but there is the law which comes in between'.

As Parliament debated the 1926 bill, one Conservative MP issued a warning. Lieutenant-Colonel Cuthbert Headlam recognized that the majority of his colleagues opposed secrecy, but he – as an adoptive father – thought it essential: 'in many cases a child will never be legally adopted unless there is a large measure of secrecy'. Headlam's judgement proved correct. Only one fifth of those who had adopted from the Mission of Hope before 1926 ultimately legalized their arrangement. Nor did the law put an end to informal adoption. More than a third of the Mission's clients up to the Second World War never obtained a legal adoption. This was despite the fact that Miss Hart, like her counterparts at the other adoption agencies, proved willing to circumvent the law in one crucial respect. She safeguarded the adoptive parents' confidentiality by omitting their names and addresses from the forms that mothers signed.

A year after Thomas Litchfield's initial inquiry about Marjorie's birth certificate, he contacted Miss Hart again. He and his wife had decided on legal adoption, but there was the matter of Marjorie's natural mother. The normal procedure was for Miss Hart to contact the birth mother to obtain her consent. But was there any way, Thomas Litchfield asked, to avoid that step? Not only would the Litchfields' name be listed ('and that is the very last thing I would wish her to know'), but Marjorie's birth mother could refuse to sign. Miss Hart knew what Thomas Litchfield did not: Daisy Harris had in fact begged for a chance to reclaim her daughter. For the benefit of the Litchfields' adoption petition, Miss Hart testified that the Mission of Hope had been unable to locate Daisy Harris. Her last contact with Marjorie's natural mother, she wrote to the Court, had been in January 1920. That was Daisy's second letter pleading for a photograph. If Miss Hart ever answered Daisy's letters or made any attempt to find her, she left no trace in the Mission's files.

Just short of her sixteenth birthday, Marjorie learned she was adopted. To Thomas Litchfield's immense relief, the news did not seem to make any difference to her. He wrote to Miss Hart: 'She is got quite a big girl now and seems to think there is nobody like her Daddy and Mummy.' Because of Marjorie's age, she had to give her consent in court to the adoption. But she asked no questions about her natural parents or where she had been born and the Litchfields volunteered nothing. Now that the truth was out, Thomas Litchfield told Miss Hart, it was perhaps all for the best. Someone else might have told her eventually anyway.

By the late 1930s, it was becoming clear how difficult it was to keep either adoption or illegitimacy a life-long secret from a child. Certified copies of the original birth certificate were increasingly required as official proof of identity – at marriage, by employers, when a man joined the army. Moreover, time and circumstance loosed the lips even of those sworn to secrecy. As the adoption societies came to recognize, it was devastating for a child to learn about the adoption years after the fact. Until she was fifteen, Janet Woodward, adopted aged four from the Mission of Hope, was 'the light of our home', as her mother put it. And then 'someone told her I was not her mother and after that she resented my control'. On the cusp of Janet's sixteenth birthday, Mrs Woodward dispatched the girl back to the Mission of Hope, declaring the adoption a failure. Barbara Smith, adopted as a baby, was fourteen when she found out. 'Someone told her a year or so ago we were not her parents and since then she has went headlong to the mischief.' Her parents, too, returned her to Miss Wallis.

Where many adoption workers had once encouraged parents to keep the secret from their children, by the Second World War they had uniformly committed to a policy of disclosure. The National Adoption Society, the largest of the registered adoption societies, 'strongly' urged parents to tell their children, at the earliest possible moment: 'It has been found that those who know from early childhood and are confident of the love and affection of their adopters accept the position quite happily and naturally.' At the Mission of Hope, the new reigning wisdom became apparent when Miss Hart retired in 1934. It was Miss Wallis's firm belief that children should know the truth about themselves. Parents whose fictions Miss Hart had once abetted Miss Wallis gently instructed to face the inevitable.

So urgent was the perceived need for the new official document that the Ministry of Health rushed to carry out a mass printing in the face of a dire paper shortage. The document was the 'short' birth certificate, proposed by the Labour government in 1947 and quickly ushered into law. Unlike the standard certificate – used in England and Wales since 1837, when the registration of births began – the short birth certificate omitted entirely the details of parentage. It listed only the child's name, sex, place and date of birth (ill. 22). Children who were legally adopted would receive a new short birth certificate under their adoptive name. To ensure that the short form was widely accepted, the government set its price at a fifth the cost of the original, in order that it would become the standard for all children. As speaker after speaker in both houses of Parliament rose to acclaim the bill, they urged that the new forms be printed immediately. As one MP put it, the children 'born, say, in 1942, are now about to go to school'.

Barely debated either in the House of Commons or in the Lords, the short birth certificate in fact marked a fundamental departure. What had once been viewed as a matter of grave public interest – whether a person was of legitimate birth – the state would now help

to conceal. The purpose of the short birth certificate was plain
enough: illegitimates and adoptees (and their families) should not be
forced to divulge the shameful facts of their birth. Mrs Ganley, MP
for Battersea, drew on her own experience working with adopted
children in the Juvenile Courts to make the case. 'A youngster who
has grown up without any real knowledge of the facts feels a sense
of shame when the true position is suddenly forced upon him.'
For the adoptive parents, it is a very great worry 'when they think
of the time when they must explain the true position. We hope
that the time will come when possession of the certificate will make
it unnecessary for such explanation to be made.'

In 1926, civil servants had ridiculed the secrecy, even wilful disre-
gard of reality, which enveloped the practice of adoption. Particularly
ludicrous was the belief that the taint of illegitimacy could be erased:
'if the eyes can be closed to facts the facts themselves will cease to
exist so that it will be an advantage to an illegitimate child who has
been adopted if in fact his origin cannot be traced.' But in the post-
war world, it no longer seemed so obvious that children should be
made to suffer for the sins of their fathers. Undoing centuries of
common law precedent, Parliament created a new right of privacy
which acknowledged the rule by which adoptive parents had for decades lived: illegitimacy was not an inherent disability, but mattered
only if it were known. Prejudice against illegitimate or adopted children could be circumvented by hiding the truth. What families long
sought to achieve with secrecy – and the Mission of Hope had abetted with Mrs Wallis's worthless forms and Miss Hart's improvisations
– had now become British law.

Just as adoptive parents had become reconciled to telling, the
government offered them the first realistic chance at life-long concealment. It was the domestic upheaval of the Second World War
that compelled British officials, as a matter of policy, to enter into the
business of concealing citizens' secrets. By the early 1940s, the vast
majority of mothers offering children for adoption were married
women whose husbands were serving overseas. The novelist Ian
McEwan's mother handed a baby over on the platform of Reading

Station to a couple who had answered a newspaper advertisement. John Lennon's mother, too, gave up a baby girl for adoption, the product of an affair with a Welsh soldier. Adoption questions no longer focused on wayward mothers, for whom public sympathy was always mixed at best, but rather on a generation of war babies who quite obviously bore no responsibility for their misfortune. Their fate had become a national predicament which rested, uneasily, in the laps of local officials. Under the 1926 law, the cuckolded husband's consent was required before the adoption could proceed. Would the courts enforce the letter of the law, with the likely result that the adoptions would never happen (and the marriages would probably fail anyway)? Or would they, in effect, collude with the wife to keep her affair a secret by allowing the adoption to proceed without her husband's knowledge?

Judges and magistrates in the provinces reacted by turning to the Lord Chancellor to resolve a question for which the law books offered no satisfactory answer. Their pleas landed on the desk of Sir Albert Napier, secretary to the Lord Chancellor. The son of a famous Victorian war hero, Napier had ended up a lifetime civil servant after his legal practice foundered. His particular responsibility was the bottom tier of the British legal system, the County Courts. Praised for both his efficiency and his humanity – 'no man, woman or child ever came to Albert Napier for advice or help and turned away empty-handed' – he understood first hand the bitter price that families paid in wartime. In 1942, as Napier took up the problem of other people's children, he had just learned that his only son was killed in battle. Napier's letters to judges operate on a personal plane that is explicitly outside precedent. 'Apart from authority,' he wrote, 'I had formed the opinion myself that the adoption court would be justified in doing its best for the child notwithstanding that the effect might be, individually, to help the mother to conceal the adultery from the husband.' In lieu of consent, proof was needed that the child was really illegitimate, that the overseas husband had no legal rights. But technical rules of evidence need not be followed. Even if flimsy or based on hearsay, the testimony of a friend or relative would suffice.

The husband's consent should be foregone, Napier advised judges, when you are satisfied that he is not the father.

Under the pressure of circumstance, local officials concluded during the war years – with Napier's help or on their own – that what mattered above all was the child's welfare. The wrongdoing of the parents, which so preoccupied prior generations, was no longer a stigma to be borne by their offspring. Granting a child a fresh start in life was the prime objective, to be accomplished by adoptions that skirted the law and birth certificates that concealed the stain of illegitimacy. For all practical purposes, the facts did indeed cease to exist if other people's eyes could be closed to them. In the long history of the destigmatization of illegitimacy, adoptive parents' conviction – that bastardy was not an intrinsic liability but mattered only if it could be known – proved prescient.

What had been the adoptive parents' secret would now be protected by a new sphere of privacy. Two years after enacting the short birth certificate, Parliament raised the walls around the adoptive family still higher. In 1949, MPs stripped away a provision that the framers of legalized adoption had twenty years earlier viewed as essential: that the birth mother consent to the adoption with full knowledge of who was taking her child and where they were going. The requirement that Miss Hart and her fellow adoption workers had often flouted would be eliminated entirely. On the papers that the birth mother signed, the identity of the adopters would now be indicated only by a serial number. According to Viscount Simon, the new measure's chief sponsor in the House of Lords, it was in the interests of the child that the natural mother could not 'haunt the home' of the new family. An 'iron curtain' should be lowered to separate the natural and adoptive families.

Over the course of a half-century, adoption had been transformed from a practice outside the law to a sanctioned and protected means of making a new family. In the decade after the war, nearly 10,000 people every year took advantage of the new procedures to adopt the children of strangers, a five-fold increase over the interwar period (ill. 23). Most adopters would probably have preferred to have their own biological children, but the distance between the two categories of parenthood was diminishing. As motherhood was redefined as a set of skills that needed to be taught, adoptive parents could reasonably feel that biological parents did not begin with an insuperable advantage. Feelings that had surprised interwar adopters – that they could love the child as their own – later generations took for granted.

Adoptive families had begun to appear normal, both to themselves and to society at large. They discovered, to their delight, that their adoptive children looked like them. The family resemblance was evident not only to family members but to strangers on the street. Irene Sterling's three-month-old adoptive daughter was the spitting image of her new mother. In a letter to the Mission of Hope about her new son, Mrs Buchanan proudly reported the reaction of her husband's relatives: 'They all think he is like my husband when he was a baby.' The baby boy she had taken from the Mission of Hope, wrote one adoptive mother, now bore a strong resemblance to her husband's family. 'Do not dare laugh at me . . . Either of my sisters in law could claim him by his resemblance to their own children.'

Family resemblance was evidence of the adoptive family's normalization, but so, too, was a new willingness to acknowledge the birth mother. With their legal status secured and anonymity guaranteed, adoptive parents' censure had mostly turned to pity. Joyce Nichols's new daughter came accompanied by a parcel of clothes her birth mother had sewn for her: 'We do think they are sweet every one of them. It made us feel a bit sad when we realized all the heartache which must have gone into the making of them.' Their own happiness, they recognized, was tied up with someone else's misfortune, even tragedy. Like many other adoptive parents, Mrs Brown sent photographs of her six-month-old daughter to be passed on to 'her mother'. 'Several times this last week or two we have said how much her mother must be thinking of her just now and wondering what she is like.' Mrs Welsford wished that her children's mothers 'could know how lovely they are and how much joy and love they have brought'. When her youngest daughter was three, she dispatched a report to the Mission of Hope, to be passed along to the birth mother if Miss Wallis thought it wise. She did not 'want our joy to cause her mother fresh pain'.

Even as the short birth certificate made concealment possible, secrecy about the fact of adoption now seemed unnecessary, even damaging. Guaranteed a measure of privacy by changes in the law, adoptive parents accepted the idea that keeping adoption a secret undermined the normal family they aimed to create. Telling remained the prescribed and accepted course for most parents, with many electing to make the disclosure at an early age, between three and nine. To counteract any sense of rejection that the child might feel, they described how they had specially chosen her from the many others available. A few adoptive parents even pursued openness with vigour, making efforts to reach across the iron curtain. Mrs Bickford asked the Mission of Hope if her daughter's mother might be willing to send a photograph of herself, to show 'the little one when she is old enough to understand'.

But if telling became the rule, adoptive parents nonetheless did not say everything. In many families, the big lie was replaced by half-truths and subjects that could not be raised. By the mid-1950s it was becoming clear to social workers how strained and incomplete communication about adoption in fact was. Children were told only once, when they were little, and adoption was never mentioned again. Or they were told in anger, after they had misbehaved, with the admonition that their adopters had lifted them from the dunghill and could return them there. In her survey of 500 adoptions, Margaret Kornitzer, editor of the flagship journal *Child Adoption*, noted how often the entire business of telling was botched, even by apparently well-adjusted adopters. She pithily summarized her findings: 'In its way, "telling" always proved the adoption. If it was done properly the consequence was that there seemed to be no consequences.'

The central issue adoptive parents sought to avoid was the old bugbear of illegitimacy. Some told children that they knew nothing about their origins, others, with the encouragement of adoption workers, that they were orphans. There was, as Kornitzer mordantly observed, a high mortality rate among parents whose children had been placed through adoption societies. Adopters 'forgot' what little information the adoption society had provided about the natural parents, even when the details might have proved reassuring to the child. They failed to ask about the child's background because, as one mother told Kornitzer, 'We wanted to start with them as our own babies.' They sought to rearrange the facts to suit their own fantasies. One couple that Kornitzer interviewed – superior adopters – corresponded with their child's working-class grandmother but of her mother frankly confessed: 'We have killed her off in a bus accident.' In many cases, they waited for children to ask questions which, as with Marjorie Litchfield, never came.

Secrecy had permitted adoptive parents to banish their children's origins. Openness, by contrast, meant that illegitimacy stayed near the surface, a fact that had to be continually confronted. To acknowledge it meant facing the consequences: an inevitable legacy of shame, as most adopters saw it, for the child. The parents of adoptive girls, especially as they entered their teenage years, worried about the birth mother's bad example. When she neared fifteen, the age at which her own mother had given birth, one adoptee became prisoner to her parents' fears about sexual immorality, shut away 'in a glass-house'. As an adoptive mother told an interviewer, 'Of course, she is sexually attractive or she wouldn't be here, would she?' In Kornitzer's view, parents' anxieties were not entirely irrational. After all, if a girl's neighbours and teachers assumed that promiscuity was heritable, wasn't it possible that an adoptee might also feel that she had a 'compulsion' to go the way of her mother?

Fears about heredity that could be submerged in an era of secrecy surfaced more insistently in an age of openness. The 'genetic anxiety' that bedevilled so many post-Second World War adoptions make a striking contrast to the faith of interwar adopters such as the Litchfields that they could make a child their own by dint of nurture and secrets – a confidence all the more extraordinary given the sway of eugenicism in the period. Secrecy did not, of course, prevent adopters from blaming bad blood when something went wrong, nor did it assure successful adoptions. But as telling became the new conventional wisdom, the advocates of openness failed to acknowledge what secrecy had protected: the ability to raise a child without a neighbour speculating as to what taint she might have inherited.

The Litchfields eventually told Marjorie that she was adopted, but like so many of their fellow adoptive parents that was the limit of their candour. At the time of the legalization proceeding, they conspired with Miss Hart to make sure that Daisy Harris was kept in the dark. Years later, when Marjorie, unmarried and still living at home, was in her twenties, her brother came calling. This was Daisy Harris's second child, the baby boy she kept when she relinquished Marjorie. Somehow Peter Harris had managed to trace his sister, but Marjorie's adoptive parents were determined to prevent any encounter with the past. They obtained an injunction to bar Peter from contacting their daughter. Legalization had given the Litchfields the confidence to tell Marjorie she was adopted. It had also given them the power to shut out her natural brother, without asking or telling.

In the early 1950s, the Scottish social worker Alexina McWhinnie set out on a pioneering investigation to evaluate systematically how children adopted in the first half of the twentieth century had actually fared. With the help of Edinburgh's general practitioners, McWhinnie identified fifty-eight adopted adults in the vicinity, whom she interviewed about their childhood and subsequent lives. Most had been adopted in the era of secrecy before 'telling' became standard practice. Her book, *Adopted Children: How They Grow Up*, was published at a propitious moment. 1967 marked both the high-point of adoption (more than 20,000 orders granted) and the year that legalization of abortion foretold adoption's precipitous decline. Based upon McWhinnie's research, there was little reason to mourn the passing of adoption. Contrary to previous surveys that had yielded largely reassuring results, McWhinnie's conclusions, as Dame Eileen Younghusband pointed out in a laudatory preface, could hardly be considered encouraging. Of McWhinnie's subjects, just one quarter made a 'successful and happy' adjustment to life.

McWhinnie's study, on the face of it, confirmed conventional wisdom: concealing the fact of adoption could have a very damaging effect. One man, who learned the truth at the age of seventeen when he needed his birth certificate to join the Navy, lost all faith in his parents: if they had told lies about 'this basic fact', why should he believe anything that they said? Another boy, told at the age of nine, 'felt that he was on his own in the world' and vowed self-sufficiency. Children revolted against their parents or drew into themselves, keeping their own secrets. They felt 'rootless' or 'besmirched and inferior'. In relationships already fraught with problems, the tardy disclosure of adoption could cause familial bonds to come entirely unravelled.

In fact, many adoptive children knew far more than anyone imagined. They overheard gossiping relatives or found legal documents, they were teased at school or wondered about the colour of their hair. They pieced together discordant facts on their own. The majority of McWhinnie's subjects learned of their adoptions from people other than their parents. Sometimes they confronted their parents with their discovery, but more often they kept silent, carrying their burdens alone. Afraid of hurting or angering their adoptive parents, they felt unable to ask. They wanted to be told. The absence of questions that Thomas Litchfield took as evidence of Marjorie's contentment says as much about the subjects she could not broach as it does about her happiness.

For McWhinnie, a strong advocate of telling, the harmful nature of secrets was evident. And yet, as her own interviews demonstrated, telling was no guarantee of success. Openness did not assure a good adoption any more than secrecy made a bad one. Adoptive families, unsurprisingly, were happiest when their parents had a happy marriage and loved the child for her own sake. It mattered whether the extended family accepted the child. Older people made worse adoptive parents, perhaps because they had taken a child to ensure that they would have someone to care for them. Children adopted after the age of two tended to fare badly. Poor outcomes were more likely when adopters had very negative attitudes towards the child's natural mother. But even in loving families where the adoptive parents were sympathetic to the birth mothers' plight, children could still feel distressed about their illegitimate birth. So common indeed was the association of adoption with illegitimacy that most adoptees assumed that their mothers were unmarried – and felt ashamed about it. In some sense, they were more exposed than their illegitimate brothers. To the extent that disclosure reached outside the home, there were few schoolfellows or neighbours who would not have suspected sexual immorality as the predicate for adoption.

Openness about adoption emerges from the raft of studies conducted in the 1950s and 1960s a trickier proposition than it first appears. Margaret Kornitzer's widely quoted proclamation – '"telling" always proved the adoption' – was contradicted by her own evidence. Success and failure, as it turned out, did not neatly correlate to disclosure. Some children, told early and often, were deeply disturbed; others, told late or not at all, seemed unbothered. If the adoptees' reactions were unpredictable, it is because neither secrecy nor openness adequately described their wishes. McWhinnie's subjects did not want their adoptive status discussed beyond the intimate family, not with relatives nor with friends. They might not wish to tell people about the adoption at all. Most were embarrassed, even humiliated, by the implication of illegitimacy. They did not want complete secrecy – 'irritating and unrealistic' – but neither did they want the adoption constantly present in their lives. They wanted forthright acknowledgement of their status within the nuclear family and then for the matter to be 'overtly apparently forgotten', in order that they could live no differently from a biological child. For all of the troubled feelings that McWhinnie and Kornitzer detected in adoptive families, the aims of adopters and their children were not, perhaps, so different after all. Parents who kept secrets had wanted their families to be thought of as normal, the same hope that adoptees expressed. The privacy adoptees sought was secrecy stripped of the stigma or the burden.

In the late 1960s, the Mission of Hope's Birdhurst Lodge – like the rest of Britain's mother and baby homes – was rendered irrelevant by legal abortion, the contraceptive pill and more permissive attitudes towards illegitimacy. After nearly a century of sheltering desperate mothers and keeping guilty secrets, the Mission of Hope wound down its adoption enterprise. Birdhurst Lodge was demolished, the Mission's adoption case files transferred to the local authorities. But if the Mission's story had come to an end, the stories in the Mission's case files have no endings. They tell of attempts to find biological mothers, of correspondence begun, of arrangements to meet, but rarely anything about what happened next. In many cases, after making a tentative contact, the adoptive child and the relinquishing mother never reported to the Mission again. So much of what mattered had been hidden in these files. It is perhaps fitting, then, that the moment of reunion happened off stage, without intermediaries.

Marjorie Litchfield never tried to trace her mother through the Mission of Hope. When she contacted the agency in 1980, more than sixty years after her adoption, it was for a different purpose. She was an unmarried lady, perhaps the schoolteacher that her adoptive parents had hoped for. Her adoption, she reported, had been on the whole successful. She was the 'cherished only child' of her parents, with whom she had 'a very happy though very sheltered upbringing'. As Daisy Harris had hoped, the little girl she gave up – her baby Vera Rose – had been 'treated kind'. Still, there was much her adoptive parents had not told Marjorie: 'I was never made aware of my background and only realized the position after their deaths.' In her letter to the Mission, Marjorie did not ask anything about Daisy Harris but wanted to know about the little boy her mother had kept: her brother Peter, left in the Birdhurst nursery in 1919. After all of these years, a 'recent powerful recall of memory' had made her aware of him.

When the Mission's social worker responded that he was unable to find any record of a brother in her file, Marjorie pressed him to search further. By now she knew not only that she had a brother, but that Peter had come looking for her years before, only to be turned away by a court order. While she did not resent her parents' interference – 'I myself was totally unaware of his existence, and I think frankly I would have been shattered if he had managed to make contact' – she now wished to find him. To her second letter Marjorie Litchfield attached a donation of sixty pounds for the Mission's work, with the plea that she be informed if the old records turned up a Peter Harris. That is the last page of the file. The search for her brother may have failed. But Marjorie had already found a way to preserve the memory of her first brief childhood. She signed her letters to the Mission with the name that her adoptive parents had long ago discarded: Vera Rose.

5. Bachelor Uncles

Among the nearly 500 diaries that the public-opinion organization Mass-Observation solicited from ordinary Britons during the Second World War is a thick bundle of typewritten pages on carbon paper, the record of the life of Anatole James between 1945 and 1949. Imprisoned three times in England for homosexual offences, James had at the end of the war moved to Edinburgh. There, he spent his days hunting out eighteenth-century objects of virtue, and living frugally in a Georgian house on Chester Street with the funds he had inherited from his paternal grandfather. The diary he sent punctually each month to Mass-Observation provided James with an opportunity to chronicle, for posterity, the life of a mid-century homosexual. Alongside descriptions of his assignations with local lads, James filled pages with the birthdays and death dates of his mother, grandmother, sisters, aunts and the father he thoroughly despised. 'Dear Grannie's Birthday. How I continue to miss her! Had she been alive she would have been 111 years old!' wrote James in 1946, 'Had she lived, how different things would have been for me!'

Families hardly figure in the history of homosexuality, despite the prominence that James and other men accorded them. This is an omission that matters, for in an era of draconian penalties and social opprobrium – when all homosexual acts between men, committed either in public or in private, were criminal offences – whether your family cast you off or not (or something in between) could make a great deal of difference in the life of an individual. If mentioned at all, the presumption is that families functioned oppressively. That the homosexual was a pariah, estranged from his relatives, was a subject upon which both social scientists in the 1950s and Gay Liberation in the 1970s could agree. And yet, queer men's own testimonies suggest a much more complex set of familial relationships – in which silence was the price of tacit acceptance – that structured their lives, and affected, too, how others saw them.

For much of the twentieth century, sex between men was the open secret par excellence. It was both known to be known, and assiduously, though inevitably imperfectly, hushed up. Officially proscribed, it was nonetheless omnipresent: in all-male settings such as schools, borstals and the army; in public toilets as in Knightsbridge clubs; and, most noisily, in the press. The travails of men arrested for 'unnatural crimes' were chronicled by a tabloid press that trafficked in disgraced parsons and schoolmasters, as well as their tearful relations. A homosexual relative in the dock was as much a family disgrace as an individual disgrace. After Anatole James's first arrest in 1917 for importuning a teenage page-boy, his father, a prominent Hull solicitor, exiled his only son from the family home: 'I'd rather you had been sent to prison for murder.'

For families, this was a secret that by definition escaped its bounds. Unlike an out-of-wedlock pregnancy or an 'idiot' child, the family had no control over the basic fact of exposure or its breadth: they had to expect that their son's queerness would be known or at the very least suspected outside the home.* To manage an open secret, then, required something more than merely a bond of secrecy. Beneath the public taboos and prevarication about sex between men lay a private sea of talk within families – occasionally with the homosexual, more often about him; sometimes momentous (banishment or acceptance), more often quotidian. How to explain the eccentric uncle who never

---

* Lesbianism was a different matter. Never outlawed in Britain, same-sex relations between women generated neither the steady thrum of scandal nor the commentary that accompanied male homosexuality. They remained shadowy, at times nearly invisible. Even in the more suspicious 1920s and 1930s – after the subject of sapphism was levered into the headlines by the libel suit brought by Maud Allan in 1918 and the 1928 prosecution for obscenity of Radclyffe Hall's *The Well of Loneliness* – love-affairs between women were still relatively easy to conceal, not least because intense female friendship had long been embedded at the heart of the family. Such was the prevailing ignorance on the subject of same-sex female desire (both real and wilful) that the headmistress and her devoted life-long deputy could through the mid twentieth century share a household in plain view.

married? Would the effeminate boy be allowed a baby carriage? A son in the dock was a catastrophe, but a quiet Sunday dinner with that son's friend could be simply a family custom.

For much of Anatole James's life, the clearly defined, nearly irreconcilable categories of 'homosexual' and 'heterosexual' that structure our sexual landscape did not order his world. Until the early 1950s, a man could have sex with another man – even love him – without considering himself in any respect abnormal. That was especially true of the working-class men and boys, 'rough trade', whom James favoured as sexual partners, for in working-class districts what made a man queer was not the kind of sex he had, but how he dressed and behaved. Whether motivated by sexual longings or just by the money that 'trade' generated, James's young guardsmen and telegraph boys moved unabashedly from homosex to conventional heterosexual marriage and sometimes back again, distinguishing themselves from the 'poufs' or 'queans', mostly working-class men, whose woman-like character, proclaimed by make-up, a 'mincing' gait or a sing-song manner of speech, announced their feminine desires. Among those men who partook of homosex in James's salad days of the 1920s and 1930s, then, there were three different types: rough trade; 'queans', a flamboyantly visible presence in interwar metropolitan society; and those so-called 'inverts' like James himself, largely middle-class men for whom homosexuality was becoming an identity defined by their exclusive attraction to other men.

Until the early 1950s, 'coming out' was something that only middle-class inverts did (and probably even then relatively rarely), for rough trade did not think about themselves as queer, and queans plainly advertised their womanlike nature. In 1925, Christopher Isherwood returned home from Cambridge, having deliberately failed his exams, to contentious discussions with his mother, Kathleen, about sexuality. Kathleen's diaries record evenings spent in bitter dispute and recrimination, punctuated by visits, in Christopher's company, to Christie's and the National Portrait Gallery. At some point in 1926, Christopher revealed to his mother his preference for men. Sex between men was hardly unknown to Kathleen: her husband's brother, Henry, had a notorious yen for guardsmen. However, in her diaries she bemoaned the change in her son's behaviour, and his alienation from her: 'I do feel so sorry for C. & understand how he is torn but it is difficult to talk about & I can't put it into words.' Although Kathleen came to recognize that Christopher would never marry, she, as Isherwood later recalled, 'did and she didn't' accept his homosexuality. While she hosted his various lovers in her house, Kathleen once confessed to Christopher that homosexuality 'didn't seem real to her'. According to Isherwood, his mother was the 'sort of person who was very good at sort of glossing things over'.

What Kathleen Isherwood could not put into words, Harold Brown found himself discussing the following year in letters, over dinners and during motoring excursions with his son, Richard (ill. 24). An expatriate American who invented the power signalling system for the London Tube, Harold Brown had since the turn of the century lived in Britain, where he and his wife raised their three sons. In August 1927, his middle child, Richard Blake Brown, was a newly ordained 26-year-old parson, unhappily ensconced in the vicarage at Portsea (ill. 25). Harold's hortatory missives to his son about pulling himself together provoked Richard to send his father 'a full, painful and awful confession . . . Telling him EVERYTHING about myself: it was a terrible task, a humiliating ordeal.' Richard had some reason to imagine his broad-minded father would view the matter sympathetically. A few weeks earlier he and his father had discussed the need to cast off 'the shocked-at-being-outraged pseudo morality that was fostered during the Victorian era'; his father had described sex as 'no conceivable sin, but the greatest, purest, and finest force in Nature'. His mother, Richard Blake Brown was confident, already knew.

The letters that Harold Brown sent back – full of expressions of paternal love – nonetheless demonstrated the wall of incomprehension that separated father and son. 'I don't know what to write to you except that I love you so very dearly . . . You will either gradually struggle up or slide down to things infinitely worse and literally break our lives, Mother and I, causing us misery that you cannot imagine. For our sakes and for our love for you, you must win your fight against yourself.' What the son viewed as a matter of fundamental identity ('The Well of Loneliness is driving me mad,' he confided to his diary the week before his confession, 'driving the homosexual truth of the <u>Tragedy</u> of myself in upon me so violently'), the father conceived of as a question of self-control. 'You must stop thinking about whether you are good or bad ... When the urge comes (to think of sexual things), the more you try to force it from you the stronger it will get. Don't waste strength in trying to force it back, use all your strength in trying to pull something else into your mind.'

The solution to his son's confession Harold Brown arrived at swiftly: marriage to Elsa, a young friend of the family. 'Her love can pull you straight ...' Richard's difficulties were 'a State of mind', which 'could not continue to exist in contact with her'. Harold amplified his earlier statements: 'The sex instinct is the most powerful, and is a fine, wholesome and clean thing. Perverted, it is filthy.' Even after Richard Blake Brown assured his father during a drive in the countryside that marriage was impossible, Harold – alongside badly needed cheques for £15 – dispatched a constant stream of missives exhorting that he conquer his 'tendency' ('a happy and successful life of any kind depends on that ...') as well as convoluted endorsements of the joys of heterosexuality: 'the actual naturalness of things will not only make them less ugly, but in the majority of cases make them attractive in their own peculiar way'. ('Surely the dear man cannot be conceivably grinding the "Elsa" axe again?' wrote the son in his diary.) Still, at the conclusion of a difficult year, Richard Blake Brown could look back on the 'invaluable and active sympathy' of his brother and sister-in-law and 'the somewhat more slowly dawning but none the less welcome understanding of my beloved Mother and Father'. 'My family have been, thank God, ever my guiding star' (ill. 26).

Just how differently such a confession could turn out the testimony of Alan Wakeman demonstrates. At the age of fifteen, in 1951,

Wakeman got up the courage to tell his mother that he was in love with one of the boys at his Surrey school. By the early 1950s, the dichotomy between the homosexual and the heterosexual was solidifying, and homosexuality was the subject of more public vitriol than when Richard Blake Brown wrote to his father. Still, Wakeman was close to his mother, closer than to his butcher father, and she had exhorted her children always to be true to themselves. She at first laughed at her son, and then tried to dissuade him. 'Oh that's just a puppy crush, you need to ignore it.' But then she did something that Wakeman had not expected: she told his father. That night, his father burst into his bedroom and beat him, 'screaming abuse that I will not repeat to another living being because it was so cruel'. He must never talk about homosexuality ever again; if he as much as said that word, his father would put him out on the street. Three decades later, Wakeman remembered that night as 'one of the worst moments in my life. I thought the world had come to an end.' The next morning, he went into breakfast, and both his parents pretended that nothing had happened.

Judging from the oral histories of gay men preserved in the British Library, Wakeman's story was relatively unusual, and so, too, was Richard Blake Brown's. Much more common were those families in which a man's queerness was unspoken, but hardly concealed. In some cases, it seemed as if a man's relatives had always known. Anatole James thought his father sensed 'instinctively' that he was 'abnormal', and was therefore intent upon rooting out any manifestation of it, such as a taste for art, while pressing 'wholesome' hobbies such as stamp-collecting upon him. By contrast, in those working-class neighbourhoods, such as London's East End, where queans had long been a well-integrated social type, a boy who seemed destined for cissyhood could be viewed as much as an immutable (and possibly amusing) outcropping of nature as a disappointment. 'Nobody ever said you can't be the princess,' remembered Mike Upton, whose working-class Bristol family encouraged his comic impersonations of famous women. David Ruffell's boyhood request for a pram, in the early 1950s, scandalized his relatives, but his mother nonetheless insisted that her son should have one for Christmas. Clad in 'bright, outrageous clothes', Ruffell felt 'a silent acceptance' – 'I was always out at home' – though it was also clear to him that his male relatives favoured his brother because he was 'more masculine'. When Ruffell's grandmother asked him when he was going to get married, his mother intervened: 'Oh, don't be stupid, you know he's not interested in women, he's perfectly happy as he is.'

Veiled references indicated to the homosexual man that his parents or siblings knew, but demonstrated, too, that they would not invite, or even permit, further confidences. One man, the product of a well-to-do socialist family, remembered that when he was fourteen, in 1940, his mother told him that 'not everyone has to get married' and 'Some people are quite happy being "everybody's uncle."' Such, however, was her own reticence about sex that he felt it impossible to pursue the subject further. He never talked with his mother about being gay, not even when he had a steady boyfriend in the 1960s and took him to stay with her. Her only open acknowledgement of his homosexuality came on that visit: 'You'll have to put up with this old double bed but you like that don't you.' John Alcock, born in Birmingham in 1927, thought that his working-class parents were not 'capable' of putting sex between men 'into words'. And yet, he acknowledged, their actions betrayed some awareness of the situation. Alcock's father, a caster in a brass foundry, carried in his wallet a snapshot of his son in full drag. When Alcock quarrelled with his first lover, his mother came to London to try to patch it up: 'Oh, don't be silly, you should be living with John, living together.'

To be accepted, the queer man often had to remain silent. In the 1950s, Tony Garrett presented his partner, the writer Angus Wilson, to his middle-class parents as his 'best friend'; as a consequence, they all 'got on extremely well'. To talk about homosexuality was either to force explicit acknowledgement (and condonation), or to provoke disapproval, even rejection. When one Welsh man, born in 1920, tried to confess to his father, a doctor, it became 'very clear that he would prefer me not to continue – and I didn't!' Antony Grey, the secretary of the homosexual rights organization the Albany Trust, always regretted having come out to his parents, which he did around the time of the Wolfenden Report; in the middle of the conversation, Grey's father started to talk about his own illness, prostate cancer: 'I wanted them to know me, but I felt like I'd inflicted such hurt on them because they didn't understand it.' To protect their parents, many men avoided the subject. The journalist Michael Davidson sought to spare his mother, the 'profile of infinite goodness', any worry, though he recognized her 'tremulous and unformulated surmise that my adventures in love, if there were any, were dangerous and unmentionable'. When he was arrested, in 1936, Davidson and his siblings constructed an elaborate falsehood to shield her from the truth. Twenty years later, Roger Fisher never wanted to discuss homosexuality with his mother, though she was very fond of his long-time lover: 'I didn't feel it was fair, so it was never mentioned.'

In the 1950s, social scientists imagined a chasm between the homosexual and his family that mirrored his alienation from society at large. The homosexual might be out to his friends, but he was 'careful to avoid arousing suspicions in the family circle'; he especially dreaded lest his parents discover. And yet, families knew more than post-war investigators credited. To be sure, homosexual men wished to avoid confronting their relations with the bald facts. To force a conversation was to risk disrupting the accommodations that allowed the suspected – or obvious – to remain unspoken. Whatever tolerance or acceptance families showed hinged upon a man's willingness (and ability) to avoid a discussion.

Queer men had the sense that homosexuality was a taboo subject in the family – and it mostly was, when they raised it. Among their relations, however, it was hardly off limits. In many families, homosexuality was apparently a subject to be identified, and discussed, even with children. During the 1940s, recollected one woman, her pianist cousin was the subject of gossip in her middle-class family. 'Gentlemanly, tall, slim and rather affected in his speech and manner, with a hyphenated surname which was the cause of some ridicule', he came to her house, accompanied by a showily dressed younger man, to give her piano lessons when she was a girl. She heard other family members describe him as a 'pansy'. When she asked her mother what it meant, she was told 'he likes other men'.

Some relatives poked fun at the 'pansies' in their midst. In other families, homosexuality was quietly acknowledged, nothing more. While her parents were old-fashioned about sex, remembered one woman, they treated in a matter-of-fact fashion her homosexual uncle, a 'very discreet' man who lived at home with her paternal grandparents. Indeed, in retrospect, it seemed to her 'surprising' that her middle-class family reacted as calmly as they did in the 1950s: 'it was not an issue, it was not a cause of embarrassment'. Queerness, of course, could also be a matter for whispers and insinuation. In one family, an uncle, well-dressed and theatrical, sent away to America in the 1940s, stoked the family rumour mill. Extended kin clucked their tongues about the misfortune of the queer man's parents. Among the Isherwoods, Christopher's mother – whose younger son, Richard, was a homosexual like his brother – was always referred to as 'poor Aunt Kathleen with those two abnormal sons'. Hostility could provoke vicious gossip. One mother warned her niece about her son's taste for young boys, urging her to keep a newborn baby away from him. Revealing a son's proclivities to relations could be construed as a matter of familial obligation.

A quean in the family provided a means of speaking about sex between men without ever using the words. Gay men interviewed in the 1980s recollected the conversations they had heard about the queans of an earlier generation. In the 1950s, David Jones's mother regaled her children with stories about her brother, Will, who as a sailor on leave during the Second World War dressed up as a woman and picked up men. Her phrase for being a homosexual was 'He's like your Uncle Will.' Roger Smith's Uncle Sid, a 'raving quean', furnished the fodder for many a tale in his family. As a young man, Sid had attracted the attention of a local grandee, and lived as a butler and footman in his stately home. Smith's grandmother was very fond of her half-brother, and recounted, with amusement, how Sid and the young lordship used to get into Victorian drag bustles, and waltz around. Though Uncle Sid was long dead by the time that Roger

Smith was a boy and the quean a rapidly disappearing cultural type, he smoothed his great-nephew's path. At a gathering of Smith's Methodist family in 1953, the subject of Roger and marriage arose. Smith, then sixteen, was not present; he heard the story from a cousin only many years later. His grandmother rapped the table and announced to the assembled relatives that they could 'forget marriage' for Roger. 'He's like Sid.'

During the interwar years, the definition of a normal family narrowed. When families hid infertility or an idiot child, it was partly because deviations from the norm appeared more shameful against the backdrop of an increasingly homogeneous set of experiences. It was also because they could: adoption provided a means of securing children and institutions a way to dispose of them. Conversely, when family members talked about their queer relations with relative frankness, it was because they could not easily look away. Even the 'discreet' homosexual could not be reliably hidden, because he operated largely outside his family's control. The writer T. C. Worsley, himself a homosexual, remembered a boyhood visit in the 1930s to an eminent relative, a retired Winchester housemaster. When Worsley, his aunt and her husband, the Canon of Southwark, arrived for a visit, 'a straw-blonde, swishing chorus boy covered with make-up', who referred to their host as 'Georgie', answered the door. Georgie's sitting room made the situation plain: on every available surface, including an easel, were photographs of the house-boy, taken in revealing poses. The Canon hardly knew where to look, while his wife, clucked and muttered, 'Look at this . . . and this one!' Rather than staying for lunch, as they had planned, they 'retired in disorder' as soon as possible.

Whether in the sitting rooms of Winchester or in the tabloid press, homosexuality was increasingly visible after the First World War. Arrests for 'gross indecency' rose steadily through the 1920s and 1930s, fuelling a rash of articles about deviant sexuality. Who the homosexual was and where he was to be found became matters for urgent discussion. The new science of sexology accorded the so-called 'invert' a prominent place, as, too, did a host of plays, novels and treatises, which exposed certain urban sites, such as urinals, as hotbeds of homosexual sex, and labelled entire professions, among them interior design, hairdressing and the stage, as refuges for pansies. By the mid-1940s, it seemed to Anatole James that talk about homosexuality had reached strange, new heights. On the one hand, there were three plays sympathetic to homosexuality running on the London stage and 'poor old' Oscar Wilde had 'become quite "respectable"'. On the other, there were skyrocketing rates of prosecution, twice to three times as many homosexuals arrested as during the interwar years, and sadistic sentences. A spate of high-profile arrests in the early 1950s – the actor John Gielgud was apprehended for soliciting in a Chelsea public toilet in October 1953, followed a few months later by the prosecutions of the young aristocrat Edward Montagu, his cousin Michael Pitt-Rivers and the journalist Peter Wildeblood for gross indecency with two Royal Air Force servicemen in Montagu's beach hut at Beaulieu – put the problem of homosexual 'perversion' insistently before the public.

So far as families were concerned, the attention paid to homosexuality in public need not have translated into discussions in private. Imbeciles, after all, had become less, not more, visible within families, when the alarm about mental deficiency intensified in the early twentieth century. However, homosexuality would prove in Britain a very different sort of stigma for the family to mental disability. The question of causation was crucial. In the glut of explanations produced in the first half of the twentieth century to account for homosexuality, no single model gained widespread acceptance among Britons – a notable contrast to the familial taint that came to characterize understandings of mental deficiency. Rather, a wide array of causes competed in expert as in public opinion; the letters that flooded the *Sunday Times* after the paper's 1953 leader on homosexuality as a 'social problem' (published in the wake of the Montagu–Wildeblood arrests) demonstrated the range. Aberrant parenting was blamed, but so, too, were single-sex male environments. Innate deviance was suspected, but so, too, were biological peculiarities particular to the affected individual. In the cacophony of opinion that characterized the debates about the origins of homosexuality, family members could feel themselves absolved, all the more so perhaps if they distanced themselves from the problem by speculating about it.

The explanation of homosexuality that in other countries indicted the family – the Freudian approach, particularly popular in the United States – had relatively limited currency in Britain until the late 1950s. Although psychoanalytic ideas seeped gradually into British public discourse from the 1920s and 1930s, when Freud himself took up residence in Hampstead, it was not until the mid twentieth century, and then only slowly, that these new understandings achieved real purchase. After the Second World War, psychoanalysts had established themselves among the country's prominent authorities on the subjects of child-rearing and deviance. Still, very few of Freud's major works were available in paperback in Britain until the late 1960s, and it was the campaigning anti-Freudian Hans Eysenck, not the psychoanalysts, who dominated the field of post-war, mass-market psychology. In the tabloids, psychoanalysts – and those who consulted them – were chiefly figures of fun. Even in the pages of highbrow publications such as *The Times Literary Supplement*, psychoanalysis more often appeared a subject for mockery than serious debate. The dominant mother, 'a familiar villainess in psychiatric literature', wearily commented one review of D. J. West's *Homosexuality* (1955), 'makes her usual appearance'. As late as 1970, the *New Statesman* referred to the Tavistock Clinic as a 'little island of American culture', as if psychotherapy was an exotic import, rather than, as the Tavistock's leadership plaintively responded, an authentically British development.

Popular psychological forays into the familial causes of homosexuality were still hesitant in the 1950s. When the *Sunday Times'* editors decided to tackle the subject, they ran an article by a mother of three sons, the wife of a Midlands businessman. What began with an apparently straightforward psychoanalytic interpretation of homosexuality – 'one of the main causes of sexual inversion is an unhealthy relationship between mother and son' – quickly departed from the Freudian orthodoxy. According to the *Sunday Times'* contributor, the sin of mothers was not that they dominated their sons (the root of the problem, as Freudians saw it) but rather that they paid too little attention to them. Her remedy harked back to the Victorians: first, for families 'to put God at the centre of our lives' and second, for mothers to exercise personal discipline (refraining, for instance, from gobbling chocolates) so that their sons, too, should learn how to resist temptation. Yet even such tentative psychological assaying provoked resistance among the *Sunday Times'* readers. While those who wrote to the paper applauded the point about the mother's 'own silent example', most were also dubious about what they saw as the tendency of 'modern psychology' to underscore the 'child's need for perfect mother-love'. The mother, letter-writers concurred, overestimated her own importance.

If psychological models were on the rise but also controversial, they had to compete with a number of older explanations, including the idea, common currency in British sexology since the early twentieth century, that inversion was congenital in nature. Well into the 1950s, homosexuality could still be conceived of in constitutional terms, as a matter of 'glands', a 'feminine bent' or, more damningly, the consequence of a 'morbid nature'. In British courtrooms, explanations common in the interwar period – that a man could succumb to homosexual 'attacks' when he was 'overworked, tired, or run down' – jostled up against ideas of neurosis, innate disposition, and the notion that homosexuality was, as the lawyer for a convicted choirmaster put it, 'something that is just as much a disease as the measles'. On occasion, causes old and new mingled together in the same case. In 1951, the Rev. Joseph Hardcastle, a 52-year-old married clergyman, pleaded guilty to a charge concerning a ten-year-old boy, explaining that his nerves 'became very bad' when he stayed at his Primrose Hill parish during the war. Giving evidence for the vicar, the Bath Police's staff surgeon added that Hardcastle required urgent surgical treatment for a 'complaint which had contributed to his actions', and thought that while he had 'abnormal leanings' and needed 'a considerable degree of mental straightening out', his wife might be 'more help than any psychiatrist'.

Far and away the most common explanation for homosexuality was conditioning. It was cited in courts and newspapers, in medical treatises and the theatre; it was combined with other factors, such as biological predisposition and deficient parenting, or presented as sufficient on its own. Early seduction by an adult homosexual could set a boy's course in life. So, too, could exposure to the rampant homosexuality of all-male environments, such as borstals, the military and the public schools. In the *Sunday Pictorial*'s infamous 'Evil Men' series (1952), such was the danger of conditioning – of a 'decadent vice' that 'spread', 'corrupted', 'tainted' and 'polluted' – that it drowned out every other cause. Public schools had long been considered a breeding ground for homosexual vice, but so alarming had the bad press become that John Wolfenden, who had spent sixteen years as the headmaster of Uppingham and then Shrewsbury, felt compelled to defend single-sex boarding schools. Structuring his argument as a response to a mother concerned about 'immorality' at school, Wolfenden neither accepted nor completely refuted conditioning. While he thought that there was very little connection between adult male homosexuality and the 'innocently' homosexual stage of schoolboy romance (which he deemed practically universal), he nonetheless acknowledged the 'danger, and it's no good concealing it, that it may go wrong'.

Just how omnipresent conditioning was as an explanation for homosexuality the reams of testimony presented during the following two years to the Wolfenden Committee indicate. Eight months after he entered the debate about schoolboy romances, Wolfenden found himself at the helm of a Home Office Committee, convened in August 1954, to investigate what changes to the law, if any, might be warranted. The Committee's members soon found themselves in a discussion about the causes of homosexuality. The witnesses they called invoked a variety of causes, ranging from endocrine troubles to constitutional deficiencies to the 'alarmingly catching' nature of the vice. The Tavistock and Davidson Clinics, alongside a handful of prominent practitioners, such as Clifford Allen and H. V. Dicks, were lonely voices for the psychoanalytic framework; outside their testimony, focused on abnormal parent–child interactions, Freud's sway was limited. Typical was the British Medical Association's memorandum, which trod lightly around the controversial subjects of genetics and early childhood relations to enumerate the eight ways – including seduction, initiation and segregation – in which homosexual habits could be acquired. According to the BMA, homosexual practices spread by contact; 'from time to time' homosexuals 'insidiously invade certain groups of the community which would otherwise be predominantly heterosexual'. Parents were not completely exonerated, but the BMA minimized their role. 'Defective homes', explanation number six on the BMA's list, resolutely avoided psychoanalytic models, citing instead the old Victorian bugbear of overcrowding and the new post-war problems of overly lax and overly strict parental authority. Excellent parents, then, could provide a bulwark against homosexual contagion, but defective families were not the root cause of the problem.

Untangling the skeins of causation increasingly seemed a thorny, perhaps hopeless, endeavour in the mid twentieth century. The Wolfenden Report struck a characteristic note, observing that neither normal nor abnormal behaviours could be attributed to a single cause. When the Albany Trust in the early 1960s surveyed public opinion on the subject, it discovered that though most people had some opinion about the causes of homosexuality, they were 'quite openly and frankly guessing'. Nonetheless, very few respondents identified innate or inheritable factors alone as principally responsible. Rather, they were divided between those who viewed homosexuality solely as a product of environmental factors and those who thought it resulted from a combination of vaguely defined 'inborn tendencies' and the environment. When pressed to explain more precisely the nature of these 'inborn tendencies', most cited glandular or hormonal abnormalities, not genetics. The environmental conditions people cited as likely to produce homosexuality had hardly changed from the late nineteenth century: all-male

communities and seduction by an older man were the two most frequently mentioned villains. As in the BMA's memo, parents could be
faulted – respondents noted both 'mother fixation' and broken homes
as factors – but they were of secondary importance, a means of weakening a man's defences rather than a root cause. Most people viewed
homosexuality as a 'contagious disease', which corrupted everyone,
but especially the young.

Unlike mental disability, which from the early twentieth century
branded families with the stigma of an innate and inheritable defect,
there was little consensus about the causes of homosexuality. However guilty or ashamed parents may have felt about their sons'
sexuality, they were not the obvious public scapegoats that the families of the mentally disabled became. In a half-century marked by
war and military service, the army, the Navy and POW camps could
all be held responsible, alongside those notorious bastions of sodomy, public schools and prisons. There were also always paedophiles
to denounce, as the alarm about sex between men and boys reached a
fever pitch in the 1940s and 1950s. Although the Wolfenden Committee found unmerited the widespread fear that seduction in youth was
the 'decisive factor' in producing homosexuals, its recommendations
nevertheless endorsed the idea that adult homosexuals posed a particular danger to children and young men. It recommended an age of
consent of twenty-one, several years higher than in other European
countries and as against a British age of consent for heterosexual sex
of sixteen; the 1967 Sexual Offences Act would increase prison sentences for those who had sex with youths under the age of twenty-one.
By contrast, the Wolfenden Report had almost nothing to say about
the responsibility of the family. In its final section on 'preventative
measures', the Committee noted simply the 'desirability of a healthy
home background', while expounding on the duty of those who
hired teachers and youth leaders to debar homosexual men from
employment, the regulation of public lavatories, and the need to
sanitize newspaper reports of criminal proceedings.

If public opinion and most experts, at least through the 1950s,
largely acquitted families of producing homosexuality, one group

did not: queer men. The vast majority of men, like Anatole James, rejected the conditioning model. As James jocularly noted in his Mass-Observation diary, in 1946: 'It is queer how many so-called, intelligent and informed, people seem to think that homosexuality is, if I may use the word, "infectious". Such people think that if once a lad is "corrupted" by a male homosexual, he, hey presto! becomes homosexual! Such an idea is completely ridiculous, as I have proved on innumerable occasions.' Based upon his own investigations, James thought that almost every male in Britain had been 'got at' by a homosexual at some point in their lives. 'Yet the average lad forgets all about it, marries and becomes a father.' None of the 127 queer men that the sociologist Michael Schofield interviewed in the late 1950s attributed their homosexuality to an early seduction.

Most often, homosexuals viewed their condition as innate. Of those men who offered Schofield an explanation for their homosexuality, by far the largest number thought it 'inborn'. Viewing their condition as congenital, Schofield observed, helped homosexuals to absolve themselves of responsibility for their actions. It also implicated their families. W. H. Auden's 'true ancestor' was his father's youngest brother, Harry, a homosexual who had got in trouble while a student in Germany. Harry Auden, like Christopher Isherwood's Uncle Henry, foretold his nephew's destiny. In his 1927 poem 'We, knowing the family history' – written the year after Auden revealed his homosexuality to his parents – he underscores the 'lethal factors that were in the stock'; he originally titled the poem, 'Family Likeness'. For Anatole James, too, it was apparent that homosexuality ran in the family: his sister and a female cousin were lesbians, while an uncle and one 'if not two' great-uncles were homosexual; he suspected, too, that his father had homosexual tendencies. His father's hostility to him James attributed to this chequered family history: his son made manifest what the family had sought to hide. 'I feel certain Father knew something of which he was ashamed in the Hudson Family. He was, of course, "peculiar" himself, and, being a human ostrich, buried his head in the sand.'

As queer men saw it, nature was culpable, but so, too, was nurture.

Even as their fellow citizens viewed psychoanalytic explanations with suspicion, many middle-class homosexuals embraced them. They were more conversant than other Britons with the international literature – the British Sexological Society's pamphlet collection included a preponderance of German, Austrian and American texts – and infinitely more likely than other Britons to come under psychological treatment. For those who had been oppressed or rejected by their families, the idea that homosexuality could be traced to aberrant child-rearing had obvious appeal. One man whose mother refused to speak to him for a decade after he came out viewed her prudishness as the source of his condition: 'it wouldn't surprise me if my mother had an effect on my gayness'. Or as Auden, psychoanalysed in 1929, humorously put it in the same year: 'The mother had wanted/To be a missionary in Africa/So the son's novel/Must be published in Paris'. But even those who had amicable relations with their parents could wonder. Peter Wildeblood speculated that the age difference between his parents was one of the factors 'which influenced my later development'.

Although Gay Liberation would, in the 1970s, reject the search for the causes of homosexuality as a mechanism of repression, homosexual men participated to a far greater degree than has been recognized in the earlier debates. More than a quarter of Schofield's respondents thought that their homosexuality had 'something to do with the way that they were brought up'. Half of those surveyed had distant or poor relationships with their fathers, while 44 per cent viewed their mothers as possessive or over-protective. Nearly all of the homosexual men the psychologist Eva Bene contacted in the early 1960s for her investigation into family life were willing to participate, a 'gratifying' result, she noted, given the harsh legal context. The eighty-three men Bene interviewed proceeded to criticize not just their fathers, but also their mothers, leading her to dispute the notion of a 'mother fixation'. The most significant difference between homosexual and heterosexual men was their attitudes towards their mothers: far more homosexual men described their mothers as nags who withheld their affection. The British studies of the 1960s that ended up finding fault with parent–child dynamics in the families of homosexuals did so in queer men's words.

Anatole James often bought the *News of the World*, as, too, did the homosexual rights campaigner George Ives, whose forty-three scrapbooks of newscuttings now housed at Yale University's Beinecke Library are indebted to the tabloid's lurid and often vicious coverage of the subjects dearest to Ives's heart. Reading the *News of the World* allowed James and Ives – and presumably many other men – to learn about the unlucky choirmasters, parsons, aristocrats and actors hauled before the courts on 'serious charges', stories that the respectable broadsheets largely avoided. James and his friends sent each other clippings from the *News of the World* and other tabloids. Based upon the facts he gleaned from the papers, James wrote letters to the Home Office and the Duke of Bedford to protest against savage sentences, and sought out, too, the families of convicted lads to offer his commiseration. He contributed a letter to the *Sunday Times*' discussion of 'A Social Problem', pointing out (erroneously) that before 1885 homosexual acts in private were not a crime. At a time when information about 'happenings' was difficult to come by, and James, newly relocated to Edinburgh, found it hard to make 'interesting friends', the tabloid press provided an unlikely means of contact. A letter James wrote to the *Sunday Pictorial* in 1948 criticizing an article on sex crimes yielded several approaches from fellow homosexuals, eager to meet its author.

The open secret was a knife edge, and living on it meant navigating constantly between concealment and revelation. The arrest was an ever-present danger, but so, too, was giving oneself away to the wrong person. To be a homosexual, the journalist Peter Wildeblood told the Wolfenden Committee, was to 'wear a mask all the time'. Like Wildeblood, self-consciously respectable homosexuals spoke of a 'double life'. Unlike the flamboyant pansies they disdained, they practised self-control, which required the rigid compartmentalization of their private and public selves. But behind the respectability that middle-class homosexuals asserted (a posture for which history

has judged them harshly) lay for many a much richer and more varie-
gated sense of difference. They embedded their sexuality within the
framework of 'distinctiveness' and 'unconventionality', which
offered both an alibi for the outside world and an internal understanding charted against the backdrop of their families of origin.

Before the First World War, it had been easier to hide in plain
sight. When the author Augustus Hare died in 1903, his obituaries
applauded his generosity in inviting boys employed in the City for
weekends at his Sussex country house, Holmhurst. Except in one
'impossible' case, Hare acknowledged in the final volume of his six-
part autobiography, he had no desire to marry; he had 'far more in
common' with the 'boys' for whom Holmhurst was the 'haven of
their lives'. In Edwardian society, a rouged quean such as Egerton
Edwards went undetected in the same upper-middle-class circles
that regarded Oscar Wilde with horror. Edwards, a Byronic-looking
figure, wore white flannel trousers, an orchid in the buttonhole of
his double-breasted jacket, and a solitaire emerald on the little finger
of his left hand; he donned mascara even to play tennis. As the novelist Beverley Nichols described him, his 'clothes, his walk, the
books he read, the company he kept – all of these proclaimed . . . the
abnormal man'. And yet, Nichols's moralistic parents remained bliss-
fully unaware. The fact that his grandfather was a baronet and his
people moved in respectable circles was sufficient to excuse any of
Edwards's peculiarities.

A spate of police raids in the 1920s on nightclubs frequented by
transvestites helped to educate the public about queans. Flamboyant
dress, make-up, a way of fluttering the eyes betrayed the quean to all
but the most innocent onlooker. So profound did the association
between effeminacy and homosexuality become, however, that other
queer men could evade detection. In the hands of the right barrister,
a man's athletic prowess became the proof of his innocence; in 1937,
Mr J. D. Cassels, KC, depicted the schoolmaster Donald Ashness-
Wells as a 'lover of strenuous, manly sports' and got his conviction
quashed on appeal. It was still a common enough experience for
queer men in the 1950s to encounter those who confidently declared

that they knew no homosexuals. But when the Albany Trust in the early 1960s surveyed public opinion on the issue, its researchers discovered that there were relatively few members of the public who trusted their intuition on the subject.

Living relatively unmolested required following the same rules as many men already observed with their families. According to one working-class man, born in 1935 in London, 'the answer was to "pretend" to be "normal" and quietly and secretly enjoy being "queer"'. In those interwar working-class neighbourhoods where queans were a familiar type, queerness could be frank and unabashed. In other settings, it required that a man tolerate a level of derision rather than actual danger. The police constable Harry Daley, a friend of J. R. Ackerley and for a time E. M. Forster's lover, met with hostility from some of his fellow policemen. But despite their animus, he continued to live with the other unmarried officers in the Section House and to entertain, 'with only slight apprehension', his unconventional friends there: 'It was only good manners to put up a pretence to the world in general, but I was not prepared to lead a life of deceit to my friends and fellow-workers.' Those well-to-do men, like George Ives, who had the resources to found unusual households had little to fear from their neighbours, especially if, like Ives, whose Primrose Hill villa was home to a menage of sexual partners, past and present, they also preserved appearances by employing the wife of a former lover to keep house.

Secrecy and disclosure were in constant tension. Ives's regimen of secrecy was obsessive: in his voluminous diaries, begun when he was nineteen, he gave all of his intimates and friends pseudonyms and employed a system of codes. Nonetheless, he chafed under the 'dark conspiracy of silence' and, throughout his life, flirted with revelation. On the eve of Oscar Wilde's trials, he published a defence of homosexuality in *The Humanitarian*: 'I will speak; see how strong the Truth must be, that they all should fear it so.' In addition to founding in the early 1890s the Order of the Chaeronea, a secret brotherhood of homosexuals, Ives also served as the secretary of the British Society for the Study of Sex Psychology, which by the interwar years had

become so identified with the cause of homosexuality that unsympathetic members resigned in disgust. Although Ives closely guarded
the identity of the Order's members in his diaries, he used his newspaper cutting collection — his 'casebooks', as he called them — to
expose those men whom he knew to be or suspected of being inverts.
A 1925 article about the late Earl of Portsmouth's attachment to a boy
tenant Ives indexed under the heading 'homosexuality'. From 1940,
he maintained an index category for 'Homosexuality and Celebrities'.

While it was no longer possible in the mid twentieth century
openly to declare, as Augustus Hare had, an excessive affection for
boys without courting suspicion, there were nonetheless those who
sought to push the envelope. Rupert Croft-Cooke was forty-nine, a
decorated war veteran with a series of detective novels to his credit,
when he published *The Life for Me* in 1952 (ill. 27). Ostensibly a book
about domestic architecture, in praise of the Georgian style and
country living, it was also an autobiographical account of Croft-
Cooke's return to Britain after the war, a 'polemical' account, as he
later put it, of an attempt to make a life in spite of the stultifying
forces of conformity. There, the reader could learn about Croft-
Cooke's passion for walking-sticks topped with silver handles, about
the glories of old timber construction, and about the revelries for
bachelors that Croft-Cooke hosted on the weekends. Among the
illustrations of mixed herbaceous borders and converted stables was a
photograph of a man Croft-Cooke identified as his Indian secretary:
Joseph Sussainathan (ill. 28).

It did not take too much reading between the lines to see in *The
Life for Me* what Croft-Cooke intended. A friend of Croft-Cooke's, a
judge in another part of England, warned him about the damage that
The Life for Me could cause him. Whether it was the parties of well-
dressed bachelors or the book itself, the next year the Sussex police
arrested both Croft-Cooke and Sussainathan on charges of gross
indecency. Croft-Cooke went to prison for six months, Sussainathan
for three. In his next book — *The Verdict of You All* (1955), an account
of his trial and imprisonment — Croft-Cooke adopted a strategy of

carefully crafted denial. He did not, he blithely asserted, 'mind in the least being thought a homosexual': 'I might have been irritated at any suggestions that I was a homosexual of the inverted, effeminate type, but that would have been because it reflected on my manhood, not because it reflected on my morals.' Fearing another arrest, he and Joseph spent the next twelve years in Tangier.

Although it eschewed a confessional tone, *The Verdict of You All* was the first account of homosexual incarceration published since Oscar Wilde's *De Profundis* and it earned Rupert Croft-Cooke queer fans. Among them was Anatole James, who wrote to Croft-Cooke to express his admiration and to ask for help with his own unpublished manuscript. His life, as he put it, had been 'extremely unusual, not to say: sensational'. He had served four prison sentences for homosexual offences. After his first conviction, in 1917, James – a solicitor in practice with his father, in Hull – had been struck off the rolls. Through the 1920s and 1930s, he held a succession of jobs, labouring in a paint factory; as a language master in a public school; as a secretary to Norman Haire, the gynaecologist and sexologist; and as a chef. When his father died in 1945, James inherited enough money from a family trust not to have to work any longer. He moved to Edinburgh, and turned to collecting antiques and to writing. Somewhere along the way, he took a pseudonym, which paid homage to his two favourite novelists, Anatole France and Henry James. For four years, he chronicled his past and present for the benefit of Mass-Observation and also composed his autobiography, an 'extremely outspoken' account of his 'abnormality'. As he wrote to Croft-Cooke, no publisher had given him any hope of it being published. And yet, 'as I "tell everything" (somewhat in the manner of a Case History) . . . it would interest quite a few people'.

Like Croft-Cooke, James conceived of the impetus to 'tell everything' as a function of his personality. He had been, as he put it, 'born original'. In a world of conformity – where, as James put it, 'originality, that used to be so highly thought of, is almost dead' – homosexuality was part and parcel of a personality that refused to be cowed. Defying convention had admittedly made his life hard and lonely. But his had been a memorable, even a 'sensational' existence. As he mused after spending Christmas day of 1945 alone: 'Strange how people, while perhaps not liking me, seem unable to forget me, once they have known me! Is B. right when he says that I can make my personality "felt" at a great distance?' Convinced that his fellow citizens could profit from the lessons he had to impart, James took an advertisement entitled 'Personality Developed' to the offices of the *Scotsman*, whose editors promptly rejected it as unsuitable for the paper. In April 1949, James's Mass-Observation diary ends abruptly; arrested yet again, he served four years in Scotland's Peterhead prison.

For men whose sexuality could not be broached, a distinctive personality offered a means of conceiving of an interchange between a private and a public self. It was a way of being queer that could encompass camp (the aesthetics of the quean) as well as the unobtrusive, 'respectable' homosexual's sense of difference. An idiosyncratic personality offered a plausible basis of deniability while always insisting upon its originality. For Rupert Croft-Cooke, the epitome of Edwardian eccentricity in the modern world was his boyhood friend, Richard Blake Brown, the agonized vicar at Portsea who had steadfastly refused his father's admonitions to pull himself together. A little over six feet tall, fair-haired with green eyes, a devoted bicyclist, Brown favoured canary-yellow gloves and scarves, and sweaters of violet or magenta. He smoked only Turkish cigarettes in a long holder, and insisted upon stationery that reflected his tastes. Among the headed writing papers that Brown had printed up was a raspberry-pink die-stamped one with a red coronet. Some of his stationery commemorated the death of Ludwig II of Bavaria with the enigmatic notation, in bold-faced black, 'L.W. DROWNED JUNE 13 1886'. Other papers announced his life-long antipathy for the telephone: 'No telephone on purpose' or 'Please write rather than telephone' (ill. 29).

A photograph of Lord Alfred Douglas pinned up over his desk, a penchant for canary-yellow gloves: Brown's queerness was barely concealed. And yet, he was not just ordained in the Church of England in 1926, but also offered a curacy in Tunbridge Wells. For a year or so, he preached there, but depressed by the Church's resistance to his efforts at gaiety, and, as he acknowledged in his diary and eventually to his father, 'gnawed with suppressed sexual desire', Brown grew disenchanted. When the Portsea archdeacon banned him from the clergy house in 1929, on the grounds that he had on his last visit read 'lurid' books on sexual abnormalities, drunk too much, and filled the residence with 'namby-pamby little pious boys', Brown – after reading his parents the archdeacon's accusatory letters – elected to resign his orders. With an allowance from his father, who supported him despite his refusal to marry Elsa, Brown decided to devote himself to writing novels, and moved to the Cotswold village of Salperton, down the lane from Rupert Croft-Cooke.

Unconventionality was both cover and revelation. It made a man's queerness so obvious that it hardly needed saying at the same time as it made use of a timeworn English stereotype, the eccentric, to parry questions. Edith Sitwell's *English Eccentrics* had just been published when Brown embarked upon the renovation of his rented blacksmith's cottage in Salperton. Its walls he painted buttercup yellow, its woodwork bright red. A tiny upstairs bedroom he outfitted with a suite of ornate gilt Empire furniture, a bust of Byron, a bronze copy of Canova's head of Napoleon, and a small Adam mantelpiece. Every evening, outfitted in a velvet smoking jacket, he descended the stairs to the kitchen, where Mrs Hodges, the amused wife of the tenant-farmer, served him his dinner. According to Croft-Cooke, these were not affectations, as Richard sought only to please himself: 'It was quite futile to judge Richard by normal standards of conduct since for him they did not exist. He had to be accepted or not – nothing was gained by criticism.'

In claiming originality as their signal feature, men such as Richard Blake Brown cast homosexuality within the broader framework of non-conformity. Whether it was Anatole James's talent for ferreting out eighteenth-century antiques, Croft-Cooke's appreciation of half-timber, or Brown's coloured stationery, they claimed tastes that ordinary people could not appreciate. It was a resolutely literary sub-culture, certainly among middle-class homosexuals, but given the large numbers of working-class men who sought out the work of Oscar Wilde and Havelock Ellis, probably further down the social spectrum as well. Booksellers and antiquarian shops became the places where the experiences of the urinal and the boyhood fling could be interpreted and conveyed. For Richard Blake Brown, two biographies – of Nietzsche and Ludwig II of Bavaria – came to his rescue after resigning his orders, spelling out a 'Bible and a creed' of 'individual & creative development' which he could 'honestly and frankly and wholeheartedly embrace'. In his turquoise-blue lacquered bookshelves Brown had the collected oeuvre of Le Queux, Carl van Vechten, Ronald Firbank, Robert Hugh Benson, Ouida, and of course also Wilde, Lord Alfred Douglas, Baron Corvo, J. A. Symonds, Edward Carpenter and Havelock Ellis.

Unorthodox figures such as Wilde, Carpenter, Ludwig II and Baron Corvo provided a rallying point as well as a focus for sociability for middle-class homosexuals of both the obviously eccentric and the more inconspicuously original sorts. For the men who gathered in the Corvine Society, which held its first banquet in 1929, it was as much the Uranian writer and artist Frederick Rolfe's iconoclastic life as his opus that was to be celebrated. A bizarre and quarrelsome genius, Rolfe (1860–1913) made his reputation as a student of the Renaissance and a fantasist with a barely veiled commitment to boy-love. Declaring oneself a Corvine was a way of announcing a liking for things queer to a like-minded circle without risking the social opprobrium that still attached to Wilde. A taste for Baron Corvo brought together men such as the retiring Cambridge librarian A. T. Bartholomew with the theatre producer and honours peddler Maundy Gregory – a man of indeterminate sexuality who, in the words of a fellow Corvian, collected the writings of 'those queer folk who in life were an anxiety & ever a terror to their friends but for the non-existence of whom the world would have been sadly poorer'. Although the membership of the Corvine Society numbered only in the hundreds, Rolfe himself became something of a cult figure. His infamously pornographic *Venice Letters* circulated in typescript amid a queer literary underground long before they were published in 1974. A. J. A. Symons's *Quest for Corvo* (1934), which tantalized the reader by claiming to expose Rolfe's secrets, proved a literary sensation.

Just as eccentricity forged bonds between queer men, so, too, did it mark out their distance from their families. Other people, James complained in his Mass-Observation diary, found his ideas interesting: 'the one exception, of course, is my own family!!' His closest relatives were his dead mother and grandmother, whom he lauded as the best example of the 'thoroughly progressive Victorian'. More than a half-century after his grandmother's death, James remembered the pink doll's house that she bought him from Hamley's: 'Dear Grannie! what a misfortune it was for me when she died! Things have never been the same for me since then.' For his father, by contrast, James had only vitriol: he had been mean and spiteful, while pretending all the while that he was the perfect parent. His three sisters James regarded with contempt. Though he and his siblings kept up regular contact, visiting each other and writing letters, James viewed them as pale and undistinguished. When his sister Brenda wrote with news about her new house, upon which she had, in the language of the women's magazine, 'impressed her personality', James scoffed: 'So far as I know she has no personality at all to impress on anything.'

Queer men often described themselves as changelings, as strange birds in the nest. Whatever affection they had for their parents did not translate into a feeling of familial closeness. Richard Blake Brown adored both of his parents, but later in life he had little to do with his brothers, both more conventional characters. He tolerated their occasional visits, but he did not seek them out. Rupert Croft-Cooke's relations with his family were similar. Although he devotedly corresponded with his mother and helped to support her in old age when he could, he felt marginal to the family. He was 'left out of the family benefits', he complained to his mother, on the ground that 'Rupert can look after himself'. When his great-aunt Xenia cut him out of her will as punishment for his arrest, redistributing his share of her sizeable estate to his two brothers and sister at a time when he was broke and living in Tangier, Croft-Cooke managed to persuade his siblings not to profit from this 'insanely cruel act', but only after a long and embittered correspondence. In the ten volumes of autobiography Croft-Cooke published while in exile in Tangier, covering the period from his childhood through the war years, his siblings hardly figure, though his parents occupy centre stage.

For those who lived as open secrets, writing proved an antidote to the constraints of daily life. Rupert Croft-Cooke's autobiography eventually stretched to twenty-five volumes, each covering just a few years of his life, each teasingly revelatory. The gadfly writer and socialite Beverley Nichols brought out six separate memoirs in addition to fifteen fictionalized autobiographies. At the *Daily Mirror*, where he got his journalistic start, and later at the *Sunday Express* and *Sunday Dispatch*, the actor and novelist Godfrey Winn chronicled for an adoring, largely female audience his daily life with his mother and terrier, Mr Sponge; his recalcitrant foxgloves; the monogrammed silk shirts he favoured; the parties he attended with famous friends; and his fruitless search for a wife, alluding every so often to the 'secret' that had been harrying him 'like a shadow'. According to Hugh Cudlipp, the editor who hired him at the *Mirror*, 'Winn believed that his most private thoughts were the ones he should share.'

What was published, however, was only the tip of the iceberg. George Ives is the most famous queer graphomaniac – his diary runs to 122 volumes, totalling approximately three million words – but there were many others. Stranded between a stultifying marriage and his longings for gondoliers and apple-cheeked Oxford undergraduates, the poet and critic John Addington Symonds was, in his own words, 'addicted' to diary-keeping, which he described as 'self-conscious, self-analytical, self-descriptive records'. In his 180-volume, four-million-plus-word diary, deposited according to the provisions of his will at Magdalene College, Cambridge, where he had been master, Arthur Benson struggled to make sense of his attractions to the undergraduates in his care. Alongside a world-class collection of Worcester-ware, the Cardiff pharmacist and antique collector Robert Drane left thirty-three volumes of diaries when he died; the archivist who received the bequest admonished his colleagues: 'Diaries of an old hermaphrodite. Do not distribute freely.' Richard Blake Brown kept his enormous diary volumes in a locked chest, within a locked chest; the volume for 1925–8 he sewed up in a yard of unbleached calico before tying it up in parchment, sealing it and sending it to his bank vault. In addition to his diaries, he also wrote eight autobiographies, which no publisher would take – the same fate that Anatole James's memoir eventually met.

Just one of Brown's autobiographical volumes was published: *Apology of a Young Ex-Parson*. It was a bowdlerized version of the diary Brown wrapped in parchment, covering the years when he took up and also resigned his orders; the material that he excised helps to indicate the function that diary-keeping served. The rhapsodical passages describing a dream about a boy become, inevitably, about a girl. His father's endorsements of sex as a life-force of humanity appear, though without the predicate of Richard's confession. Brown's desire for a 'human-being to love and be loved by'; the thoughts of his 'own unlovableness and sexual solitude and hidden bitterness' that his brother's happy marriage provoked; his musings about Wilde, 'If it is wrong, it is at least deep-rooted in many of God's children': none of these appear, even in veiled form, in the published *Apology*. Nor does the faux Pathé newsreel his family filmed one July day in 1927 with a newly acquired movie camera: Richard in the role of Queen Mary (his mother took the part of Lady Bertha Dawkins).

More surprising, perhaps, is what Brown left in. His zeal at the redecoration of the vicarage dining-room at Portsea, which he had distempered in a flame-orange. A description of his hair as 'deliciously crisp and fluffy and coy'. A quote from Lord Alfred Douglas. The 'marked value' he placed on privacy and the Yale lock he had put on his door. For some reviewers, the import of these details was all too clear. Denouncing Brown's 'exhibitionism and megalomania', the *Sphere*'s enraged reviewer wondered 'how such a buffoon was allowed to turn the chancel into a vaudeville stage'. But evident, too, in the book's clutch of bad press was the alibi that unconventionality provided. Brown's story was in poor taste, frivolous and vulgar, but not necessarily immoral or deviant. His non-conformity was 'headlong', thought the more positively disposed critics: 'it is the portrait of an entirely admirable and lovable man, very English, very modern, and withal quite unlike the majority of parsons – a "character" in every sense of the word'.

According to his friend Croft-Cooke, Richard Blake Brown's most notable characteristic was his self-sufficiency. The 'secret life' that he chronicled in his diaries was his wellspring. He lived in a 'radiant private world' of his own making. Self-sufficiency was the term that A. J. A. Symons used, too, to describe the antiquarian bookseller Christopher Millard, whose multiple imprisonments and poverty never diminished his 'air and dignity'. Self-sufficiency was a corollary to independence and non-conformity; it refuted the suspicion that the homosexual was a herd creature, and warded off the implication of tragic loneliness. Most importantly, it also reflected, or so Anatole James believed, the armament necessary for a queer life. He had never cared 'a row of pins' what other people thought of him; the mythical lady next door who ruled other people's lives had never governed his behaviour. And yet, he who wished to live in defiance of the rules of society had to be prepared for social isolation. 'I would never, never, advise anyone to flout the before-mentioned "lady",' warned James in his Mass-Observation diary, 'UNLESS they have the courage to spend most of their life, quite alone.' 'I have led a strange, eventful life, and I suppose, I shall continue to do so until the end of the chapter.'

There were better and worse endings. Released from Peterhead prison, Anatole James was met at the gates by a guardsman-friend (now married) with whom he had consorted before the war. With the help of the guardsman, James re-established life on Chester Street. He lived to see the decriminalization of private homosexual acts and the Gay Liberation movement, which together rendered biographies such as his own prematurely anachronistic; the editors at *Jeremy*, the swinging 'magazine for young men', had no use for the

article James submitted on 'homosexuality now and then'. Evidence
that attitudes were changing James greeted with a victor's satisfaction: 'I can't help wondering what Father would have had to say
about this.' He died in Cheltenham in 1979 at the age of eighty-seven.
He never found 'the great friend' for whom he had longed⊢ 'Probably I have tried too hard to gain this person' – but in his last years
was cared for by the former guardsman and his wife. Rupert Croft-
Cooke also died in 1979. In 1967, he and Joseph had separated after
twenty-three years together. Sussainathan was depressed and drinking heavily, and Rupert paid for him to leave Tangier and return to
his family in India, in the hope that time away would restore his
health. Rupert's unsympathetic brother Geoffrey disparaged the
investment: Joseph was 'going to the "dogs" & whatever you spend
on him it will be a waste of money'. But Sussainathan, after three
failed rapprochements, returned to Rupert in the end, and the pair,
after nearly two decades in exile, settled in England once more.
There, in Bournemouth, the erstwhile outlaw discovered to his
'happy surprise', as the *Times* obituary put it, 'fewer disadvantages
and more delights than he had supposed'.

After three years in his fantastical Cotswold cottage, Richard
Blake Brown elected to resume his orders. He took a curacy in a
Derbyshire mining village, and, believing that nepotism was the
means to advancement in the Church, at the start of the Second
World War he married the daughter of a bishop; the pair quickly
separated. In the Navy, Brown served as a chaplain, and after the war,
when his marriage ended, he secured the Chaplaincy of Bristol
Prison. His official duties hardly diminished his passion for eccentric
stationery, his intrigues with 'nice-looking' boys, or his pleasure at a
new Lent hood he designed of magenta lined with rosebud-pink
satin. 'How cross it will make people.' To his prisoners Brown was
devoted. He spent his inheritance helping difficult cases, and for the
thousands of 'REAL tragedies', 'the men who matter', he exhausted
himself. When he finally retired from Bristol Prison, after twelve
years of service, he was in chronic pain from sciatica and nearly broke.
He had given up all hope of publishing his memoirs. As he wrote to

Croft-Cooke: 'I have largely lost my old ZEST FOR LIFE and am full of an incurable sadness, only relieved, alas, by costly GIN.' He drank to fall asleep at night, but could no longer afford it, 'believe it or not, I NEED being cheered up after having spent most of my life cheering OTHERS UP'. The arrival of Rupert Croft-Cooke's latest volume of memoirs, *Wild Hills*, with its affectionate portrayal of the years they spent in the Cotswolds was a bright spot. His life had not been altogether wasted: who 'could possibly wish for a better more fragrant OBITUARY NOTICE?' When he died in 1968, from burns incurred by falling into his fire, Brown owed the wine merchants of Bristol a small fortune.

A few years before John Wolfenden opined in the *Sunday Times* on the subject of sexual misbehaviour in public schools, his eldest child, Jeremy, involved in a schoolboy contretemps at Eton, had been forced to lay all his 'cards on the table' for his father: he was a homosexual. A brilliant student on his way to Oxford, Jeremy Wolfenden was eighteen. Hair dyed fair, his eyes hidden behind dark clip-on glasses, dressed in a trademark felt hat, dark shirt and light tie, Jeremy Wolfenden cultivated a look of elegant menace (ill. 30). His model was the Maquisard, the guerrilla fighter of the French Resistance, his credo (as his friend Neal Ascherson put it) that of the 'moral nomad'; he was intrigued, too, by the world of the double-agent and espionage.* Before taking up the Home Office chairmanship, John Wolfenden – as Jeremy told the story – sought to extract a promise from his son. It would be best if they were to 'stay out of each other's way for the time being'. He purportedly pleaded with Jeremy, too, to 'wear rather less make-up'.

In 1957, Wolfenden's Home Office Committee offered what appeared at the time a pioneering recommendation. Homosexual acts in private between consenting adults should be decriminalized. Echoing John Stuart Mill's distinction between acts likely to harm

* Nervy and reckless, Jeremy would lead a short life of espionage and counterespionage in Moscow, London and Washington; he was dead of acute alcoholism at the age of thirty-one.

others and those that harmed only oneself, the Committee concluded that it was not the 'function of the law to intervene in the private lives of citizens'. The sphere of privacy that had been extended to illegitimates after the war would now cloak the activities of consenting and discreet homosexuals as well. The Wolfenden Report has been viewed as the triumph of 'respectable', middle-class homosexuals who sought new rights for themselves at the expense of their fellow queers too flamboyant or abject to be able to conduct their sex lives in private. But both the Wolfenden Report and the Sexual Offences Act that enacted its agenda a decade later reflected just as much, if not more so, the wishes of the respectable homosexual's family.

Only a right to privacy could protect the homosexual (and his family) from the predations of those who threatened the secret. As the eighth Earl of Arran spearheaded the Sexual Offences Act through the House of Lords, he cited the many letters he had received from parents terrified that their son would be arrested or blackmailed: 'I live in a world of perpetual fear and anxiety lest one of his contacts, who are unknown to me, should in some way expose him.' Arran explained his conclusions as the product of deep reading. But like John Wolfenden, he too had his own first-hand knowledge of the subject: his elder brother, Sir Arthur Gore, barely closeted and hounded by their parents after a series of unsuitable relationships, had died in mysterious circumstances in a Devon nursing home. Arran's admonition to homosexuals after the passage of the 1967 Act, to 'show their thanks by comporting themselves quietly and with dignity', was nothing more than the rule that respectable families had long sought to impose upon their queer relatives. Both in its principles and in its sentiment, the Sexual Offences Act was the decriminalization that relatives made.

As in the case of adoption, what had been a family secret would become simply private. It was nobody's business, and neither Wolfenden nor Arran ever acknowledged anything more than a public-policy stake in the subject. Five years after the passage of the Sexual Offences Act, Arran mused in *Encounter* about why he had taken on an unpopular campaign that had injured his reputation. Conceding 'I do not know my own motives anymore', he suggested that his involvement with the issue derived from his unhappiness 'at that time over a purely domestic matter (nothing to do with homosexuality!)'. Such, however, was the nature of an open secret that it could not remain long hidden. It was not just the way that Sir Arthur Gore had lived. Arran himself invited discovery; he referred to his bill by the pet name of 'William': the long-form for Bill, but also the title of Sir Arthur Gore's roman à clef, *William, or More Loved Than Loving* (with himself in the title role). In a memoir published the year after Arran's article in *Encounter*, Leo Abse, who steered the Sexual Offences Act through the Commons, told of his own puzzlement about Arran's motivations 'until by chance, through my wife, I met a man who for many years had been the lover of Arran's older brother: then all was clear'.

Jeremy Wolfenden evaded arrest and exposure, but he did not entirely stay out of his father's way. In the summer of 1956, as John Wolfenden's Committee prepared its report, his son exploited the high-wire act of the open secret to critique the entire enterprise. In an article in the Oxford student magazine, *The Isis*, Jeremy mocked the efforts of the 'Great British public' to come to terms with the 'homosexual predicament' (a phrase he ironically imprisoned in quotes). As John Wolfenden strove to make the world safe for respectable homosexuals and their families, Jeremy took aim at what counted as a respectable homosexual ending: the love-affair between men of approximately the same age that concludes 'happily, or at least nobly, in a basement flat in Earl's Court'. But where did that leave everyone else? Advertising a familiarity with the subject that exceeded the casual newspaper reader's grasp, Wolfenden enumerated the 'underworld's' unrespectable types: 'the frustrated choirmaster, or the perpetually disappointed hunter, or the National Serviceman who wants a pound or two, and the chance of a watch or a fountain pen if he wakes up first in the morning'. If there was a homosexual predicament at all, concluded Jeremy Wolfenden, it 'arises not because homosexual love is different in kind from normal love, but because, being similar, it is treated and regarded differently'. His was a retort from the inside, a pre-emption of the Wolfenden Committee's charge. There was nothing for his father to investigate that he could not learn at home.

PART 3

Secret No More?

6. Talking It Out

In the palmier days of the 1920s, when the parson Richard Blake Brown cut a figure by cycling to Claridge's in a checked suit, he and his new sister-in-law, Cecilia, exchanged confessions. Shortly before he sealed up his latest volume of diaries, Brown in 1929 read to Cecilia from its gilt-edged pages. A modern woman with her hair bobbed short, Cecilia reciprocated by offering him her own volume of confessions: most notably, that she and his brother had slept together before they were married. Like Brown's father, Harold, with his up-to-date attitudes about the joys of (heterosexual) sex, Richard and Cecilia were casting off what they saw as Victorian humbug, the prudishness about what could and could not be done (or, more to the point, discussed). Frankness, as Brown put it, was 'courageous'. It was also ever more common, for from the late 1920s the so-called 'new morality' was characterized as much by its trademark candidness about personal lives as by the rapid adoption of the short hemline and the cocktail.

On its own, confession was nothing new. The Church of England's rule had long been 'none must, all may, some should'. The commandment to wash one's dirty linen at home became a favourite injunction of the 1890s precisely because the old strictures were breaking down. But by the 1930s what had been a trickle of unseemly revelations had become a torrent: the mass-market confession was born. From the agony aunts to the tabloid 'I confess' competitions, from memoirs to marriage guidance centres, the notoriously reserved British proved not just willing but apparently eager to spill their secrets. 'Ours is an age,' observed the poet Stephen Spender, 'where many people feel a need to confess the tensions of their inner lives.' Swept away was the Victorian autobiographical tradition of circumspection in personal matters. The most successful interwar memoirs were also the most candid ones. Female readers especially, it was said, liked to read about family skeletons. Such 'extreme intimacies', observed the novelist Trevor Allen in 1934, no longer remained 'hidden at the bottom of the inkwell'; frankness – he predicted – would be the twentieth century's most valuable contribution to literature.

Through the early twentieth century, a family's privacy had been safeguarded by its secrets. Skeletons, the Victorians recognized, were inevitable and, as a sign of family unity, even laudable. By the First World War, what privacy meant was in flux. Partly it was that reticence about personal affairs seemed anomalous when so many mourned and others feared a knock on the door: a peacetime luxury, like eggs and silk stockings. It was also that the cherished skeleton in the closet was acquiring a fusty air of Victorianism. While some people still confused secrecy and privacy, observed the *Saturday Review* in 1918, it was 'only to the inquisitive that the private is the secret'. 'Privacy is good sound metal, but secrecy is its rust due to some corroding influence without.' During the 1930s, secrecy and privacy pulled further apart, as conduct that had furnished the terrain of family secrets was increasingly redefined as a legitimate area of privacy. People still kept secrets, but more and more they imagined that their intimate doings were no one else's business.

The interwar period marked not just the first modern age of confession, but a sharpening public contest over the control of personal information. Successive governments eager to collect information time and again confronted hostile citizens who protested at this violation of their right to be left alone. The most infamous of the snoopers was the prying means inspector of the Slump, whose investigations into the living situations of the unemployed made him one of the most hated figures in working-class communities. But much less consequential incursions proved just as controversial. When in 1937 the National Government, alarmed by the declining birth rate, sought to empower local Registrars of Births and Deaths to inquire for statistical purposes into the details of family life (asking, for instance, about the previous marriages of a mother registering a newborn child, or, in the case of an illegitimate baby, other bastards she had borne), the furore occupied the papers and Parliament for nearly two weeks. It was the 'Nosey Parkers' Charter', as the *Daily Express* dubbed the bill. As a mother of two and the wife of a London shopkeeper put it, 'It sounds like Russia. And I have no skeletons in my cupboard.' Chastened, the government quickly withdrew the original bill, trimming the permitted questions to a few, and guaranteeing the confidentiality of the information.

The phalanx of social scientists who fanned out across Britain after the Second World War would identify privacy as the most cherished attribute of marital life. Privacy was not yet defined, as it would be in the late twentieth century, as the right to live as you wished. But neither was it any longer the Victorian concept – by lore, choked with subjects that could not be mentioned and dark secrets. The privacy of the mid twentieth century joined a new democratic language of a right to non-interference with the conviction that talking problems out was a means to better relationships. Bolstered by the conviction that husbands and wives deserved a protected space, it was privacy as the precondition of marital intimacy. Confession, then, was a way of ridding privacy of its secrets, of purging in public (often anonymously) the hidden forces that burdened family life.

By the time that Vivian Simon, the managing director of a firm of champagne importers, entered the Divorce Court, he had – in writing – confessed his sins. Among the papers that Simon's lawyers submitted to the Court was a new sort of document, a so-called 'discretion statement', which not only identified Simon's young paramour, but enumerated as well the dates and places (Cannes, winter of 1929–30), where he and Miss Norah Huntley Walker had carried on their affair. Still, Simon asked the Court to forgive his mistakes and to award him a divorce. His wife's misconduct, he charged, was worse than his own: Mrs Simon had had three affairs, only one of which, with a former RAF officer, in a hotel in South Devon, she admitted to the Court.

After six days of charges and counter-charges in the autumn of 1935, during which the Simons accused each other of concealing additional wrongdoing from the Court, the disgusted judge ferreted out the facts. Mrs Simon had indeed lied to the Court, insisting that her visits to Percy Shaw's flat, the cocktails she drank there, her payment of his Ascot debts were all entirely innocent – until Shaw's cousin came forward to testify that he had caught the pair in bed together. Mr Simon, meanwhile, was telling the truth when he denied a second affair with young Miss Joan Nurick. True, he had wooed the wily Miss Nurick with furs, redeemed items out of pawn for her, and treated her to lavish restaurant meals. However, she had taken advantage of him, not the other way around. Mr Simon, observed the judge, was 'trying to buy something which he never actually succeeded in getting'. Simon was a rogue and an adulterer, but his saving grace in the Divorce Court was that he had confessed it all. For admitting his marital vices and leaving nothing out, he would be rewarded with a divorce.

Seventy-four years earlier, when Harriett Capel appeared in the Divorce Court, a petitioner's adultery had served as an absolute bar to divorce. In line with Justice Cresswell's dictate, divorce was reserved for innocent parties; the only option for those whose virtue was even slightly blemished was to lie. So firmly had Cresswell shut the door that in the half-century that followed Harriett's case, only forty-five people (of the nearly 25,000 who sought a divorce) even dared to ask the Court to excuse their adultery. But after the First World War the Divorce Court was changing, along the lines that Sir George Lewis had urged in the Royal Commission hearings (ill. 31). Circuit courts in the provinces were permitted to issue divorce decrees, and legal counsel was made available to the poor; as of 1923, wives were granted the right to divorce on the same grounds as their husbands, bringing an end to the sexual double standard; and in 1926 Parliament had taken the extraordinary step of closing the Divorce Court to daily reporting. Sixty years of press reports had entirely discredited the hopeful Victorian idea that stories of wrongdoing would have a salutary effect on public morality.

Even the old dogma that prohibited adulterers from seeking the Court's favour had weakened. Dismayed by evidence of widespread collusion and falsehood, the Royal Commission had instructed individual judges to exercise their discretion to grant relief even when both parties had traduced their vows. What had started as a slow trickle had become, by the 1920s, a worrisome trend: of the 34,500 divorce cases filed from 1920 to 1929, 690 were accompanied by an acknowledgement of the petitioner's own adultery. The numbers, though small, were alarming enough, but the variation in judges' decisions, magnified by the extension of jurisdiction to the provinces, threatened to launch an era of consensual divorce.

Under what conditions, then, should the marriages of misbehaving spouses be severed? That was the question that confronted the Divorce Court in 1929, six years before the flagrantly adulterous Simons passed through its portals. The presiding judge was the elderly Lord Merrivale. Self-made, tall and commanding, a slow and deliberate speaker, Lord Merrivale seemed a relic of dignified days gone by. The man whose case would establish a new rule in the Divorce Court – the reign of confessions – was the estate agent Frank Apted. When Apted appeared before Merrivale, he attempted to cast his matrimonial troubles in the most sympathetic light possible. On active duty with the Territorial Force in 1917, Apted had learned that his wife, the mother of his two daughters, had been unfaithful and planned to desert him. He had retaliated, or so he said, with a single act of adultery. Upon his return home, believing (erroneously) that his wife had obtained a divorce, Apted took up with a new partner with whom he had lived happily, albeit adulterously, for a decade. Now Apted asked the Court to excuse his mis-steps so that he could remarry and live an upright life.

Behaviour that might have been excusable among those 'in the poorest of circumstances', pronounced Merrivale, was unacceptable for the well-to-do. Moreover, Merrivale had his doubts as to whether he had the full story from Apted. He called in the King's Proctor and then the Attorney General to question the estate agent. Under blistering cross-examination, the truth came out: Apted was no jilted ex-serviceman but a serial adulterer and blatant perjurer. Before the war, while living at home with his wife and children, Apted had indulged in 'gross' sexual promiscuity. During the war, he had written to his wife, 'You can do as you please; I have been unfaithful to you not once but many times since we parted in 1914.' Not only would Apted be denied a divorce, but his entire case – the lies he had told, his partial admissions – proved the need for a new principle. Petitioners who asked the Court to forgive their sins, the Attorney General proclaimed, 'should make a clean breast of it and hold nothing back'. Henceforth, those who sought a divorce would be required to file with the Court a 'discretion statement' setting forth the particulars of their adultery.

The Divorce Court had always trafficked in revelations, but before the Apted decision, it was the innocent victims who told their stories. The shame they revealed was the disgrace of an unfaithful spouse and a failed marriage. Now it was the adulterers and bigamists who were required to tender to the Court a sexual autobiography, complete with an inventory of the occasions, with dates, names and places. Making a clean breast of one's transgressions would be both a purgative and a punishment. Even more importantly, the full confession of the guilty would – or so imagined Lord Merrivale and the Attorney General – restore order to a system bedevilled by secrets and lies. Policed by the prying eye of the King's Proctor, the discretion statement would shut the Court once and for all to people who were unwilling to lay their sexual lives completely bare.

Unintended consequences were the rule in the Divorce Court, and like its other innovations the discretion statement did not function according to plan. Though in theory the discretion statement was sealed, available only to the judge and the King's Proctor, in practice – and especially in the most titillating cases – it often ended up a part of the judge's ruling and hence fair game for reporters. The result was a proliferation of the scandalous reports that Parliament had sought to contain. Major Grigg admitted his own adultery, but charged that his wife had cuckolded him with a professional dancing partner at a bungalow near Virginia Water five times in one week. Mr and Mrs Merton not only both committed adultery – she with the 'tall, strong, middle-aged' (and married) Mr Cross, he with his fetching and flirtatious nurse-masseuse Miss Jones – but they continued to sleep with each other amidst their dalliances.

Not only did the discretion statement undermine the effort to turn off the spigot of revelations from the Court, but it failed to discourage divorce. Divorce petitions continued their inexorable climb upwards through the 1930s, while discretion statements became their increasingly routine companion. According to one judge, that was because the people who pleaded for discretion had no shame. The people who appeared in his Court, fumed the bachelor Justice Charles of the Leeds Assizes Court, were 'filthy' people of whom the 'county should be heartily ashamed'. They had 'no more decency than a lot of cattle'.

All of that would have been bad enough, but it quickly became clear that the discretion statement had failed to banish liars and scoundrels from the Divorce Court. Like the Apteds, both Elizabeth and Richard Blunt had violated their wedding vows repeatedly by the time they appeared in the Divorce Court in 1942. Married in 1936, the Blunts had very soon proved an ill-matched pair. Richard Blunt, an aspiring horse trainer, expected his gentle-born wife to entertain drunken jockeys and grooms in their cottage on the Berkshire Downs; he refused to pay the doctors who attended his sick infant son. Within a few years, the Blunts' marriage was a disaster; at the start of the Second World War, both turned to other partners. Adultery was rife during the war, and the disintegration of the Blunts' marriage demonstrates how romances begun in canteens and air-raid shelters and fed by a fatalistically inspired hedonism helped to unravel already unhappy unions. Elizabeth fell in love first with an officer quartered near their cottage, then, after she moved to London, with a married musician. Richard Blunt, meanwhile, expecting any day to be called up, found solace in the arms of a Miss Dean.

But when the Blunts each filed for divorce in 1942, neither owned up to adultery. The obligatory discretion statement was missing from their suits. It was not an oversight but a deliberate attempt on the part of both parties to deceive the Court. As the charges and cross-charges of adultery mounted, their lawyers hastened to remedy the obvious omission. Mrs Blunt submitted her discretion statement four days before the hearing was to begin; her husband filed his statement, acknowledging two acts of adultery with Miss Dean, the day before the hearing started. Even then, there was reason to doubt that the Blunts had revealed the full extent of their adulterous conduct. After a probing cross-examination, Richard Blunt admitted to the Divorce Court judge, Charles Hodson, that he had not yet told the entire truth because he resented the opposing counsel's intrusive questioning. Still dubious about Mrs Blunt's charges but convinced that he had finally 'got the truth' from her husband, Justice Hodson decided to grant Blunt his divorce.

That should have been the end of the matter, for never before in such a case had the Divorce Court judge's decision been overturned. But the Lords Justice of the Appeal Court took the unprecedented step of reversing Hodson's judgment. All three Justices agreed that the key requirement for discretion was a 'full and frank' confession. That was the 'one rule which must obviously obtain'. For Hodson, it was enough to have got the truth out of Blunt in the first place. The Lords Justice, by contrast, insisted that the petitioner who hoped for discretion had voluntarily to surrender his secrets to the Court. 'He must approach the court, when he first seeks it, in a white sheet,' wrote Lord Justice Mackinnon. Richard Blunt had 'entirely failed to play the penitent game'. Beyond that, Blunt's conduct towards his wife, his coarseness and indecencies, wrote Mackinnon, were very bad. He had 'behaved as a cad', and if a man who conducted himself in that way could be granted a divorce, who would be denied? Surely not every confession, no matter how indecent or dilatory, warranted a divorce decree. The Blunts, ruled the Court of Appeal, would have to remain married.

Aghast to find their marriage bond intact when all they had sought was to blame each other, both Blunts took their case to the House of Lords. It fell to the Lord Chancellor, Viscount Simon, to make some legal sense of the mass of conflicting decisions. Though John Simon is today excoriated as one of Neville Chamberlain's appeasers, his pragmatic, even amoral, approach to questions of the family fundamentally reoriented British social policy during the 1940s. Though recognizing 'full and frank' disclosure as a fundamental requirement, Simon saw Blunt's confession as merely tardy not involuntary. So far as Blunt's bad morals went, why, Simon asked, should his abhorrent behaviour preclude the Court from weighing the other factors that courts had deemed relevant in the past: the prospects of reconciliation, the interests of the children, the possibility of the petitioner remarrying. Simon then introduced what he termed a new principle of 'primary' importance that would in short order eclipse all the rest. The Court was to determine a 'true balance' between the sanctity of marriage and the 'social considerations' that militated against the continuation of a union that had 'utterly broken down'. Since the Blunts' marriage was manifestly broken, they would get their divorce.

Richard Blunt's case would become a landmark in British law, laying the intellectual groundwork for the consensual divorces that the Court's Victorian framers had always feared. The line between the sinners and the righteous still mattered, for an entirely innocent spouse could block a divorce. But, after Blunt, mutual adultery, once a moral disqualification, had become the surest sign that a decree was warranted. In such cases, the discretion statement ought not to have mattered. What difference did it make if adulterers omitted a hotel room or two, if the marriage was plainly wrecked? Still, in decision after decision in the 1950s and 1960s, judges clung to it as a moral anchor, reiterating the necessity of a 'full and frank' confession. People who confessed everything got their divorces. Those who sought to conceal a portion of their misbehaviour risked not just the prying investigations of the Queen's Proctor, but the rejection of their divorce suits. Failing to tell the whole truth was the principal way – in time, just about the only way – that a divorce case could flop.

From the 1930s, then, it was not adultery that the Court punished, but the failure to confess adultery. Confession had been transformed from the means to the truth to a central purpose of the Divorce Court. The discretion statement kept alive the Court's moral purpose by imposing the penalty of self-revelation upon the petitioner. But that was a penalty that people were increasingly willing to accept in return for freedom. And rather than stigmatizing adultery, the discretion statement most likely helped to normalize it. In the 1930s, adulterers who read the news knew that they had plenty of company. By 1965, 12,000 British men and women, nearly a third of all divorce applicants, filed the requisite sexual autobiographies. So unexceptional had a confession of adultery become that only a handful of discretion statements even made the papers: those of celebrities or a man with forty lovers. What was once a deadly secret would become a routine disclosure, as telling all replaced lying as the signature strategy of Divorce Court petitioners.

In the twentieth century as in the nineteenth, the Divorce Court would prove an inadvertent trailblazer: the playground of perjurers became the court of confession. Dogged by secrets and lies since its founding, the Victorian Divorce Court had mounted an extraordinary apparatus of moral regulation, the Queen's Proctor, to root out liars. But the Proctor had backfired as often as he succeeded, as relatives contriving to thwart intervention instead created a new generation of family secrets. The discretion statement, too, was intended to ensure the integrity of the Court's operations. But unlike the Proctor, the discretion statement eventually worked, though not at all in the way expected. It stopped lies by rewarding truth-telling; the chance to start life afresh was well worth the price of disclosure, especially when so many other people were also offering up confessions. And so, when the Attorney General in 1930 admonished petitioners to 'make a clean breast of it', he issued a call which was, as it turned out, thoroughly modern. The idea that a family's troubles ought to be aired rather than concealed – and that ridding yourself of secrets could lead the way to a better private life – was about to become common sense.

It was a short stroll eastwards from the neo-Gothic Royal Courts of Justice, where the discretion statement took hold in the Divorce Court, to the extravagantly tiered, wedding cake premises of Geraldine House. There, at the *Daily Mirror*'s headquarters in Fetter Lane, another experiment in confession was in the mid-1930s just getting underway. In 1934, the *Mirror* was the backwater in the Rothermere press empire. Once the world's bestselling daily, by the early 1930s the *Mirror* had a plummeting readership of less than 800,000 at a time at which its competitors racked up sales of more than two million. The news photographs that before the First World War propelled the *Mirror* to the top (most famously a two-page spread of the corpse of Edward VII) had been superseded by newsreels. Oblivious to the changing times, the *Mirror*'s editors continued to cater to a staid and ageing, ever diminishing middle-class readership. It was the paper of 'retired colonels, dowagers, professional gentlemen and schoolmistresses', those who 'enjoyed the long weekend, had tea at the tennis club and motored the country' – or so judged the reporter Hugh Cudlipp, who arrived at Geraldine House in 1935 as a 21-year-old in a hurry (ill. 32).

The *Daily Mirror* had either to change or fail, but by 1936 it had done something far more daring. Thundering black headlines and short, snappy stories, a graphic flavour borrowed from *film noir* paired with the salacious and shocking: Britain's modern tabloid newspaper had arrived. When the *Mirror* more than doubled its readership in five years, shedding many of the retired schoolmistresses but gaining a young and largely working-class audience, there was plenty of credit (or blame, depending upon your perspective) to go around. Some of the new elements, especially the strip cartoons and the far-fetched headlines, were borrowed from the New York tabloids, of which the paper's new publisher, Harry Guy Bartholomew, had made a study. The Anglo-American advertising firm J. Walter Thompson contributed design flair, and sent over the mercurial genius Basil Nicholson, who brought an adman's sensibility to the task of luring readers. But most important of all was the determination shared by the revamped *Mirror*'s editors, young men from working- and middle-class provincial families – 'lay psychologists', as Cudlipp put it – who aimed to 'get under the readers' skin and to stay there'.

Readers' confessions proved one of the *Mirror*'s most popular and durable features through the late 1930s, a formula to which the tabloid returned over and over as its circulation mounted. The paper's 'pledge of secrecy', inaugurated in 1935, was a promise of confidentiality intended to entice – and reassure – potential contributors. Your secrets were safe with the *Mirror*. With the added temptation of a payment of 10s. 6d., you could also bare your confidences to the reading public. 'What is the skeleton in your cupboard?' queried the *Mirror* in one running feature through 1936, noting both the purgative value of confession and the warning such tales of woe served for others. 'I CONFESS', read the headlines, with scraps torn from handwritten letters offering the visual evidence of wrongs that had haunted the conscience of apparently ordinary Britons (ill. 33). Then there were the contests: for the most intimate pages of your diary, for the secrets you dared not tell your mother, for the 200 words of truth you wished you could speak to your spouse. Confessions about affairs and illegitimate children, parents who were not who they claimed to be, all better out than 'bottled up', all to be dispatched to the *Mirror* under the rubric 'SECRETS'.

The men who stewarded the *Mirror*'s revolution – Cecil Thomas, Harry Guy Bartholomew and Hugh Cudlipp – were by virtue of temperament and upbringing uniquely attuned to the power of confession. It wasn't just that they shared the background of their readers. Rather, they had a visceral understanding of the intimacy that secrets created between complete strangers. For Cecil Thomas, the *Mirror*'s editor, the idea that confession was, as the *Mirror* put it, 'good for the soul' came as second nature: he was the son of a Cambridgeshire rector. The irascible and dictatorial Harry Guy Bartholomew, a self-made man who worked his way up from art assistant to the *Mirror*'s helm, had a 'psychopathic passion for mystery, concealment, intrigue and surprise'. And during the two explosive years that Hugh Cudlipp served as the *Mirror*'s features editor, he lived the sort of dramatic tale of familial shame that he sought to elicit from readers. Cudlipp's wife carried on an affair with another man early in their marriage and died in childbirth; the baby was not his.

Confessional headlines such as 'I Smashed a Good Woman's Life' or 'Where is My Daughter?' were shocking, especially for a public unaccustomed to such fodder, but the *Mirror*'s strategy for wooing readers went beyond mere sensationalism. Getting under the reader's skin meant getting him or her to imagine having disowned a pregnant daughter or concealed a youthful love-affair from a new spouse. Unlike the third-person revelation, in which the similarly guilty might take solace while the morally unbesmirched tut-tutted, the 'pledge of secrecy' series drew the reader into the confessant's dilemma. The *Mirror* explicitly encouraged that sort of identification, asking readers, 'What would YOU do?' and soliciting readers' replies. Reading about other people's guilty secrets had always been a winning ploy in the marketplace, but imagining oneself the possessor of such a secret proved equally successful. Curiosity about how people 'like themselves' would react kept readers returning to the paper. Readers' letters proved the single most popular feature of the relaunched *Mirror*, outpacing even the comic strips and cartoons.

For Hugh Cudlipp, this democratization was the *Mirror*'s greatest virtue. The paper had proved that the experiences of ordinary men and women, rendered in their own words, could make 'exciting reading'. According to Cudlipp, it wasn't the prize of 10s. 6d. that attracted readers' confessions, but the prospect of airing their troubles in a national newspaper sympathetic to their own views. In an age that increasingly valued expertise, the *Mirror* – it was true – devoted a substantial number of its pages to readers' opinions; according to the eminent historian A. J. P. Taylor, it was in Bartholomew's tabloid that 'the English people at last found their voice'. It was undeniably also the case that the most exciting thing that the *Mirror*'s readers had to contribute to the paper was their deepest secrets. As bishops and politicians wrung their hands about the 'new morality', the *Mirror* solicited the life-stories of those who had trampled upon social conventions. Confessions piled up from husbands who illicitly maintained two households and mothers who disliked their children and dreamed of hedonistic escape.

Retailed prominently in the *Mirror*'s pages were the wrongs that family members committed against each other. The curly-haired darling who visited the childless couple several evenings a week? Little did the unsuspecting husband imagine, but she was his wife's illegitimate daughter, 'the outcome of a foolish intrigue'. For years, confessed the apparently dutiful spinster, she had stolen money from her widower father. Left at home to care for him, aggrieved that she was 'growing old through living his life', she squirrelled away the banknotes she pilfered each week, burdening his old age with money worries, and depriving her siblings of a fair share of their inheritance. The 'crime' that tortured the guilty father was that he had driven his pregnant and unmarried daughter from the house. Unable to 'stomach' his wife's idea that their daughter should have her baby at home, he insisted that the girl had 'made her bed and she had better lie in it'. When the girl wrote to him, begging for help, he did not reply, and from his wife he had concealed their daughter's plea for assistance.

And yet, even as the *Mirror* encouraged its readers to tell all (in print), it differentiated between the confession intended for public consumption and revelation in private. After a barrage of married readers wrote in to tell the secrets they kept from their spouses, the *Mirror*'s psychologist, Henry Harris, issued a warning. It could be a 'sin', he instructed, to tell the truth. Confessing all to the *Mirror*, or to a doctor, psychologist or priest, could help to purge your conscience. But telling your husband that you had an abortion before you married, or that your brother was not your biological kin, served no purpose. It could inflict pain and raise unsavoury questions better avoided. 'Whom does it really concern,' Harris demanded, 'that there is a family skeleton that cannot affect the present generation?' Your past was your own affair, and circumspection in private matters was justified.

The line that Henry Harris drew – between matters to be discussed within the family and secrets to be divulged outside it, between the cleansing value of confession and the individual's right to privacy – was an increasingly familiar distinction in the 1930s. It was a staple of the bestselling British advice columnist of the era: Leonora Eyles, whose problem page in *Woman's Own* was the most popular of the era. Introduced in *Woman's Own*'s first issue as 'the woman who understands', Eyles headed a long line of agony aunts whose own chequered pasts outfitted them for the role (ill. 34). Eyles was born into a comfortable middle-class Staffordshire china-manufacturing family in 1889, but her youth was marked by tragedy and upheaval. Her mother died when Leonora was still a girl. Against vehement familial protests, her father married his dead wife's sister, who resented being saddled with her nieces and nephews. After her father drank himself to death, Eyles ran away from her detested stepmother to London, and from there to Australia, where she worked as a domestic servant and made an unsuitable marriage to a man who later abandoned her with three small children. Eyles returned to England a divorcee and took employment as a munitions worker during the First World War. In the 1920s, her fortunes turned around: she became a successful journalist, novelist and crime writer and married the editor of *The Times Literary Supplement*.

Not until Eyles published her autobiography at the end of her life were her youthful travails common knowledge, but the lessons she had learned were evident in every column she wrote. You couldn't change a drunkard; if you were stuck in a miserable marriage, you had to be prepared to start a new life, even in middle age; be sensible and forgive a man who strayed occasionally; sex is important to a successful marriage; don't let your childhood unhappiness warp you. Above all, though, she laid down rules about when to talk – and when to remain silent. Pregnant girls she urged to confide in their mothers. A woman made infertile from an operation had to tell her fiancé. In quite a different category, though, were earlier love-affairs, insane family members, even illegitimate babies. Your past was 'your own affair' and you owed no explanations, nor should you press a husband-to-be for details. The tale of Bluebeard's wife was 'a very true story of human life'. Transgressions of the moment were a harder call, especially when the betrayed party was a soldier, but even then Eyles tended to counsel circumspection. To the otherwise happily married wife who had committed adultery while her husband was away in the war, Eyles strongly discouraged disclosure; a confession would only hurt him, and she had now learned her lesson.

Eyles's rule about truth-telling could, she recognized, seem 'contrary to morals'. It was certainly a break with Victorian dictates. For the Victorians, a person's past was emphatically not their own private business, but of grave concern to the family they would enter and relevant, too, to their public standing. The transgressions that for the Victorians were of communal interest, to be protected by family secrets, Eyles – like the *Daily Mirror*'s editors and Viscount Simon – defined as a legitimate area of individual privacy. That did not mean that you could live as you wished, only that you were entitled to draw very broadly the boundaries of what constituted your own individual affairs. Demarcating that right to privacy did not, however, mean that a person had to keep everything 'bottled up'. If it was unnecessary, even impossible, to tell your husband or your mother, you could (and probably should) confess all to the *Daily Mirror* or an agony aunt. As the secrets of the past were redefined as private matters, the need for confessional channels only increased: they were the means by which taints and wrongdoing would be rendered nobody's business and everyone's reading pleasure.

The premises of the Edinburgh Marriage Guidance Centre were marked discreetly, with a small brass plaque. For the man who hurried into the Georgian building in October 1951, already in a nervous condition, the 'homely' fittings – the sofas and neutral wallcovering intended to put clients at their ease – may not have mattered much. He had come to talk. Over the course of the interview, the 37-year-old chartered surveyor, a father of three, confided in the counsellor the secrets he dared not discuss with anyone else. His wife drank too much, and so, too, perhaps, did he. On a variety of occasions, he had struck her. 'This applicant came in mostly to relieve his mood by talking about his troubles,' noted the counsellor in her case notes. She recommended that he consult Alcoholics Anonymous, a recent American import to Edinburgh, and advised him to make another appointment to see her; she urged him, too, to bring along his wife next time. But the surveyor's first appointment was also his last. His troubles aired, he did not call on the marriage counsellor again.

It was one thing to expose your darkest secrets anonymously to the *Daily Mirror* or to barter a sexual autobiography for a divorce, quite another to discuss your personal and familial shame face-to-face with a perfect stranger. But how else would the British family withstand the crisis that – it was commonly agreed – had engulfed it? First detected in the 1930s, the breakdown of the family had become nearly a truism by the following decade. There were the so-called 'problem families', whose acute poverty and neglected children brought them to the attention of the authorities. Even worse, though, were the signs of a moral breakdown among the populace at large. Skyrocketing rates of illegitimacy; a huge rise in the number of divorces; an epidemic of juvenile delinquency, personified by the spectacle of degenerate and rebellious Teddy Boys; an influx of colonial subjects with their own distinctive patterns of familial life; bombed-out families doubling up and getting on each other's nerves: everywhere the fragility – but also the centrality – of family life was apparent. If family was the bedrock of national life, the place where the virtues of post-war democratic citizenship should be inculcated (as a host of influential commentators argued), then Britain was in serious trouble.

Putting the British family right would require a heroic effort on the part both of the state and of its citizens. It necessitated a work of psychic reconstruction no less profound than the restoration of the national economy – or so claimed the army of ministers, doctors, lawyers, social scientists, psychologists and respectable married ladies who volunteered themselves for duty. What was required was an intervention into the most private realm of marriage. The marriage guidance centre would be the antidote to the Divorce Court. It was time for the British to learn how to resolve their private troubles.

But would people talk about their intimate lives with strangers? Working-class families were accustomed to the prying investigations of moral-welfare workers and district nurses, whose scrutiny of household expenditure and inquiries into sleeping arrangements were the price paid for aid delivered in times of need. So resented, however, was this meddling that the precedent was not encouraging:

it hardly seemed likely that poor people would yield up their confidences voluntarily. And as far as 'counselling' went – the word itself was an American import – the middle classes were nearly virgin territory. They might confide in a clergyman or doctor, perhaps a lawyer. But with the exception of a tiny set of 'advanced' types who patronized psychiatrists and a slightly larger number who took a troublesome son or daughter to one of the new child guidance clinics founded in the 1930s, middle-class Britons lived their lives outside social work's grasp.

Still, it seemed plausible in the late 1940s that people might be more willing to consult a counsellor than they would have been before the war. Evacuation and bombing had made it much more acceptable among all classes of society to seek help outside one's own family. Plenty of people, too, had problems they could not confide in their intimates. There were hasty marriages to be repented at leisure and extramarital affairs that disrupted apparently contented partnerships. Wives who had done things their own way during the war years struggled with returning husbands eager to assert their control. As marriage itself became more difficult, expectations of marriage had soared, buoyed by a relentless advice industry that deemed sexual satisfaction as important for wives as for their husbands; the ideal couple enjoyed perfect mutuality in all things, from their hobbies to the bedroom. How drastically far short the reality fell of the ideal the overstuffed mailbags of the agony aunts demonstrated. By the end of the war, Britain's aunties were deluged with correspondents. Leonora Eyles received 35,000 letters a year. At *Woman*, a special branch of the magazine's 100-person correspondence department was kept busy answering 1000 letters that arrived each week for the agony aunt 'Evelyn Home', 90 per cent of whose authors requested a private reply.

For those who had toiled without success in a nascent marriage-counselling movement before the war, the so-called 'crisis of the family' offered a golden opportunity. Responsible people, proclaimed the ex-Methodist minister David Mace, were not taking the booming divorce rate 'lying down'. 'We know how to fight battles in

Britain, and we're getting ready to fight the Battle of the Family.'
Founded in 1946, the National Marriage Guidance Council that Mace
headed was the work of sexologically minded doctors and moderate
clergymen who aimed to reconcile Christian ethics with a joy in sex.
According to Mace and his compatriots, the key to victory was permanent monogamous marriage. Fertile, pleasurable connubial sex
had to be promoted; parenthood was both the fulfilment of marriage's 'racial end' and one of its deepest satisfactions. The Marriage
Guidance Council envisioned not just counselling for troubled
unions, but a technocratic intervention in the institution of marriage
itself. Marriage guidance centres would prepare young couples for
wedlock and 'service' their marriages in the years to come.

The Edinburgh Marriage Guidance Centre, where the chartered
surveyor called in to discuss his troubles, was an offshoot of the
national enterprise, one of the eighty-plus centres that mushroomed
across Britain. As Mace had recommended, it was located in a busy
part of the city, where people could travel without arousing suspicion. The centre's counsellors were all voluntary workers, local
professionals and worthies who had joined the enterprise in 'the
spirit of a crusade'. Volunteers were a necessity since there was never
enough money to pay staff, but they were also a virtue, since clients,
or so it was imagined, would feel more at ease with people who had
a 'calling' for the work. Counsellors were to be recruited from
people of unimpeachable reputation, the 'morbidly curious' to be
avoided at all costs. Most importantly, counsellors had to be sympathetic and friendly so that they could establish the rapport necessary
to win clients' trust.

The naysayers had forecast that no one (or no one of intelligence
or sense) would voluntarily submit to marriage counselling, but it
did not take long for them to be proved wrong. Edinburgh's marriage
counsellors were soon inundated by confessions and complaints,
delivered up by immaculately coiffured doctors' wives as by dishevelled machinists. Affairs, drunkenness, illegitimacy, venereal disease,
domestic violence, incest: every type of family secret was aired. The
wife of an engineer came to unburden herself about her husband's

dalliances. The clerk acknowledged that he drank too much and occasionally hit his wife. The chartered accountant's spouse admitted that she had threatened her husband with suicide. Even those, like the newsagent Mr Green, who seemed at first glance unlikely to avail themselves of counselling had plenty to say: 'I wondered how & when he would open his mouth,' the counsellor recorded in her case notes, 'he just looked at me rather dumbly – like a sick cow – but after a few remarks by me – he suddenly started & for about an hour & a half didn't stop.'

Far from being unwilling to talk, the centre's clients were (as one counsellor put it) 'bursting' to tell their stories. 'It is surprising,' noted a 1959 counselling manual, 'how much people will disclose even in a first interview of the facts of their life and marriage, hardly aware that they are doing so and with little or no direct questioning by the counsellor.' Although women were more likely to visit a marriage-counselling centre than men, the husbands who came – frequently after their wives had left them – hardly hesitated before plunging into their tales. Occasionally of course callers were reticent: a teacher who acknowledged that it was like 'drawing teeth' to get her to talk, a salesman who blurted out 'it was like going along to sit an exam!' But these were very much the exceptions. Sometimes it was even difficult for the counsellor to get a word in edgewise. On many occasions an exhausted volunteer had to escort a voluble client to the door.

The problem for counsellors was not that people said too little but that they said too much. While most problems that people brought to the Edinburgh centre were garden-variety, counsellors also confronted categories of trouble that neither the taboo-breaking editors of the *Daily Mirror* nor the most forthright agony aunts of the era ever dared to touch publicly. What to do, for instance about the revelation that Mrs Cooper's husband had sexually abused their ten-year-old daughter for the past four years? Well versed in the advice literature on marriage – a course of lectures on sex and family relationships was required for all counsellors – the centre's volunteers were hardly prepared for complex pathologies. Their approach was commonsensical and practical; they tended in the 1940s and 1950s to be suspicious of psychology. A woman who suspected that her husband was having an affair was told to make herself and her home as attractive as possible and to pretend that she suspected nothing. A man whose wife had left home after his mother took up residence with the couple was advised to pull himself together and 'stop the "self-pity" attitude he was showing'. The husband who hit his wife occasionally most counsellors treated as a fact of life rather than a crisis.

Marriage counselling's motto was 'You find the answer by getting on with the job', and despite its improvisations the movement gathered strength. At the local centres, the client rosters increased steadily. By 1961, the Edinburgh Marriage Guidance Council treated more than 600 cases a year, a four-fold increase from 1947, the year it was founded. Beginning in 1948, the Home Office provided the National Marriage Guidance Council substantial grants to fund their counselling work. The grants were both a boon for an organization perpetually short of funds and an indication of the post-war state's deep concern about the fate of the nuclear family. Most importantly, the Home Office grants served to legitimize the idea that Britons would benefit from discussions with strangers about their private lives.

But even as the National Marriage Guidance Council confidently proclaimed counselling the solution to the 'disease' of marital disharmony, records from local centres such as Edinburgh revealed a disturbing fact. The vast majority of clients – like the chartered surveyor – attended only once or twice. The Council's standard practice was to see troubled spouses separately, but it was rare that a case ever proceeded so far. Much more customary was the chartered surveyor's sole visit. People came in a crisis, told the counsellor in a great rush about their problems, and never returned. Or they visited the clinic a couple of times, but failed to keep follow-up appointments. So common was this outcome that the Edinburgh counsellors could spot clients who had no intention ever of calling again. Though Mrs Mackenzie had booked another counselling session after having tearfully divulged her problems, the counsellor suspected (and was right) that she would not be back.

Curing marital corrosion was obviously impossible in a session or two, especially, as in the vast majority of cases, when only one spouse was seen. So what then was the purpose of marriage counselling? Faced with the dismal statistics about the numbers of repeat customers – information that the Council omitted from its published reports – the leaders of marriage guidance emphasized the useful services they could provide. Counselling, they argued, allowed people to vent feelings that would otherwise be bottled up. It provided an opportunity for catharsis, a Freudian term defined in ordinary parlance as the emotional release that followed an unburdening of one's troubles. This purging was especially important for unhappily married spouses, who rarely had anyone to whom they could confide. 'To those who have carried some secret worry or resentment for years, festering like a sore in their deepest thoughts,' wrote David Mace, 'it is an enormous and unspeakable relief to be able . . . to pour it all out and begin for the first time to see it objectively and in perspective.'

Catharsis had always been envisioned as part of the counselling process. Increasingly, however, it became an end in itself. In 1948, with the first 800 cases in London behind him, Mace acknowledged that there were those clients who thrived on catharsis, on the 'pleasure of making confessions'. The job of the counsellor was to move clients from catharsis to elucidation, from purgative release to understanding their behaviour. As it became clear how intractable many marital problems were, Mace's successors settled on more modest aims. J. H. Wallis, who headed the National Marriage Guidance Council's training programme after Mace decamped to the more therapeutically inclined shores of the United States, suggested that the counsellor's most important task was to listen without 'fuss, embarrassment or alarm'. Ideally discussion would pave the way for self-revelation and change. But often it was enough for clients to express what they had long kept hidden. The simple fact of being heard was sufficient to comfort many people in distress.

Marriage guidance's turn to catharsis was a reorientation born of necessity, for the chance 'to pour it all out' was what those who visited its centres sought. Like Mrs Lawson, who called at the Edinburgh centre, they doubted that the counsellor could do anything concrete to help, but nonetheless had to talk to someone. They recognized that secrets were damaging if hidden, and thought that they would feel better for having discussed their troubles. By the time that they came for marriage counselling they had often tried other sources of assistance without success. When Mr Connell broached with his minister the fact that his wife refused to speak to him, he received the dour reply 'this was his lot & he would have to put up with it'. Finding a sympathetic listener was, as advertised, a great relief, especially for those who imagined that their problem was unique. For one newly married ex-serviceman, just confessing his trouble – a secret history of venereal disease, concealed from both his bride and his minister – was enough to assuage his guilt. 'Perhaps the relief of having unburdened himself to a counsellor will for him do instead of confession to wife or clergyman?' observed the volunteer to whom he revealed his plight.

Although the counsellor felt that there was much more to discuss, and contacted the man for another appointment, the ex-serviceman drifted away. His secret dealt with, he could return to business as usual. He had no intention of involving the marriage guidance people in further discussion of his sex life or in the plans he and his wife were making for a baby. Mace and his compatriots had originally imagined that the challenge was to get clients through the door and talking. But if people appeared in marriage guidance offices eager to discuss their problems, they were not prepared to entertain the counsellors' questions or to return for more probing scrutiny of the issues. Even the most apparently forthcoming of clients very quickly clammed up when the counsellor pressed them for more information. Mrs Thomas 'talked on and on' about how her husband neglected her, but turned 'resentful' and 'indignant' when the counsellor inquired further about her childhood. Mr Williams had no difficulty confessing that he had sex with a prostitute. But in spite of his 'open expression', his face went 'furtive at any attempt to ask questions about anything beyond what he has already told'. The more questions a counsellor asked, the more resistance they encountered. People did not want to 'lose face', as Wallis put it, by yielding access to their private lives.

Above all, the experiment in marriage counselling made clear how much could not be discussed within the family itself. However guarded clients were when counsellors asked questions, they were even more bottled up at home. Problems festered for years, and silence or sniping substituted for communication. What began as an effort to save marriages revealed that familial relationships were in a sorrier state than even the pessimists had imagined. Unhappy husbands and wives could not talk to each other and there was very little a counsellor could do – other than listen. Although they bristled at the comparison, the National Marriage Guidance counsellors served much the same function in the 1940s and 1950s as the agony aunts. They provided a means of confessing secrets without answering questions, of getting things off one's chest without compromising privacy.

The tall, slim woman with the pronounced German accent who appeared in Fulham in 1948 hardly seemed the most likely recipient of Londoners' marital confidences. Lily Pincus spoke like the enemy, and in a borough ravaged by the Blitz, that fact alone aroused suspicion (ill. 35). She was forty-four, married but childless, a Jewish refugee from Hitler's Germany whose world-view had been forged in the bohemian precincts of Weimar Berlin. Quietly imposing and meticulously self-aware, Pincus had a rare talent for glimpsing the 'human being behind the hostile fact'. When the Charity Organisation Society hired Pincus as a caseworker in 1943, she had been in Britain just five years, and had no training in social work.

Long Britain's largest and most powerful philanthropic body, the Charity Organisation Society was at a crossroads. With the advent of the welfare state, people's basic needs for food, shelter and employment would now be met. But caseworkers were confronting new problems, especially widespread family breakdown, for which their training in hygiene and weekly budgeting had left them unequipped.

That the nuclear family would become the new focus of social work was already evident; in recognition of the fact, the Charity Organisation Society renamed itself the Family Welfare Association in 1945. Like the National Marriage Guidance Council, the newly christened Family Welfare Association wished to intervene in troubled relationships before families crumbled. But how was it to be done?

For the iconoclastic social worker Enid Eichholz, who ran inner London's Citizens Advice Bureaux during the war, the next frontier for social work was the intimate dimensions of human unhappiness. Even more devastating than bombs, Eichholz had learned during the war, was the erosion of relationships. Eichholz had heard about Lily Pincus – 'a quite exceptional, unobtrusive but wise caseworker' – and picked her out of 400 applicants to staff the experimental project she had cajoled the Family Welfare Association into funding. In working-class Fulham and in middle-class Hendon, Pincus and two colleagues were to visit maternity clinics, Mothers' Institutes, youth organizations, sports clubs and hospitals, in order to interview both the 'healthy' parts of the community and distressed people in disintegrating relationships. Their mission was to investigate marital unhappiness and how it might be dealt with. 'I am sure that never again did we do quite so much talking than at that time when we really did not know what we were talking about,' wrote Lily Pincus a decade later.

All too soon Pincus and Eichholz made the same discovery as the marriage guidance counsellors. In group meetings, the ostensibly 'healthy' parts of the community talked with great avidity about the difficulties confronting a 'cousin', 'brother' or 'friend', never themselves. On the rare occasions when people made follow-up appointments, they did not appear. Participants in the early group meetings had suggested that the new initiative be named the 'Family Discussion Bureau' because it would be less offputting than direct reference to marital problems. But while most thought that there was an urgent need for such a service, they could not fathom what good it would do. By 1951, when the Family Discussion Bureau took a lease on two floors at 4 Chandos Street in London's West End, the challenge was clear. As Pincus saw it, 'help was needed, but . . . there was little hope that help could be given'. In the very Continental setting of the Chandos Street premises, outfitted with teak Knoll chairs and polished wooden floors, new techniques for deciphering families and improving marital relationships would have to be discovered.

Where marriage counsellors took the role of confessors, the Family Discussion Bureau's workers viewed themselves as detectives. What people said about their troubles was merely the beginning, for the caseworker was to be equally aware of what clients didn't say – and why. Unlike the Marriage Guidance Council, the aim was not necessarily to save marriages, but to help couples understand their behaviour. Much to the Family Welfare Association's chagrin, its experimental station edged closer to the Tavistock Clinic, Britain's mecca of psychotherapy. Eichholz, who was already in analysis herself, drafted the eminent Hungarian analyst Michael Balint to lead weekly case conferences with the Bureau's social workers. Pincus was an enthusiast: psychoanalysis was part and parcel of the Weimar common sense she had imbibed in Berlin. The job of the caseworker, wrote Pincus, was to figure out the 'irrational unrecognized motives, the carry-over into the matrimonial relationship of unresolved childhood problems'.

That marriage was the 'most direct heir of childhood relationships' became the mantra of the Family Discussion Bureau. The man with the domineering mother chose a wife who smothered him. A woman whose mother died when she was young sought out a husband who compulsively philandered. By its very nature, marriage was 'collusive' (that bugaboo of the Divorce Court) because husbands and wives sought in their marriage partners an opportunity to re-enact the past. 'This constantly repeated experience of how well people fit,' observed Pincus, 'how even in the most unhappy marriages, husband and wife fill each others' needs, has been a revelation to us all.' The 'fit' that exponents of mutuality had extolled was not the result of wise choices or hard work, but the legacy of early childhood. All marriages were made in heaven – even the bad ones.

In treating the marital pair, the Family Discussion Bureau's workers were striking out in unknown territory. The focus of psychoanalysis was individuals, not couples or families. Although John Bowlby, Britain's leading child psychologist, mooted the idea of family therapy in 1949, he thought it too complicated to pursue in practice. Pincus likened her fellow caseworkers to drunks who tottered out of a bar clutching on to each other as they lurched hesitantly forward. The Marriage Guidance Council was hostile to the Family Discussion Bureau, especially after the Home Office elected to fund its efforts. Digging up the roots of problems in childhood, complained J. H. Wallis, hardly helped clients in the here and now. The Family Discussion Bureau's caseworkers, in turn, viewed Wallis's counsellors as hopelessly naïve and very poorly trained: 'Ultimately, their claim to be counsellors lies in the belief of their own emotional stability and their own good marriages – a terribly fragile foothold, and one we dared not shake too much.'

The Family Discussion Bureau would always be small-scale, research-oriented and dependent upon a charismatic leader. Not long after the Bureau moved to Chandos Street, the Family Welfare Association forced Enid Eichholz's resignation. She had left her husband for Michael Balint; as a veteran of the Divorce Court, she was now 'unsuited' for work in the Bureau. When Balint, too, resigned in disgust, Lily Pincus was left to carry on the work that they had begun. This would be a fertile period in the Bureau's history. In 1956, the Bureau severed its relations with the Family Welfare Association and came under the Tavistock's wing. Pincus and her colleagues had also developed the idea of 'conjoint' therapy. Two caseworkers were allocated to each marital pair, in order to check the unconscious feelings of identification and hostility that marriage problems inevitably raised among counsellors themselves. The Family Discussion Bureau had an average of 300 referrals every year and employed eight caseworkers, preponderantly married women. Although treatment at the Bureau was free, clients tended to be professionals or white-collar workers; both husband and wife were urged to participate. The typical case involved a minimum of ten interviews.

It was a labour-intensive process, and success was far from assured.

Some couples were able to come to a more realistic understanding of
their marriage, to break from childish fantasies and accept the bad
parts of themselves, to see how the dynamics of the marriage refracted
the past. On the whole, though, marriages proved more difficult to
mend than individual lives. Statistics gathered in the early 1950s demonstrated that among those couples who continued past the first
three sessions, 37 per cent showed some improvement in their marital
relationships, while nearly twice as many individuals made a better
adjustment in other dimensions of their lives. Even in the cases
selected for publication, the Bureau recognized the precariousness of
the achievement. The lessening of tensions was sometimes all that
could be expected; many difficulties remained unsolved. 'In quite a
high proportion of cases,' noted the Bureau bleakly in 1954, 'little
help can be given.'

Indeed, the more the Family Discussion Bureau investigated, the
worse its assessment of familial relationships became. Notwithstanding all of the attention paid to so-called 'problem families', the
apparently healthy and the disturbed segments of the community
had much more in common than anyone had recognized. All were
plagued by unresolved conflicts and unconscious anxieties, trapped
by dimly understood childhood longings and secrets both inevitable
and universal. Couples maintained 'mutual misperceptions' to avoid
recognizing their underlying problems. They used each other to
carry their own 'repressed parts'. Caseworkers themselves fell prey to
marital collusions because of their own intrinsic vulnerabilities.
Rather than the bulwark of British national strength, marriage
lurked behind many of the country's difficulties. 'Marital problems
are frequently expressed in concealed ways and have indirect mani-
festations.'

At the end of a long life of thinking about marriage, it was the
secrecy of the family that most struck Lily Pincus. Three years before
she died, Pincus published with the psychiatrist Christopher Dare
her final book on the family, entitled *Secrets in the Family* (1978). It was
both a summary of her life-work and a provocative extension of it.
Secrets, Pincus and Dare suggested, were inherent in every family.

Incestuous longings, for the most part repressed, accounted for the intense secrecy that attached to the oedipal situations of childhood. Oedipal desire, in turn, was the wellspring of the unconscious motives that guided the choice of a marriage partner. For that reason, marriage itself was always a 'cradle for secrets'. Secrecy was not necessarily bad – it could function protectively – but it was inevitable and could for that reason never be purged from the family. Every family re-enacted the patterns of the past, transmitting the burden of its secrets to an unwitting new generation.

Was it liberating to confess or was it, as the philosopher Michel Foucault famously claimed, an unrelenting 'obligation', 'carefully tailored to the requirements of power'? Discomfited by the assumption – a staple of 1970s consciousness-raising – that talking about shameful subjects was personally liberating, Foucault made the influential argument that secrets, once announced, became targets of heightened scrutiny, sites for drawing the line between deviance and normality. At first glance, the history of the mass-market British confession seems to prove Foucault's point. Accompanying the narrowing definition of normality in the interwar years was the drive to confess one's transgressions. Voluntary confessions were on the rise, but so, too, were the variety extracted by the police and in courts of law. In the Divorce Court, as in Assizes trials of homosexual offenders, confessions were becoming an ever more significant dimension of the machinery of moral regulation. Confessions in the 1930s and 1940s about sex between men were substantially more detailed than they had previously been, obtained by police who because of the revelations that had come before knew the right questions to ask. Against that backdrop, the giddy confidences that Richard Blake Brown exchanged with his flapper sister-in-law necessarily appear in a different light.

Still, such was the nature of confession that it could serve many masters and with unpredictable consequences. Those who sought to extract confessions in the Divorce Court ended up succeeding beyond their most extravagant imaginings – but with entirely different effects from what they intended. Confession, moreover, was not a one-way street: talk in one sphere did not necessarily lead to more talk in another; silence also proved conducive to labelling and stigmatizing, as the history of mental disability demonstrates. What is noteworthy is the desire many people felt – very evident first in the 1930s, today a cultural mainstay – both to talk out loud about shameful subjects and to stake a claim to their inviolable privacy. Anatole James wanted, as he put it, to 'tell everything', while also fervently arguing that the law had no business intervening in the private lives of British citizens. To treat him as a dupe is to ignore the fact that it was his vision of privacy that had by the late twentieth century prevailed. As the line between what was sinful and what was merely socially unacceptable was being redrawn, talking and reading about other people's secrets wasn't just the site at which governance was made intense. It was also the way that norms shifted.

Between the 1930s and the 1950s, privacy and secrecy parted ways. This divergence was evident in the tidal wave of confessions that swept through the tabloids and welled up in marriage-counselling clinics. It was clear, too, in the new status privacy was accorded both in social relations and in public life. While privacy was not a free-standing right in Britain until 2000, it was nonetheless protected by a set of targeted defences: the camouflage of the short birth certificate, the fortress constructed by the Wolfenden Committee. Increasingly safeguarded by the state, privacy was also the marital couple's prized prerogative. Secrets, by contrast, were burdensome, probably damaging to the individual, a barrier to marital closeness, and better off expelled. Secrecy, in sum, degraded privacy.

Talking problems out was supposed to purge the individual conscience and provide the means to better relationships. It probably did both things, at least to some extent. But the more people talked about their problems, the thornier they seemed, and the harder to resolve. The pioneers of marriage counselling began with bold hopes and settled for catharsis, which during the 1940s and 1950s, when few people kept more than one or two appointments, was probably the best that they could manage. Meanwhile, the Divorce Court's discretion statements indicated how widespread, even normal, adultery had become; it was easier to confess your sins in public than fix your marriage in private. Although agony aunts continued to exhort husbands and wives to talk to each other, the strains of communication within the family were all too evident. So much could not be discussed. And if Lily Pincus and the psychoanalysts were right and marriage was the heir of childhood relationships, wasn't the family, then, at the root of the problem?

7. The Repressive Family

Edmund Leach, ever a 'roughneck in argument', liked a good controversy, but the firestorm he provoked in the autumn of 1967 exceeded even his intentions. Fifty-seven years old, newly elected to the Provostship of King's College, Cambridge, Leach – one of Britain's leading experts on theories of kinship – was the first anthropologist selected to deliver the BBC's prestigious Reith Lectures. At Cambridge, students crowded into lecture halls to hear Leach, 'hair flying and dressed in a dishevelled pinstripe suit', discourse about the mating patterns of the Highland Burmese and tear into the dogmas of his field. In his first two Reith lectures, the controversialist seemed to disappoint; his soliloquies on the philosophical, even esoteric, subjects of men and nature and men and machines garnered respectful, if subdued, reviews in the papers. In late November, however, Leach sharpened his knives for bigger quarry.

The ostensible subject of Leach's third Reith lecture was the youth rebellion that was just, in 1967, making itself felt in Britain. The London School of Economics had been the target of a sit-in for nine days earlier that spring, and across the country 100,000 people had demonstrated to protest against the Labour government's plans to raise university fees for overseas students. It was standard post-war fare to ascribe the phenomenon of disruptive and delinquent youth to poor parenting, but Leach unequivocally rejected the conventional wisdom. The problem, he argued, lay not with teenagers or their parents, but with the modern British family. Contrary to the 'soppy propaganda about the virtue of a united family life' disgorged by psychologists, doctors, schoolmasters and clergymen, the family was not a 'universal institution' or 'the very foundation of organized society'. He urged his listeners to attend to the realities, rather than the pieties, of modern British family life. As a consequence of unprecedented residential mobility, Leach argued, the post-war British household was now disastrously isolated, the inward-looking family seethed with emotional tension. 'The strain is greater than most of us can bear.' He continued: 'Far from being the basis of the good society, the family, with its narrow privacy and tawdry secrets, is the source of all of our discontents.'

This one sentence would become Leach's most famous utterance, quoted by antagonists and admirers alike long after everything else he had written had gone out of print. Most of the 500-plus correspondents who filled the King's College postbags in the years 1967 and 1968 were moved to write because of Leach's comments about the family. Almost immediately the anthropologist began to back-pedal. In the published version of his Reith lectures, Leach claimed rather implausibly that what he intended by 'tawdry secrets' was the omnipresence of a hire-purchase system that forced Britons to live beyond their means. But there was no stuffing that particular genie back into the bottle. With his attack on the family, Leach had given voice to the concerns that others less bold had felt but dared not express. 'I clapped my hands when I heard your statements regarding the family as the unit in society,' wrote one appreciative female correspondent. 'I questioned it long ago, but only voiced my opinion in private and that in a limited way.'

Criticism of the family as an institution was not entirely novel before Leach's Reith lecture, but it was confined to an avant-garde. At the 'Dialectics of Liberation' congress held at the Chalk Farm Roundhouse in the summer of 1967, the renegade psychiatrists R. D. Laing and David Cooper, who implicated the family in mental illness, joined forces with the intellectuals of the New Left, who blamed it for perpetuating capitalist tyranny. By the late 1960s and early 1970s, the notion of the family's repressive character and penchant for secrecy had migrated from long-haired bohemia to the mainstream. Penguin published for the mass market David Cooper's treatise *The Death of the Family* in 1971, the same year that Ken Loach made *Family Life* for the cinema, Roger Graef shot the fly-on-the-wall documentary *Family* (part of his *The Space between Words* series) for the BBC, and Philip Larkin penned his most famous lines: 'They fuck you up, your mum and dad. / They may not mean to but they do. / They fill you with the faults they had. / And add some extra just for you.' Feminists and gay rights activists sharpened the indictment by identifying the family as the source of a particularly intimate and systematic form of oppression. Whether the subject was the origins of schizophrenia, women's subordination, the perpetuation of social class, or the persecution of homosexuals, at the root of the trouble was the modern nuclear family.

In the aftermath of the Second World War, the family was widely regarded as vulnerable but vital, the building block of society. By the early 1970s, the terms of the debate had shifted radically: now the family was powerful and destructive, perhaps even unnecessary. From his self-imposed American exile, the marriage counsellor David Mace marvelled at the 'curious cult that seeks to vilify' the nuclear family, remembering the battle he had fought to save it. In this turn-about, Leach's phrase – 'narrow privacy and tawdry secrets' – foretold the sea-change. By lambasting the family's privacy, Leach attacked precisely that characteristic most often viewed as its greatest virtue. Moreover, he insisted that the family, despite several decades of confession and counselling, was still riddled with secrets. Families, it was becoming clear, could no longer be trusted with privacy; only the individual should be vested with that prerogative. There was a new definition of privacy in the works, which insisted upon individual autonomy and the right to live as you wanted to rather than on the unbreachable fortress of familial discretion.

Geoffrey Maddox's psychiatrist was frustrated. The 25-year-old clerk appeared at the Tavistock Clinic in 1958 because he was getting in debt and cheating his friends. But Maddox refused to talk about his childhood. 'When I invited him to tell me about his early life he digressed to the tendency of psychiatry to lay the blame on parents or upbringing, and he wanted to make it clear that this was no good in his case – he couldn't possibly hold his parents to blame for his present way of going on.' The psychiatrist, persevering, managed to discover that Maddox had been his mother's sole support during the war, and that there had been a period of strife when his father returned home from the Front. Despite the psychiatrist's best efforts, Maddox refused any 'interpretation' of this family dynamic: 'he shrugged off the significance of this, however, along with the rest of his childhood'.

Geoffrey Maddox's psychiatrist was R. D. Laing, soon to be the most famous exponent of the repressive family hypothesis, then a thirty-year-old trainee psychoanalyst at the Tavistock, newly arrived in London from Glasgow. Founded to treat shell-shocked soldiers of the Great War, the Tavistock was from the early 1920s at the centre of psychotherapy in Britain. When Carl Jung visited Britain in 1935, it was by invitation of the Tavistock. Here, amid the avowedly eclectic atmosphere of the Clinic, John Bowlby developed his famous theories of mother–child attachment, and here, too, the first British experiments in group therapy were made. The Tavistock was a place for heterodox Scots and émigrés who had their training in Vienna, Berlin and Budapest. For the striving young Glaswegian disenchanted by what he had seen of mainstream psychiatric practices of insulin-induced comas, straitjackets, electroshock and tranquillizers, the Tavistock promised a more congenial environment in which to test his own ideas about mental illness.

At the Tavistock in the 1950s, all of the discussion was about families. The family, as John Bowlby wryly put it, had been 'rediscovered', and the Tavistock was at the fore. At the Tavistock's Department for Children and Parents, so renamed in 1953 to publicize the still controversial proposition that parents 'conditioned' the new generation of children, it was the policy that mothers, and to a lesser extent fathers, who brought disturbed children to the clinic would be offered psychological treatment as well. The Tavistock's staff included psychiatrists such as Bowlby, then in the midst of his infant-bonding research, as well as more orthodox analytic types who found 'red-hot oedipal situations' in the fantasy lives of their patients. For Laing, the ideas would prove transformative, shaping the research on schizophrenia that made him a household name. He had not considered investigating the families of schizophrenics, he later acknowledged, until John Bowlby suggested it.

Because of the scepticism with which many Britons still regarded psychotherapy in the 1950s, the Tavistock necessarily drew its patients from a relatively narrow band of the British population. Although treatment was free, it was the younger members of the middle class – engineers, schoolmasters, housewives and students – who partook of the clinic's services. Given the presumably self-selecting nature of the clinic's patients, it is all the more surprising how many, like Geoffrey Maddox, resolutely refused to discuss their parents. Such patients, nearly all men, were a minority, but still common enough to vex their psychiatrists, for whom childhood furnished the essential interpretive key. Edward Bruce, a 34-year-old engineer, suffered from recurrent depression but maintained that his upbringing had nothing to do with it: 'He does not see the point of raking up things about childhood or parents,' wrote the psychiatrist who led his group session. Ronald Brook, a foreman in his mid-thirties, came to the clinic because of attacks of guilty anxiety. When David Malan, the psychiatrist who saw him, asked about his childhood, Brook parried the inquiry: 'he gave the amazing answer that he did not remember anything before the age of 16'. Brook added that he felt 'very warmly' towards his mother and described his relationship with his father as good.

At the other end of the spectrum were those patients who arrived at the Tavistock with a keen awareness of the correlation between their parents' flaws and their own troubles. In her application to the clinic, Miss Marion Sharpe, a young schoolteacher, described her problem as an 'anxiety neurosis and a father complex'. Her session with the Tavistock's psychiatrist was consumed by discussion of her 'terrible parents', always feuding with each other: 'They are to blame for my being adolescent and for my being so afraid of men.' Even those who lacked Miss Sharpe's conversance with the language of complexes could hold their parents responsible for their present difficulties. Mrs Standiford, a 32-year-old housewife, thought her frigidity was due to the fact that 'she had never had any affection from her parents'. According to Ronald Greene, an engineer in his thirties, the fact that his career had stumbled was a product of his mother's over-ambitious expectations for him, combined with his father's complete neglect.

By far the largest number of the Tavistock's patients in the 1950s, however, did not identify their parents as the source of their problems when they first walked through the clinic's doors. Most people left blank the first question on the clinic's application form: 'Did you experience any special difficulties or changes in the home in your early years?' They presented their problems – anxiety, sexual difficulties, depression – without implicating either their parents or their upbringing. Robert Mitchell, a 32-year-old insurance agent who came to the Tavistock because he was unable to have an orgasm in intercourse, described his family as 'happy' and 'united', a depiction that Laing, Mitchell's psychiatrist, thought 'a stereotyped idealisation'. The laboratory technician John Fletcher, who sought treatment at the Tavistock for his embarrassment and anxiety, passed the entire preliminary interview without, until directly questioned, making mention of his parents.

And yet, after a few sessions, many of the Tavistock's patients appear to have readily acceded to an interpretation that indicted their parents, especially their mothers. Miss Margaret Watson, a university student, came to the clinic with the complaint of headaches and tension, but very soon, Laing, her psychiatrist, had discovered her unexpressed hatred of her mother. Though Miss Watson at first dismissed the diagnosis as 'nonsense', it later, she admitted to Laing, 'struck her with revelatory force'. Harold Webb, a 26-year-old teacher, had difficulty in concentrating; he cried during the intake interview with the psychiatric social worker, who suggested to him that he 'felt in desperate need to be looked after and receive sympathy, and that this was something he must have lacked throughout his childhood'. Though Webb at first rejected the interpretation, very quickly he began to talk all about his mother's own difficult childhood. Mrs Sheila Booker was a 24-year-old housewife who sought help for her recurrent nightmares about spiders and aversion to sex.

On her original application, she – like Miss Watson and Webb – reported no problems in childhood, but after a course of treatment she started to express her ambivalence about her mother. By the next month, she had realized 'what a tyrant' her mother was.

That mothers could damage their children's lives was for the Tavistock's young middle-class patients hardly a conceptual stretch, for they were themselves – as parents – the audience for a psychologically inflected literature on child-rearing. Among the geographically mobile middle classes of the 1950s, social scientists agreed, there was ever less certainty about how children ought to be treated, and more resort to experts, such as the psychoanalyst Donald Winnicott, whose BBC broadcasts vividly evoked the emotional lives of babies and small children. Young mothers and fathers were both much more self-conscious than previous generations about the importance of child-rearing, and more anxious to get it right. 'Nowadays, if they don't turn out right you wonder where you've gone wrong, don't you?' confessed one young mother. 'It used to be . . . if things went wrong it was the child's fault, not the parents', they could never be wrong. I think we're not so happy about *ourselves* these days, we blame ourselves, not the child. I do, I know, I wish I didn't sometimes.'

For the new mothers and fathers of the 1950s, turning their child-rearing anxieties back against their own parents who 'could never be wrong' made nearly irresistible sense. But it depended upon larger transformations, both the rising tide of psychotherapeutic consciousness and the waning of religious belief. As long as Christians were tasked with responsibility for the state of their own adult souls, the influence accorded upbringing had necessarily been limited. The emphasis was on independence and self-sufficiency, the strength of character necessary to emerge unscathed from personal trials. The few Victorians who wrote (with circumspection, often posthumously) about familial mistreatment underscored their own imperviousness to the parent's harmful conduct. J. S. Mill's account of his father's punishing intellectual regimen in his posthumously published *Autobiography* (1873) served to explain an unhappy childhood, not a life-long emotional deformity. The same is true of Edmund Gosse's *Father and Son* (1907). By publishing an account of his father's deficiencies as a husband and parent, the younger Gosse scandalized his Edwardian contemporaries, but the book, unsparing in its descriptions of the father's rigidity, does not admit of any damage to the son.

If for Gosse it was inconceivable to imagine himself indelibly stamped by his father's influence, a half-century later it seemed far-fetched to deny it. In the 1950s, it was becoming more and more plausible that parents, even well-meaning ones, could 'fuck you up'. It was not yet a generational assumption, as it would become in the late 1960s and early 1970s. Teenagers of the 1950s, or so thought the cultural critic Richard Hoggart, displayed a heartening degree of attachment to Mum, Dad and Grandma; it was one of the few redeeming qualities of a youth culture he otherwise found distasteful. The Angry Young Men's manifesto, *Declaration* (1958), barely mentioned the family. Even in the Tavistock's rosters there were plenty of patients who like Geoffrey Maddox disavowed any parental role in their troubles. But on the whole young people, especially unhappy ones, were relatively easy to persuade that their parents' influence was so formative that it had crowded out everything else. Blaming your parents for your problems was a new phenomenon in mid-twentieth-century Britain, and it opened the way for a broader assault on the once hallowed privacy of the family.

As befitted a man who made a career out of the mystifications of the family, R. D. Laing entered the world entirely legitimate, but a secret. When he was born, in 1927, his parents had been married a decade. For her entire pregnancy, his mother, Amelia, concealed her condition from relatives and neighbours, hiding her expanding belly beneath the man's overcoat she always wore. In the lower-middle-class neighbourhood where the Laings lived, a respectable Glasgow district of sandstone tenements where people knew each other's business, it was a deception of astonishing hubris. Only when the baby was a few days old did R. D. Laing's parents confess to his existence.

It was the start of a childhood that upended many of the early twentieth century's pieties about family love. An only child, Laing was raised around the corner from both sets of grandparents, his uncles, aunts and cousins. Contrary to the happy stereotype of the close-knit kinship network, though, proximity did not make for harmonious relations among the Laings; the extended family, riven by old feuds, went for long periods of time without speaking. Laing's family life was nuclear by default: young Ronnie, his unhappily married father, and at its centre Amelia. By lore, 'Mum' was resilient and loyal, beloved by her children, and the linchpin of family and neighbourhood. Instead, Amelia, as Laing told it, was his tormentor. She excelled both in forced affection and silent manipulation. Her devotion to him was suffocating: it took a family scene before Laing, aged fifteen, was permitted to wash his own back. In later life, Laing hinted to friends about 'darker skeletons in the family cupboard ... of a particularly anguishing kind'.

Laing would escape Glasgow but not its lessons. As he acknowledged, his own upbringing led him to emphasize how the apparently 'normal' clan unit served as the locus of insanity. Still, less than a decade after arriving in London, he was well on his way to professional success. In the early 1960s, R. D. Laing was a qualified psychoanalyst and psychiatrist with a private practice in fashionable Wimpole Street, five young children and a marriage that was falling apart. His first book, *The Divided Self* (1960), which sought to make intelligible the process of going mad, had garnered appreciative notices. The *Times Literary Supplement*'s reviewer thought that if the young author tempered philosophical insight with scientific method he might well make a 'contribution of the first order to the growth of psychological medicine'.

But Laing had ambitions far beyond the confines of the Tavistock and British psychiatry. 1964 was the year that he became a celebrity. In January, he stirred up controversy with a speech at the Institute of Contemporary Arts, in which he exposed the 'forces of outrageous violence, called love' to which the twentieth-century mother subjected her 'stone-age baby': 'The initial act of brutality against the average child is the mother's first kiss.' The book that catapulted him to fame, *Sanity, Madness and the Family*, co-authored with his fellow Glaswegian, Aaron Esterson, was published that spring. Suddenly, Laing – thin, charismatic and intense, with a beaky nose, a disarming if rare smile, and eyebrows permanently raised – was ubiquitous. He appeared on British television five times that year, performed star turns at international conferences, hob-nobbed with London's literati, and, hard on the heels of the Beatles, embarked upon a tour of the United States.

The argument of *Sanity, Madness and the Family* was often rendered in the shorthand 'families cause madness', but its point was more subtle and its indictment more precise. Dubious about whether there was in fact a disease of 'schizophrenia' at all, Laing and Esterson sought to investigate the familial interactions of those patients who had been diagnosed as schizophrenic. In eleven detailed case studies, all of women, Laing and Esterson dissected the family dynamics that rendered a patient's behaviour 'intelligible'. Maya Abbott, labelled a 'paranoid schizophrenic', was the victim of parents who colluded to undermine her autonomy with an unconscious but plainly visible 'series of nods, winks, gestures, knowing smiles'. Claire Church was listless, her expression vacant, and her thoughts 'disordered' because her domineering mother constantly invalidated her feelings. 'Mrs Church tended to destroy not only her own inner world but Claire's, since she was so largely living in and through Claire.' According to Laing and Esterson, the fears and delusions that so-called schizophrenics suffered were in fact rational responses to family members, especially mothers, who suppressed, even obliterated, them.

All of the virtues claimed for the post-war family Laing and Esterson exposed as illusory, or, in a perverse fashion, damaging. The close relationship of a daughter with her mother was not preparation for adult life, but a threat to it. Families sabotaged autonomy instead of fostering it. Communication in families – rather than the basis of intimacy – was hopelessly muddled, characterized by non-sequiturs and mystifications. 'What Mrs Church says she says is bewilderingly incongruent with what she says.' The fear of shame and scandal that parents instilled in their children did not create socially beneficial conduct but disorientation. Family solidarity was not praiseworthy, but suspicious; relatives joined together to isolate the schizophrenic patient in order to shore up their view of themselves as a sane, respectable, normal and loving family. Despite the oft-repeated argument that 'Victorian' secrecy had been purged from modern relationships, large tracts of family life were in fact forbidden territory, enshrouded in silence. Under the cloak of familial privacy, fathers and particularly mothers were oppressing their children.

That families needed privacy, indeed were entitled to it, had been a guiding presumption of the post-war period. But look, Laing and Esterson remonstrated with their readers, what use privacy served! The more the family functioned as a 'closed system', turning in upon itself, the more likely it was to create 'untenable' situations for its weaker members. In *The Divided Self*, Laing had described individual privacy – 'genuine privacy', the knowledge that 'within the territory of ourselves there can be only our footprints' – as the basis of genuine relationships. In *Sanity, Madness and the Family*, he and Esterson extended the idea further: in families that shut out the outside world, individual privacy, recognized as the prerequisite of autonomy, was not tolerated. Parents listened in on their daughters' telephone conversations, policed their interactions with acquaintances, insisted upon accompanying them on errands down the street, all in the name of 'protection' and 'concern'. The individual's privacy, her autonomy and ultimately her sanity were the sacrifices made for the family's cohesion.

Sanity, Madness and the Family was ostensibly a book about a particular type of family. But whether all families shared in these characteristics – whether families inevitably brutalized their members – was the subject that Laing teasingly danced around in his cult figure days, generalizing wildly here, and retreating to specificity, with the researcher's indignant empiricism, there. He objected vociferously when he was credited with the theory that families 'scapegoated' one of their members into schizophrenia. At the same time, he insisted that for those of his generation childhood 'was very largely one long persecution which one was supposed to feel grateful for and if one persisted in feeling persecuted by this persecution you were sent along to see a psychiatrist'.

What made Laing a guru of the 1960s and early 1970s was this full-throated critique of the family (ill. 36). So drastically has his reputation collapsed, so discredited are his ideas, that it is easy to forget how influential a figure he in fact was. Laing's 'extraordinary following', judged the psychiatrist Anthony Clare, came from 'flailing society and berating witch-like parents for driving their offspring mad'. Many of the horns Laing tooted had already been sounded by others: by sociologists who worried about the isolation of the nuclear family or psychiatrists who traced the maladies of children to the obsessional conduct of their mothers. His rapid ascendancy, however, was a sign that conceptions of the family were shifting, in some quarters rapidly. It was not just teenagers, the legendary rebels of the previous decade, who were in danger of turning against their parents. Among middle-class adults in their twenties and thirties, too, social scientists in the early 1960s detected a marked chill in inter-generational relations. The people they interviewed – married couples with young children in London – viewed their own parents 'surprisingly without illusion'. While the vast majority (85 per cent) judged their filial relations 'good or reasonably equable', that figure included expressions of 'superficial harmony' that covered an inability to discuss intimate matters. They viewed their parents coolly and rationally; they lacked an 'emotionally sticky' attachment to them. The 'commonest' stereotype of all in English family life – mother–daughter love – did not withstand scrutiny. When relations had soured, it was most often because adult children, especially daughters, could not abide their mothers.

The detachment with which middle-class people viewed their parents was surprising but perhaps not shocking. The sociological studies in the 1950s had indicated that young married couples were willing to move geographically far away from their families in pursuit of better careers; indeed, distance from their own parents contributed to the home-centred, marital privacy that they cherished. Much more unexpected, however, was the discovery in the early 1960s that many young, working-class people, too, found fault with their upbringing. Contrary to the staple image of the working-class 'Mum' as ever-reliable confidante and helpmeet, they told researchers about loveless filial relations and harsh discipline. They acknowledged the difficulties their mothers had in raising too many children on paypackets too small, but nonetheless underscored the lack of affection and 'rod of iron' that had marred their younger years. Even those who recognized their parents' sacrifices felt that they were fundamentally remote. As the wife of a machine operator put it: 'I could never hold a conversation with my mother, well even now I can't – seems as though we're distant somehow, funny isn't it?'

The 'generation gap', as it was coming to be known, had many causes, among them the effects of affluence, which dug a gulf between the lives of the post-war baby boomers and their elders. But one of its undoubted effects was to cast doubt on the cheery platitudes of family life. Those who wrote to Edmund Leach after his Reith lecture – both his admirers and his critics – recognized that the sacred cow of the family was heading to slaughter, at least rhetorically. Leach's fans greeted his lecture as the dawn of a new era. 'Most of all', wrote one London woman, 'I was delighted with what you have to say about the family. This has been my conviction also for some years, but I have never found anyone however broadminded, who would brook any criticism of an established British tradition, always held to be the unquestioned basis of the good, wholesome life.' Others compared Leach to Laing, as well as other heroes of the international counter-culture, the American anarchist Paul Goodman and the Sicilian radical Danilo Dolci, noting that they had all probed 'what is outside habit but within the lump in our windpipe'. Mothers of four and youth leaders alike wrote of their own enthusiasm for the kibbutz idea, and their experiments in communal living beyond the nuclear family. Richard Blake Brown, ailing with sciatica, elected to drink Coca-Cola instead of gin so that he could keep awake for the next lecture and, as he wrote to Leach appreciatively, hear 'that magnetic voice'. 'I much liked your phrase "narrow privacy and tawdry secrecy" among many others.'

Leach's critics recognized that the value of the family could no longer be taken for granted; what was in the previous decade unquestioned, even unquestionable, now had to be defended. What did Leach with his 'only child and in a cloistered atmosphere of academic absurdities', raged one Birmingham man, know about the family? 'The great strength of this country is its FAMILY LIFE whilst in the press, television etc., and from such as yourself everything is being done to undermine the Family position. I for instance cannot have normal relations with my wife without a feeling of revulsion brought on by the sick Press or Television.' Some correspondents responded to his lecture as a personal attack. 'Please tell us, just what are our tawdry secrets,' a Home Counties woman caustically inquired. 'We are dying to know. P.S. Have my husband and I failed as parents?' After her eleven-year-old daughter asked about the family's tawdry secrets, one working-class mother chastized Leach. It was easy for him, with 'the means of higher education' to attack the family, but parental devotion was all that her children had. 'Do not talk them along the path of rebellion.' While she agreed with Leach that the family was 'isolated, looks inward and is quite a strain' (though she thought that was hardly a new phenomenon), she pleaded with him to give 'moral' support 'To those families. That are trying.'

So rapid was the pace of change that sentiments that seemed daring to express in 1967 were entirely commonplace by the early 1970s. The idea that the family repressed its members – that 'behind the comfortable façade of family life there simmers a sulphurous and barely containable cauldron of frustrated desires' – was, as the *Times'* theatre critic observed in 1970, by now a 'familiar starting point'. This was the high tide of psychoanalytic influence in Britain, borne along a crest of blue-spined Pelican editions that resuscitated Freud, Wilhelm Reich and J. A. Hadfield for the mass market. The 'dangers of enclosed family life' were everywhere apparent: in television programmes, on the stage, in newspaper articles, in the manifestos of feminist and gay rights groups, and in a new style of memoir, most famously J. R. Ackerley's posthumously published *My Father and Myself* (1968) and Beverley Nichols's *Father Figure* (1972), which defiantly exposed the skeletons, or, according to the *Spectator*, 'putrescent' corpses, of the past. Not even the corridors of Whitehall and Parliament were immune: the tone of the 1975 Children's Bill, complained the 62-year-old Labour peer Lord Winterbottom, was 'of angelic children being mishandled and brutalized by demonic parents'. 'Is the family really the nearest thing to hell on earth?' asked a Thames Television advertisement in 1972, promoting an interview with R. D. Laing.

After a year devoted to Buddhist meditation in Sri Lanka and India, Laing had returned to England. In the Thames Television interview, he insisted that he was not, nor had ever been 'anti-family': 'Some of the happiest and most fulfilling, rewarding, pleasant and memorable experiences have been in families in which I have lived myself.' But his followers had outpaced their guru. While Laing delved into Eastern theology in the foothills of the Himalayas, his friend and collaborator, the South African psychiatrist David Cooper, charged ahead. The family, wrote Cooper in his *The Death of the Family* (1971), was the enemy of individual autonomy and the maidservant of 'imperializing capitalism'. It had to be dismantled both because it forced conformism (the 'chronic murder' of the self) and because it replicated itself through every other social institution. The 'age of relatives is over', proclaimed Cooper, 'because the relative invades the absolute centre of ourselves'. A few months later came Ken Loach's film *Family Life*, which depicted a young, suburban girl driven inexorably to schizophrenia by her over-protective mother and weak-willed father. It was a cinematic reprise of Laing and Esterson's *Sanity, Madness and the Family*, without the hedging or the veneer of scientific objectivity. Loach's title made his argument: this was the nature of family life. 'Middle-class notions of what constitutes good behaviour, respect for authority, parental discipline, the whole blood-is-thicker-than-water syndrome, are stripped bare and shown as the destructive cancerous diseases they are,' wrote the *Spectator*'s critic approvingly.

By the early 1970s you did not need to be a Marxist or a feminist, an anthropologist or a playwright (or any combination thereof), to imagine that the family, in its current form, was outmoded. In a 1973 lecture, the eminent Glaswegian child psychiatrist Frederick H. Stone marvelled at how quickly the prognosis for the family had changed. Only a decade earlier, the idea that the family as an institution had 'outlived its usefulness [was] something I think no one could seriously have suggested'. And yet, given the 'hell' of many marriages, Stone observed, it was 'a very hard case to answer'. Cooper's *The Death of the Family* was roundly panned in the broadsheets as woolly and polemical (Leach dismissed it as 'drivel'), but some reviewers followed the *New Statesman*'s critic in wishing that Cooper had landed sounder blows against objects of 'legitimate attack', such as 'rigid family structure'. Even so, the book was a commercial success; it was reprinted three times in paperback between 1972 and 1978.

Cooper, like Laing and Leach, was most avidly read by the young and proudly non-conformist, but the new conventional wisdom about the inhibiting confines of the family extended far beyond their numbers. That was evident in negative portrayals of family life on the television and in the papers, but even more starkly, in the decisions that millions of Britons made about marriage, divorce and child-bearing in the 1960s and 1970s. Divorce rates had been steadily climbing through the 1960s, but with the passage of the 1969 Divorce Act Britain inaugurated a new era of no-fault, consensual divorce, and hundreds of thousands of people proceeded to abandon their marriages. In 1972, 119,025 (45,385 men and 73,220 women) sued for a divorce, an increase of more than 140 per cent from the figure for 1969 (51,310), which was itself more than double the total of 1960 (23,868). Before the 1969 Act, women frequently filed 30–40 per cent more divorce petitions than men; between 1970 and 1980, however, they initiated as many as seven of every ten divorce cases.

'Marriage, I am sure, has never been more difficult,' wrote a middle-class mother in Bath to *The Times* in 1970. By the following year, it seemed to the feminist Juliet Mitchell that the sexual revolution had permeated further in England than in other countries: 'there is a renunciation of marriage not to be found in America'. After 1972, first-marriage rates for both men and women plunged; the total number of marriages fell from 404,700 in 1971 to 283,000 in 1995. Although illegitimacy was on the rise (in part a consequence of patterns of cohabitation rather than marriage), birth rates still fell sharply after 1971 as the post-war baby boom came to an abrupt end. For the first time since the Second World War, there were fewer than two children per family.

Taking a long view of history, O. R. McGregor, Britain's leading sociologist of the family, had in 1968 comfortingly described most families as 'little democracies', commending the 'freedom of choice' that was the 'essential habit of their lives'. Like the *Times*' 1857 homily about the happiness of English marriage, it was a statement quickly belied by events, for, in the decade that followed, criticisms of the family would only intensify. The family's newest critics, feminists and gay rights activists, had at their disposal the psychological arsenal that radical psychiatry and its allies had forged. But as they tackled the issue about which Laing had always equivocated – whom the family victimized – they would develop an analysis that both demolished McGregor's optimism and turned the critique back against their comrades and lovers. In the process, they would also reclaim hidden experiences as the basis for a reconstructed definition of the family.

In his fan letter to Edmund Leach, the prison chaplain Richard Blake Brown – enthusiastic as he was about the phrase 'narrow privacy and tawdry secrets' – nonetheless showed his loyalty to a different era. Because of his work, Brown wrote to Leach, he saw first hand the estrangements of the contemporary family. He often asked young prisoners whether they were on good terms with their parents, only to hear the reply: 'Oh, I don't bother with them now.' When Brown 'gently' asked, 'but didn't they bother with you when you were a baby', the prisoners just shrugged their shoulders. 'It all seems strange to me,' Brown told the Reith lecturer, and it made him reflect all the more gratefully upon his own parentage. He and his two brothers had been brought up 'marvellously' – with 'discipline and love, THE combination'.

Extolling the virtues of one's upbringing was increasingly unusual fare in the late 1960s and early 1970s, especially among homosexual men. The two most visible 'liberation' movements of the era – feminism and gay liberation – identified the family as the leading cause of subordination. 'How many of us have been pressured into marriage, sent to psychiatrists, frightened into sexual inertia, ostracized, banned, emotionally destroyed – all by our parents?' read the Gay Liberation Front's manifesto of 1971. Feminists and gays sharpened the critique that radical psychiatry had developed: the victims of the family were no longer generic individuals, driven mad by a familial micro-politics of mystification or browbeaten into conformity, but entire categories of people, whose status as women and as homosexuals rendered them uniquely vulnerable to the family's machinations. Their parents were the agents of oppression, but so, too, were members of their own generation, especially left-wing men whose vision of a new order was predicated upon patriarchal and heterosexual supremacy. Early on, Juliet Mitchell, British feminism's most influential theorist and for a time David Cooper's partner, identified radical psychiatry's blindspot: 'rich as it is in understanding intergenerational conflict, so is it poor in even noticing inter-sexual tensions'.

For the Women's Liberation movement, already on the boil in the late 1960s and newly visible after its first conference at Oxford's Ruskin College in 1970, the family's oppressive character was a first principle. All of the discussions in the inaugural London Women's Liberation Workshop, reported Michelene Wandor, a mother of two young children, led back 'to what had happened to us as children in our families with our parents or to what was happening now to those of us who were with men and/or children'. Like Wandor, whose marriage to the radical publisher Ed Victor was breaking up in the late 1960s, many feminists had cut their political teeth in the counter-culture or labour movements, only to be sidelined by patterns of personal relationships – affairs for men, housework for women – that were, if anything, worse than what their mothers had to endure. If Women's Liberation talked more about intimate repression than

exploitation at work, it was not because of 'personal hangups', protested a Bristol women's group, but because 'family and relations
with men are the areas which define the oppression of women'. Not
only had families 'squashed' women into roles, but these relationships set the pattern for the subjugation of women in society more
broadly: 'Other groups are discriminated in the world of production
but only women are discriminated against because of their role in the
family' (ill. 37).

Like the women's movement, the Gay Liberation Front – organized in London in 1970 on the model of post-Stonewall protest in the
United States – also denounced the family as the starting-point of
oppression. Families, wrote the socialist Don Milligan in a widely
reproduced 1973 pamphlet, ensnared their children in heterosexual
norms, rigidly repressing any sign of sexual non-conformity. It was
in the family that homosexuals learned to conceal and disguise themselves, taking on the burdens of shame. Whatever 'tolerance' gays
and lesbians found in their families came at the price of silence. Parents worried more about what the neighbours would think than their
own offspring's happiness. Unlike other oppressed groups, 'Jews and
Blacks', who could find solace in the family, homosexuals were perpetually 'outside the family': 'For the homosexual there is never the
comforting "We" stretching back through generations of achievement and pride; only the vulnerable "I".'

Hand in hand with these attacks on the family came broadsides
against its hallowed privacy, delivered up by people with a claim to
know intimately the suffocating confinement of domestic life. It was
the 'extreme, violent privacy of the family', wrote Michelene Wandor, which drove women mad. Privacy was another word for
isolation and oblivion. Gay liberationists agreed. When the
Wolfenden Committee in 1957 proposed the decriminalization of
homosexual acts in private (a principle enshrined in the 1967 Sexual
Offences Act), its members imagined they had struck a blow against
intrusive Victorian moralism. Little more than a decade later, however, the ostensible beneficiaries of a newly legalized private sphere
of homosexual conduct protested at their confinement. Privacy was

not a refuge, but a personality-deforming exile. Practically speaking, argued gay liberationists, privacy was the same as secrecy: the law legitimated only the 'discreet, secretive or furtive homosexual', as the Scottish Minorities Group put it, not the open homosexual.

Since silence enforced privacy, the vehicle of liberation would be talk. For both gay liberation and feminism, small-group discussion or so-called 'consciousness-raising' was a strategy to transform the hidden realms of life into the basis of collective action. What was private had to be brought out into the open, what had been kept a secret forthrightly proclaimed. Untangling the skeins of repression was a psychological exercise as much as a sociological one, in which 'speaking the unspoken' was a means of wresting control for oneself. Unlike the furtive, highly confidential confessions made to marriage counsellors in the 1940s and 1950s, which outed secrets while preserving privacy, consciousness-raising groups launched full-scale assaults on the entire notion of familial privacy. According to the ground-rules of most consciousness-raising groups, the testimony had to be personal. Though participants might start off tentatively – 'we circled about like seagulls afraid to dive and swoop onto our innermost thoughts and secrets,' reported a member of the Bristol Women's Liberation workshop – they were soon, much to the alarm of their spouses, discussing sex, masturbation, orgasm, lesbianism, children and of course husbands.

Unburdening oneself of secrets had since at least the 1920s been construed as a psychic (as opposed to simply spiritual) relief, but consciousness-raising staked a much larger claim. Secrets about sexuality, family and victimization were not incidental – to be purged by a letter to the *Daily Mirror* or a visit to a marriage counsellor – but fundamental to personality. They lay at the heart of identity. Only by refusing the 'self-oppression' of silence could a person live authentically and honestly. For gay men and lesbians, that meant coming out of the closet, a first step upon which liberationists of all stripes, from Trotskyist to Conservative, could agree. For feminists, it required exposing the family skeletons, especially incest, rape and domestic violence, which lurked in private cupboards. The single 'cardinal rule' of Erin Pizzey's first battered-women's shelter, founded in 1972 in Chiswick, was that no one kept secret their particular ordeal. Whether she was a barmaid or the wife of a renowned barrister, every woman had the obligation to break her 'long-held marital loyalties'. Shared confessions would transform abused wives and girlfriends from victims to the vanguard of a new movement.

Amid the exhilaration of consciousness-raising, however, there were those who worried that the volley of revelations and confessions was a political dead-end. The most famous sceptic was the French philosopher Michel Foucault, himself a homosexual, who cast a jaundiced eye over his generation's belief in the liberatory power of confession. Self-revelation, warned Foucault, was not the path to freedom, but simply the site at which people submitted to even more intense social regulation. Even those who heartily endorsed consciousness-raising, like Juliet Mitchell, recognized the danger that it could serve as catharsis and nothing more. 'Individual – small group – individual. Lonely women have left home and gone back home.'

The alchemy by which pain was transformed into politics indeed proved a slower and more painstaking process than it had appeared at the time. From the vantage point of the 1980s, feminists and gays marvelled at their youthful optimism that personal relationships could be changed so easily. Most of the communes envisioned as the experimental alternatives to the nuclear family had broken up and the lure of the kibbutz had faded. The de-closetings of the 1970s, meanwhile, had shifted the family relations of the time far less dramatically than the Gay Liberation Front's fiery manifestos had predicted. Given how many parents knew about a child's homosexuality but avoided discussing it, coming out 'officially' to one's mother and father could seem unnecessary, even to the most ardent liberationists. Others arrived at newly negotiated compromises. Jonathan Blake, aged twenty-one in 1970, sent his middle-class and conservative Jewish parents books about homosexuality until they objected that it was 'one thing to know and it was one thing to tolerate it, but me asking them to read books was just pushing it too far. So I thought fair enough, we'll leave it at that.'

Although a critique of the repressive family had been the glue that held together the various strands of both gay liberation and feminism, called upon to spell out the alternatives, liberationist movements splintered. While the Gay Liberation Front had campaigned for the abolition of the nuclear family, the avowedly apolitical and much larger organization of the 1970s – the Campaign for Homosexual Equality – aimed instead for inclusion. To one gay socialist, recoiling in 1975 at the 'gloomy' aspiration to 'gay pairbonds and marriages, with in-laws welcoming both partners to dinner', it seemed that gays had come out of the closet only to conduct themselves like heterosexuals. Homosexuality would be tolerated only if it could be fitted within a familial framework.

If the liberationist rhetoric about lives 'outside the family' had never quite matched the autobiographies of many gay men and lesbians, neither – as radical feminists discovered to their disgust – did the women's movement intend to 'fuck the family'. While radicals went the way of separatism, most feminists sought to reform, not to destroy the family. For feminists with small children, discarding the family was by and large not an option; the vilification of mothers among Laing and his left-wing allies sat uneasily, too, with those who like Mitchell herself had mothers of a 'proto-feminist' type. Even as they criticized men for shirking their familial responsibilities, remembered the historian Catherine Hall, then a young mother and academic spouse in Birmingham organizing the city's first women's liberation playgroup, they sought to remake the realm with which they had been saddled: 'we were absolutely claiming the sphere of children and home as ours and redefining it'.

Because of the vehemence of their attacks on the family, feminists and gay liberationists were viewed in the 1970s as threats to its survival. The irony, rather, is how much they did not to abolish the family, but to reform it. In 1966, Juliet Mitchell had envisioned families that would match the 'free invention and variety of men and women': 'Couples living together or not living together, long-term unions with children, single parents bringing up children, children socialized by conventional rather than biological parents, extended kin groups, etc.' The ravages of the enclosed family were diagnosed in the 1960s, but the explicit reconstruction of its boundaries got underway only in the following decade, as certain categories of family secrets – Mitchell's list of 'unlegitimised experience' – became simply family. Cohabitation, civil partnership, separation, divorce, remarriage, lone parenthood: whether celebrated or deplored, these have become for most Britons in the early twenty-first century the unexceptional patterns of family life. Of all of the changes in the watershed decades of the 1960s and 1970s, it was perhaps this widening definition of a family that was most unanticipated and has been most durable.

Although the British family – measured by its capacity for physical isolation – had by 1970 attained an unprecedented level of privacy, families had an ever harder time holding on to their secrets. More than half of British families owned both their own home and a car at the start of the decade. And yet, high privet hedges and sound-proofed transport could only do so much to contain the fall-out of permissiveness. Concealing shameful behaviour from outsiders became all the more difficult when there was more of it. Even as the authority that parents wielded over their children diminished, Parliament ensured that they could be kept further in the dark; in 1969, medical confidentiality was granted to those aged sixteen and older and the age of majority was reduced from twenty-one to eighteen. The silence that families had succeeded in imposing upon their members broke down under the pressures exerted by liberationist movements. A decade after Erin Pizzey founded the country's first battered-women's shelter in Chiswick, there were more than 170 refuges operating under the auspices of Women's Aid. In 1977, the London Gay Switchboard (one of a handful of such services in Britain) answered over 177,000 calls. An incest crisis-line opened in London in 1978.

The claim that the family needed and deserved privacy – a funda-

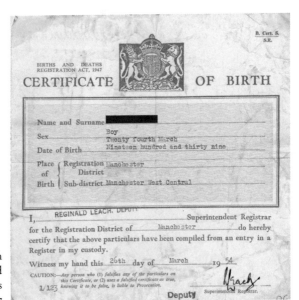

BIRTHS AND DEATHS
REGISTRATION ACT, 1947

CERTIFICATE OF BIRTH

Name and Surname ▇▇▇▇▇▇▇▇

Sex ___ Boy

Date of Birth ___ Twenty fourth March
Nineteen hundred and thirty nine

Place ⎰ Registration ___ Manchester
of ⎱ District
Birth ⎰ Sub-district ___ Manchester West Central

I, ___ REGINALD LEACH, DEPUTY ___ Superintendent Registrar
for the Registration District of ___ Manchester ___ do hereby
certify that the above particulars have been compiled from an entry in a
Register in my custody.

Witness my hand this 26th day of March 19 54.

CAUTION:—Any person who (1) falsifies any of the particulars on
this Certificate, or (2) uses a falsified certificate as true,
1/123 knowing it to be false, is liable to Prosecution.

Deputy Superintendent Registrar.

22. The short birth certificate, introduced in England and Wales in 1947

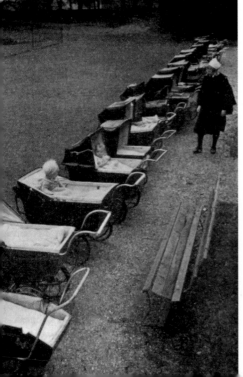

23. The matron of Birdhurst with her charges, 1950

24. Harold Brown, father of Richard Blake Brown, in 1925

25. A Hollywood-style photograph of the curate Richard Blake Brown, 1929

26. Richard Blake Brown with his mother, taken from his diaries, 1920s

27. The young Rupert Croft-Cooke, *c*.1930

28. Joseph Sussainathan (also Susei Mari), Croft-Cooke's Indian secretary, pictured in *The Life for Me*

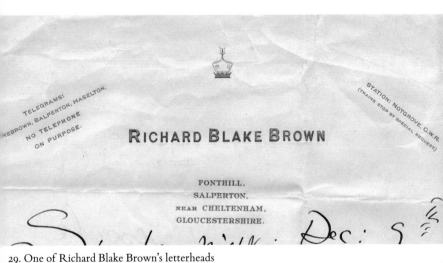

RICHARD BLAKE BROWN

FONTHILL,
SALPERTON,
NEAR CHELTENHAM,
GLOUCESTERSHIRE.

29. One of Richard Blake Brown's letterheads

30. Jeremy Wolfenden at Oxford, *c.*1956

31. The Divorce Court in the 1920s

32. Hugh Cudlipp (*centre*) as a young reporter in 1931

The secret I dare not tell my mother!

Prizes for Postcards

The letter you see above is the true confession of a nineteen-year-old girl reader of the "Daily Mirror."

Day in, day out, she is living in the shadow of a great deception—a secret which must be kept at all costs from the one person in the world she most not hurt—her mother!

Thousands of girls will read and sympathise because they KNOW this girl's predicament.

Have YOU a secret you dare not tell your mother?

Simply—on a postcard—write it down and send it to the "Daily Mirror" ("True Confession", Geraldine House, Fetter-lane, London, E.C.4. No photos can be returned.

For each confession published we will pay 10s. 6d. Names and addresses will not be printed—each confession will appear under the "Daily Mirror" pledge of secrecy.

JOHN DANNHORN suggests a cure for A WOMAN WHO *NAGS!*

"To read your article," a friend said to me the other day, "one would think you had only met people who had made a success of their lives —have you never met one of life's failures?"

I knew a man once—a butcher who had failed. He tried to chop his own head off with a meat chopper.

He was one of life's

The other day a woman wrote to me.

She was full of complaints. Everyone had treated her badly, from her husband, who had left her, to a Judge in the High Courts.

"Can you tell me," she wrote, "why my husband has . . . why my son has . . . Why my daughter has . . . Why Lord Justice ——— said. . . ."

After pages of this she finished up with:

"Now my doctor tells

33. From the *Daily Mirror*'s contest, 'Secrets I Dare Not Tell My Mother', March 1938

34. Leonora Eyles, photographed by Howard Coster, 1934

35. Lily Pincus as a young woman in Germany

36. R. D. Laing, photographed by John Haynes, 1971

37. 'Nuclear Family, No Thanks!' badge, late 1970s. A play on the anti-nuclear slogan, 'Nuclear Power, No Thanks!'

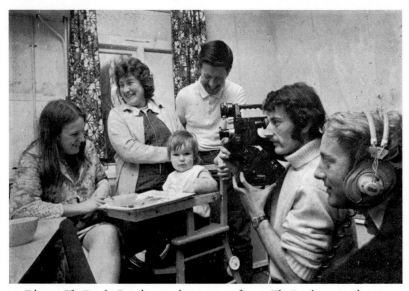

38. Filming *The Family*. Broadcast in the summer of 1974, *The Family* attracted seven to ten million viewers a night

39. *Who Do You Think You Are?* logo. The show that made genealogy prime-time television

mental, nearly unquestioned premise for at least a century – had been badly dented by its indictment in secret-keeping. In the 1970s, privacy was being redefined to emphasize the autonomy of the individual rather than the unbreachable sanctity of the familial sphere. When Parliament in 1970 appointed a committee headed by the aristocratic Labour MP Kenneth Younger (an advocate of the iron curtain in adoption and a leading proponent of homosexual law reform after Wolfenden) to investigate whether Britain needed a statutory right to privacy, the change was made manifest. As the Younger Committee conceived of the issue, familial privacy hardly had a look-in, except as a derivative of the rights of the individual. One of the few mentions of the privacy of the family came from the testimony of the British Council of Churches, which noted the 'undue obsession with personal or family privacy' of former times. Indeed, excessive privacy, the Younger Committee observed, was as damaging as too little privacy. 'The result is likely to be loneliness, estrangement from society and the growth of secretiveness and introversion.' 'Keeping to oneself', a few decades earlier viewed as sensible, even virtuous, was now suspect: what started off as privacy could end as secrecy.

The public opinion survey that the Younger Committee commissioned confirmed a generational shift in progress. Asked to define privacy, survey respondents identified a number of key components: the ability to keep your private affairs to yourself, other people minding their own business, preserving confidentiality, being allowed to live your own life as you want to, not having to mix with other people, having your own home, doing what you liked in your own home and garden. Although definitions often overlapped, the single most important determinant in people's responses was their age. Where older people defined privacy much as the sociological surveys of the 1950s indicated – the right to keep your affairs to yourself, freedom from nosey parkers – their grandchildren instead underscored an expansion of individual liberties. Young people were much more likely than their elders to define privacy as 'leading your life as you want to lead it', an understanding of privacy also more common among the better-educated, non-manual groups and men. To older people in the early 1970s it seemed that privacy was threatened. It was harder than ever, they told survey takers, to preserve confidential information from friends and neighbours. Younger people were much less concerned about invasions of privacy, believing, by contrast, that their privacy had increased with independence from their parents.

The debates about privacy that flared up in the late 1960s and early 1970s pitted one good of the permissive era, the right of non-intervention, against another: the drive to openness. Unlike in the United States, where the notion of privacy became the ideological guarantor of the sexual revolution, in Britain openness with its venerable Utilitarian lineage gained the upper hand. Recommending against a general legal right to privacy, the Younger Committee judged the 'unimpeded circulation of true information' and 'the right to tell the truth freely' at least as important to the well-being of society as privacy. It was a calculus that extended to personal relationships as well. Trust between people, wrote David Cooper, depended upon transparency: 'This means an end to secrets, no relationship-act carried out behind anyone else's back, although privacy, antithetic to family-modelled secrecy, always remains a possibility.' If privacy meant leading your life as you wanted to lead it, it could be made compatible with openness. Defined, however, as the ability to keep your affairs to yourself, privacy militated against the honesty and authenticity that seemed the key to better personal relationships.

Openness was an argument-winning proposition, while privacy, especially when it shaded into secrecy, met with suspicion. Adoption once again provided the leading edge. To protect the privacy of the adoptive family, Parliament had in 1949 dropped an iron curtain between the birth mother and the new family: the relinquishing mother would not know to whom her child had gone, and the short birth certificate camouflaged the fact of adoption from everyone else. However, as post-war adoptees came of age, they pressed for the right to trace their natural parents. That openness and privacy were difficult to reconcile adoptees already knew. But why, they argued, should adopted people be deprived of fundamental information about their families? Why should the state be complicit in keeping the family secrets of the past? The Parliamentary committees which considered the issue were sympathetic, acknowledging the need for 'greater openness about adoption'; in 1971, the Houghton Committee recommended that adopted adults eighteen and older be permitted a copy of their original birth certificate.

The Houghton Committee's proposal forced Parliament to decide whether the birth mother's secret trumped her child's right to know, whether her privacy superseded the illegitimate child's genealogical quest. Opponents of the new provision doggedly raised objections, warning of the 'disastrous effect' on a mother and her family should an illegitimate child whose existence she had hidden for decades turn up on her doorstep. In the end, however, the mother's stake in the matter merited little more than expressions of perfunctory regret. The fact that she might have kept the illegitimate birth a secret, indeed, weighed against her. If the mother had persisted in concealing her past from her husband, observed one woman MP, a matrimonial lawyer, 'should not she take the consequences? Why, because she chose to make that decision, should her child be deprived of his rights?' In 1975, Parliament turned John Simon's iron curtain into a one-way mirror. Adoptees could search for their biological families, but not until 1997 were birth parents entitled to attempt to trace the children they had relinquished.

How fundamentally openness pervaded social relationships in the 1970s a set of concurrent developments made clear. In the sexually revolutionary decade of 1968–78, adultery became much more common, but so, too, did the habit of telling one's wife. According to one survey of middle-class marriages, while less than half of those men who first committed adultery before 1965 told their wives, 60 per cent did so when the affair took place between 1965 and 1974, and 78 per cent did so when the affair commenced between 1974 and 1983. (For women, by contrast, there was little change, though the rates, just under 70 per cent, were correspondingly high.) The idea that people in intimate relations ought not to keep secrets from each other informed a new approach to death as well as sex. Where it had formerly been established medical practice to hide from the dying (but not from their relatives) the knowledge of their prognosis, a burgeoning hospice movement insisted on truth-telling.

And yet, if openness seemed an unalloyed virtue, it proved much more difficult to live by. It was one thing to enjoin other people to forsake their secrets, quite another to dispense with one's own. Openness, David Cooper warned his readers, was no 'euphoric myth', but entailed 'a lot of hard work' as well as a 'considerable amount of suffering'. It was a discovery that a great many people made first hand as they sought to build familial relations in an age of openness. Even those who seemed most confident about the iniquity of secrecy faltered in the matter of consistency. When R. D. Laing's 21-year-old daughter Susie was diagnosed with leukaemia in 1975, he insisted – against the strong objections of his estranged ex-wife, his daughter's fiancé and her doctors – that she be told that she was dying. After Susie's mother refused to comply, Laing arrived in Glasgow to tell his daughter himself. When, on the other hand, Susie's sister, Fiona, had a nervous breakdown in 1977, and was taken to Gartnavel Mental Hospital for treatment, Laing went out of his way to conceal his daughter's condition.

By the end of the 1970s, the secrets of the nuclear family had few defenders. But for those who had experimented with transparency the ideal of intimate relationships without boundaries, too, had worn thin. A university lecturer, who talked to his girlfriend about everything, discontentedly described a relationship 'which doesn't allow space for privacy and any privacy becomes secrecy'. It would be better, he thought, to forswear affairs than to do without either privacy or secrecy: 'the telling, the confessional thing is more dangerous than the sexual abstemiousness rule. I mean I prefer to have rules that say no sex than rules which say no secrets or no privacy.' Openness had its own invasive logic. What began as a critique of the family's proclivity for secrets had advanced into the prerogatives of its members.

The Wilkins family had nothing to hide because they had done nothing to be ashamed of. That was what they told the papers when the producer Paul Watson chose them from fifty other contenders to star in *The Family*, the programme often called Britain's first reality TV show. Broadcast on the BBC in the spring and summer of 1974, *The Family* attracted huge audiences, between seven and ten million a night, who tuned in to see the rowdy Wilkinses – bus driver Terry; his wife Margaret, a part-time greengrocer; and their four children – lay themselves bare. The nation soon knew as much about the Wilkinses' domestic life as the nosiest of the family's next-door neighbours. The couple's younger son, Christopher, aged nine, was the product of his mother's extramarital affair, the details of which she provided in a ghost-written memoir serialized, tantalizingly, in the *Sun*. Their elder son had married at the age of sixteen because his girlfriend was pregnant. One daughter was living with her ne'er-do-well boyfriend in the family's crowded flat. Another daughter was dating an Afro-Caribbean man (ill. 38).

It is entirely fitting that reality TV took as its first subject the family unit, for by the early 1970s what had once been the citadel of privacy was the place to mount an invasion. Margaret Wilkins proved as fearless a foot-soldier as the most militant consciousness-raiser. Airing the family's dirty laundry was, for Margaret, the point of participating in the programme. 'If we helped even one person to get rid of a worry, then it's all been worth while.' Hers was not an ideological position: she disdained feminism, but objected, too, to what she saw as the silences about family problems, the constraints of propriety that made people feel alone. It was the rough's answer to the respectables; television, said Margaret, gave the Wilkins family a 'platform' on behalf of the '60 per cent of ordinary people who would like their voices to be heard'. Many of the show's critics, for their part, objected that the Wilkinses had been taken advantage of. The family's members had sacrificed their privacy without understanding the ramifications of doing so. That was a point that Margaret would later in life acknowledge but without ever regretting the family's summer of fame. All three of the Wilkins marriages – her own, her son's and her daughter's – broke up a few years after the show aired.

Presented to the nation as an 'ordinary' British family, the Wilkinses were hardly typical. Although a significant minority of the population in the 1970s had affairs and divorced, bore illegitimate children and cohabited before marriage, many fewer were prepared to talk about it, let alone reveal their secrets on television. The Wilkinses' willingness to tell all, Margaret recognized, distinguished them: 'other people didn't do that sort of thing, then, but we did.' The moralists of the era could not help but worry about the dreadful example the Wilkins family set. Long gone was the confidence that exposing transgressions to view would rein in other people's bad behaviour. Still, in the Wilkinses' solidarity, in their cohesiveness in the face of adversity, there was reassurance for those inclined to look on the bright side. Despite all of the spats and the wrongdoing, neither the Wilkins children nor their parents had given up on the family. They talked with each other about their problems. Their affairs might be sordid but they had no tawdry secrets, and as for privacy, theirs was not narrow but either non-existent or so capacious that it could withstand the scrutiny of millions. They might have strayed far from the nuclear ideal, but at least they stuck together. And then they didn't.

Epilogue: Genealogy and Confessional Culture

Two decades after R. D. Laing forsook Glasgow for London, another ambitious young Glaswegian left behind his upbringing. In 1977, fresh off the radicalization of Glasgow University student politics, Alex Graham arrived in London. It was a good moment to make a career in television: what had been a bastion of Oxbridge privilege was soon to be forced open to the talented outsider. And Graham himself was eager to get away from home. Steeped in 'that Laingian, Freudian moment', the family was for Graham, as for many other post-war progeny, a 'repressive institution that we want nothing to do with and that we're going to free ourselves from'. Families were 'something not to be relied on'.

It was a Laingian sceptic who turned genealogy into international blockbuster television. Graham's programme, *Who Do You Think You Are?*, averages five to six million viewers, capturing as much as a quarter of the TV audience. The show has been cloned for audiences in the United States, Canada, Australia, South Africa, Israel, Sweden, Norway, Denmark, the Netherlands, the Czech Republic, Poland and Ireland, and on British television has spawned a host of imitators (ill. 39). There is a *Who Do You Think You Are? Magazine* and an annual three-day exhibition that attracts more than 12,000 visitors. Many of the UK's celebrities, including the notoriously publicity-shy J. K. Rowling, have taken their turns on the programme, delving into the difficult lives their ancestors led. Family secrets are at the heart of the quest. For Rowling, the emotional climax was the discovery of a line of ancestors who were, as the creator of Harry Potter had herself been, lone mothers. For the comedian Bill Oddie, it was finding out about a hidden elder sister, a baby whose death precipitated his mother's life-long institutionalization.

If the memoir is the purview of the elite and seriously damaged, the talk show is reserved for the brazen and the blog for youth, for everyone else there is genealogy. More than a third of all Britons, it is estimated, have researched their ancestors online. One in six has discovered something that a previous generation had sought to hide. Never has the 1970s maxim about the family's predilection for secret-keeping looked more accurate. Ancestry, the world's largest genealogical website, tempts prospective subscribers with the lure of secrets to be ferreted out. 'Who knows what amazing family secrets you'll discover with a free 14 day trial . . . Just be prepared for some shocking revelations.' Combing through numbing census lists and deciphering the crabbed writing of birth and death certificates now hold the promise of intimate discovery. If you cannot find a celebrity in your own past, wryly commented one retired librarian, you might be happy with a skeleton in the cupboard. Conversations about family history with friends always reveal 'skeletons hidden which turn out to be hilarious', reported a retired personal assistant; even if the tales are exaggerated, 'it does make for brilliant after-dinner chat'. Discovering long-forgotten miscreants lurking in the family's past is no longer a dread embarrassment: it is the reward at the end of a determined search.

The prospect that genealogy would open up a new front of tell-all culture hardly seemed likely before the turn of the twenty-first century. An enthusiasm of the late-Victorian period, genealogy came into vogue again in the early 1970s, when family history societies sprouted up all over the country. The American television programme *Roots* (a hit in the UK, with nineteen million viewers), together with the opening of the 1871 census, helped to publicize the pursuit. Still, the membership tended to the upper middle class, even pedigreed: it was a hobby for professional men and their wives and the occasional maiden aunt, a congenial occupation, especially in retirement, for those with the leisure, money and education to ramble through old graveyards and embark upon a research project. Among the founding members of the South East Hampshire Genealogical Society were a colonel with a double-barrelled name, whose 'principal concern is to prove succession eventually to the title of

Baron Vernon', and a gentleman who after three decades of research into the blood lines of European royalty had turned his attention to the history of his family.

At a moment when the family was often regarded with suspicion, amateur genealogists in the 1970s insisted upon the majesty and relevance of lineage. They underscored the importance of preserving familial traditions, of talking with elderly relatives, of locating the family heirlooms, of keeping or making contact with far-flung kin. It was with the 'commendable aim of letting our uprooted children know something of where they came from', according to one man, that he and his wife had embarked upon their research. The possibility of stumbling upon a family secret was acknowledged, but the real ambition was an ancestor of distinction. An article on researching noble lineage aimed to 'whet the appetites' of those 'who have no idea what worthy ancestors are hidden in their cupboards'.

So why are millions of people riffling around in their ancestral cupboards today? The digitization of records and the advent of genealogical databases – ancestry.com launched in 1999 and ancestry.co.uk in 2002 – vastly expanded the opportunities for family history research. It is not only much easier and cheaper to get hold of records, but entire segments of the populace previously very difficult to locate (especially the unpropertied and women) readily yield up their traces; the conviction long nourished by social history that ordinary people's lives matter has made their stories seem worth telling. Driving the genealogy boom, too, is a better-educated populace, beneficiaries of the expansion of university education, in addition to the spur that programmes such as *Who Do You Think You Are?*, which aired first in 2004, provided. Though genealogy still skews upmarket, it is no longer the exclusive province of the older and comfortably situated; it draws recruits in their thirties and forties as well as retirees, working-class people as well as the middle class.

But if technology helped to democratize genealogy, the family history boom required something more: the desire to know and, for many, a need to tell. 'I wanted to know what makes me "me",' explained the actress Amanda Redman, profiled in the first season of

Who Do You Think You Are? For Redman, as for a great many others, genealogy is a means of deciphering identity. Secrets are crucial to the enterprise, for it is the shadowy and suppressed, the mysteries of previous generations, which unlock the clue to the family, and, by extension, the searcher's own personality. Ancestry.co.uk emphasizes secrets because it is the sense of intimate discovery that hooks people on family history research. Users tend to start with the idea of genealogy as something quite impersonal, a finite process 'like a jigsaw puzzle', explains Ancestry's spokesman, Daniel Jones. But once they discover something that was hidden, it draws them in, and 'goes to the core of their identity'. The prospect of uncovering a connection to the royal family still reels in subscribers. But more alluring (and realistic) is the idea of finding the missing clue that explains what has been transmitted down the generations. For one amateur genealogist in her early sixties, that is the appeal of family history: 'We are who we are, but all of our physical and mental patterns are made up from all the generations who have gone before, and left part of themselves inside our beings.'

Harnessing genealogy to the quest for personal identity is a logical follow-on to the Narcissistic Nineties. The airing of private troubles, the outing of secrets: the techniques of consciousness-raising had, by the 1990s, swept up far more people in their wake. It was perhaps as much the self-perception as the reality of British life that was jolted by the very public unravelling of the marriages of the Waleses and the Yorks. Where Penguin's psychology editor would through the 1970s reject self-help titles as 'too American', whatever distance there had once been between the revelatory habits of the two countries was by the end of the century fast evaporating. When Marje Proops, Britain's best-known agony aunt, in 1992 confessed to a two-decade-long extramarital affair, admitting, too, her loveless marriage with 'Proopsie', whose domestic habits she had affectionately chronicled in her columns, it was the final canny publicity stunt by a woman who had made a career of anticipating the changing social mores of her fellow citizens. That a drive to openness would eventually colonize the past as well as the present was to be anticipated, for if you are willing to talk about your own shame, why not also reveal your ancestor's?

Still, why so many people seek to anchor their own identity in a family tree is more of a puzzle. 'That connection over time,' acknowledges *Who Do You Think You Are?*'s Alex Graham, 'I still find quite mysterious.' It was not until he produced the first show, the film about Bill Oddie, that Graham recognized that his original conception – family history as a means of encapsulating the broader social history of, say, industrialization or the First World War – missed the mark. 'I began to understand that there was an emotional and psychological power in people's family relationships.' When the flinty Jeremy Paxman was brought to tears by his great-grandmother's death certificate, the mystery of that 'gravitational pull from one person to another' for Graham only deepened. 'Nobody seems to stop and think I had thirty-two great-great-great grandparents, but that's the one they connect with.'

Genealogy is inevitably a search for belonging, but one that looks different after four decades of permissive, mobile society from how it did either to the late Victorians or to the pioneers of family history in the 1970s. In the early days of *Who Do You Think You Are?*, Graham recounts, a sceptic objected to the premise of the show. Who doesn't know the names of their grandparents? The whole idea of the show seemed implausible: it was inconceivable that people could be so detached from their immediate family. Graham was at first chastened, but then thought about his own family. 'And then I realized that I had no idea.' He didn't know the proper names of his mother's parents. His maternal grandmother had died when he was three, and her husband had deserted the family when his mother was a girl.

Although the liberationist vision of kibbutzes in Kidderminster proved short-lived, family break-up is now a permanent and visible fixture of modern British society. After the tidal wave of the early 1970s, divorce rates inched steadily upwards through the 1980s, eluding efforts on both the Left and Right to preserve marital bonds. Ties to extended kin have also attenuated, a consequence of the Second World War, which scattered families; of social and geographic mobility; and of the premium placed on individualism and self-determination. For many of those who responded to the 1984 Mass-Observation survey on 'Relatives, Friends and Neighbours', family – rather than an inevitable set of bonds – had become a set of relationships to be chosen, or not, according to individual affinity. Reflecting upon the differences between her own attitudes and those of her parents and grandparents, the 31-year-old wife of a mechanic in 1984 emphasized the 'more relaxed, informal approach' of her generation: 'We keep in close contact with those we love and have something in common with and have little to do with all the others.'

Contrary to the old saying, you could, at least to some degree, choose your family, at least the extended and mythical version of it. The compensation for the weakening of extended kin was that those relations that remained were all the stronger for being freely chosen; this was an element in the reconstruction of the family that Juliet Mitchell had in 1964 imagined. It was, thought one man, like chopping the dead wood out of a tree in order to make it stronger. At the turn of the twenty-first century, when, as a divorced carer put it, 'Family is anything you want it to be', genealogy, despite the immutable appearance of those bold vertical and horizontal lines, can be pressed into service. At odds with siblings and parents who had made her feel 'inadequate and inferior', one 45-year-old woman had traced her mother's family back to the fifteenth century: 'The blip of nastiness around the latest part of this story becomes less important.'

This most recent genealogy boom bespeaks, it has been said, the rootlessness of modern society. Yet this rootlessness is not simply a generic by-product of contemporary life, but was for many people, especially the upwardly mobile, something they chose. The sentiment that the family was either an irrelevant or a repressive institution not only accompanied social and geographic mobility. It also justified it. 'I was quite selfish. I wanted a career, I wanted to come to London, from early on I was ambitious and stroppy,' reflects Alex Graham, who was in the early 1970s the first person in his family to attend university. 'As soon as I could, I got out of Glasgow.'

Focusing a genealogy show around celebrities was in some sense an obvious choice because they're more telegenic and presumably also more interesting than the rest of us. But Graham's masterstroke was to recognize that celebrities enact the family drama of social mobility, living an exaggerated version of the phenomenon that millions of their fellow citizens have experienced in the last half-century. Cocooned in their protected worlds, at a remove from the lives their parents and grandparents led, celebrities are, as Graham points out, 'an extreme example of what social mobility does'.

While *Who Do You Think You Are?* started off with a conventional post-permissive premise – all families have secrets and revealing secrets makes good television – family secrets do not function on the show as either liberationists or the therapeutic prophets of openness would have predicted. Secrets do not estrange the celebrities from their kin, but draw them in closer. That is true whether the secrets are at a comfortable remove in the distant past or whether, as in Bill Oddie's case, they are wrapped up in the tragedy of recent times. Unearthing what has been hidden offers the celebrities an opportunity to talk back across the generation gap and the distance that social mobility has opened up. This is what they went through, we didn't and couldn't understand. 'Such an extraordinary amount of awful things to happen to people,' says Amanda Redman as she untangles a multi-generational history of illegitimacy, abandonment and alcoholism. 'Their lives have been so affected by this.' The family secret that had once been the indictment becomes, when exposed, the bond and also the explanation.

The story of the last thirty years, as Alex Graham now sees it, is of the 'family reasserting itself'. At the end of their genealogical journeys, the show's subjects often explain their own trajectory in familial terms. The actress Sue Johnston's left-wing sympathies reflect the harsh conditions of her own family's working-class past, her decision to thwart her parents' plans and become an actress mirrors the path her great-grandfather also took; J. K. Rowling's true ancestors are the women in her line forced by circumstance to raise children on their own. What is true of celebrities is also true of ordinary folk; as Ancestry's Daniel Jones explains it, if you get divorced and then you find a bigamist in your past, that discovery helps to forge a connection. It is this sort of bond that can give family history a spiritual dimension: a sense of higher purpose, all the more powerful when laced with the modern gospel of genetics. We are but the recombined bits of people now long gone, whose lives – knowingly or unknowingly – we carry with us. As an aficionado in his thirties explains it, genealogy is 'one of the things to believe in that has sprung up in the last hundred years, as Christianity has waned'.

And yet, the irony is that in the past half-century the accumulated weight of family history has probably played less of a role in determining people's lives than ever before. If *Who Do You Think You Are?* proves anything, it is that the family's hold was not inescapable: prosperity and the welfare state, the opening of higher education and the vagaries of individual talent made for existences that are not delimited by the experiences of previous generations. The emotional habits of the past, too, could be kicked over, so thoroughly as to make them nearly unfathomable. That Stephen Fry's great-great-grandfather was a pauper and jailbird matters as little to his genius as Britain's forsaken post-industrial landscapes, a constant backdrop in the show's episodes, do to the future of the country's biotech sector. Nevertheless, there is that longing to 'get back to the garden', observes Alex Graham, invoking Joni Mitchell. Telling the family's secrets works for us moderns in much the same way as keeping them did for the Victorians: it forges the bonds of kin.

The need to tell and the duty to keep quiet: this was a conundrum that a 77-year-old pensioner, a retired Yorkshire newspaper editor, found inescapable. The genealogical craze of the early twenty-first century had swept through his own relations: one niece had contacted him for information, another had borrowed old family photographs for the collection she was assembling in her hall. When a cousin whom he had barely seen in decades telephoned him out of the blue to announce that she was bringing by a box of old family mementos, rescued from the rubbish heap, he could hardly wait. He carried the box to his office and tipped its contents out on the desk: photographs and tattered birthday and Valentine cards, all smelling of the starchy scent of old face powder. And there in the dim light of the day 'were the nuggets I had hoped to see': pictures of his beloved paternal grandmother in her mob cap and pinafore, posed outside her fish-and-chip shop on the coronation day of George VI; his grandfather in his blacksmith's apron; his father's timber lorry; his uncle pushing him in a blue toy pedal car; and scores of his ancestors – forbidding Victorians in heavy dresses and children entombed in lace, young men looking appraisingly at the photographer – whose names he would never know.

As the man sorted through the photographs, though, he could not escape a sense of unease. He resented intrusions into his own privacy, whether the 'cold eye' of the omnipresent CCTV or local governments with their computerized data. 'So how do we know that our nosey-parkering among long-dead ancestors is any more acceptable to their spirits?' It was more, though, than a scruple about disturbing the dead. Sickened by the perfume given off by the pictures, 'I realized that I didn't relish touching them again.' He had dearly loved his paternal grandparents and his uncle, but, eager to make his way in the world, he had drifted away from them when he started work far away at the age of fourteen. 'I now felt that those dear people were lost to me. I had had my place amongst them, but I had lost it.' Recognizing that his ancestors needed to be left in peace, he did one final thing. Neither his wife nor his daughter knew it, but for the past two decades he had been writing a book of family history for the benefit of his descendants. He took a few photographs from the box and put them in the first volume. His daughter would never know how unsettled the pictures made him feel.

This has been a book about how shame was lived: about the terrors and also the failures of moral regulation, about families that chastized and concealed, about the resonance of interactions played out behind locked doors. At its core, the book has explored how the first-hand knowledge gained in families about stigmatized subjects did (and did not) extend beyond their boundaries. It puts thousands of hidden-away familial encounters alongside the public turning-points of protest movements and new laws to argue for the significance of an intimate history of why social mores changed.

That families instil shame is a commonplace. About this – if little else – early-nineteenth-century evangelicals and late-twentieth-century psychoanalysts could agree. Repression lies close to the surface, its marks readily apparent. The testimony of individuals can tell us how families have stifled and suppressed their members, banishing, as did Anatole James's father, a homosexual son or hiding away an 'imbecile' daughter. When Elizabeth Scott-Sanderson's mother delivered her to Normansfield in 1921, she did so in large measure because in her upper-middle-class circles it was more acceptable to put away a disabled person for ever than to acknowledge her existence.

Equally important if far less well known are the ways in which the meaning of shame was transformed within families. Defiant acts of loyalty – Charlotte Capel's unflinching support of her wayward daughter – were the most shocking in the moment. More frequent were attempts at protection intended to be unseen: Thomas and Gertrude Litchfield deceiving their friends about their adoptive daughter Marjorie's illegitimate origins. Or the still more familiar mixture of silence, support and disapproval: Harold Brown sending cheques alongside remonstrations to his errant son in a Cotswold cottage. Family secrets were pacts with unintended consequences. They required deviations from rules and improvisations such as forged birth certificates. They, too, worked the levers of social change.

The protection secrets offered was often as much about the family's reputation as the individual's well-being. Defects recognized as innate proved more dangerous to families than bad behaviour, especially in the early twentieth century, when hereditarianism held sway. It was on the whole easier to be a relativist when morality rather than genetics was at stake. Either way, though, keeping secrets bolstered the idea that the deficiencies or transgressions of your intimates were nobody else's business – not your neighbours' and not the state's. Secrets laid the groundwork for legitimate claims to privacy.

In the many books devoted to the subject of privacy, secrets have hardly figured. The invention of privacy has been recounted in a heroic key. Heralded as a milestone of modern civilization, it came about, historians agree, in early modern Europe, as the medieval world of clan and community yielded to a household centred upon the nuclear family and the individual. Newly inward-looking and literate, disciplined by the Protestant Reformation and ever more susceptible to the incursion of powerful states, people retreated to a domestic sphere, where they took refuge in self-cultivation and built corridors to safeguard personal quarters, developed bells for servants and newfangled locks for furniture. Privacy, it has been claimed, was the precondition for individualism; it promoted creativity and intro-spection, and fostered the inner life.

And yet, to accord privacy an idealized pedigree is to obscure the secrecy and deception that lay at its heart. While Victorians extolled the virtues of privacy, they took for granted the need for secrecy. Privacy was manifestly insecure, they recognized, without stout walls and close-mouthed relatives. Even for the comfortably situated middle and upper orders, bedrooms with doors and back hallways hardly guaranteed that a family could exchange confidences with security. Still more importantly, a legal system that prized transpar-ency forced a family's shame out into the open. Mechanisms such as the Queen's Proctor designed to dispel lies succeeded only in creating more liars. That privacy and secrecy were inextricably intertwined was a Victorian certainty. That they would come apart has been the work of their children and grandchildren.

Rethinking the relationship between secrecy and privacy is all the more useful because laments over the demise of privacy have become an early-21st-century staple. Since the 1970s, citizens of both the United Kingdom and the United States have consistently ranked the protection of privacy as a priority. At the same time, the deluge of talk shows, memoirs, blogs, reality television programmes, Facebook updates and Twitter feeds has turned the family secrets of yesteryear into the social media fodder of today. Some of the same people who reveal their own intimate matters to all comers also decry the inva-sions of CCTV or Google's infringements upon personal data, leading bemused commentators to speculate about the Janus-face of a populace that apparently cherishes privacy even as it takes gleeful part in self-exposure. Conceptions of privacy, argues Facebook's founder, Mark Zuckerberg, have changed dramatically over the past five years: 'People have really gotten comfortable not only sharing more information and different kinds, but more openly and with more people.' The era of privacy, it has been variously claimed, is 'over' or 'dead'.

But from the vantage point of the past two centuries, what is most remarkable is not that privacy is endangered (or obsolete) but its long expansion. To have privacy, as we now define it, is to be able to conduct your affairs and develop your personality without significant social detriment; the right to privacy presupposes that our neighbours and our government have agreed, within limits, not to care what we do. In the early twenty-first century, privacy is not the ability to hide but the right to tell without cost. Confessional culture marks not the end of privacy but its broadened expression: the right to be let alone shorn of the shame and secrecy.

The apparently puzzling coexistence of tell-all culture and the high value we place on privacy, then, is neither so paradoxical nor so new. It predates both the social media revolution and the 1960s, for it was a cultural shift before it was a technological one. From the 1930s, people defended a right to be left alone even as they came to believe that secrets were better off out (whether in the anonymous confines of the *Daily Mirror* or the confidential setting of the Marriage Counselling Centre) than for ever bottled up. The high-ranking government officials who decided in the 1940s and 1950s that transparency in family matters was less important than privacy and marital harmony – that birth certificates need not disclose illegitimacy and that a wife's wartime affair could be legally papered over – knew their J. S. Mill. They took their cue, too, from a populace that deployed a new democratic language of non-interference to buttress the argument that their doings were their own and no one else's to reveal. Telling all, then, was a personal privilege exercised for the right price (a divorce or a season of fame) or simply for the satisfaction of emerging from the shadows.

The writer J. R. Ackerley was enough of a modern to write a memoir that intertwined the revelation of his own homosexuality with the outing of his father's secret lives. And, born in 1896, he was old-fashioned enough to worry about the propriety of publishing it; he started the book in 1933 and would work on it for more than thirty years. When *My Father and Myself* finally appeared in 1968, the year after Ackerley died, it marked out a frank new frontier of confessional literature. Still, after nearly a decade of untwisting his father's deceptions, of unwinding the secrets that had cemented his parents' union but also ruined his family, it was the futility of the effort that confronted Ackerley. Investigations led to more questions, answers to more puzzles. For Ackerley, the search for the truth was the first principle, but the limitations of his endeavour, he acknowledged, were inescapable. 'Of my father, my mother, myself, I know in the end practically nothing.' About families and their secrets, much can be known, but much more is silence.

References

Introduction

p. xi 'I intend': Letter to Miss Hart, 27 October 1920, Mission of Hope files, Fostering and Adoption Service, Croydon Council [henceforth CC].

p. xi 'splendidly': Index Books, 1916–1922, CC.

p. xi This is a book: The best history of 'official' secrecy and, more generally, the relationship between the control of information and the liberal polity is David Vincent's superb, wide-ranging *The Culture of Secrecy: Britain, 1832–1998* (Oxford, 1998). Also Clive Ponting, *Secrecy in Britain* (Oxford, 1990); James Michael, *The Politics of Secrecy* (London, 1982). In selecting particular family secrets, I have been guided by two criteria: prevalence, and relevance to the nature/nurture debates that form the heart of the book.

p. xii But what of the British: Peter Mandler, *The English National Character: The History of an Idea from Edmund Burke to Tony Blair* (New Haven and London, 2006), 100–101, 166–70, 211–13.

p. xii 'give themselves away': Brian Harrison, 'The Public and the Private in Modern Britain', in Peter Burke, Brian Harrison and Paul Slack, eds., *Civil Histories: Essays Presented to Sir Keith Thomas* (Oxford, 2000), 340.

p. xii Eleven of the country's: Liz Bury, 'Tugging at Heart Strings', *The Bookseller*, 22 February 2007; Stefanie March, 'I Confess: I Have Not been Agonising About Madeleine', *The Times* (London), 1 June 2007.

p. xii But secrecy as a familial strategy: See, for instance, 'Should Family Secrets Remain Hidden', *Psychologies Magazine*, http://www.psychologies.co.uk/family/secrets-in-the-family. For an overview of the psychological literature, Naima Brown-Smith, 'Family Secrets', *Journal of Family Issues* 19 (1998), 20–42.

p. xiii 'Nothing changes more': Elizabeth Bowen, 'Preface to Dr. Thorne' (reprint, 1959), in *Seven Winters: Memories of a Dublin Childhood & Afterthoughts* (New York, 1962), 126.

p. xiii secrecy tends to run: A point made by Georg Simmel in his essay 'Secrecy', in Kurt H. Wolff, trans. and ed., *The Sociology of Georg Simmel* (New York, 1950), 335–6.

p. xiii Incest, the most shocking: 'Overcrowded Cottages', *Examiner*, 11 May 1861, 291; James Anthony Froude, 'The Agricultural Labourer', *Fraser's Magazine*, n.s. 1:4 (1870), 429; A.W. L., 'Slum Overcrowding and the Repeal of the Legislative Restrictions on Railways', *Westminster Review* 158:3 (1902), 259; Beatrice Webb, *My Apprenticeship* (Cambridge, 1979 [1926]), 321, n. 1; Anthony S. Wohl, 'Sex and the Single Room: Incest among the Victorian Working Class', in Wohl, ed., *The Victorian Family* (London, 1978), 197–218; Louise Jackson, *Child Sexual Abuse in Victorian England* (London, 2000), 7–8, 43, 46–50, 57–8, 66–7, 120–21; Mary Jean Corbett, *Family Likeness: Sex, Marriage and Incest from Jane Austen to Virginia Woolf* (Ithaca, 2008); Stephen Marcus, *The Other Victorians: A Study of Sexuality and Pornography in Mid-Nineteenth-Century England* (London, 1966), 245; Adam Kuper, *Incest and Influence: The Private Life of Bourgeois England* (Cambridge, Mass., 2009). On brother–sister intimacy, Leonore Davidoff, *Thicker Than Water: Siblings and Their Relations* (Oxford, 2011), 197–224.

p. xiii Similarly, domestic violence: Ellen Ross, *Love and Toil: Motherhood in Outcast London, 1870–1918* (Oxford, 1993), 85–6; Gill Hague, *The Silenced Pain: Domestic Violence, 1945–1970* (Bristol, 1996); Marjorie Homer, Anne Leonard and Pat Taylor, *Private Violence, Public Shame: A Report on the Circumstances of Women Leaving Domestic Violence in Cleveland* (Cleveland Refuge and Aid for Women and Children, 1984); Paul Lockley, *Counselling Women in Violent Relationships* (London, 1999).

p. xiii And yet, the distinction: On contemporary conceptions of secrecy, Sissela Bok, *Secrets: On the Ethics of Concealment and Revelation* (New York, 1983); Carol Warren and Barbara Laslett, 'Privacy and Secrecy: A Conceptual Comparison', in Stanton K. Tefft, ed., *Secrecy: A Cross-Cultural Perspective* (New York, 1980), 25–34. Of the vast literature on privacy, see especially Walter F. Pratt, *Privacy in Britain* (Lewisburg, 1979); Philippe Ariès and Georges Duby, gen. eds., *A History of Private Life*, vols. I–V (Cambridge, Mass., 1987–91), esp. vol. IV, Michelle Perrot, ed., *From the Fires of Revolution to the Great War* (Cambridge, Mass., 1990); Patricia Meyer Spacks, *Privacy: Concealing the Eighteenth-Century Self* (Chicago, 2003); John Brewer, 'This, That and the Other: Public, Social and Private in the Seventeenth and Eighteenth Centuries', in Dario Castiglione and Lesley Sharpe, eds., *Shifting the Boundaries: Transformation of the Languages of Public and Private in the Eighteenth Century* (Exeter, 1995), 1–21; Amanda Vickery, *Behind Closed Doors* (New Haven and London, 2009), 25–48; Harrison, 'The Public and the Private'; Vincent, *Culture of Secrecy*, 18–25; Mervyn Jones, ed., *Privacy* (Newton Abbott, 1974); Linda Pollock, 'Living on the Stage of the World: The Concept of Privacy among the Elite of Early Modern England', in Adrian Wilson, ed., *Rethinking Social History: English Society, 1570–1920* (Manchester, 1993), 78–96; John Barrell, *Spirit of Despotism: Invasions of Privacy in the 1790s* (Oxford, 2006); Faramerz Dabhoiwala, *The Origins of Sex: A History of the First Sexual Revolution* (New York, 2012), 84, 91–3, 108–10, 329–34; Ferdinand David Schoeman, *Privacy and Social Freedom* (Cambridge, 1992).

p. xiii 'state of being secret': Samuel Johnson, *A Dictionary of the English Language* (London, 1755–6), vol. 2.

p. xiii 'In this country': 'The Vernon Case', *Spectator*, 11 July 1863, 2224.

p. xiv For the Victorians: Alexander Welsh, *George Eliot and Blackmail* (Cambridge, Mass., 1985), 33–109; H. G. Cocks, *Nameless Offences: Homosexual Desire in the 19th Century* (London, 2010 [2003]), 115–54; Angus McLaren, *Sexual Blackmail: A Modern History* (Cambridge, Mass., 2002); Barbara Leckie, *Culture and Adultery: The Novel, the Newspaper and the Law, 1857–1914* (Philadelphia, 1999); Karen Chase and Michael Levenson, *The Spectacle of Intimacy: A Public Life for the Victorian Family* (Princeton, 2000), 3–17, 143–55, 201–13; John Tosh, *A Man's Place: Masculinity and the Middle-Class Home in Victorian England* (New Haven and London, 1999), 32, 38.

p. xiv 'at the queer': Sir Arthur Conan Doyle, *Adventures of Sherlock Holmes* (New York, 1892), 56; Welsh, *George Eliot*, 75.

p. xiv 'necessary and justifiable secrecy': Holyoake, *A New Defence of the Ballot* (1868), cited in Vincent, *Culture of Secrecy*, 316; Albert D. Pionke and Denise Tischler Millstein, *Victorian Secrecy: Economies of Knowledge and Concealment* (Farnham, 2010), 1–14; John Kucich, *The Power of Lies: Transgression in Victorian Fiction* (Ithaca, 1994), 4–38.

p. xiv 'Every house has its skeleton': W. M. Thackeray, *The History of Pendennis* (Leipzig, 1849), vol. II, 25.

p. xiv 'There are private histories': Sarah Stickney Ellis, *The Daughters of England: Their Position in Society, Character and Responsibilities* (New York, 1842), 193.

p. xv secrecy forged: Georg Simmel, 'The Secret Society' in Wolff, ed., *Sociology*, 345–76; also Vincent, *Culture of Secrecy*, 14–25.

p. xv a portrait endorsed by the many histories: Notable exceptions are John Gillis, *For Better, for Worse: British Marriages, 1600 to the Present* (Oxford, 1985); Leonore Davidoff and Catherine Hall, *Family Fortunes: Men and Women of the English Middle Class, 1780–1850* (Chicago, 1987). On this problem, interpreted as a legacy of structural-functionalist explanations, Steven Mintz, *Prison of Expectations: The Family in Victorian Culture* (New York, 1983).

p. xv most people confronted illicit behaviours: Erving Goffman, *Stigma: Notes on the Management of Spoiled Identity* (Englewood Cliffs, 1963), 30–31; Leonore Davidoff, Megan Doolittle, Janet Fink and Katherine Holden, *The Family Story: Blood, Contract and Intimacy, 1830–1960* (London, 1999), 244–65; Ginger Frost, *Living in Sin: Cohabiting as Husband and Wife in Nineteenth-Century England* (Manchester, 2008), 2–3, 62–3, 100–103.

p. xvi As privacy was written into law: There was no general right to privacy in English law until 2000, when the European Union's Human Rights Act came into effect, a contrast to the free-standing rights to privacy established in the US and some Continental European countries. In English law, targeted provisions (such as slander, libel and trespass) provided some guarantees, as did those measures (such as the development of the short birth certificate) that this book traces. On international comparisons, Report of the Younger Committee, Appendix J.

p. xvi 'a secret, so long': 'Sensation Novels', *Quarterly Review* 113 (April 1862) [H. L. Mansel – Wellesley attribution]: 497.

p. xvi Who should be told: D. A. Miller, *The Novel and the Police* (Berkeley, 1988), 206; Luise White, 'Telling More: Lies, Secrets and History', *History & Theory* 39:4 (December 2000), 11–22.

p. xviii 'no domestic secrets': 'Misery Out of Town', *Hunt's London Journal*, 2 November 1844, 217.

p. xviii Reticence, an attribute: Mandler, *English National Character*, 145, 166–7, 173.

p. xviii 'talked about their troubles': John Osborne, 'They Call It Cricket', in Tom Maschler, ed., *Declaration* (New York, 1958), 64.

p. xix Writing about the families of the past: Leonore Davidoff, 'The Family in Britain', in F. M. L. Thompson, ed., *The Cambridge Social History of Britain, 1750–1950*, (Cambridge, 1990), vol. II, 71–121.

p. xix As the Victorians exalted: A. James Hammerton, *Cruelty and Companionship: Conflict in Nineteenth-Century Married Life* (London, 1992), 1–2, 8, 82, 102, 116.

p. xx As debates about nature versus nurture: Mathew Thomson, *Psychological Subjects: Identity, Culture, and Health in Twentieth-Century Britain* (Oxford, 2006); Nikolas Rose, *The Psychological Complex: Psychology, Politics and Society in England, 1869–1939* (London, 1985); Nikolas Rose, *Governing the Soul: The Shaping of the Private Self* (London, 1989).

p. xx 'in the name of pity': Gwendoline Pitkin, '2 Questions', *Daily Mirror*, 13 August 1936, 12.

1. The Nabob's Secrets

p. 3 'You never beheld': Robert Bruce to John Bruce, 15 March 1781, GD152/35A, National Archives of Scotland (henceforth NAS). All GD citations refer to collections held at the NAS.

p. 3 'his little black connections': Robert Bruce to John Bruce, 19 June 1784, GD152/35A, NAS; also Robert Bruce to John Bruce, 16 June 1782, GD152/213/3, NAS. On the subject of liaisons between native women and British men, Durba Ghosh, *Sex and the Family in Colonial*

India: The Making of Empire (Cambridge, 2006); C. J. Hawes, *Poor Relations: The Making of a Eurasian Community in British India 1773–1833* (Richmond, 1996); William Dalrymple, *White Mughals: Love and Betrayal in Eighteenth-Century India* (London, 2002); Indrani Chatterjee, 'Colouring Subalternity: Slaves, Concubines and Social Orphans in Early Colonial India', *Subaltern Studies X* (1999), 49–97; Herbert Alick Stark, *Hostages to India, or The Life Story of the Anglo-Indian Race* (Calcutta, 1936); Ann Laura Stoler, *Carnal Knowledge and Imperial Power: Race and the Intimate in Colonial Rule* (Berkeley, 2002); Peter Robb, *Clash of Cultures? An Englishman in Calcutta in the 1790s* (London, 1998), 40–43; Peter Robb, 'Children, Emotion, Identity and Empire: Views from the Blechyndens' Calcutta Diaries (1790–1822)', *Modern Asian Studies* 40:1 (2006), 175–201.

p. 4   The nabob was a controversial: Vilified for their rapacity and lust, nabobs became embroiled in a host of public contretemps, culminating in the seven-year-long impeachment trial of Warren Hastings, the first Governor-General of Bengal. James Mayer Holzman, *The Nabobs in England: A Study of the Returned Anglo-Indian* (New York, 1926), 37–45, 70–83; T. G. P. Spear, *The Nabobs: English Social Life in 18th Century India* (New York, 1963); E. M. Collingham, *Imperial Bodies: The Physical Experience of the Raj, c. 1800–1947* (Cambridge, 2001), 3–113; Tillman Nechtman, *Nabobs: Empire and Identity in Eighteenth-Century Britain* (Cambridge, 2010), 92–139; Anna Clark, *Scandal: The Sexual Politics of the British Constitution* (Princeton, 2004), 84–112.

p. 4   A ferret belonging: Nechtman, *Nabobs*, 79.

p. 4   There were over 20,000: Robert Grant, *The Expediency Maintained of Continuing the System by which the Trade and Government of India are now Regulated* (London, 1813), 182; P. J. Marshall, 'British Immigration into India in the Nineteenth Century', in P. C. Emmer and Magnus Mörner, eds., *European Expansion and Migration: Essays on the Intercontinental Migration from Africa, Asia and Europe* (New York, 1992), 182; Raymond K. Renford, *The Non-Official British in India to 1920* (Delhi, 1987), 4–11; P. J. Marshall, *East Indian Fortunes: The British in Bengal in the Eighteenth Century* (Oxford, 1976), 15–28.

p. 4   They left a rich human: Hawes's calculation takes the period from

1767 to 1782. Hawes, *Poor Relations*, 4; Ghosh, *Sex and the Family*, 40. On the terms 'half-caste' and 'Eurasian', Hawes, *Poor Relations*, 89–90.

p. 4 'There are no secrets': 'Sir John's Troubles', *All the Year Round* 19:453 (December 1867), 68.

p. 5 In 1786, the two fathers: 'Condition of the Trust between Col. Bruce Capt. Denby and Messrs. Jackson Deare & Wells', GD152/143.

p. 6 'now be easy': Robert Bruce to Jean Bruce, 4 January 1769, GD 152/214/4.

p. 6 'somebody': Robert Bruce to John Bruce, 6 May 1782, GD152/213/3.

p. 6 While still a youth: See Memorial by John Bruce, GD152/213/1.

p. 6 'I have fought': Robert Bruce to John Bruce, 29 December 1787, GD152/213/4.

p. 6 'She is not like other': Robert Bruce to Peggie, 13 July 1786, GD152/35A.

p. 7 It was also a product of the intimacy: Margot Finn, 'Family Formations: Anglo India and the Familial Proto-State', in David Feldman and Jon Lawrence, eds., *Structures and Transformations in Modern British History* (Cambridge, 2011), 100–117; Emma Rothschild, *The Inner Life of Empires: An Eighteenth-Century History* (Princeton, 2011), 170–96; Sarah Pearsall, *Atlantic Families: Lives and Letters in the Later Eighteenth Century* (Oxford, 2008), 111–78. For a later period, Elizabeth Buettner, *Empire Families: Britons and Late Imperial India* (Oxford, 2004).

p. 7 So far preferable: Will Hollond to Frank Fowke, 7 December 1784; Joseph Fowke to Frank Fowke, 14 October 1785; Joseph Fowke to Frank Fowke, 29 July 1785; Francis Fowke to Frank Fowke, 25 January 1781, all Mss. Eur. D11, Asia, Pacific and Africa Collections (henceforth APAC), British Library (henceforth BL).

p. 7 Single men in India: Between 1813 and 1833, 819 of the 5925 writers and cadets appointed to the Company were the British sons of Company servants. Hawes, *Poor Relations*, 63; Marshall, *East Indian Fortunes*, 15; Margot Finn, 'The Barlow Bastards: Romance Comes Home from the Empire', in Margot Finn, Michael Lobban and Jenny Bourne Taylor, eds., *Legitimacy and Illegitimacy in Nineteenth-Century Law, Literature and History* (Basingstoke, 2010), 25–47.

p. 7 'below their station': Peggie Bruce to John Bruce, 22 August n.y., GD152/214/3.

p. 8 'he is rather more cool': Peggie Bruce to John Bruce, 24 May n.y., GD152/214/3, Bundle III.

p. 8 'my Mother thinks': Peggie Bruce to John Bruce, 23 March n.y. [1788 or 1789?], GD152/213/9; Peggie Bruce to John Bruce, 13 April n.y. [1792?], GD152/214/3.

p. 8 'be kind to her': Peggie Bruce to Robert Bruce, 26 November 1794, GD 152/214/4.

p. 8 'like our Mother': John Bruce to Robert Bruce, 20 October 1794, GD152/213/6.

p. 8 'I am as much attached': John Bruce to Robert Bruce, 23 September 1794, GD152/213/6.

p. 8 'she never shall want a mother': Peggie Bruce to Robert Bruce, 5 April 1795, and Peggie Bruce to Robert Bruce, 26 November 1794, GD152/214/4.

p. 8 'Margaret Stuart I am frightened': Peggie Bruce to John Bruce, 11 August n.y. [1791?], GD152/214/3, Bundle III.

p. 8 'may so sensibly degenerate the race': Innes Munro, *Narrative of Military Operations on the Coromandel Coast in 1780* (London, 1789), 50–55, cited in Spear, *Nabobs*, 63.

p. 9 'the duty of every man': J. H. Cochrane to his son James, 21 March 1801, GD1/594/1.

p. 9 'think what a terrible thing': Peggie Bruce to John Bruce, 6 January 1790, GD152/214/3, Bundle III.

p. 9 'she knows what she is': Peggie Bruce to John Bruce, 24 May n.y. [1791?], GD152/214/3, Bundle III.

p. 9 'as it will set people': Peggie Bruce to John Bruce, 2 March n.y. [1792?], GD152/214/3.

p. 9 'as she begins to be': John Bruce to Robert Bruce, 20 January 1795, GD152/213/6.

p. 10 'I have nothing but my little heart': Margaret Bruce to Robert Bruce, 25 March 1795, GD152/213/8/6.

p. 10 'constant study': Margaret Bruce to Robert Bruce, 26 January 1796, GD152/213/8/8.

p. 10 'to secure to her': Memorial & Queries for Miss Bruce & Others, 1797, GD152/112/4.

p. 10 The Beachcroft children: TS 11/763, The National Archives [henceforth TNA]. *Beachcroft v. Beachcroft*, 8, 11, 23 April 1816, 56 *English Reports* 159 (8, 11, 23 April 1816), 159–64.

p. 11 Henry Dundas's Eurasian niece: On Mary/Maria Dundas, Charles Stuart to James Stuart, 16 March 1774, GD235/9/20/10. Michael Fry, *The Dundas Despotism* (Edinburgh, 1992), 112.

p. 11 'old Servant': Capt. Alston to Major Bruce, 3 December 1796, postscript Major Bruce to John Bruce, GD152/213/1; Robert Bruce to John Bruce, 1 February 1800, GD152/112/6.

p. 12 'In a case of so much': Copy letter from Mr Bruce to Col. Bruce, 23 February 1810, GD152/112/7.

p. 12 John's cousin in India: Parry, Sub Treasurer, paper no. 88, dated 12 December 1798, GD152/112/6.

p. 12 'she is lively and agreeable': Ursula Low, *Fifty Years with John Company: From the Letters of General Sir John Low of Clatto, Fife, 1822–1858* (London, 1936), 62.

p. 13 'nothing but being unknown': Peggie Bruce to Margaret Bruce, 21 July n.y. [1820], GD152/35B. In the same file, also Peggie's letters of 26 May n.y. and 23 June n.y. This is a marked contrast to the warm reception apparently accorded Kitty Kirkpatrick. Dalrymple, *White Mughals*, 374–6. On the social tribulations of the wealthy David Ochterlony Dyce Sombre, see Michael Fisher, *Counterflows to Colonialism: Indian Travellers and Settlers in Britain 1600–1857* (Delhi, 2004), 318–37.

p. 13 Onesiphorus Tyndall's courtship: W. Gordon to Walter Hamilton, December 1827, GD152/205/1/11; J. Hamilton to Walter Hamilton, 19 July 1827, GD152/151.

p. 13 'a most provoking': H. Bull to Onesiphorus, 10 October 1826, GD152/53/1/4/3.

p. 13 Onesiphorus pursued her: Robert Lemon to William Waddel, 8 December 1827, GD152/76/28.

p. 13 'Methodest': Peggie Bruce to Margaret Bruce, 7 June n.y., GD152/35B; Onesiphorus Tyndall-Bruce to Peggie Bruce, 5 July 1828, GD152/35A.

p. 13 'allowed themselves to rest': Margaret Tyndall-Bruce to Onesiphorus Tyndall-Bruce, 22 June, n.y. [after 1833 and probably before 1848], GD152/204/2/1.

p. 14 'dark complexion': William Dun, affidavit, 5 September 1804, GD152/143.

p. 14 'I am only a poor Cleanser': William Jackson to John Denby, n.d. [received 2 July 1801], GD152/143; also John Denby, affidavit, 10 September 1804, GD152/143.

p. 14 His father even tried: Copy Mr Sale's remarks respecting Col. Denby's claim on the Fund, GD152/143.

p. 15 'inconveniences attending': Francis Fowke to his nephew Francis Fowke, 27 July 1782, Mss. Eur. D11, APAC. In demurring, Uncle Francis did not explain himself further.

p. 15 The first two generations of Fowkes: On the Stracheys, Barbara Caine, *Bombay to Bloomsbury* (Oxford, 2005), 17–79; on the Fowkes, Eileen and Harry Green, *The Fowkes of Boughrood Castle: A Study in Social Mobility* (Tenby, 1973).

p. 16 'comfortable independancy': Francis Fowke to Francis Fowke, 20 December 1774, Mss. Eur. E3, APAC.

p. 16 'May you get rich': Francis Fowke to Francis Fowke, 27 July 1782.

p. 16 there were vastly more white men: In 1810, Thomas Williamson estimated that there were 250 European women in Bengal for the 4000 'European male inhabitants of respectability'. Outside the Presidency towns, there were even fewer white women. Collingham, *Imperial Bodies*, 63; Renford, *Non-Official*, 10–11.

p. 16 'A young beautifull girl': Robert Bruce to John Bruce, 15 March 1781, GD152/35A.

p. 16 'necessity': Samuel Beachcroft to his brother, 15 March 1798, cited in Answer of Defendants Matthews Beachcroft et al., in *Beachcroft v. Beachcroft*, filed 30 March 1816, TS11/763, TNA.

p. 16 In Britain, a young buck: Michael Mason, *The Making of Victorian Sexuality* (Oxford, 2003 [1994]), 83–103, 109–15; Karen Harvey, *Reading Sex in the Eighteenth Century: Bodies and Gender in English Erotic Culture* (Cambridge, 2004), 54, 74–7, 224–5; Vic Gatrell, *City of*

Laughter: Sex and Satire in Eighteenth-Century London (London, 2006), 23–156.

p. 16 'as I have so good an Opinnion': J. P. Hoare to F. Fowke, 1786, Mss. Eur. E7, APAC. See also Claud Alexander to David Anderson, 9 June 1783, Add. Mss. 45424, BL.

p. 17 'ancient housekeepers': As Ghosh explains, *bibi* meant, when used by speakers of Hindi or Urdu, 'wife' or 'lady'. In eighteenth-century colonial society, it could also denote the female companion (Indian or European) of an Englishman. Although Begum means women of high rank, specifically those who were also Muslim, in the eighteenth century, it was used interchangeably with *bibi*.

p. 17 'imprudent connection': Samuel Beachcroft to his brother, 15 March 1798.

p. 17 race was not yet: Roxann Wheeler, *The Complexion of Race: Categories of Difference in Eighteenth-Century British Culture* (Philadelphia, 2000), 2–48, 138–75, 289–302; David Arnold, 'Race, Place and Bodily Difference in Early Nineteenth-Century India', *Historical Research* 77:196 (May 2004), 254–75; Kathleen Wilson, *Island Race: Englishness, Empire, and Gender* (London and New York, 2003); Nechtman, *Nabobs*, 37–54.

p. 17 'Asiatic tawny': Robert Bruce to Peggie Bruce, 1 February 1769, GD152/214/4.

p. 17 'passably well': Francis Fowke to Margaret Fowke, 15–27 May 1788, D. 546/26, APAC.

p. 18 'All that I can do for you': William Hollond to Francis Fowke, 26 November 1782, Mss. Eur. F3, APAC. On Hollond, see also Mr Justice C. G. H. Fawcett, 'The Two Hollonds of Madras and Their Dubash', *Journal of Indian History* 5 (1927), 189–97.

p. 18 'poor girl it cannot be done': William Hollond to Francis Fowke, 26 November 1782.

p. 18 from the East as well as the West Indies: On mixed-race children sent to Britain from the West Indies, Daniel Livesay, 'Children of Uncertain Fortune: Mixed Race Migration from the West Indies to Britain, 1750–1820', PhD diss., University of Michigan, 2010. Livesay estimates that by the end of the eighteenth century as many as a quarter of rich Jamaicans with children of colour sent them abroad.

p. 18 'and his seat of honour': Samuel Beachcroft to his brother, 15 March 1798.

p. 19 Aboard the ship *Barwell*: Journal of the Ship *Barwell*, 23 September 1782–11 September 1784, IOR/L/MAR/B/420A, APAC.

p. 19 Boys 'White and Brown': Frank Fowke to Margaret Fowke, 17 August 1787, D. 546/26, APAC.

p. 19 'My love to the young brownies': Francis Fowke to Francis Fowke, 29 April 1788, D. 546/31, APAC.

p. 20 'modest, handsome': Frank Fowke to Margaret Fowke, 28 August 1788, D. 546/26, APAC.

p. 20 'pride revolting': William Hollond to Frank Fowke, 2 August 1788, D. 546/31, APAC.

p. 20 'a blundering lover': Margaret Benn to Frank Fowke, 7 July 1788, D. 546/31, APAC.

p. 20 'I see you are both doomed': Francis Fowke to Frank Fowke, 23 August 1788, D. 546/31, APAC.

p. 20 Twenty-four years: E. Strachey to F. Fowke, Torquay, 4 October 1813, Mss. Eur. F3, APAC; Frank Fowke to Margaret Benn-Walsh, 5 October 1813, D. 546/29, APAC.

p. 20 The children of Frank Fowke: John Benn-Walsh, First Baron Ormathwaite, Memoir of Lady Walsh, vol. 1, 125, Mss. Eur. Photo Eur 032, APAC.

p. 21 Travelling in France: Margaret Benn to Francis Fowke, 17 September 1789, Mss. Eur. E8, APAC.

p. 21 her cousin Edward Hollond: Upon his arrival in England, Edward was taken directly to court, where his bail was fixed at an astronomical £400,000. Will and Frank showed up to post the entire bond that same morning, a sum equal to £38m today. Ultimately acquitted, Edward fled to the Continent where he could enjoy his India-made fortune unmolested. His two Eurasian daughters he left behind in Will's care, expanding still further the Fowke–Hollond collection of imperial children. See Margaret Benn to Francis Fowke, 17 September 1789, Mss. Eur. E8, APAC; 'Court Circular: London', *The Times*, 17 June 1791, 2.

p. 21 'indulgence for irregular pleasures': Margaret Benn to Francis

Fowke, 17 September 1789, Mss. Eur. E8, APAC. Also Benn-Walsh, Memoir, vol. 2, 81–7.

p. 21 'W. Hollond, Sir Henry Strachey'; 'The flaunting grasping': Benn-Walsh, Memoir, vol. 1, 122–3.

p. 22 During the two generations: Green, *Fowkes*, 20–22.

p. 22 Alice Meadows Taylor: 'The Indian Connection', Presented by W. Acworth, 26 March 1980, FL3/PA/267, Photo Eur 191, 12, APAC. Colonel Meadows Taylor, *The Story of My Life, edited by his daughter*, 2 vols. (Edinburgh and London, 1877).

p. 22 Anna Leonowens: Susan Morgan, *Bombay Anna: The Real Story and Remarkable Adventures of the King and I Governess* (Berkeley, 2008).

p. 22 Only William Thackeray's intimates: Theodore Taylor, *Thackeray: The Humourist and the Man of Letters* (London, 1864); Lewis Melville, *William Makepeace Thackeray* (London, 1889); Sir W. W. Hunter, *The Thackerays in India* (London, 1897); Malcolm Elwin, *Thackeray: A Personality* (London, 1932).

p. 23 The family's entry: Sir Bernard Burke, *History of the Landed Gentry of Great Britain & Ireland*, vol. 1 (London, 1875), 638.

p. 23 'an English gentleman of honorable descent': Henry A. Boardman, *In Memoriam: Harriet Hollond* (Philadelphia, 1871), 5.

p. 24 As Raheim Bibi told the story: Bill of Complaint of Henry Moorhouse, 2–3; also described in Affidavit of Thomas Chauntler in *Moorhouse v. Colvin*, filed 17 November 1857, C31/1277/M3333, TNA.

p. 25 'I can only say': Raheim Bibi to James Colvin, March 1847, Answer of Alexander Colvin, to Bill of Complaint of Henry Moorhouse and Susan his wife in *Moorhouse v. Colvin*, paragraph 84, filed 19 February 1857, C15/315/M73, TNA. All of the letters cited from Peter Cochrane to his sister Joanna are included in this document.

p. 25 'luxuries without pain': Peter Cochrane to his sister, 28 May 1801, cited in Answer of Alexander Colvin, paragraph 14.

p. 25 'Can you procure me': Peter Cochrane to his sister Joanna, 2 June 1807.

p. 25 'Habits of much indulgence': Peter Cochrane to his sister Joanna, 28 February 1796.

p. 26 'My father was right': Peter Cochrane to his sister Joanna, 1797 or 1798.

p. 26 'are not the less nearly allied': Peter Cochrane to his sister Joanna, 3 April 1808.

p. 26 'substitutes': Peter Cochrane to his sister Joanna, 13 April 1808.

p. 26 'afford a chance': Peter Cochrane to his sister Joanna, 24 August 1809.

p. 26 'my heart had nothing': Cochrane's Journal, cited in Answer of Alexander Colvin, paragraph 20.

p. 26 'Pleasing': Peter Cochrane to his sister Joanna, 15 December 1817.

p. 27 'We shall bring her': Peter Cochrane to his sister Joanna, 24 August 1809.

p. 27 According to Susan: This description of the living arrangements is asserted in Bill of Complaint of Henry Moorhouse, 5–6. Crucially, it is not denied by Alexander Colvin, Answer of Alexander Colvin, paragraphs 64 and 65.

p. 27 'Madame Cochrane': Answer of Alexander Colvin, paragraphs 64–8.

p. 28 'the little girl Susan Cochrane': Answer of Alexander Colvin, paragraph 49.

p. 28 Unwilling to disguise her affair: *Lord v. Colvin* [366], 1857, 1858, 1859, HeinOnline – 62 Eng. Rep. 141 1815–1865, 147–8.

p. 29 'nor will that be all': Peter Cochrane to William Thomas, 6 July 1825, Answer of Alexander Colvin, paragraph 50.

p. 29 During the five years they lived: *Lord v. Colvin*, 155–6.

p. 30 'I apprehend Mrs Cochrane': 'House of Lords', *The Law Times*, 25 April 1863, 216.

p. 31 'with all his heart': 'Law Report, Court of Chancery', *The Times*, 3 July 1852, 6.

p. 31 But, in 1790: Indrani Chatterjee notes that in nineteenth-century Bengal, *nikah* was regarded as an inferior sort of marriage, often with slaves, as opposed to *shadi*, which was celebrated with festivities and regarded as a more legitimate form. This distinction appears not to have been drawn by either side in the Cochrane case or by the various Courts. While the distinction is not made in the Cochrane case, it may nonetheless have coloured how the *nikah* was regarded. Indrani Chatterjee, *Gender, Slavery and Law in Colonial India* (Delhi, 1999), 27, 82, 85–90.

p. 32 'Nothing but native testimony': 'Lord v. Colvin – Vice Chancellor's

Court', *The Times*, 21 December 1853. His grandmother, Jemima Kindersley, observed in her *Letters from the Island of Teneriffe* (London, 1777) that pretty Eurasian women could marry Europeans but that they did not like to have their descent remembered.

p. 32 'body shaking with palsy': Supplemental Bill of Complaint, Filed 13 October 1857, 20; also C15/315/M73, TNA.

p. 33 She was his mistress: Answer of Alexander Colvin, paragraphs 62, 64, 65, 75, 90.

p. 33 'Could it be believed': 'Vice-Chancellor's Court, July 31', *The Times*, 1 August 1862, 10.

p. 33 'whole case': 'Vice-Chancellors' Courts, Feb. 14', *The Times*, 15 February 1859, 12.

p. 33 'of very great interest': The litigation was complex, enduring for thirty years in Chancery, and occupying in total seventy-three days of argumentation. By the time that the House of Lords heard the case, the printed record alone came to more than 2,200 pages. 'Appeals: House of Lords, March 2', *The Times*, 3 March 1863, 13.

p. 33 'almost impossible for any': 'Moorhouse v. Lord', *Law Times Reports*, vol. 8, new series 25 April 1863, 218.

p. 34 'constantly formed connexions': 'Appeals: House of Lords, March 2'.

p. 36 Even in British India: Ghosh, *Sex and the Family*, 36; Sudipta Sen, 'Colonial Aversions and Domestic Desires: Blood, Race, Sex and the Decline of Intimacy in Early British India', *South Asia* 24 (2001), 25–45; Kenneth Ballhatchet, *Race, Sex and Class under the Raj: Imperial Attitudes and Policies and Their Critics, 1793–1905* (New York, 1980), 96–122, 144–59; Collingham, *Imperial Bodies*, 74–7, 182–3; Ronald Hyam, *Empire and Sexuality: The British Experience* (Manchester, 1990), 116–21.

p. 36 By the 1830s, just one: Ghosh, *Sex and the Family*, 41; Hawes, *Poor Relations*, 4, 17. David Arnold, 'European Orphans and Vagrants in India in the Nineteenth Century', *Journal of Imperial and Commonwealth History* 7: 2 (1979), 104–27.

p. 36 'white as marble': John Lang, *Will He Marry Her?* (London, 1858), 55.

p. 36 'it was as black': Lang, *Will He*, 445.

p. 37 'the mother's heart': [Selina Bunbury], 'A Legend of Forfarshire', *Fraser's Magazine for Town and Country* 35 (February 1847), 238.

p. 37 'her mother Poor Soul': Affidavit of Henry Hauseal, 19 August 1857, M31/3062, TNA.

2. Revelation in the Divorce Court

p. 38 In the newspapers: *Lloyd v. Lloyd and Chichester*, 164 Eng. Rep. 862 1752–18652, 1 SW & TR 566–72, 862–5; reports in *The Times*, 26 and 27 November 1859.

p. 38 Barred from remarrying: 'London Correspondence', *Belfast News Letter*, 15 October 1861; 'Suicide of Lord Forth', *Aberdeen Journal*, 16 October 1861.

p. 38 'very name of divorce': 'The Law of Divorce', *The Times*, 27 January 1857. As with so much else in law pertaining to the family, Scotland – where divorce had been permitted since the Reformation – was very different from England and Wales. Divorce was available in Scotland equally to men and women on grounds of adultery and later also desertion. On divorce, see especially Roderick Phillips, *Putting Asunder: A History of Divorce in Western Society* (Cambridge, 1988), 95–133, 227–40, 412–22; A. James Hammerton, *Cruelty and Companionship: Conflict in Nineteenth-Century Married Life* (London, 1992); and Allen Horstman, *Victorian Divorce* (New York, 1985).

p. 39 'laid upon the breakfast-table': A. C. Horstman and Viscount Esher, eds., *Letters of Queen Victoria* (London, 1907), vol. 3, 482.

p. 40 'neighbourhood of voluntary spies': Jane Austen, *Northanger Abbey* (London, 1833), 164.

p. 40 As soon as the doors opened: Henry Edwin Fenn, *Thirty-Five Years in the Divorce Court* (London, 1911), 35, 88–9; 'London Correspondence', *Belfast News Letter*, 7 June 1860.

p. 42 A curmudgeonly bachelor: On Cresswell, Joshua Getzler, 'Sir Cresswell Cresswell', *Oxford Dictionary of National Biography*; Edward Foss, *The Judges of England*, vol. IX (London, 1864), 184–6; 'A Lady and a Judge', *Punch*, 5 December 1857, 234; and 'A Manchester Man', 'The

Philosophy of Marriage, Studied under Sir Cresswell Cresswell', *Fraser's Magazine* 62:371 (November 1860), 555–6.

p. 42 'soured and cynical': 'Sketches of the English Bench and Bar', *London Society* 11:64 (April 1867), 344.

p. 43 'We cannot conceive': 'Scenes from the Divorce Court', *Lloyd's Weekly Newspaper*, 4 December 1859.

p. 43 Without an apparatus: John George Phillimore, *The Divorce Court: Its Evils and the Remedy* (London, 1859), 14–15, 20.

p. 44 'to doubt the reality of our eyesight': 'Manchester Man', 'Philosophy', 556–7.

p. 44 'misery which was silently': Leader, *The Times*, 26 December 1859, 6.

p. 44 'strange revelation of the secret': Leader, *The Times*, 12 December 1859, 8.

p. 45 Mr Samuel Alexander: 'Court for Divorce and Matrimonial Causes, Nov. 19', *The Times*, 21 November 1859, 9.

p. 45 The confectioner Mr Wilton's: 'Court for Divorce and Matrimonial Causes, Nov. 22', *The Times*, 23 November 1859, 9.

p. 45 The engraver Alfred Bacon: 'Court for Divorce and Matrimonial Causes, Nov. 28', *The Times*, 29 November 1859, 11.

p. 45 Mr Allen, a military: 'Court for Divorce and Matrimonial Causes, Dec. 5', *The Times*, 6 December 1859, 9.

p. 45 'as nothing to Baron Cresswell': *Morning Chronicle*, 29 November 1859.

p. 45 'spicy' pages: Sir G. H. Lewis, 28 February 1910 in *Minutes of Evidence Taken before the Royal Commission on Divorce and Matrimonial Causes*, vol. 1 (London, 1912) [Cd 6479], 75.

p. 45 'gross unregenerate British': Matthew Arnold, 'The Function of Criticism', in *The Complete Prose Works of Matthew Arnold*, vol. III, ed. R. H. Super (Ann Arbor, 1990 [1962]), 281.

p. 45 The *Daily Telegraph* printed: G. A. Cranfield, *The Press and Society* (London, 1978), 207.

p. 46 'afraid of the monster': Hon. Mrs Hardcastle, ed., *Life of John, Lord Campbell* (London, 1881, 2 vols.), vol. II, 361, cited in Gail Savage, 'Erotic Stories and Public Decency: Newspaper Reporting of Divorce Proceedings in England', *Historical Journal* 41:2 (1998), 513.

p. 46 Two proposals occupied: On the Queen's/King's Proctor, see Gail Savage, 'The Divorce Court and the Queen's/King's Proctor: Legal Patriarchy and the Sanctity of Marriage in England, 1861–1937', in *Historical Papers: A Selection from the Papers Presented at the Annual Meeting of the Canadian Historical Association*, eds. Dana Johnson and Andrée Désilets (Ottawa, 1989), 210–27; Wendie Ellen Schneider, 'Secrets and Lies: The Queen's Proctor and Judicial Investigation of Party-Controlled Narratives', *Law & Social Inquiry* 27:3 (Summer, 2002), 449–88.

p. 46 If the Divorce Court could be shut: Barbara Leckie, *Culture and Adultery: The Novel, the Newspaper and the Law, 1857–1914* (Philadelphia, 1999); Savage, 'Erotic Stories and Public Decency', 513–16.

p. 46 'should continue to appear as models': Hansard, *Parl. Deb.* (Commons), vol. 156, 7 February 1860, 621.

p. 47 It was originally envisioned: Lord Cranworth, Hansard, *Parl. Deb.* (Lords), 21 July 1859, 146.

p. 48 'prepossessing': 'Court of Probate and Divorce', *Observer*, 21 April 1861, 3.

p. 49 In exasperation: 'Drummond, Commonly Called Viscountess Forth v. Drummond, Commonly Called Viscount Forth', *The Times*, 18 April 1861.

p. 50 'I have a very bad memory': 'Court of Probate and Divorce', *Daily News*, 19 April 1861.

p. 51 'this lady': 'Court of Probate and Divorce', *The Times*, 9 May 1861.

p. 51 'I think a wife guilty': *Drummond v. Drummond*, 2 SW & TR 267, 1001.

p. 52 'an air of mystery hung': 'Suicide of Viscount Forth', *Aberdeen Journal*, 16 October 1861; 'London Correspondence', *The Belfast News Letter*, 15 October 1861.

p. 53 'so much attention': 'The Suicide of Viscount Forth', *The Times*, 12 October 1861, 4.

p. 53 'that mysterious and awful': 'London Correspondence', *Belfast News Letter*, 15 October 1861.

p. 53 At the age of twenty: Among others, 'Suicide of Lord Forth', *Liverpool Mercury*, 15 October 1861; 'The Late Lamentable Suicide', *Morning Chronicle*, 15 October 1861; 'The Late Viscount Forth and Mrs. Lloyd', *Observer*, 20 October 1861.

p. 55 As Fearon told the story: 'Court for Divorce and Matrimonial Causes', *The Times*, 6 June 1868, 11. Captain Fearon was the nephew of Margaret Fearon, wife of Peter Cochrane. While Fearon was testifying in the Divorce Court, his family's stake in the Cochrane estate was being finally decided in Chancery.

p. 56 'with vengeance clearly written': 'Gamma', 'Divorce a Vinculo; or, the Terrors of Sir Cresswell Cresswell', *Once a Week* 2:35 (February 1860), 186; also Carolyn Steedman, *Master and Servant: Love and Labour in the English Industrial Age* (Cambridge, 2007).

p. 56 'greedy watchfulness': 'Respondents and Co-Respondents', *London Review*, 6 August 1864, 142. The neighbours were also included.

p. 57 'she should go mad': 'Court for Divorce and Matrimonial Causes', *The Times*, 6 June 1868, 11.

p. 57 'unvarying kindness': 'A Divorce Case in Fashionable Life', *Reynolds's Newspaper*, 7 June 1868.

p. 58 Dering ought not to be yoked: 'Court for Divorce and Matrimonial Causes', *The Times*, 8 June 1868; *Dering v. Dering and Blakeley, The Queen's Proctor and Others Intervening*, Courts of Probate and Divorce [L R] 1 P&D 531, 7 July 1868.

p. 58 There would be a time: 'The Pleasures of Memory' [from the *Saturday Review*], *London Reader* 2:45 (March 1864), 603–4.

p. 59 'great want of caution': Court for Divorce and Matrimonial Causes', *The Times*, 6 June 1868.

p. 60 A discreet tip: Between one half and one third of the charges brought to the Queen's Proctor before 1880 came from people within the case, either parties to the litigation and their immediate families or solicitors on behalf of former litigants. See TS 29/1 and TS 29/2, TNA; Savage, 'Divorce Court and the Queen's/King's Proctor', 225.

p. 60 'full vigour': 'The End of Miserable Story', *Liverpool Mercury*, 10 July 1868.

p. 60 'one of the greatest scandals': 'Romantic Termination of a Divorce Case', *Aberdeen Journal*, 15 July 1868.

p. 61 'aggravating feature': 'The Man about Town', *Sporting Gazette*, 20 June 1868.

p. 61 Her lover was: Mary S. Millar, *Disraeli's Disciple: The Scandalous Life of George Smythe* (Toronto, 2006), 280–81.

p. 61 By the end of the will-reading: Margaret Blunden, *The Countess of Warwick* (London, 1967), 8–10; Last Will and Testament of The Rt. Hon. Henry Viscount Maynard (d. 19 May 1865), Principal Registry, First Avenue House.

p. 62 'golden bloom': The Hon. Julia Maynard, 'On the Portrait of the Hon. Mrs. Adolphus Capel', *Ladies' Companion*, 4 (July 1853), 16–17.

p. 62 'people we are in the habit': 'Sensation Novels', *Quarterly Review* 113 (April 1862), [H. L. Mansel – Wellesley attribution], 489; Jenny Bourne Taylor, *In the Secret Theatre of Home: Wilkie Collins, Sensation Narrative, and Nineteenth-Century Psychology* (London and New York, 1988).

p. 63 The novelist Charles Reade: 'Facts Must be Faced', Charles Reade, letter to the Editor, *The Times*, 31 August 1871, 4.

p. 63 For masters of the art: William M. Clarke, *The Secret Life of Wilkie Collins* (London, 1988); Wilkie Collins, *The Woman in White*, eds. Maria K. Bachman and Don Richard Cox (Peterborough, Ont., 2004), 624–5.

p. 63 What was a convention: Tamara S. Wagner, 'Detecting Business Fraud at Home: White-Collar Crime and the Sensational Clergyman in Victorian Domestic Fiction', in Albert D. Pionke and Denise Tischler Millstein, *Victorian Secrecy: Economies of Knowledge and Concealment* (Farnham, 2010), 115–33; Karen Chase and Michael Levenson, *The Spectacle of Intimacy: A Public Life for the Victorian Family* (Princeton, 2000), 201–13; Alexander Welsh, *George Eliot and Blackmail* (Cambridge, Mass., 1985), 59–334.

p. 63 'I only wish I could': To Charles Bray, 26 September 1859, quoted in Welsh, *George Eliot,* 131.

p. 64 'public duties': 'Facts Must Be Faced', editor's response, *The Times*, 31 August 1871, 4.

p. 64 'man of many secrets': Harry How, 'Illustrated Interviews: XXIX, Sir George Lewis', *Strand Magazine* 6 (July 1893), 645. Also John Juxon, *Lewis and Lewis* (London, 1983).

p. 65 'generally the regard': Report of the Royal Commission on Divorce and Matrimonial Causes (London, 1912) [Cd 6478], 2.

p. 65 'savage and barbarous': George H. Lewis, 'Marriage and Divorce', *Fortnightly Review* 37:221 (May 1885), 653.

p. 66 'spectacle that these two': Royal Commission, vol. 1, 76.

p. 67 Still, Alverstone insisted: ibid., vol. 2, 129.

p. 67 'I confess feeling the greatest doubt': ibid., vol. 2, 141; also H. J. A. Cuffe, the Earl of Desart, and His Daughter, Lady Sybil Lubbock, *A Page from the Past: Memories of the Earl of Desart* (London, 1936), 164–5.

p. 69 'conceived by men': E. S. P. Haynes, 'Abolish the King's Proctor', *Spectator*, 24 February 1933, quoted in Savage, 'The Divorce Court and the Queen's/King's Proctor', 216.

p. 69 'Considering the nature of the issues': Prosecution of Offences Acts, 1879 and 1884, Return to an Address of the Honourable the House of Commons (London, 1892), 25.

p. 70 'unsavoury': Leader, *The Times*, 12 December 1859, 8.

p. 70 'familiarized the public mind': Alfred Austin in *Temple Bar*, quoted in Leckie, *Culture*, 109.

p. 71 boon companion: 'A Romance of the Peerage', *Lloyd's Weekly Newspaper*, 14 August 1887. In some reports, Eliza Harrison (Lewis) was older – as old as twenty-eight. 'She Clings to Her Child', *New York Times*, 2 September 1887.

p. 72 'I cannot understand': 'The Late Lord Forth', *Aberdeen Weekly Journal*, 2 September 1887.

p. 72 'dull, inexpressive' face: 'Lord Drummond's Story', *New York Times*, 7 August 1887.

p. 73 'The old Earl': 'An Heiress of Lord Perth', *New York Times*, 2 March 1902.

p. 73 'Lady Drummond': 'Romance of a Peerage', *New York Times*, 25 January 1899; 'An Heiress of Lord Perth', John Haynes, ed., *Scottish Notes and Queries*, vol. XI (Aberdeen, 1898), 187–8.

3. Children Who Disappeared

p. 77 'imbeciles from birth': In this chapter, I use – both for the purposes of quotation and to convey changing sensibilities – terminology of the time about learning difficulties which we today deplore. 'Idiot', 'imbecile' and 'feeble-minded' generally marked out a sliding scale of disability, with idiot indicating the worst-off, and the feeble-minded a 'higher-grade' intellect. See P. Martin Duncan and William Millard, *A Manual for the Classification, Training and Education of the Feeble-Minded, Imbecile, and Idiotic* (London, 1866).

p. 77 'bright lovable': Letter of 8 February 1884, H29/NF/A1/4/462, London Metropolitan Archives (henceforth LMA). All citations to the Normansfield papers in this chapter are from the LMA collection unless otherwise noted.

p. 77 Elizabeth also arrived: Letters dated 26 May 1922, H29/NF/A/01/227; 14 November 1932, H29/NF/A/01/246.

p. 77 64,000 mentally deficient: Margaret Bone, Bernie Spain and F. M. Martin, *Plans and Provisions for the Mentally Handicapped* (London, 1972), 35.

p. 78 Like Elizabeth, they came: The Registrar General, *Statistical Review of England and Wales for the Two Years 1952–3, Supplement on Mental Health* (London, 1958), 28; The Registrar General, *Statistical Review of England and Wales for the Three Years 1954–6, Supplement on Mental Health* (London, 1960), 161–2; Mathew Thomson, *The Problem of Mental Deficiency: Eugenics, Democracy, and Social Policy in Britain, c. 1870–1959* (Oxford, 1998), 248. The Registrar General's Office did not separately enumerate 'mental defectives' until 1949. My generalization refers to 'idiots' and 'imbeciles', not the merely feeble-minded.

p. 78 'to open out fresh': Cited in 'Opening Ceremony of the Normansfield Training College for the Feeble in Mind', *Christian Union*, 27 June 1879, Normansfield Press Cutting Book, Langdon Down Museum of Learning Disability. On the history of Normansfield, Andy Merriman, *Tales of Normansfield: The Langdon Down Legacy* (Teddington, 2007), and O Conor Ward, *John Langdon Down: A Caring Pioneer* (London, 1998). On mental disability more broadly, see especially David Wright, *Mental Disability in Victorian England* (Oxford, 2001); Thomson, *Problem*; Dorothy Atkinson, Mark Jackson and Jan Walmsley, *Forgotten Lives: Exploring the History of Learning Disability* (Kidderminster, 1997); Dorothy Atkinson et al., *Good*

Times, Bad Times: Women with Learning Difficulties Telling Their Stories (Kidderminster, 2000); Mark Jackson, *The Borderland of Imbecility: Medicine, Society, and the Fabrication of the Feeble Mind in Late Victorian and Edwardian England* (Manchester and New York, 2000); David Wright and Anne Digby, eds., *From Idiocy to Mental Deficiency* (London, 1996); Peter Bartlett and David Wright, *Outside the Walls of the Asylum: The History of Care in the Community 1750–2000* (London, 1999); Lindsay Brigham et al., eds., *Crossing Boundaries: Change and Continuity in the History of Learning Disability* (Kidderminster, 2000); Maggie Potts and Rebecca Fido, *A Fit Person to be Removed* (Plymouth, 1991); Sheena Rolph et al., *Witnesses to Change: Families, Learning Difficulties and History* (Kidderminster, 2005); Michael Barrett, 'From Education to Segregation: an Inquiry into the Changing Character of Special Provision for the Retarded in England, c. 1846–1918', PhD thesis, University of Lancaster, 1986; Andy Stevens, 'The institutional care and treatment of people categorized as mentally defective before and after the Second World War: the Royal Eastern Counties Institution', PhD thesis, University of Essex, 1998; and Anne Borsay, *Disability and Social Policy in Britain since 1750* (Basingstoke, 2005).

p. 79 'resolution to have': 'Care for Imbecile Children', *Christian World*, 27 June 1879, Normansfield Press Cutting Book.

p. 79 The idea that idiots: Wright, *Mental Disability*, 137–54. Among the many articles, esp. Charles Dickens, 'Idiots', *Household Words* 7:167 (4 June 1853), 313–17; 'Idiots Again', *Household Words* 9:212 (April 1854), 197–200; 'Education of Idiots', *Chambers's Edinburgh Journal* 193 (September 1847), 169–71; [Edwin Sidney: Wellesley attribution], Article II, *Edinburgh Review* 122:249 (July 1865), 37–74.

p. 79 'afflicted with idiocy' and 'idiots had been found': 'Visit of the Members of the British Medical Association', n.d., Normansfield Press Cutting Book.

p. 79 'idiocy was becoming': 'Old Bloomsbury', *Moments of Being*, 198, cited in Hermione Lee, *Virginia Woolf* (London, 1996), 102.

p. 80 'contrivance': Letter of 22 February 1882, H29/NF/A1/4/189.

p. 80 When at home: Letter of 28 July 1882, H29/NF/A/01/008; letter of

30 August 1901; letter of 12 June 1909, H29/NF/A/01/152; letter of 23 November 1904, H29/NF/A/01/124; letter of 29 December 1890, H29/NF/A/01/050.

p. 80 'All our friends': Letter of 1 February, n.y. [1896?], H29/NF/A01/078.

p. 81 'as those she has': Letter of 31 January 1884, H29/NF/A1/4/476.

p. 81 'I like Cecilia': Letter of 24 October 1901, H29/NF/A/01/104.

p. 81 'a little bit waved': Letter of 10 April 1902, H29/NF/A/01/104.

p. 81 'longed': Letter of 31 January 1902, H29/NF/A/01/104.

p. 81 'strong manly': Letter of 31 January 1882, H29/NF/A01/008; letter of 22 August 1900, H29/NF/A/01/98.

p. 81 'look a bit more': Letter of 3 May n.y. [1896?], H29/NF/A01/078.

p. 81 'we all wish': Letter of 27 November 1883, H29/NF/A1/4.

p. 81 'little stretch': Letter of 7 October n.y. [1883?], H29/NF/A1/4/405.

p. 82 'I would prize': Letter of 20 May 1883, H29/NF/A01/008.

p. 82 'I am sorry': Letter of 16 January 1882, H29/NF/A1/4/391.

p. 82 'as they may be smashed': Letter of 5 December 1883, H29/NF/A1/4/403.

p. 82 'You can imagine': Letter of 14 June 1883, H29/NF/A1/4/432.

p. 82 'has never been accustomed': Letter of 7 October 1883, H29/NF/A1/4/405.

p. 82 'strange dreams' and 'a child who enjoys': Letter of 11 May 1901, H29/NF/A/01/104.

p. 83 'dreadful trial': Letter of 11 May 1901, H29/NF/A/01/104.

p. 83 According to the conventional: 'Our Ladies' Column by One of Themselves', *Bristol Mercury & Daily Post*, 11 September 1880.

p. 83 'I should give him': Letter of Friday, n.d. [1883?], H29/NF/A01/008.

p. 83 'I felt when I left': Letter of 7 October n.y. [1883?], H29/NF/A1/4.

p. 83 At 150 guineas: In 1912, Eton charged a boarder £166 and Harrow £153. Beverley Ussher, ed., *Public Schools at a Glance, Boarding Schools at £80 and over: A Guide for Parents and Guardians in Selecting a Public School for their Boys* (London, 1912), 25, 33, 39.

p. 83 'so many conflicting duties': H29/NF/A1/4/179.

p. 84 Just 40 per cent: H29/NF/B/1/2.

p. 85 'Our dear boy': Letter of 27 May 1902, H29/NF/A/01/104.

p. 86 'pre-eminently a lady': 'Care for Imbecile Children'.

p. 87 When Mary Langdon Down: Ward, *Langdon Down*, 198.

p. 87 'providential': 'Opening Ceremony'.

p. 88 All correspondence: Ward, *Langdon Down*, 123–7. John Langdon Down generally did not hyphenate his name. Reginald Langdon-Down always used the hyphen.

p. 88 When his son: 'South-Eastern Division', *Journal of Mental Science* 62 (1906), 187–90.

p. 88 'gruff': Medical Case Book, H29/NF/B13/010.

p. 89 For half a century: Reginald Langdon-Down, 'The Feeble-Minded', in T. N. Kelynack, ed., *Human Derelicts: Medico-Sociological Studies for Teachers of Religion and Social Workers* (London, 1914), 73–98; also testimony before the Royal Commission on the Care and Control of the Feeble-Minded, *Minutes of Evidence*, vol. 1 (London, 1908) [Cd 4215], 537–8.

p. 89 'It was,' she wrote, 'to be deplored': Mary Dendy, 'The Feeble-Minded', *Economic Review* 13:3 (July 1903), 257–79, cited on 259; Jackson, *Borderland*, 56–78.

p. 89 A prominent member: See, for instance, 'Correspondence: Sterilization of the Unfit', Letter to the Editors, C. P. Blacker, R. A. Fisher, R. A. Gibbons, R. Langdon-Down and J. A. Ryle, *British Medical Journal*, 26 July 1930, 159–60; 'Marriage of Defectives', Letter to the Editors, R. Langdon-Down, J. A. Ryle, C. P. Blacker, *British Medical Journal*, 25 October 1930, 710; 'Insanity and Heredity', Letter to the Editor, Bernard Mallet, Leonard Darwin, C. J. Bond, R. Langdon-Down, J. A. Ryle and C. P. Blacker, *The Times*, 3 October 1930, 8.

p. 89 When he moved: Ward, *Langdon Down*, 141.

p. 90 'I am sure': Letter of 6 March 1925, H29/NF/A/01/227.

p. 90 'with God nothing': Letter of 25 May 1883, H29/NF/A01/008.

p. 90 'really the most tragic thing': Noel Annan, *Leslie Stephen: The Godless Victorian* (New York, 1984), 122; Lee, *Woolf*, 100.

p. 90 At Normansfield, education: Prospectus, dated June 1935, H29/NF/A1/308.

p. 90 'there is nothing served': Letter of 13 January 1911, H29/NF/A/01/156.

p. 91 'a limited rather than': Letter of 29 October 1900, H29/NF/A/01/98.

p. 91 'Boy': Letter of 21 September 1901, H29/NF/A/01/104.

p. 91 'I wish he would': Letter of 10 April 1902, H29/NF/A/01/104.

p. 91 'all such a struggle': Letter of 14 August 1905, H29/NF/A/01/131.

p. 91 'I cannot help': Letter of 21 September 1901; letter of 30 July 1907, H29/NF/A/01/137.

p. 92 'a better chance': Letter of 27 August 1912, H29/NF/A/01/171.

p. 92 'such a longing': Letter of 21 April 1907, H29/NF/A/01/137.

p. 92 'You see his wig': Letter of 7 August 1907, H29/NF/A/01/137.

p. 93 'the dear fellow': Letter of 3 September 1907, H29/NF/A/01/137.

p. 93 'Poor': Letter of 14 July 1907, H29/NF/A/01/137.

p. 93 'all the facts': John Langdon Down, *On Some of the Mental Affections of Childhood and Youth: Being the Lettsomian Lectures Delivered before the Medical Society of London in 1887 Together with Other Papers* (London, 1887), 54.

p. 94 'had he been': Letter of 12 August 1902, H29/NF/A/01/110.

p. 94 'predispose': Letter of 4 June 1905, H29/NF/A/01/124.

p. 94 The siege: Langdon Down, *Mental Affections*, 58.

p. 94 Thumb-sucking: 'On Idiocy and Its Relation to Tuberculosis', *Lancet*, vol. ii, 1867, republished in Langdon Down, *Mental Affections*, 218. David Wright, '"Childlike in His Innocence": Lay Attitudes to "idiots" and "imbeciles" in Victorian England', in Wright and Digby, *From Idiocy*, 127–9.

p. 94 'slowly, very slowly': Dendy, 'Feeble-Minded', 8.

p. 94 5 per cent of all cases: H29/NF/B/1/2, LMA.

p. 95 Worst of all: Dendy, 'Feeble-Minded', 259–60; Jackson, *Borderland*, 78.

p. 95 133,000 mental defectives: Thomson, *Problem*, 21.

p. 95 'depended largely': *British Medical Journal*, 9 March 1901, 616.

p. 96 'It is so sad': Letter of 12 April 1908, H29/NF/A/01/145.

p. 96 Between 1900: H29/NF/B/1/2. There are no admissions/discharge registers extant for the period after October 1914.

p. 97 Private attendants: Akihito Suzuki, *Madness at Home: The Psychiatrist, the Patient and the Family in England, 1820–1860* (Berkeley, 2006), 108–11; Charlotte MacKenzie, *Psychiatry for the Rich: A History of Ticehurst Private Asylum, 1792–1917* (London, 1992); Harriet Sturdy and William

Parry-Jones, 'Boarding-out Insane Patients: The Significance of the Scottish System, 1857–1913', in Wright and Digby, eds., *From Idiocy*, 88–112; R. A. Houston, '"Not Simple Boarding": Care of the Mentally Incapacitated in Scotland during the Long Eighteenth Century', in Bartlett and Wright, eds., *Outside the Walls*, 19–44.

p. 97 The codification: Gillian Sutherland, *Ability, Merit and Measurement: Mental Testing and English Education* (Oxford, 1984); Adrian Wooldridge, *Measuring the Mind: Education and Psychology in England, c.1860–c.1990* (Cambridge, 1994), 18–72.

p. 97 'wise': Letters of 11 January and 18 February 1921, H29/NF/A1/211.

p. 98 Registrar-General's survey: See Registrar General, *Statistical Review of England and Wales for the Two Years 1952–3*, 28; Registrar General, *Statistical Review of England and Wales for the Three Years 1954–6*, 161–2; Thomson, *Problem*, 248.

p. 98 '[Y]oung, disturbed': Brian Rix, *My Farce from My Elbow: An Autobiography* (London, 1975), 106–7; Rolph et al., *Witnesses to Change*, 77.

p. 98 'One cannot but': Letter of 8 March 1921, H29/NF/A/01/218.

p. 98 'well looked after': Letter of 11 January 1921, H29/NF/A1/211.

p. 99 'I felt like a murderess': Rene Harris, on her decision to send her son Colin to Bronham Hospital in the 1950s. Rolph et al., *Witnesses to Change*, 50.

p. 99 With 1700 patients: Leaflet from Stoke Park Colony, AR11/2, Croydon Local Studies Library and Archives Service (henceforth CAS). For Botley Park rules, AR11/1, CAS.

p. 100 'it is possible': Letter of 19 March 1934, H29/NF/A1/308.

p. 100 'I thought she': Letter of 16 August 1924, H29/NF/A/01/234.

p. 100 'extraordinary progress': Entry dated 9 May 1922, Medical Case Book, H29/NF/B13/005.

p. 101 'I have not felt': Letter of 20 April 1922, H29/NF/A/01/227.

p. 101 Brian Rix: Rix, *Farce*, 18; on silence, Rolph et al., *Witnesses to Change*, 57–8, 77, 86, 114.

p. 101 'most upset': Letters of 20 April 1937 and 23 April 1937, H29/NF/A/01/321.

p. 102 'There were people': Rolph et al., *Witnesses to Change*, 53; Simon Olshansky, 'Chronic Sorrow: A Response to Having a Mentally

Defective Child', *Social Casework*, 43: 4 (April 1962), reprinted in Eileen Younghusband, ed., *Social Work with Families* (London, 1965), vol. 1, 87–91; Sheila Hewett with John and Elizabeth Newson, *The Family and the Handicapped Child* (London, 1970).

p. 102 David Towell: 'Brothers and Sisters as Change Agents', in Brian Rix, ed., *All About Us! The Story of People with a Learning Disability and Mencap* (London, 2006).

p. 102 'not to hear any more': Medical Case Book, H29/NF/B13/008; Reginald Langdon-Down to Dr G-A., 16 January 1942, H29/NF/A/01/352; letter of 5 November 1943, H29/NF/A/01/359.

p. 103 'carriers': The term 'carrier' became a staple of the discussion of mental deficiency. Among many examples, see 'Mental Disease: The Problem of Heredity', A. F. Tredgold, Letter to the Editor, *The Times*, 1 October 1930, 8.

p. 103 total of more than 300,000: *Report of the Interdepartmental Committee on Mental Deficiency, 1925–1929* [Wood Report] (London, 1929), 175.

p. 104 The poet Louis MacNeice: Jon Stallworthy, *Louis MacNeice* (London, 1995), 39; Louis MacNeice, *The Strings are False* (London, 1982), 120–22.

p. 104 The fact that his son: On Mountenoy Wellcome, Robert Rhodes James, *Edward Wellcome* (London, 1994), 335–8, and Gerald McKnight, *The Scandal of Syrie Maugham* (London, 1980), 42–52.

p. 104 For two decades: E. J. Lidbetter, *Heredity and the Social Problem Group* (London, 1933), vol. 1; Jackson, *Borderland*, 138–48; for the post-Second World War period, C. P. Blacker, ed., *Problem Families: Five Inquiries* (London, 1952).

p. 104 'because I mind people': Letter of 9 February n.y. [1911?], H29/NF/A/01/161.

p. 105 'the benefit of the doubt': Letter of 24 June 1924, H29/NF/A/01/234.

p. 105 Given the shortage: Thomson, *Problem*, 260–64; Pamela Dale, 'Assistance and Resistance: Making Sense of Inter-War Caring Strategies', in Duncan Mitchell et al., eds., *Exploring Experiences of Advocacy by People with Learning Disabilities* (London, 2006), 196; Joyce Leeson, 'Place of the Hospital in the Care of the Mentally Subnormal', *British Medical Journal*, 16 March 1963, 713–18.

p. 106 'as it will just': Letter of 7 June 1928, H29/NF/A/01/264.

p. 106 'difficult and heavy': Medical Case Book, 3 March 1955, H29/NF/B13/011; Medical Case Book, 28 August 1941, H29/NF/B13/008.

p. 106 'it is a bit like the Victorian': Moira Keenan, 'A Hospital is Not a Home', *The Times*, 4 August 1971, 9. On Oswin, Sheena Rolph and Dorothy Atkinson, 'Maureen Oswin and the "Forgotten Children" of the Long-Stay Wards: Research as Resistance', in Mitchell et al., eds., *Exploring Experiences of Advocacy*.

p. 107 In the typical ward: Maureen Oswin, *Children in Long-Stay Hospitals* (Lavenham, 1978), 76–128; Maureen Oswin, *The Empty Hours: A Study of the Weekend Life of Handicapped Children in Institutions* (London, 1971), 138; Jack Tizard, 'Quality of Residential Care for Retarded Children', in Jack Tizard, Ian Sinclair and R. V. G. Clarke, eds., *Varieties of Residential Experience* (London, 1975); Roy D. King, Norma V. Raynes and Jack Tizard, *Patterns of Residential Care: Sociological Studies in Institutions for Handicapped Children* (London, 1971), 85–103.

p. 107 'Come *here*, lady': Oswin, *Empty Hours,* 148, 142. Also Report on Ida Darwin Hospital, Cambridge (31 August–22 September 1975), MO/1/3, 156, Open University Archive [henceforth OUA]. All citations to Oswin's unpublished reports are to records held at the OUA.

p. 107 'Think . . . how a child like this': Oswin, *Empty Hours*, 129.

p. 107 'He'll be right': Oswin, *Children*, 109.

p. 107 'corpse': Oswin, Report on Calderstones, Lancashire, Autumn 1975, 250, MO/1/4.

p. 107 One afternoon: Oswin, *Children*, 122.

p. 108 Worst off: On visiting, Oswin, *Children*, 8–18; Oswin, Report on Prudhoe Hospital, Northumberland, MO/1/2, 228; Pauline Morris, *Put Away: A Sociological Study of Institutions for the Mentally Retarded* (New York, 1969), 107–207; Department of Health and Social Security Memorandum, *Children in Hospital: Maintenance of Family Links and Prevention of Abandonment*, January 1972 (HM 72.2).

p. 108 The orthopaedic: Oswin, Report on Calderstones.

p. 108 'dumped': Oswin, *Empty Hours*, 205–6; Oswin, *Children*, 8–13; Oswin, Report on Ida Darwin Hospital, Cambridge (31 August–22 September 1975), MO/1/3, 170.

p. 108 'Nobody can guess': Oswin, Report on Calderstones.

p. 108 But the medical case: See, for instance, H29/NF/A/01/321; Medical Case Books: H29/NF/B13/009–012.

p. 109 'nauseatingly': *Report of the Committee of Inquiry into Normansfield Hospital, Presented to Parliament by the Secretary of State for Social Services by Command of Her Majesty*, November 1978 (London, 1978), Cmnd 7357, 15; Merriman, *Tales*, 185–202.

p. 109 'just as if Dickens': *Report of the Committee*, 27.

p. 109 'I was shocked': ibid., 28.

p. 110 In an era: Michael Anderson, 'Social Implications of Demographic Change', in F. M. L. Thompson, ed., *The Cambridge Social History of Britain, 1750–1950*, vol. II (Cambridge, 1990), 41.

p. 110 By the 1920s: Anderson, 'Social Implications', 28–9, 66–70; Pat Thane, 'Happy Families? History and Policy', History & Policy, http://www.historyandpolicy.org/papers/policy-paper-107.html.

p. 111 Yet even at the height: Bone, Spain and Martin, *Plans and Provisions*, 29; Jack Tizard and Jacqueline C. Grad, *The Mentally Handicapped and Their Families: A Social Survey* (London and Oxford, 1961).

p. 112 To combat the stigma: Rolph et al., *Witnesses to Change*, 79–80; 82–3. On Mencap: Liz Tizard, 'Resistance in Mencap's History', in Mitchell et al., eds., *Exploring Experiences*; Sheena Rolph, *Reclaiming the Past: The Role of Local Mencap Societies in the Development of Community Care in East Anglia, 1946–1980* (Milton Keynes, 2002).

p. 112 one of the largest: Rolph et al., *Witnesses to Change*, 117.

p. 112 'Poor child': Letter of 30 June 1938, H29/NF/A/01/329.

4. Other People's Bastards

p. 113 'an illegitimate child': Letter to Mrs Ransome Wallis, 29 May 1919, CC.

p. 113 an estimated 65,000: Lionel Rose, *Massacre of the Innocents: Infanticide in Great Britain, 1800–1939* (London, 1986), 23. On illegitimacy more generally, the special issue of *Women's History Review* on 'Lone Mothers', 20:1 (February 2011), eds. Tanya Evans and Pat Thane; Pat Thane and Tanya Evans, *Sinners? Scroungers? Saints: Unmarried Motherhood in*

Twentieth-Century England (Oxford, 2012); Ginger Frost, '"The Black Lamb of the Black Sheep": Illegitimacy in the English Working Class, 1850–1939', *Journal of Social History* 37:2 (2003), 293–322; Kathleen Kiernan, Hilary Land and Jane Lewis, *Lone Motherhood in Twentieth-Century Britain: From Footnote to Front Page* (Oxford, 1998), 27–8; Janet Fink, 'Natural Mothers, Putative Fathers, and Innocent Children: The Definition and Regulation of Parental Relationships outside Marriage, in England, 1945–1959', *Journal of Family History* 25:2 (April 2000), 178–95; Pat Thane, 'Unmarried Motherhood in Twentieth-Century England', *Women's History Review* 20:1 (February 2011), 11–29; John Gillis, *For Better, for Worse: British Marriages 1600 to the Present* (Oxford, 1985), 231–59; Ginger Frost, *Living in Sin: Cohabiting as Husband and Wife in Nineteenth-Century England* (Manchester, 2008), 9–31; Margot Finn, Michael Lobban and Jenny Bourne Taylor, *Legitimacy and Illegitimacy in Nineteenth-Century Law, Literature and History* (Basingstoke, 2010); Deborah Derrick, ed., *Illegitimate: The Experience of People Born outside Marriage* (London, 1986); Stephen Cretney, *Family Law in the Twentieth Century: A History* (Oxford, 2003), 545–65; Virginia Wimperis, *The Unmarried Mother and Her Child* (London, 1960); Alysa Levene, Thomas Nutt and Samantha Williams, eds., *Illegitimacy in Britain, 1700–1920* (Basingstoke, 2005); Janet Fink, 'Condemned or Condoned? Investigating the Problem of Unmarried Motherhood in England, 1945–60', PhD thesis, University of Essex, 1997; Mary Hopkirk, *Nobody Wanted Sam: The Story of the Unwelcomed Child, 1530–1948* (London, 1949).

p. 113 Sexual immorality in a parent: Ernest James Lidbetter, *Heredity and the Social Problem Group* (London, 1933); Frost, 'Black Lamb', 304–5. The authoritative history of adoption in interwar England is Jenny Keating, *A Child for Keeps: The History of Adoption in England, 1918–45* (London, 2009); also George Behlmer, *Friends of the Family: The English Home and Its Guardians, 1850–1940* (Stanford, 1998), 272–316.

p. 113 'I am very anxious': Letter to Mrs Wallis, 11 March 1895, AR11/1, CAS.

p. 113 'Please mark': Letter to Madam, 18 April 1917, T box – old series, CAS.

p. 114 'If it would ease': Quoted in Mission of Hope, 1924 Report, S70 (362.7) MIS, 6, CAS.

p. 114 tens of thousands: There are no official statistics as to the number of children adopted extra-legally before the 1926 Adoption Act, though the records from the Mission of Hope, which arranged 2000 adoptions before 1926, suggest that the total from all of the societies involved could be as high as 15,000. In the first nine years after the legalization of adoption, between 1927 and 1936, 41,914 adoption orders were granted. *Report of the Departmental Committee on Adoption Societies and Agencies, 1936–7* [Horsbrugh Committee], Cmd 5499, 4, 6.

p. 114 'She seemed to take': Letter to Mr and Mrs Beesley, 12 July 1919, CC.

p. 114 'She speaks sometimes': Letter to Mr Beesley, 5 November 1919, CC.

p. 115 'Saint Joan': 'What She Could: Being a Brief Sketch of the Life and Work of Mrs. Ransome Wallis', by Two of Her Daughters and including the 35th Annual Report of the Mission of Hope, 1928, 8, 16.

p. 116 Although the position: The 1926 Legitimacy Act provided that children whose parents were free to marry when they were born could be legitimated by a later marriage. It omitted those whose parents had been carrying on adulterous affairs. As Frost points out, rather than collapsing the distinction between 'legitimate' and 'illegitimate', it created another category: the legitimated. See Frost, 'Black Lamb', 315. Also Ginger Frost, '"Revolting to Humanity": Oversights, Limitations and Complications of the English Legitimacy Act of 1926', *Women's History Review* 20:1 (February 2011), 31–46.

p. 116 'important considerations': Letter by William Baker (Hon. Director), Barnardo's, 27 November 1914, AR 11/1, CAS.

p. 117 'as reachable and salvable': 'What She Could', 24.

p. 117 'I the Lord': Mission of Hope, 'With the King for His Work', 56th Annual Report, 1949, n.p.

p. 118 'It grieves me': Application, 1919; Letter to Madam, 15 April 1919, CC.

p. 118 For Miss Hart: Letter from Miss Hart, 2 January 1926, T box – old series, CAS. On secrecy in adoption, Murray Ryburn, 'Secrecy and

Openness in Adoption: An Historical Perspective', *Social Policy and Administration* 29:2 (June 1995), 151–68.

p. 118 'who loves the child': Index Book, 1916–1922, 30 January 1924, CC.

p. 118 Edwin Jones: Index Book, 1903–1909, July 1905, CC.

p. 118 'The child was well cared': Index Book, 1903–1909, 14 February 1925, CC.

p. 118 'terrified in case': Index Book, 1903–1909, 16 May 1926, CC.

p. 119 'You may always rest': Letter from Miss Hart, 19 May 1926, CC.

p. 119 'subsequently made a nuisance': Testimony of the Chief Education Officer of Birmingham, cited in *Report of the Departmental Committee*, 16.

p. 120 Mrs. Burr: Letter to Miss Hart, n.d. [February 1924], CC.

p. 120 'one of the sweetest': Letter to Miss Hart, 17 July 1933, CC.

p. 120 'Of course she knows': Index Book, 1916–1922, 20 November 1933, CC.

p. 120 'feelings should never be hurt': Letter to Mrs Wallis, 31 May 1908, AR11/1, CAS.

p. 120 'it might make all': Letter to Miss Wallis, 10 December 1934, CC.

p. 121 'as anxious as': For example, Index Book, 1924–7, 22 December 1924, CC.

p. 121 'practically forgotten': Index Book, 1916–1922, 15 June 1924, CC.

p. 121 'Was Charlotte's': Letter to Miss Hames, n.d. [1911?], CAS.

p. 121 'refinement': Inspection Report by F. E. Lauder, 24 June 1928; letter from Miss Hart, 12 September 1928, T box – old series, CAS.

p. 121 'both by her ways': Letter to Miss Hart, 12 March 1931, CC.

p. 121 'very superior': Letter from Miss Hart, 13 March 1931, CC.

p. 121 'I have tried': Letter to Miss Hames, 24 September 1919, CAS.

p. 121 'with a certain heredity': Associated Societies for the Care and Maintenance of Infants, *Report of the Select Committee Appointed to Examine the Principle and Practice of Child Adoption* (London, 1920).

p. 122 'no one knows': Letter to Miss Hames, 2 November 1910, CAS.

p. 122 Cooperative ministers: Letter to Miss Hart, n.d. [November 1917], T box – old series, CAS.

p. 123 'This is what a great': Letter from Miss Hart, 28 July 1924, CC; letter from Miss Hart, 24 June 1924, CC.

.

p. 123 'extreme' friendliness: COS report, signed D.T., 25 October 1927, A/FWA/C/D258/8, LMA.

p. 123 'How I wish': Letter to Miss Wallis, 23 October 1919, CC.

p. 123 'I have been waiting': Letter to Madam, n.d. [received 31 January 1920], CC.

p. 123 'every means': Testimony of Mr F. W. Sherwood, Recorder of Worcester, cited in *Report of the Select Committee Appointed to Examine the Principle and Practice of Child Adoption*, 19.

p. 124 'their business': Letter to Mrs Ransome Wallis, 20 January 1916, T box – old series, CAS.

p. 124 Florence Mayne: Letter to Miss Smith, 12 August 1947, AR 11/2, CAS. Thane and Evans, *Sinners?*, 35–9.

p. 125 Mrs Shaw: Letter to Miss Wallis, 2 September 1947, AR 11/2, CAS.

p. 125 'flatly refused': Letter to Miss Hart, 25 April 1924, CC.

p. 125 'Last night': Letter to Mrs Ransome Wallis, 12 July 1913, AR11/1, CAS.

p. 126 All that we know: Letter to Miss Wallis, 13 June 1926, CAS.

p. 126 'Very superior': 'One Such Little Child', 1923 Report (31st Annual Report), Mission of Hope, S70 (362.7) MIS, CAS.

p. 126 'unfortunate past': Letter to Miss Edith Hart, 4 May 1920, AR11/2, CAS.

p. 126 'exceedingly anxious': Letter to Miss Edith Hart, February 1921, AR11/2, CAS.

p. 126 'No one is more sorry': Letter from Miss Hart, 9 May 1924, CC.

p. 127 'no one can realize': Letter to Miss Hart, 4 February 1924, CC.

p. 127 'It is very rare': Letter to Miss Wallis, 7 May 1935, CAS.

p. 128 'hiding up things': Judge Edward Abbott Parry's testimony to the Hopkinson Committee, quoted in Keating, *Child for Keeps*, 80.

p. 128 'wholly unnecessary': Child Adoption Committee, First Report (London, 1924–5), Cmd 2401, 9.

p. 129 'is so much my boy': Letter to Miss Hart, 25 June 1933, CC.

p. 129 'in our hearts': Letter to Miss Hart, n.d. [August 1934], CC.

p. 129 'in many cases': Hansard. *Parl. Deb.* (Commons), 26 February 1926, 944.

p. 129 'and that is': Letter to Miss Hart, 12 March 1931, CC.

p. 130 'She is got': Letter to Miss Hart, 3 July 1931, CC.

p. 130 'she resented my control': Letter to Miss Hart, 28 December 1927, AR11/2, CAS.

p. 130 'Someone told her': Letter to Miss Wallis, 20 August 1923, AR11/1, CAS.

p. 131 'It has been found': NAS Annual Report, 1940 [June, 1941], LCO2/2642, TNA.

p. 131 So urgent: Mr Key, Parliamentary Secretary to the Ministry of Health, Hansard, *Parl. Deb.* (Commons), 7 February 1947, 2110.

p. 131 Unlike the standard: The short birth certificate was introduced in Scotland in 1934, over the objections of the English Home Office, which also resisted the efforts of the Child Welfare Committee of the League of Nations to implement such a document, on the grounds that it was against the interests of public policy to curtail the amount of information on a birth certificate (which could lead to more fraud) in order to minimize embarrassment for illegitimates. See S.P.V., 'Abridged Birth Certificates', 21 February 1934, RG 48/2300, TNA.

p. 131 'born, say': Lieut-Colonel Lipton (Brixton), Hansard, *Parl. Deb.* (Commons), 7 February 1947, 2119.

p. 132 'A youngster': Hansard, *Parl. Deb.* (Commons), 7 February 1947, 2115.

p. 132 'if the eyes': Child Adoption Committee, First Report, 9.

p. 133 'no man, woman': G.P.C. [George Coldstream], 'Hon. Sir Albert Napier', *The Times*, 21 July 1973, 14.

p. 133 'Apart from authority': Napier to Fraser Harrison, 20 July 1942, LCO2/2642, TNA.

p. 134 'haunt the home': Hansard, *Parl. Deb.* (Lords), 21 July 1949, 362.

p. 134 'iron curtain': Home Office brief, forwarded to H. Boggis-Rolfe in the Lord Chancellor's Office by H. H. O. Prestige, MH/102/1875, TNA.

p. 135 'They all think': Letter to Miss Smith, 20 October 1944, CC.

p. 135 'Do not dare': Letter to Miss Smith, 6 September 1953, CC.

p. 135 'We do think': Letter to Miss Smith, 29 July 1945, CC.

p. 135 'Several times': Letter to Miss Smith, 9 February 1944, CC.

p. 136 'want our joy': Letter to Miss Smith, 23 May 1957, CC.

p. 136 Telling remained: Lois Raynor, *The Adopted Child Comes of Age* (London, 1980), 91.

p. 136 'the little one': Letter from Miss Smith, 16 February 1944, CC.

p. 136 '"telling" always proved': Margaret Kornitzer, *Adoption and Family Life* (London, 1968), 226.

p. 137 'forgot': Raynor, *Adopted Child*, 95.

p. 137 'We wanted to start': Kornitzer, *Adoption and Family Life*, 205.

p. 137 'We have killed': ibid., 131.

p. 137 'in a glasshouse': ibid., 140.

p. 137 'Of course': Raynor, *Adopted Child*, 120.

p. 137 'compulsion': Kornitzer, *Adoption and Family Life*, 38.

p. 137 'genetic anxiety': M. Humphrey and C. Ounsted, 'Adoptive Families Referred for Psychiatric Advice', *The British Journal of Psychiatry* 109 (September 1963), 550–55.

p. 138 1967 marked: There were 22,802 adoption orders granted in 1967: 7189 to parents and 15,613 to others. 1968 was the apogee of adoption, with 24,831 orders granted. Registrar General's *Statistical Review*, pt II, Table T5, quoted in Eleanor Grey in collaboration with Ronald M. Blunden, *A Survey of Adoption in Great Britain: Home Office Research Studies* (London, 1971), 3.

p. 139 'felt that he was': McWhinnie, *Adopted Children*, 114–15, 163, 227.

p. 139 'rootless': ibid., 129, 135; Kornitzer, *Adoption and Family Life*, 205.

p. 141 'cherished only child': Letter to Director, Mission of Hope, 16 February 1980, CC.

p. 141 'I myself was': Letter to social worker, 15 January 1981, CC.

5. Bachelor Uncles

p. 143 'Dear Grannie's': D5122, Diary for 6 March 1946, MOA.

p. 143 Families hardly: An exception in the British literature is Charles Upchurch's chapter in *Before Wilde: Sex between Men in Britain's Age of Reform* (Berkeley, 2009), 21–49, which explores the wide range of responses in early-nineteenth-century families, from defence to banishment.

p. 144 It was both known: On the open secret, D. A. Miller, *The Novel and the Police* (Berkeley, 1988), and Anna Clark, 'Twilight Moments', *Journal of the History of Sexuality* 14:1/2 (2005), 139–60.

p. 144 'I'd rather': Timothy d'Arch Smith, 'Introduction', unpublished TS, author's collection.

p. 144 (fn) Lesbianism was: Laura Doan, *Fashioning Sapphism: The Origins of a Modern English Lesbian Culture* (New York, 2001); Sharon Marcus, *Between Women: Friendship, Desire and Marriage in Victorian England* (Princeton, 2007); Martha Vicinus, *Intimate Friends: Women Who Loved Women, 1778–1928* (Chicago, 2004).

p. 145 For much of Anatole: Matt Houlbrook, *Queer London: Perils and Pleasures in the Sexual Metropolis, 1918–1957* (Chicago, 2005), 1–13, 139–218.

p. 146 'I do feel so': Kathleen Isherwood, Diary, 14 December 1926, Harry Ransom Center, University of Texas [henceforth Ransom].

p. 146 'didn't seem': James J. Berg and Chris Freeman, *Conversations with Christopher Isherwood* (Jackson, Miss., 2001), 172–3.

p. 146 'a full, painful': Richard Blake Brown, 15 August 1927, Diary 1925–8 [The Tide in the Bay], 131. The diaries of Richard Blake Brown [henceforth RBB] are held in two private collections.

p. 146 'no conceivable': RBB, 30 July, Diary 1925–8, 105–6.

p. 146 'I don't know what': RBB, 17 August, Diary 1925–8, 141.

p. 147 'driving the homosexual': RBB, 9 August 1928, Yellow Dawn (#44).

p. 147 'You must stop': RBB, 17 August, Diary 1925–8, 142.

p. 147 'Her love': Harold Brown to RBB, 19 August 1927. Entry dated 27 August 1927, Diary 1925–8, 160–66.

p. 147 'Surely the dear': RBB, Diary 1925–8, 321.

p. 147 'invaluable and active': RBB, 5 March 1928, Diary 1925–8, 394.

p. 148 'Oh that's just': Alan Wakeman, b. 1936, C1159/05, 'Before Stonewall: A Lesbian, Gay, Bisexual and Transgendered Oral History', Sound Archive, BL.

p. 148 'instinctively': Fragment of a TS autobiography of Anatole James [1972?], #7660 Box 1, Rare and Manuscript Collections, Carl A. Kroch Library, Cornell University, 1, 21.

p. 148 'Nobody ever said': Mike Upton, b. 1941, C1159/82 C1, 'Before Stonewall'.

p. 149 'bright, outrageous': David Ruffell, b. 1940, C456/011/01-02, Hall-Carpenter Oral History Archive, Sound Archive, BL.

p. 149 'Some people': b. 1926, National Lesbian & Gay Survey, Series 3, Code 382, Special Collections, University of Sussex Library.

p. 149 'into words': John Alcock, b. 1927, C456/003/01-02, Hall-Carpenter; Hall-Carpenter Archives Gay Men's Oral History Group, *Walking After Midnight: Gay Men's Life Stories* (London, 1989), 41–55.

p. 149 'best friend': Tony Garrett, b. 1929, C456/090/01-02, Hall-Carpenter.

p. 149 'very clear': b. 1920, National Lesbian & Gay Survey, Series 2, Code 212, Box 1.

p. 150 'I wanted them': Antony Grey, b. 1927, C456/071/01-03, Hall-Carpenter.

p. 150 'profile of infinite': Michael Davidson, *The World, The Flesh and Myself* (London, 1977 [1962]), 22–3.

p. 150 'I didn't feel': Roger Fisher, b. 1935, C1159/09 C1, 'Before Stonewall'.

p. 150 In the 1950s: Chris Waters, 'The Homosexual as a Social Being in Britain, 1945–1968', *Journal of British Studies* 51:3 (2012), 685–710; Eustace Chesser, 'Society and the Homosexual', *International Journal of Sexology* 7 (1954), 214; Liz Stanley, *Sex Surveyed, 1949–1994: From Mass-Observation's 'Little Kinsey' to the National Survey and the Hite Reports* (London, 1995), 199–200.

p. 150 'careful to avoid': Gordon Westwood [Michael Schofield], *A Minority: A Report on the Life of the Male Homosexual in Great Britain* (London, 1960), 40.

p. 150 'Gentlemanly, tall': T. 2543, b. 1933, Gays and Lesbians in the Family – Autumn 2000, MOA; also B-2240, b. 1921.

p. 151 'pansies': L. 1697, b. 1943, ibid.

p. 151 'it was not': B. 1475, b. 1943, ibid.

p. 151 In one family: A. 1706, b. 1946, ibid.

p. 151 'poor Aunt Kathleen': Peter Parker, *Isherwood* (Basingstoke, 2004), 473.

p. 151 One mother: D. 1697, b. 1923, Gays and Lesbians in the Family – Autumn 2000, MOA.

p. 151 'He's like your': David Jones, b. 1941, C1159/42 C1, 'Before Stone-wall'.

p. 151 As a young man: Roger Smith, b. 1937, C1159/28 C1, 'Before Stone-wall'.

p. 152 'retired in disorder': T. C. Worsley, *Flannelled Fool: A Slice of Life in the Thirties* (London, 1967), 118–19.

p. 153 'poor old': D5122, Diary for 23 June 1946 and 24 October 1947, MOA.

p. 153 Rather, a wide array: *A Reprint of the Leading Article under the Title 'A Social Problem' from the Sunday Times. November 1, 1953, Together with a Comprehensive Selection of Letters Received from Readers Following Its Publication.*

p. 154 After the Second World War: Chris Waters, 'Havelock Ellis, Sigmund Freud and the State: Discourses of Homosexual Identity in Interwar Britain', in Lucy Bland and Laura Doan, eds., *Sexology in Culture: Labelling Bodies and Desires* (Chicago, 1998), 65–179. On child-rearing, see Michal Shapira, *The War Inside: Child Psychoanalysis and the Democratic Self in Britain, 1930–1960* (Cambridge, forthcoming); Deborah Thom, 'Domestic Life, Psychological Thinking and the Permissive Turn', in Lucy Delap, Ben Griffin and Abigail Wills, eds., *The Politics of Domestic Authority in Britain since 1800* (Basingstoke, 2009), 261–81.

p. 154 Still, very few: Published in Britain in paperback before 1970 were: *Psychopathology of Everyday Life* (Pelican, 1939); *Totem & Taboo* (Penguin Books, 1938); *Two Short Accounts of Psycho-Analysis* (Penguin Books, 1963); and *Leonardo* (Pelican, 1966). More broadly, see Nikolas Rose, *The Psychological Complex: Psychology, Politics and Society in England, 1869–1939* (London, 1985); Mathew Thomson, *Psychological Subjects: Identity, Culture and Health in Twentieth-Century Britain* (Oxford, 2006), 20–23, 46–7, 81–3, 258–62; Dean Rapp, 'The Early Discovery of Freud by the British General Educated Reading Public, 1912–1919', *Social History of Medicine* 3: 2 (1990), 217–45; Dean Rapp, 'The Reception of Freud by the British Press: General Interest and Literary Magazines, 1920–1925', *Journal of the History of the Behavioural Sciences* 24: 2 (1988), 191–201; John Forrester, 'Freud in Cambridge', *Critical*

Quarterly 46:2 (2004), 1–26; John Forrester, '1919: Psychology and Psychoanalysis, London and Cambridge', *Psychoanalysis and History* 10:1 (2008), 37–94; and Sandra Ellesley, 'Psychoanalysis in Early Twentieth Century England: A Study in the Popularisation of Ideas', PhD thesis, University of Essex, 1995. For a contrary view, Graham Richards, 'Britain on the Couch: The Popularization of Psychoanalysis in Britain, 1918–1940', *Science in Context 2* 13 : 2 (2000), 183–230.

p. 154 'a familiar villainess': Review of D. J. West, *Homosexuality*, *The Times Literary Supplement*, 26 August 1955.

p. 154 'little island': 'Crux', 'London Diary', *New Statesman*, 9 October 1970, 448; R. Gosling, Letter to the Editor, 'The British Tavistock', *New Statesman*, 522.

p. 154 'one of the main causes': 'Mothers and Sons', *Sunday Times*, 6 December 1953, 6.

p. 155 'child's need': Among many others, Mother of Daughters, Letter to the Editor, 'Child Psychology', *Sunday Times*, 13 December 1953, 6; Mother in Dundee, Letter to the Editor, 'The Father's Role', ibid.

p. 155 If psychological: Waters, 'Havelock Ellis', 166–71; Chris Waters, 'Disorders of the Mind, Disorders of the Body Social: Peter Wildeblood and the Making of the Modern Homosexual', in Becky Conekin, Frank Mort and Chris Waters, eds., *Moments of Modernity: Reconstructing Britain, 1945–64* (London, 1999), 134–51; Waters, 'Homosexual as a Social Being in Britain, 1945–1968', esp. 702–5.

p. 155 'glands', a 'feminine bent': D. R. Morgan, Letter to the Editor, *A Reprint of the Leading Article under the Title 'A Social Problem' from the Sunday Times. November 1, 1953, Together with a Comprehensive Selection of Letters Received from Readers Following Its Publication*; 'Schoolmaster Sentenced to Ten Years', *News of the World*, 22 July 1951, 2.

p. 155 'something that is': 'Five Years Ban', *News of the World*, 14 December 1941, George Ives, Clipping Album, GEN MSS. 426, vol. 43, Beinecke Rare Book and Manuscript Library, Yale.

p. 155 'abnormal leanings': '"Devoted" Vicar Will Not Be Gaoled', *News of the World*, 23 December 1951, 6.

p. 156 'decadent vice': Douglas Warth, 'Evil Men', *Sunday Pictorial*: 25 May 1952, 6; 1 June 1952, 12; 8 June 1952, 12.

p. 156 'danger, and it's no good': J. F. Wolfenden, 'Sons, Mothers & Schools', *Sunday Times*, 3 January 1954, 6.

p. 156 'alarmingly catching': Bishop of Rochester to J. F. Wolfenden, Esq., 8 August 1956, HO 345/2, TNA.

p. 156 The Tavistock: Document No. CHP/96 – the Tavistock Clinic Memorandum of Evidence, HO 345/8 – CHP Papers 40–81, TNA; also the ISTD and the Portman joint memo (CHP/90) and the British Psychological Society memo (CHP/91); Frank Mort, *Capital Affairs: London and the Making of the Permissive Society* (New Haven and London, 2010), 151.

p. 157 Typical was: HO 345/9 – CHP Papers 82-109. Document No. CHP/95 – British Medical Association Memorandum, 7–8, TNA. The BMA distinguished between 'essential' and 'acquired' homosexuals, and it was the former group in whom both genetics and an abnormal early childhood figured.

p. 157 'insidiously invade': Document No. CHP/95 – British Medical Association Memorandum, 7–8, TNA. The BMA's memo did observe that homosexuals themselves often identified disturbances in early childhood relations (especially 'too intense relationships' with mothers), a pattern which, it noted, psychoanalysts had confirmed. Unlike the BMA's confident discussion of the perils of segregation and initiation, on the significance of such emotional disturbances in early childhood it hedged: 'The extent to which these psychological factors are fundamental to the production of homosexuals is difficult to assess.' See Doc. No. CHP/05, 19.

p. 157 Untangling the skeins: See, for example, 'A Difficult Topic', *The Times Literary Supplement*, 9 March 1956, 152; Ivor Brown, 'Goings On' [review of 'The Green Bay Tree'], *Week-End Review*, 4 February 1933, George Ives, Clipping Album, GEN MSS. 426, vol. 32; *Report of the Committee on Homosexual Offences and Prostitution* [henceforth *Wolfenden Report*], Cmnd 247 (London, 1957), 15, 37. On the Wolfenden Committee, Mort, *Capital*, 139–96; Patrick Higgins, *Heterosexual Dictatorship: Male Homosexuality in Postwar Britain* (London, 1996), 15–58.

p. 157 'quite openly': British Market Research Bureau Limited, *Homosex-*

uality: Report on a Pilot Attitude Study, September 1963, 4, HCA/AT 12/7, London School of Economics Archives.

p. 158 age of consent: Stephen Jeffery-Poulter, *Peers, Queers and Commons: The Struggle for Gay Law Reform from 1950 to the Present* (London and New York, 1991), 81–3, 87–8; H. Montgomery Hyde, *The Other Love: An Historical and Contemporary Survey of Homosexuality in Britain* (London, 1970), 269; Higgins, *Heterosexual Dictatorship*, 63–5; 72–3; Dagmar Herzog, *Sexuality in Europe: A Twentieth-Century History* (Cambridge, 2011), 77–82.

p. 158 'preventative measures': *Wolfenden Report*, 77–8.

p. 159 'It is queer': D5122, Diary entry for 15 November 1946, MOA.

p. 159 None of the 127: Westwood, *Minority*, 60.

p. 159 'Family Likeness': W. H. Auden, *Juvenilia: Poems, 1922–1928*, ed. Katherine Bucknell (London, 1994), 217.

p. 159 'if not two': Anatole James to Rupert Croft-Cooke, 29 January 1956, Croft-Cooke Collection, Ransom; James, TS Autobiography, 43–4.

p. 159 '"peculiar"': D5122, Diary entry for 13 November 1946, MOA.

p. 160 'it wouldn't surprise': C1159/91 C1, 'Before Stonewall'.

p. 160 'The mother had': Richard Davenport-Hines, *Auden* (New York, 1995), 31.

p. 160 'which influenced': Peter Wildeblood, *Against the Law* (London, 1955), 8.

p. 160 'something to do': Westwood, *Minority*, 60.

p. 160 'gratifying': Eva Bene, 'On the Genesis of Male Homosexuality: An Attempt at Clarifying the Role of the Parents', *British Journal of Psychiatry* 111 (1965), 804.

p. 161 George Ives: Ives was the illegitimate grandson of the Hon. Emma Ives, who raised him. Emma Ives was the sister of Charlotte Capel.

p. 161 'wear a mask': HO 345/13 – CHP Transcripts: CHP/TRANS/24 – Mr. Peter Wildeblood, 24 May 1955, TNA.

p. 162 When the author: 'Mr Augustus Hare: Death of a Notable Author', *Daily Chronicle*, 23 January 1903, and 'Here, There and Everywhere: The Late Mr. Augustus Hare', *Westminster Gazette*, 23 January 1903, George Ives, Clipping Album, GEN MSS. 426, vol. 3.

p. 162 'far more in common': Augustus Hare, *The Story of My Life*, vol. 6 (London, 1900), 530.

p. 162 'clothes, his walk': Beverley Nichols, *Father Figure* (London, 1972), 87–9.

p. 162 'lover of strenuous': 'Teacher Wins Appeal', *News of the World*, 26 September 1937, George Ives, Clipping Album, GEN MSS. 426, vol. 39.

p. 163 But when the Albany: British Market Research Bureau Ltd, *Homosexuality*, 10.

p. 163 'the answer': b. 1935, National Lesbian & Gay Survey, Series 4, Code 432, Box 5.

p. 163 'with only slight': Harry Daley, *This Small Cloud* (London, 1986), 112–13, 158, 231.

p. 163 'dark conspiracy': 10 January 1895, Ives diary – vols. 21–5, Ransom; also 25 March 1897, Ives diary – vols. 26–30, f. 3232. On Ives, see Matt Cook, *London and the Culture of Homosexuality, 1885–1914* (Cambridge, 2008), and Matt Cook, 'Families of Choice? George Ives, Queer Lives and the Family in Early Twentieth-Century Britain', *Gender and History* 22:1 (April 2010), 1–20.

p. 164 Joseph Sussainathan: Also known as Joseph Susei Mari.

p. 165 'mind in the least': Rupert Croft-Cooke, *The Verdict of You All* (London, 1955), 68.

p. 165 'extremely outspoken': Anatole James to Sir Compton Mackenzie, 19 July 1956, Compton Mackenzie Collection, Ransom.

p. 165 'as I "tell everything"': Anatole James to Rupert Croft-Cooke, 29 January 1956, Croft-Cooke Collection, Ransom.

p. 165 'born original': D5122, Diary entry for 4 December 1945, MOA.

p. 165 'originality': D5122, Diary entry for 4 January 1948, MOA. On domesticity and distinctiveness, Matt Cook, 'Domestic Passions: Unpacking the Homes of Charles Shannon and Charles Ricketts', *Journal of British Studies* 51:3 (2012).

p. 166 'Strange how': D5122, Diary entry for 25 December 1945, MOA.

p. 166 'Personality Developed': D5122, Diary entry for 13 January 1947, MOA.

p. 166 In April 1949: d'Arch Smith, 'Introduction', 6.

p. 166 'No telephone': Rupert Croft-Cooke, *The Wild Hills* (London, 1966), 88–104.

p. 167 'gnawed with suppressed': RBB, 26 January 1929, Diary, 1929.

p. 167 'It was quite': Croft-Cooke, *Wild Hills*, 94.

p. 168 'Bible and a creed': RBB, Diary, 1927–9, 9–11.

p. 168 'those queer folk': Robert Cust to Theo Bartholomew, 28 December 1929, A. T. Bartholomew Scrapbook in Rolfe Collection, Misc., Ransom.

p. 169 'the one exception': D5122, Diary entry for 13 November 1946, MOA.

p. 169 'thoroughly progressive': D5122, Diary entry for 6 March 1946, MOA.

p. 169 'Dear Grannie': D5122, Diary entry for 27 May 1946, MOA.

p. 169 'So far as I know': D5122, Diary entry for 13 May 1946, MOA.

p. 169 'left out': TS to mother, 30 January 1946, Croft-Cooke Collection.

p. 170 'insanely cruel': Rupert Croft-Cooke (RCC), to Olive Cooke, 7 January 1955; Olive to RCC, 11 January 1955; RCC to Olive, 17 January 1955; RCC to Olive, 18 April 1955, Croft-Cooke Collection.

p. 170 'secret': Godfrey Winn, 'Personality Parade', *Daily Mirror*, 18 June 1937, 11, cited in Ryan Linkof, '"These Young Men Who Come Down from Oxford and Write Gossip": Society Gossip, Homosexuality, and the Logic of Revelation in the Interwar Popular Press', in Brian Lewis, ed., *British Queer History: New Approaches and Perspectives* (Manchester, forthcoming); Hugh Cudlipp, *Publish and be Damned* (London, 1953), 113.

p. 170 George Ives: Cook, *London and the Culture of Homosexuality*, 143.

p. 170 'addicted': J. A. Symonds, *The Memoirs of John Addington Symonds*, ed. and intro. Phyllis Grosskurth (London, 1984), 154.

p. 170 180-volume: David Newsome, *On the Edge of Paradise: A. C. Benson, the Diarist* (London, 1980); Percy Lubbock, ed., *The Diary of Arthur Christopher Benson* (London, 1926); F. McD. C. Turner, *A. C. Benson* (Cambridge, 1992).

p. 171 'Diaries of an old': On Drane, Deborah Cohen, *Household Gods: The British and Their Possessions* (New Haven and London, 2006), 145–69.

p. 171 enormous diary: Croft-Cooke, *Wild Hills*, 93.

p. 171 'If it is wrong': RBB, 8 July 1927, Diary 1925–8.

p. 171 'marked value': Richard Blake Brown, *The Apology of a Young Ex-Parson: Extracts from His Private Diary of Three Years in Anglican Orders* (London, 1932), 59, 67, 135, 172.

p. 171 'exhibitionism': *Sphere*, 21 May 1932, pasted into Richard Blake Brown's 1931–2 Diary [In a Rococo Room].

p. 172 'headlong' and 'a character': *Expository Times*; James L. Grant, *Socialist Review*, Summer Number, 1932, 1931/2 Diary.

p. 172 'secret life': Croft-Cooke, *Wild Hills*, 93.

p. 172 Self-sufficiency: A. J. A. Symons, *The Quest for Corvo* (London, 1940 [1934]), 11.

p. 172 'I would never': D5122, Diary entry for 4 December 1945, MOA.

p. 173 'I can't help': D5122, Diary entry for 14 March 1949, MOA.

p. 173 'going to the dogs': Geoffrey Cooke to Rupert Croft-Cooke, 10 November 1968, Croft-Cooke Collection.

p. 173 'fewer disadvantages': 'Rupert Croft-Cooke', *The Times*, 17 December 1979, 15.

p. 173 'How cross': RBB to RCC, 7 February 1962, Croft-Cooke Collection.

p. 173 'REAL tragedies': RBB to RCC, 11 September 1960 and 20 February 1963, Croft-Cooke Collection.

p. 174 'I have largely': RBB to RCC, 8 October 1965, Croft-Cooke Collection.

p. 174 'believe it or not': RBB to RCC, 19 February 1966, Croft-Cooke Collection.

p. 174 'more fragrant': RBB to RCC, 22 February 1966, Croft-Cooke Collection.

p. 174 'cards on the table': Sebastian Faulks, *The Fatal Englishman: Three Short Lives* (London, 1997 [1996]), 226.

p. 174 'moral nomad': Neal Ascherson, 'A Tale of Two Arrogant Eton Boys Who Tried Hard Not to Do Their Best', *Independent on Sunday*, 5 May 1996; Philip French, 'Bunnymooning', *London Review of Books*, 18:11, 6 June 1996, 19–20.

p. 174 'wear rather': Faulks, *Fatal*, 242.

p. 175 'I live': Hansard, *Parl. Deb.* (Lords), 28 October 1965, 682.

p. 176 'I do not': Lord Arran, 'The Sexual Offences Act: A Personal Memoir', *Encounter*, March 1972, 3.

p. 176 Arran himself: Paul Sudley [Sir Arthur Gore], *William, Or More Loved Than Loving* (London, 1933).

p. 176 'until by chance': Leo Abse, *Private Member* (London, 1973), 150.

p. 176 come to terms: Jeremy Wolfenden, 'A Sensitive Treatment', *The Isis*, 30 May 1956, 19. For a short profile, 'Jeremy Wolfenden', *The Isis*, 25 April 1956, 18.

6. Talking It Out

p. 181 'courageous': RBB, 30 July, Diary 1925–8; 12 July 1929, Diary 1929.

p. 181 'Ours is an age': Stephen Spender, 'Task of an Autobiographer', *Listener*, 14 September 1950, 350.

p. 182 'extreme intimacies': Trevor Allen, '"These "Revelations": Need Memoirs be Quite So Candid?', *Daily Mirror*, 17 January 1934, 10.

p. 182 'only to the inquisitive': 'On Privacy', *Saturday Review*, 2 February 1918, 91.

p. 183 'Nosey Parkers': Population (Statistics) Bill, Hansard, *Parl. Deb.* (Commons), 29 November 1937, 1717–1837.

p. 183 'It sounds': 'Women Say "No" to Nosey Parker', *Daily Express*, 3 December 1937, 7.

p. 183 The phalanx: Eliot Slater and Moya Woodside, *Patterns of Marriage: A Study of Marriage Relationships in the Urban Working Classes* (London, 1951), 24; Elizabeth Bott, *Family and Social Network: Roles, Norms, and External Relationships in Ordinary Urban Families*, 2nd edn (New York, 1971 [1957]), 84, 88, 96; Charles Madge, 'Private and Public Spaces', *Human Relations* 3 (1950), 187–99; Peter Willmott and Michael Young, *Family and Class in a London Suburb* (London, 1960), 31–2, 201–3. On the significance accorded marital privacy, Kate Fisher and Simon Szreter, *Sex before the Sexual Revolution: Intimate Life in England, 1918–1963* (Cambridge, 2010), 2–3, 53, 359–60, 386, 242–3. On interwar privacy more generally, Alison Light, *Forever England* (London, 1991).

p. 184 'trying to buy': 'Judge Says Wife Lied', *Daily Mirror*, 30 October 1935, 5; 'High Court of Justice', *The Times*, 30 October 1935, 4.

p. 184 only forty-five people and of the 34,500: *Apted v. Apted and Bliss*, Probate, Divorce and Admiralty Division [1930] P 246, 19 May 1930.

p. 184 Sixty years of press: Gail Savage, 'Erotic Stories and Public

Decency: Newspaper Reporting of Divorce Proceedings in England', *Historical Journal* 41:2 (1998), 511–28; Anne Humphreys, 'Coming Apart: The British Newspaper Press and the Divorce Court', in Laurel Brake, Bill Bell and David Finkelstein, eds., *Nineteenth-Century Media and the Construction of Identities* (Basingstoke, 2000), 220–31; Adrian Bingham, *Family Newspapers? Sex, Private Life and the British Popular Press, 1918–1978* (Oxford, 2009), 133–44.

p. 185 'in the poorest' and 'make a clean breast': *Apted v. Apted and Bliss*; 'High Court of Justice. Probate, Divorce and Admiralty Division, Discretion in Divorce and Obligations of Marriage', *The Times*, 17 May 1929, 5; 'High Court of Justice. Probate, Divorce and Admiralty Division, Discretion in Divorce: Principles Reviewed', *The Times*, 16 April 1930, 5; 'High Court of Justice. Probate, Divorce and Admiralty Division, Discretion in Divorce: Judgment Reserved', *The Times*, 17 April 1930, 5.

p. 186 Major Grigg: '£700 for His Wife – on Terms', *Daily Mirror*, 28 November 1939, 16.

p. 186 'tall, strong': 'Divorce Judge Speaks of "Scandalous Behaviour" of Husband and His Nurse-Companion', *Daily Express*, 11 December 1935, 9.

p. 187 Divorce petitions: Between 1930 and 1937, when A. P. Herbert's Matrimonial Causes Act of 1937 made divorce available to men or women showing 1) adultery, 2) three years' desertion, 3) cruelty, or 4) unsound mind, the number of divorces rose each year except for 1935 and 1937. In 1930 there were 3,563 divorces; in 1936, there were 5,146. 'Divorces: 1858–2003, Number of Couples Divorcing, By Party Petitioning/Granted Decree', Office for National Statistics, Dataset Na PVH41.

p. 187 'filthy': 'Mothers Who Like to See Sons Sinning', *Daily Mirror*, 22 July 1936, 1.

p. 188 'got the truth': *Blunt v. Blunt and Farrow; Blunt v. Blunt*, Court of Appeal [1942] 2 All ER 613, 6 November 1942.

p. 188 'He must approach': *Blunt v. Blunt and Farrow; Blunt v. Blunt*; 'Discretion in Divorce Suits; Court of Appeal's Right to Review', *The Times*, 7 November 1942, 2.

p. 189 'social considerations': *Blunt v. Blunt et e contra*, House of Lords [1943] AC 517, [1943] 2 All ER 76, 9 June 1943.

p. 189 'full and frank': For instance, 'Discretion in Cases of Divorce', *The Times*, 19 February 1953, 2; 'Court of Appeal, Divorce Appeal Fails, Discretion Refused, *Moor v. Moor*', *The Times*, 26 May 1954, 3; *Bull v. Bull* (Queen's Proctor Showing Cause), Probate, Divorce and Admiralty Division [1968] P 618, 21 December 1964; *Williams v. Williams and Harris*, Court of Appeal [1966] P 97, [1966] 2 All ER 614, [1966] 2 WLR 1248, 5 April 1966; 'High Court of Justice: Probate, Divorce and Admiralty, Discretion with Reluctance', *The Times*, 8 May 1964, 27.

p. 190 By 1965: The Law Commission, *Reform of the Grounds of Divorce: The Field of Choice: Report on a Reference Under Section 3(1)(e) of the Law Commissions Act 1965, Presented to Parliament by the Lord High Chancellor by Command of Her Majesty* (London, 1966), Cmnd 3123, 12.

p. 191 Once the world's: Bingham, *Family Newspapers*, 19; Hugh Cudlipp, *Publish and be Damned! The Astonishing Story of the Daily Mirror* (London, 1953); Chris Horrie, *Tabloid Nation: The Birth of the Daily Mirror to the Death of the Tabloid* (London, 2003).

p. 191 'lay psychologists': Cudlipp, *Publish*, 82.

p. 192 'I CONFESS': 'I Confess', *Daily Mirror*, 19 October 1936, 14.

p. 192 'good for the soul': Cudlipp, *Publish*, 67.

p. 192 'psychopathic': Hugh Cudlipp, *Walking on the Water* (London, 1976), 71.

p. 193 Readers' letters: Cudlipp, *Publish*, 122–3.

p. 193 According to Cudlipp: Cudlipp, *Publish*, 86.

p. 193 'English people': A. J. P. Taylor, *English History, 1914–1945* (Oxford, 1976 [1965]), 548–9.

p. 194 'the outcome': 'Dare She Tell Him the Child is Hers?', *Daily Mirror*, 9 March 1937, 14.

p. 194 'growing old': 'A Woman Confesses: "I Robbed My Father!"', *Daily Mirror*, 16 October 1936, 16.

p. 194 'crime': 'Where is My Daughter?', *Daily Mirror*, 14 October 1936, 12.

p. 194 'sin': Henry Harris, 'A Sin to Tell the Truth', *Daily Mirror*, 18 March 1937, 12.

p. 194 'woman who understands': Leonora Eyles, *The Ram Escapes: The Story of a Victorian Childhood* (London, 1953).

p. 195 You couldn't change: *Woman's Own*, 19 November 1932, 228; 29 October 1932, 120; and 20 January 1934, 460. Also Leonora Eyles, *Is Your Problem Here?* (London, 1947), 24–34.

p. 195 Pregnant girls: *Woman's Own*, 'In Trouble', 30 January 1942, 22.

p. 195 infertile: ibid., 'Afraid to Tell', 4 April 1936, 1016.

p. 195 'your own affair': ibid., 'No Real Danger', 4 February 1933, 592; ibid., 'No Point in Telling', 4 May 1934, 128; ibid., 'Forget the Past', 11 May 1935, 196; ibid., 'You Need Not Tell Him', 14 September 1935, 832; ibid., 'Should She Tell', 11 January 1936, 572; ibid., 16 January 1942, 22; ibid., 'In Fear', 6 February 1942, 22; ibid., 27 March 1942, 22.

p. 195 'very true': ibid., 'Forget It', 30 September 1933, 788.

p. 195 To the otherwise: ibid., 'Don't Tell Him', 23 April 1943, 22.

p. 196 'contrary to morals': Eyles, *Is Your Problem Here?*, 31.

p. 196 'This applicant': No. 682, 24 October 1951, GD386/6, NAS. All references to the Edinburgh Marriage Guidance Centre case files are to NAS. On Scottish marriage guidance, Ann Eyles, *Picking Up the Pieces: The Scottish Marriage Guidance Council, 1948–1988* (Edinburgh, 1988).

p. 197 'problem families': Tom Stephens, ed., *Problem Families: An Experiment in Social Rehabilitation* (Liverpool and Manchester, 1947); A. F. Philp and Noel Timms, *The Problem of 'The Problem Family'* (London, 1962); A. F. Philp and Douglas Woodhouse, *Family Failure: A Study of 129 Families with Multiple Problems* (London, 1963).

p. 197 signs of a moral breakdown: Janet Finch and Penny Summerfield, 'Social Reconstruction and the Emergence of Companionate Marriage', in David Clark, ed., *Marriage, Domestic Life and Social Change* (London and New York, 1991), 7–32; Jordanna Bailkin, 'The Postcolonial Family? West African Children, Private Fostering, and the British State', *Journal of Modern History* 81:1 (March 2009), 87–121; Nick Thomas, 'Will the Real 1950s Please Stand Up: Views of a Contradictory Decade', *Cultural and Social History* 5:2 (April 2008), 227–36; Pat Thane, 'Family Life and "Normality" in Postwar British Culture', in Richard Bessel and Dirk Schumann, eds., *Life After Death: Approaches to a Cultural and Social History of Europe during the*

1940s and 1950s (Cambridge, 2003), 193–210; Angela Davis, 'A Criti-
cal Perspective on British Social Surveys and Community Studies
and Their Accounts of Married Life *c.*1945–70', *Cultural and Social
History* 6:1 (January 2009), 47–64; Michael Peplar, *Family Matters: A
History of Ideas about Family since 1945* (London, 2002), 17–38; Chris
Harris, 'The Family in Post-War Britain', in James Obelkevich and
Peter Catterall, eds., *Understanding Post-War British Society* (London,
1994), 45–57; Claire Langhamer, 'Adultery in Post-war England',
History Workshop Journal 62 (2006), 86–115.

p. 197 It necessitated: Jane Lewis, David Clark and David H. J. Morgan,
'Whom God Hath Joined Together': The Work of Marriage Guidance
(London and New York, 1992), 44–88; Jane Lewis, 'Public Institution and Private Relationship: Marriage and Marriage Guidance,
1920–1968', *Twentieth-Century British History* 1:3 (1990), 233–63.

p. 198 perfect mutuality: Marcus Collins, *Modern Love: An Intimate History
of Men and Women in Twentieth-Century Britain* (London, 2003),
90–133; Claire Langhamer, 'Love and Courtship in Mid-Twentieth-
Century England', *Historical Journal* 50:1 (2007), 173–96; Fisher and
Szreter, *Sex*, 34–44, 196.

p. 198 Leonora Eyles: Eyles, *Is Your Problem*, 1.

p. 198 'Evelyn Home': Peggy Makins, *The Evelyn Home Story* (London,
1975), 184.

p. 198 'We know how': David Mace, 'What Britain is Doing', *Marriage and
Family Living* 10:1 (February 1948), 6.

p. 199 'racial end': 'Memorandum on the Work of the National Marriage
Guidance Council, 1948', Archives: Min. of Health, Beaumont St/
Chandos St, FWA etc., Tavistock Centre for Couple Relationships
[henceforth TCCR].

p. 199 'spirit of a crusade' and 'calling': Mace, 'What Britain', 6. Lewis,
Clark and Morgan, *Whom God*, 78; A. Herbert Gray, 'Looking
Backwards', *Marriage Guidance*, December 1949, 2.

p. 199 'morbidly': David Mace, *Marriage Counselling: The First Full Account of
the Remedial Work of the Marriage Guidance Councils* (London, 1948),
103–4. Also on the selection of counsellors, J. H. Wallis and H. S.
Booker, *Marriage Counselling: A Description and Analysis of the Remedial*

Work of the National Marriage Guidance Council (London, 1958); John H. Wallis, Training Officer, NMGC, April 1956, paper prepared for International Union of Family Organisations' Commission on Marriage Guidance, meetings in London on 25/26 May, 1956, Archives: Min. of Health, Beaumont St/Chandos St, FWA etc., TCCR.

p. 199 Edinburgh's: No. 3850 – 27 April 1961, GD386/16; No. 656 – 10 July 1951, GD386/5; No. 108, 3 July 1947, GD386/3.

p. 200 'I wondered how': No. 3852 – n.d. [April/May 1961], GD386/16.

p. 200 'bursting': No. 6751 – 3 November 1966, GD 386/33.

p. 200 'It is surprising': W. L. Herbert and F. V. Jarvis, *A Modern Approach to Marriage Counselling* (London, 1969 [1959]), 116.

p. 200 Although women: According to the Marriage Guidance Council's records for 1952–3, the women made the first approach 57–8 per cent of the time, NMGC Report, Not for Publication, July 1955, 55/74, 2, TIMP/TCCR Archive – Prof. Cohen's Box, TCCR.

p. 200 Sometimes it: No. 3828 – 18 April 1961, GD386/15.

p. 200 What to do: No. 3652 – 11 January 1961, GD386/12. The family's GP had advised against psychiatry, advising that the girl was far more disturbed by her mother's distress than her father's abuse. The counsellor had to tread carefully, as she disagreed but could not undermine the patient's faith in her own doctor.

p. 201 A woman who suspected: No. 602 – 20 March 1951, GD 386/4.

p. 201 'stop the "self-pity"': No. 1518 – 21 March 1956, GD386/7.

p. 201 The husband: No. 3759 – 18 March 1961, GD386/14. Severe violence (strangulation and beating to unconsciousness) they treated as a matter for the police. No. 4048 – 29 January 1962, GD386/20.

p. 201 'You find': Mace, *Marriage Counselling*, 9.

p. 201 The vast majority: National Marriage Guidance Council, paper prepared for the International Union of Family Organisations' Commission on Marriage Guidance, meetings in London on 25/26 May 1956, 'The Task Confronting the Marriage Counsellor', Min. of Health, Beaumont St/Chandos St, FWA etc., TCCR. On national statistics, Lewis, Clark and Morgan, *Whom God*, 100.

p. 202 'it is an enormous': Mace, *Marriage Counselling*, 66.

p. 202 'pleasure of making': ibid., 67.

p. 202 'fuss, embarrassment': J. H. Wallis, *Marriage Guidance: A New Introduction* (London, 1968), 131; J. H. Wallis, *Someone to Turn To: A Description of the Remedial Work of the National Marriage Guidance Council* (London, 1964 [1961]), 32–3, 37.

p. 203 Like Mrs Lawson: No. 1536 – 27 April 1956, GD386/7.

p. 203 'this was his': No. 1622 – 20 July 1956, GD386/9.

p. 203 'Perhaps the relief': No. 6544 – 16 June 1966, GD386/29.

p. 203 'talked on and on': No. 6811 – 13 December 1966, GD386/34.

p. 203 'open expression': No. 6302 – 5 January 1966, GD386/24.

p. 204 'lose face': Wallis, *Marriage Guidance*, 92.

p. 204 'human being': Paul Pengelly, 'Lily Pincus Remembered', *Tavistock Gazette: House Journal of the Tavistock Clinic* 8 (1982), TIMP/TCCR Archive; Lily Pincus, *Verloren-gewonnen: Mein Weg von Berlin nach London* (Stuttgart, 1980).

p. 205 'a quite exceptional': Pengelly, 'Lily Pincus Remembered'.

p. 205 'healthy': Enid Eichholz, 'A Description of the Development of the Family Discussion Bureaux', September 1950, Old MGE Welfare Cttee Box; Christopher Clulow, 'The Tavistock Institute of Marital Studies in Retrospect', and Douglas Woodhouse, 'The Tavistock Institute of Marital Studies: Evolution of a Marital Agency', in *Marriage: Disillusion and Hope: Papers Celebrating Forty Years of the Tavistock Institute of Marital Studies* (London, 1990), 13–22, 71–100.

p. 205 'I am sure': Mrs Pincus, 6 December 1957, 'Talk to Staff of the Tavistock Clinic and Institute', TCCR.

p. 205 'Family Discussion Bureau': 'Notes: The Institute of Marital Studies, Formerly the Family Discussion Bureau: The Development of a Non-Medical Path into Work with Marital and Related Family Problems', Archives: Min of Health, Beaumont St/ Chandos St, FWA etc., TCCR; Pincus, 'Talk to Staff of the Tavistock Clinic'.

p. 206 'help was needed': Lily Pincus, 'Talk for Family Planning Assn, 15 March 1955', TCCR.

p. 206 What people said: Pincus, 'Talk to FWA Admin. Council, December 1952', TCCR; 'An Essay in the Elucidation of the Methods of the Family Discussion Bureaux and the Assumptions on Which They are Based', April 1949, TIMP/TCCR archive – History of Clinic Book.

p. 206 'irrational unrecognized': Lily Pincus, talk to London Senior Probation Officers, 'Psychological Background to the Marriage Relationship', 19 November 1960, TCCR; *Institute for Marital Studies, The Marital Relationship as a Focus for Casework* (London, 1962).

p. 206 'most direct heir': Lily Pincus, 'Hendon Talk', 1957?, TCCR.

p. 207 Although John Bowlby: John Bowlby, 'The Study and Reduction of Group Tensions in the Family', *Human Relations* 2 (1949), 123–9.

p. 207 Digging up: Wallis, *Marriage Guidance*, 126–7. Meeting of the Family Discussion Bureau Advisory Panel, 10 February 1960 and 31 May 1961, Archives: Min. of Health, Beaumont St/Chandos St, FWA etc., TCCR.

p. 207 'Ultimately, their claim': 6 December 1957, talk given by Mrs Bannister to the Staff of the Tavistock Clinic and Institute, TCCR.

p. 207 'unsuited': Marriage Welfare Committee, FWA minutes, 16 October 1952, TCCR.

p. 207 300 referrals: 'Family Discussion Bureau', 'Overview', undated and unsigned, Tavistock MCC/HS/MH/23, LMA.

p. 207 Although treatment: 'Summary of Assessment of One Hundred Cases', 1955, and 'Nat. Marriage Guidance Council', May 1955, Bannister, TCCR.

p. 208 37 per cent: 'Tentative Draft of what seemed to Emerge from the Evening Meeting on January 11th, 1955, as a basis for discussion at the Marriage Welfare Committee Meeting on Wednesday, 2nd February, 1955', 4, TCCR.

p. 208 The lessening: Lily Pincus, ed., *Marriage: Studies in Emotional Conflict and Growth* (London, 1960), 83, 206.

p. 208 'In quite': 'Training. 1954. Early Draft for Book', Old MGE Welfare Cttee Box, TCCR.

p. 208 'mutual misperceptions': Kathleen Bannister and Lily Pincus, *Shared Phantasy in Marital Problems: Therapy in a Four-Person Relationship* (London, 1971), 5.

p. 208 'repressed parts': Pincus, *Marriage*, 57.

p. 208 'Marital problems': 'Notes on the Discussion with reference to the

Bureau's future relationship with the Health Services' n.d. [1959?], Ministry of Health folder, Archives: Min. of Health, Beaumont St/ Chandos St, FWA etc., TCCR.

p. 209 'cradle for secrets': Lily Pincus and Christopher Dare, *Secrets in the Family* (London, 1978), 123.

p. 209 'obligation': Michel Foucault, *The History of Sexuality: An Introduction*, vol. 1, trans. Robert Hurley (Harmondsworth, 1990 [1978]), 60, 72.

p. 209 Assizes trials: Patrick Higgins, *Heterosexual Dictatorship: Male Homosexuality in Postwar Britain* (London, 1996), 159–60, 168.

p. 210 Increasingly safeguarded: On limits placed upon press intrusion, including Clause 39 of the 1925 Criminal Justice Act (which banned photographs both inside courts and in their immediate vicinity) and the 1947 Lea ruling, Ryan Linkof, 'The Public Eye: Celebrity and Photojournalism in the Making of the British Tabloids, 1904–1938', PhD diss., University of Southern California, 2011, 323–400.

7. The Repressive Family

p. 212 'roughneck in argument': Noel Annan, *Our Age: Portrait of a Generation* (London, 1990), 259.

p. 212 'hair flying': Stephen Hugh-Jones, *Edmund Leach, 1910–1989. Memoir Prepared by Direction of the Council of King's College, Cambridge* (Cambridge, 1989), 24.

p. 212 In his first two: 'Now Man is Like a God', *Daily Express*, 13 November 1967, 11; 'Men with "The Power of Gods"', *The Times*, 13 November 1967, 2; 'Machines "Part of Men"', *The Times*, 20 November 1967, 10.

p. 212 London School: Ronald Fraser, ed., *1968: A Student Generation in Revolt: An International Oral History* (New York and London, 1988), 128–35; Nick Thomas, 'Challenging Myths of the 1960s: The Case of Student Protest in Britain', *Twentieth-Century British History* 13:3 (2002), 277–97; Chad Martin, 'Paradise Now: Youth Politics and the British Counterculture, 1958–1974', PhD diss., Stanford University, 2003.

p. 212 'soppy propaganda': Edmund Leach, *A Runaway World? The Reith Lectures 1967* (London, 1968), 42.

p. 213 'Far from being': ibid., 44

p. 213 This one sentence: On the Reith lectures, among many others, Angus Maude, 'Dr Leach's Instant New Jerusalem', *Spectator* 219:7277 (15 December 1967), 743; 'Against Leach, Letter by Mary Whitehouse', *Listener*, 7 December 1967, 755; Robert Pitman, 'In My Opinion', *Daily Express*, 29 November 1967, 8; Angus Calder, 'Anti-Gerontocrat', *New Statesman* new series 75 (10 May 1968), 617–18; Ronald Fletcher, *The Abolitionists: The Family and Marriage under Attack* (London, 1988), 1–9.

p. 213 'tawdry secrets': Leach, *Runaway World?*, 44–5.

p. 213 'I clapped': Margaret MacLean to Leach, 27 November 1967, ERL/6/1/156 Box 1, King's College Archive Centre, Cambridge.

p. 214 'They fuck you up': Loach's *Family Life* and Graef's *The Family* were shot in 1971 and screened the following year. Larkin, 'This be the Verse', *New Humanist*, August 1971.

p. 214 'curious cult': David Mace, 'What I Have Learned About Family Life', *The Family Coordinator* 23:2 (April 1974), 191.

p. 215 'he shrugged': Interview with Dr Laing, 16 June 1958, H57/TV/Box 1/B2766, LMA. All references to Tavistock case files are to records held at the LMA.

p. 215 Founded to treat: H. V. Dicks, *Fifty Years of the Tavistock Clinic* (London, 1970); Frank C. P. van der Horst, *John Bowlby – From Psychoanalysis to Ethology: Unravelling the Roots of Attachment Theory* (Oxford, 2011); W. R. Bion, *Experiences in Groups and Other Papers* (New York, 1961); Malcolm Pines, ed., *Bion and Group Psychotherapy* (London, 1985).

p. 215 'rediscovered': John Bowlby, 'The Rediscovery of the Family', November 1954, in *Rediscovery of the Family and Other Lectures: Sister Marie Hilda Memorial Lectures, 1954–1973* (Aberdeen, 1981), 3.

p. 215 'conditioned': Dicks, *Fifty*, 264.

p. 215 'red-hot': 14 May 1952 – Balint report, H57/TV/Box 1/A9514.

p. 215 For Laing: 'Kingsley Hall, transcript of tape recorded discussions between RD Laing, Sid Briskin, Leon Redler', Ms. Laing DT40 (1), Glasgow University Archive Services.

p. 216 'He does not see': 4 February 1958 – H57/TV/Box 2/B2190.

p. 216 'very warmly': H57/TV/Box 2/B1231.

p. 216 'anxiety neurosis': H57/TV/Box 4/B2220.

p. 216 'They are to blame': 2nd interview with Dr Gosling, 16 May 1957, H57/TV/Box 4/B2220.

p. 216 'she had never had': H57/TV/Box 22/B3083.

p. 217 According to Ronald Greene: Interview with Dr Gosling, 29 October 1956, H57/TV/B/01/007B1957.

p. 217 Most people left: This is true of intake forms from the 1950s, which are the ones represented in the LMA – see H57/TV/Box1/B2766.

p. 217 'stereotyped idealisation': Report of Dr Laing, 12 September 1957, H57/TV/Box 1/B2420; also see Mr Broeham's report of 20 November 1956, H57/TV/Box 1/B1990.

p. 217 The laboratory: Report of Dr Malan, 5 May 1954, H57/TV/Box2/B644.

p. 217 'nonsense': 4 February 1958, H57/TV/Box 2/B2062.

p. 217 'felt in desperate': H57/TV/Box22/B582.

p. 218 'tyrant': 10 April 1961, H57/TV/Box 2/B1231, LMA.

p. 218 That mothers: Michal Shapira, *The War Inside: Child Psychoanalysis and the Democratic Self in Britain, 1930–1960* (Cambridge, forthcoming); Mathew Thomson, *Psychological Subjects: Identity, Culture, and Health in Twentieth-Century Britain* (Oxford, 2006), 135–9; D. W. Winnicott, *The Child, the Family, and the Outside World* (London, 1964).

p. 218 'Nowadays': John and Elizabeth Newson, *Infant Care in an Urban Community* (London, 1963), 239. See also J. M. Mogey, *Family and Neighbourhood: Two Studies in Oxford* (Oxford, 1956), 50–76.

p. 218 'influence accorded': Exceptions include progressive educationalists such as A. S. Neill and Dora Russell – convinced that children ought to 'grow up untrammelled by the damaging influences of the parents'. James Drawbell, *A Gallery of Women* (London, 1933), 41.

p. 219 Angry Young Men's: Tom Maschler, ed., *Declaration* (New York, 1958). Exception is 137.

p. 219 For her entire: Adrian Laing, *R. D. Laing: A Life* (Thrupp,

2006 [1994]), 5–6; Bob Mullan, *Mad to be Normal* (London, 1995), 12–84.

p. 220 'darker skeletons': Quoting Clancy Sigal, John Clay, *R. D. Laing: A Divided Self: A Biography* (London, 1996), 12; also R. D. Laing, *Wisdom, Madness and Folly: The Making of a Psychiatrist* (New York, 1985), 47, 55.

p. 220 'contribution': Prof. O. L. Zangwill, 'Review of R.D. Laing's *Divided Self*', *Times Literary Supplement*, 9 December 1960, 801.

p. 220 'forces of outrageous': Published as R. D. Laing, 'Violence and Love', *Journal of Existentialism* 5:20 (1965), 417–22.

p. 221 'intelligible': R. D. Laing and Aaron Esterson, *Sanity, Madness and the Family: Families of Schizophrenics,* 2nd edn (London, 1970 [1964]), 16; Aaron Esterson, *The Leaves of Spring: Schizophrenia, Family and Sacrifice* (London, 1972 [1970]); Daniel Burston, *The Wing of Madness: The Life and Work of R. D. Laing* (Cambridge, Mass., 1996), 70–75.

p. 221 'Mrs Church tended': Laing and Esterson, *Sanity*, 83.

p. 221 'What Mrs Church': ibid., 73.

p. 222 'closed system': ibid., 213.

p. 222 'genuine privacy': R. D. Laing, *The Divided Self: An Existential Study in Sanity and Madness* (London, 1960), 38.

p. 222 'protection': Laing and Esterson, *Sanity*, 109–14.

p. 222 'scapegoated': Adrian Laing, *Laing*, 132–3.

p. 222 'was very largely': *Psychiatry and Violence*, Peter Robinson Productions, 1970.

p. 223 'extraordinary': Anthony W. Clare, 'Laing Returns to the Fold', *Spectator* 230:7545 (3 February 1973), 148; Nick Crossley, *Contesting Psychiatry: Social Movements in Mental Health* (New York, 2006), 112–25.

p. 223 Many of the horns: Stephen Coates, 'Rebels in Christendom', *Listener*, 31 May 1962, 935–7; Hannah Gavron, *The Captive Wife: Conflicts of Housebound Mothers* (London, 1966); E. M. Goldberg, *Family Influences and Psychosomatic Illness* (London, 1958); Colin Rosser and Christopher Harris, *The Family and Social Change: A Study of Family and Kinship in a South Wales Town* (London, 1965), 20–32; Peter Lomas, ed., *The Predicament of the Family: A Psycho-Analytical Symposium*

(London, 1967), 16, 18; Paul Halmos, *Solitude and Privacy: A Study of Social Isolation, Its Causes and Therapy* (New York, 1969 [1953]).

p. 223 It was not just teenagers: Ministry of Education, *The Youth Service in England and Wales* (London, 1960); Dominic Sandbrook, *Never Had It So Good: A History of Britain from Suez to the Beatles* (London, 2005), 408–26; Mark Donnelly, *Sixties Britain* (Harlow, 2005), 1–14, 116–30.

p. 223 'surprisingly without': Raymond Firth, Jane Hubert and Anthony Forge, *Families and Their Relatives: Kinship in a Middle-Class Sector of London* (London, 1969), 458.

p. 223 'superficial harmony': ibid., 400, 404.

p. 223 'emotionally sticky': ibid., 458.

p. 223 'commonest': ibid., 13, 400, 403.

p. 223 The sociological studies: Peter Willmott and Michael Young, *Family and Class in a London Suburb* (London, 1960), 28–35; Josephine Klein, *Samples from English Cultures*, vol. 1 (London, 1965), 377.

p. 224 'I could never': Newson, *Infant Care*, 229.

p. 224 'generation gap': On the generation gap, Catherine Ellis, 'The Younger Generation: The Labour Party and the 1959 Youth Commission', *Journal of British Studies* 41:2 (April 2002), 199–231; Lawrence Black, 'The Lost World of Young Conservatism', *Historical Journal* 51:4 (December 2008), 991–1024; Jonathon Green, *All Dressed Up: The Sixties and the Counterculture* (London, 1999); Sandbrook, *Never Had It*, 407–13, 425–6; Dominic Sandbrook, *White Heat, A History of Britain in the Swinging Sixties, 1964–70* (London, 2006), 198–200, 441–2, 537–45.

p. 224 'Most of all': Letter to Leach, 7 May 1968, ERL/6/1/156 Box 1.

p. 224 'what is outside': Letter to Leach, 26 November 1967, ERL/6/1/156 Box 1.

p. 224 Mothers of four: Letters to Leach, 27 November 1967 and 28 November 1967, both ERL/6/1/156 Box 1.

p. 224 'magnetic voice': RBB to Leach, 27 November 1967, 2 December 1967 and 17 December 1967, ERL/6/1/156 Box 1.

p. 225 'only child': Letter to Leach, 27 November 1967, ERL/6/1/156 Box 1.

p. 225 'We are dying': Letter to Leach, 27 November 1967, ERL/6/1/156 Box 3.

p. 225 'Do not talk': 'A Mother' to Sir, 27 November 1967, ERL/6/1/156 Box 3.

p. 225 'behind the comfortable': Irving Wardle, 'Calculated Study of Emotional Waste', *The Times*, 13 May 1970, 16.

p. 225 'dangers of enclosed': Alan Blyth, 'Dangers of an Enclosed Family', *The Times*, 13 November 1968, 8. Among the plays, David Storey's oeuvre, especially *In Celebration*, John Hopkins's *Find Your Way Home*; Peter Nichols's *The Gorge* and Roy Minton's *Sometime Never*.

p. 226 'angelic children': Hansard, *Parl. Deb.* (Lords), 3 March 1975, 1142.

p. 226 'Is the family': Advertisement, 'Next Week: The Authentic RD Laing?', *New Statesman* 84:2178 (15 December 1972), 917.

p. 226 'anti-family': Quoted in Clare, 'Laing', *Spectator*, 149.

p. 226 'age of relatives': David Cooper, *The Death of the Family* (Harmondsworth, 1974 [1971]), 151.

p. 226 'Middle-class notions': Tony Palmer, 'Unholy Family', *Spectator* 228:7488 (1 January 1972), 18. *The Times*' reviewer was more sceptical – 'A Death in the Family', *The Times*, 14 January 1972, 8.

p. 227 'outlived': Frederick H. Stone, 'Challenge of Parenthood', November 1973, in *Rediscovery of the Family*, 98–9, 100.

p. 227 'legitimate attack': Philip Graham, 'Nuclear Disaster', *New Statesman*, 11 June 1971, 811; also 'Family Failure', *The Scotsman*, 26 June 1971; Geoffrey Hawthorn, 'Vicious Paradox', *New Society*, 27 May 1971, 924–5; Martin Fagg, 'Generation Gap', *Church Times*, 11 June 1971; Edmund Leach, 'The Millennium', *Listener*, 17 June 1971, 770; Nigel Dennis, 'Relatively Speaking', *Sunday Telegraph*, 30 May 1971; 'The Giddy Limit', *Times Literary Supplement*, 6 August 1971; Charles Rycroft, 'Noes, Noses, Nonsense', *Guardian*, 27 May 1971. For positive reviews, *Time Out*, 18–24 June 1971, 20, and David Hart, 'The Family as a Frightened Group', *The Teacher*, 24 September 1971, Death of the Family File, Penguin Archive, Special Collections, Bristol University Library.

p. 227 Cooper, like Laing: See, for instance, Fred Halliday – C896/01; David Triesman – C896/05; Ronald Fraser interviews, '1968 – A Student Generation in Revolt', C896 Sound Archive, BL; Fraser, ed., *1968*, 69; David Martin, 'R. D. Laing' in Maurice Cranston, ed. *The New Left* (London, 1970), 179–208; Juliet Mitchell, *Psychoanalysis and Feminism* (New York, 1974), xv–xix, 277–9; Anthony Clare, *In the Psychiatrist's Chair* (London, 1992), 113; Frank Musgrove, *Ecstasy and Holiness: Counter Culture and the Open Society* (London, 1974), 32–4.

p. 227 In 1972: B. Jane Elliott, 'Demographic Trends in Domestic Life, 1945–87', in David Clark, ed., *Marriage, Domestic Life and Social Change: Writings for Jacqueline Burgoyne (1944–88)* (London and New York, 1991), 92–3; David Coleman, 'Population and Family', in A. H. Halsey with Josephine Webb, eds., *Twentieth-Century British Social Trends* (Basingstoke, 2000), 55–65; Dominic Sandbrook, *State of Emergency: The Way We Were, Britain, 1970–1974* (London, 2010), 436–9.

p. 227 'Marriage': Rosemary Cornford, 'Family Life and Politics of Morals: The Real Test', *The Times*, 3 August 1970, 7.

p. 227 'there is a renunciation': Juliet Mitchell, *Woman's Estate* (New York, 1971), 140.

p. 227 After 1972: Coleman, 'Population and Family', 58.

p. 228 'little democracies': O. R. McGregor, *Evening Standard*, 29 March 1968, 11. Writing after the first clause in the Divorce Law Reform Bill was approved by Parliament, McGregor was applauding the notion of 'moral freedom' as opposed to the sanctions (religious as well as legal and social) that used to be thought necessary to undergird family life.

p. 228 'Oh, I don't': RRB to Leach, 2 December 1967, ERL/6/1/156 Box 1.

p. 229 'How many': 'Gay Liberation Front Manifesto', London 1971, 2, HCA/CHE12/15, LSE.

p. 229 'rich as it': Mitchell, *Woman's*, 166; Mitchell, *Psychoanalysis*, 282–92.

p. 229 'what had happened to us': Michelene Wandor, 'The Small Group' in Wandor, ed., *The Body Politic: Writings from the Women's Liberation Movement in Britain, 1969–1972* (London, 1972), 109.

p. 230 'family and relations': Bristol Groups, 'The Oppression of Women in the 1970s', Papers Presented at the Women's National Co-ordinating Committee Conference Held 15–17 October 1971, McIntosh 1/2, LSE.

p. 230 'Other groups': Jan Williams, Hazel Twort and Ann Bachelli, 'Women and the Family', in Michelene Wandor, ed., *Once a Feminist: Stories of a Generation* (London, 1990), 227; Bristol Groups, 'The Oppression'.

p. 230 Families: Don Milligan, 'The Politics of Homosexuality', 1973, 3, GD467/2/1/7, NAS. On GLF, Jeffrey Weeks, *Coming Out: Homosexual Politics in Britain from the Nineteenth Century to the Present* (London, 1983 [1977]), 185–237.

p. 230 It was in the family: Jack Babuscio, *We Speak for Ourselves: Experiences in Homosexual Counselling* (London, 1976), 96.

p. 230 'tolerance': Scottish Homosexual Rights Group, 'The Right to Live as We Choose', 11/1978, GD467/2/1/7, NAS; Stephen Etherington, 'Inside Viewpoint', HCA/AT, 18/7, LSE.

p. 230 'For the homosexual': 'Gay Liberation Front Manifesto', London, 1971; 'Psychiatry and the Homosexual: A Brief Analysis of Oppression', Gay Liberation pamphlet no. 1, HCA/CHE/12/15, LSE.

p. 230 'extreme, violent': Michelene Wandor, 'Family everafter', *Spare Rib*, November 1972, 13.

p. 230 When the Wolfenden: Weeks, *Coming Out*, 165–78; Stuart Hall, 'Reformism and the Legislation of Consent', in *Permissiveness and Control: The Fate of the Sixties Legislation*, ed. National Deviancy Conference (London, 1980), 12–21; John Wolfenden, *Turning Points: The Memoirs of Lord Wolfenden* (London, 1976), 146.

p. 231 'discreet, secretive' and 'speaking the unspoken': Scottish Minorities Group, 'The Case for Homosexual Law Reform in Scotland', n.d. GD 467/2/1/7, NAS.

p. 231 Untangling the skeins: Indebted to radical psychiatry's emphasis upon healing and empowerment through community (Laing and Cooper, alongside Wilhelm Reich and Herbert Marcuse, were staples on liberation reading lists), British consciousness-raising was on the whole more psychologically inclined than its American cousin. Whereas in the United States liberationists shunned Freud as part and parcel of an oppressive status quo, their British counterparts – who lived in a country in which psychoanalysis could, as late as 1970, be viewed as an exotic foreign import – found it potentially useful. Thomson, *Psychological Subjects*, 278–87, 293; Mitchell, *Woman's*, 62; 'Why Marxism', *Gay Left* 5 (Winter 1977), 2–5.

p. 231 'we circled': Jill Robin, 'Another Point of View', *Enough: Journal of Bristol Women's Liberation Group*, 7LIM/1/04: Pamphlets, Women's Library; Sue Bruley, 'Women Awake: The Experience of Consciousness-Raising', April 1976; Carole Brasset, 'Bristol Women's Liberation Group: Consciousness-Raising Group', 1972, Papers for the Manchester Women's Liberation Conference, McIntosh 1/4, LSE.

p. 231 'self-oppression': R. Kincaid, 'Coming Out Politically', *Gay Left* 1 (Autumn 1975), 10.

p. 232 'cardinal rule': Jill Tweedie, 'Beaten Up Women and Their Children', *Spare Rib*, June 1973, 12.

p. 232 'Individual – small': Mitchell, *Woman's*, 63.

p. 232 From the vantage point: Sheila Rowbowtham, *The Past is before Us: Feminism in Action since the 1960s* (London, 1989), 17; Anna Coote and Beatrix Campbell, *Sweet Freedom: The Struggle for Women's Liberation* (London, 1987 [1982]), 88; David Fernbach and Simon Watney, 'Two Letters on Freud', *Gay Left* 7 (Winter 1978/9), 23.

p. 232 Given how many: Derek Jarman, *At Your Own Risk: A Saint's Testament*, ed. Michael Christie (Woodstock, NY, 1993), 36.

p. 232 'one thing to know': Jonathan Blake (1949–), C456/104/01-05, Hall-Carpenter, BL.

p. 233 'gloomy': Emmanuel Cooper, 'CHE in Close-Up', *Gay Left* 1 (Autumn 1975), 12; 'Fuck the Family', n.d., 7LIM/1/04: Pamphlets, Women's Library.

p. 233 'proto-feminist': Juliet Mitchell and Audrey Wise in *Once a Feminist*, 108, 205; Sheila Rowbotham, *Promise of a Dream: Remembering the Sixties* (London, 2000), 102.

p. 233 'we were absolutely': Catherine Hall in *Once a Feminist*, 177; Eve Setch, 'The Face of Metropolitan Feminism: The London Women's Liberation Workshop, 1969–79', *Twentieth-Century British History* 13:2 (2002).

p. 233 The irony: Coote and Campbell, *Sweet*, 88. The alternative, as Michèle Barrett and Mary McIntosh saw it, was to make the family less necessary. *The Anti-Social Family* (London, 1982), 132–3; Jane Lewis, *The End of Marriage? Individualism and Intimate Relations* (Northampton, Mass., 2001).

p. 233 'Couples living': Juliet Mitchell, 'Women: The Longest Revolution', *New Left Review*, 1966, reprinted in Mitchell, *Women: The Longest Revolution. Essays in Feminism, Literature and Psychoanalysis* (London, 1984), 54.

p. 234 The ravages: Carol Smart, *Personal Life: New Directions in Sociological Thinking* (Cambridge, 2007), 6–52; Jacqui Gabb, *Researching Intimacy in Families* (Basingstoke, 2010 [2008]), 15–17, 70–81; Alison Park et al., *British Social Attitudes: Public Policy, Social Ties: The 18th Report* (Aldershot, 2002); Central Statistical Office, *Social Trends 1994* (London, 1994).

p. 234 170 refuges: Coote and Campbell, *Sweet*, 37.

p. 234 In 1977, 'Switchboard', *Gay Left* 6 (Summer 1978), 28.

p. 235 'The result is likely': Committee on Privacy (Younger Report; Cmnd 5012, 1972), 33.

p. 235 Asked to define: Committee on Privacy, 234.

p. 235 'leading your life': A definition of privacy that the Committee did not initially contemplate when it commissioned the survey. Committee on Privacy, 'Research into Public Attitudes on Privacy, Brief for the Organisation Conducting the Research', Part A, HO 411/8, Office for National Statistics Library.

p. 236 Younger people: Committee on Privacy, 241.

p. 236 'This means an end': Cooper, *Death*, 48.

p. 237 Houghton Committee: Home Office, Scottish Education Department, *Report of the Departmental Committee on the Adoption of Children, 1971–2*, Cmnd 5107, 85–6; Jane Lewis, 'Adoption: The Nature of Policy Shifts in England and Wales, 1972–2002', *International Journal of Law, Policy and the Family* 18: 2 (2004), 235–55.

p. 237 'disastrous': Hansard, *Parl. Deb.* (Lords), 20 June 1975.

p. 237 'should not she': Mrs Winifred Ewing (Moray and Nairn), Counselling in Scotland for Adopted Person Seeking Information about His Birth, Hansard, *Parl. Deb.* (Commons), 28 October 1975, 1369.

p. 237 According to one survey: Annette Lawson, *Adultery: An Analysis of Love and Betrayal* (Oxford and New York, 1988), 232.

p. 237 Where it had formerly: Pat Jalland, *Death in War and Peace: A History of Loss and Grief in England, 1914–1970* (Oxford, 2010), 190–94, 217, 250–51.

p. 238 'euphoric myth': Cooper, *Death*, 48.

p. 238 When R. D. Laing's: Adrian Laing, *Laing*, 180–81, 193.

p. 238 'which doesn't allow': Lawson, *Adultery*, 253.

p. 238 'the telling': Law: 2:13, Special Collections – Lawson, ESDS Qualidata, UK Data Archive, University of Essex.

p. 238 That was what: James Murray, 'Meet the Family', *Daily Express*, 9 March 1974, 8. On *The Family*, Su Holmes, '*The Family* and Reality TV', in Julie Anne Taddeo and Ken Dvorak, eds., *The Tube Has Spoken: Reality TV and History* (Lexington, 2010), 98–122; Margaret Wilkins, with Sue Freeman, *Family Affair* (London, 1975). *The Family* was modelled on the American series *An American Family*, which aired in 1973.

p. 239 between seven and ten million: Colin Young, '"The Family"', *Sight and Sound* 43:4 (Autumn 1974), 206.

p. 239 'If we helped': James Murray, 'Now a Few More Home Truths about "The Family"', *Daily Express*, 12 October 1974, 14.

p. 239 'platform': James Thomas, 'Meet the Family', *Daily Express*, 9 March 1974, 8.

p. 239 Many of the show's critics: Young, 'The Family', 208–9; Dennis Potter, 'Back to Nature', *New Statesman,* new series, 88: 2274 (18 October 1974), 549–50; Philip Purser, 'Approximately Themselves?', *Sight and Sound* 44:1 (Winter 1974/5), 48–9.

p. 239 That was a point: Paul Revoir, 'The *Family*'s Margaret Wilkins, "First Lady" of Reality TV, is Dead', *Daily Mail* Online, 19 August 2008.

p. 240 Although a significant minority: Peggy Makins, Report on 'Contact', n.d. [1970s], R6/222/3, BBC Written Archives Centre.

p. 240 'other people': Revoir, '*Family*'s'.

Epilogue: Genealogy and Confessional Culture

p. 241 It was a good moment: Peter Bazalgette, 'Smallscreen', *Prospect Magazine* 175 (22 September 2010).

p. 241 Steeped: Interview with Alex Graham, CEO, Wall to Wall Media, London, 5 December 2011.

p. 241 five to six million: Paul Kalina, 'You're Not Always Who You Think You Are', *The Age* (Melbourne), 22 March 2007, 20; Anne-Marie Kramer, 'Mediatizing Memory: History, Affect and Identity in *Who Do You Think You Are?*', *European Journal of Cultural Studies* 14:4 (2011), 428–45.

p. 242 More than a third: Catherine Jones, 'Be Prepared for the Family Secrets You May Uncover, Genealogists Warn', *Western Mail*, 15 September 2007, 16.

p. 242 One in six: 'Secrets in the Family Closet for 1 in 6 Britons', *Daily Telegraph*, 13 September 2007, http://www.telegraph.co.uk/news/uknews/1563004/Secrets-in-the-family-closet-for-1-in-6-Britons.html.

p. 242 'Who knows': Free 14-Day Trial for Ancestry.co.uk, http://landing.ancestry.co.uk/offers/uk/trial/trial.aspx.

p. 242 If you cannot: H2637, Reply to Summer 2008, Pt 1 Directive (Doing Family History Research), MOA.

p. 242 'which turn out to be hilarious': H1703, Reply to Summer 2008 Directive, Pt 1 (Doing Family History Research), MOA.

p. 242 An enthusiasm: Twenty-five Family History Societies were founded between 1973 and 1975 alone. *Berkshire Family History Society* 1: 1 (October 1975), 7. On the relative lack of interest in genealogy among middle-class north Londoners in the early 1960s, see Firth et al., *Families and Their Relatives,* 119–32.

p. 242 *Roots*: Interview with Else Churchill, Society of Genealogists, 7 December 2011.

p. 242 'principal concern': 'Our Members', *The Family History Journal of the South East Hampshire Genealogical Society* 1 (1974), 3, 4.

p. 243 They underscored: 'A Few Anecdotes', *Berkshire Family History Society* 1:1 (October 1975), 7; D. A. Palgrave, 'Why Indulge in

Genealogical Research', *Norfolk & Norwich Genealogical Society* 5 (April 1974), 75–6; J. G. Shenton, 'Acquiring Family Heirlooms', reprinted from the *Cheshire Family Historian* in *The Family History Journal of the South East Hampshire Genealogical Society* 3:1 (May 1976), 5.

p. 243 'commendable aim': Alwyn James, 'There was an Englishman, a Scotsman, a Welshman and an Irishman', *The Journal of the Hereford-shire Family History Society* 1:12 (Winter 1983), 275.

p. 243 'whet the appetites': R. E. Hooker, 'Noble Ancestry', *The Family History Journal of the South East Hampshire Genealogical Society* 2:3 (November 1975), 39.

p. 243 'I wanted': Jackie Brown, 'How I Discovered My Family Secrets', *The Express*, 14 October 2004, 52.

p. 244 'like a jigsaw': Interview with Daniel H. Jones, VP, Content Strategy & Acquisition, ancestry.co.uk, 16 December 2011.

p. 244 'We are who': A1706, Reply to Summer 2008 Directive, Pt 1 (Doing Family History Research), MOA.

p. 244 Narcissistic Nineties: Boyd Tonkin, 'English Roads to Hell – and Paradise', *Independent*, 2 February 2002, 10.

p. 244 'too American': Julia Vellacott files, 'Psychology Rejects', 1978, Penguin Archive.

p. 244 When Marje Proops: Angela Patmore, *Marje: The Guilt and the Gingerbread* (London, 1993).

p. 245 Ties to extended kin: Colin Bell, *Middle Class Families: Social and Geographical Mobility* (London, 1968), 68–126; Jane Hubert, 'Kinship and Geographical Mobility in a Sample from a London Middle-Class Area', *International Journal of Comparative Sociology* 6:1 (March 1965), 61–80; Barrie Stacey, 'Some Psychological Aspects of Inter-Generational Mobility', *Human Relations* 20:1 (February 1967), 3–12.

p. 246 For many: See, for example, B690, B1254, A773, B1028, C110, D157, A1323, A855, B1215, Relatives, Friends, Neighbours – Replies to Winter Directive, 1984, MOA; Mike Savage, *Identities and Social Change in Britain since 1940* (Oxford, 2010), 46–7, 184.

p. 246 'more relaxed': B1215, Reply to Winter Directive, 1984 (Relatives, Friends, Neighbours), Women Box, MOA.

p. 246 chopping the dead: A773, Reply to Winter Directive, 1984 (Relatives, Friends, Neighbours), Men Box, MOA. This participant does not permit direct quotation from his response.

p. 246 'Family is anything': C1191, Reply to Autumn 2000 Directive (Gays and Lesbians in the Family), MOA.

p. 246 'blip of nastiness': M1201, Reply to Summer 2008 Directive, Pt 1 (Doing Family History Research), MOA.

p. 248 'one of the things': H4235, also B3227, Replies to Summer 2008 Directive, Pt 1 (Doing Family History Research), MOA.

p. 249 'were the nuggets': B1654, Reply to Summer 2008 Directive, Pt 1 (Doing Family History Research), MOA.

p. 252 'People have really gotten': Mark Zuckerberg, interview with Michael Arrington, TechCrunch, 8 January 2010, http://www.youtube.com/watch?v=Z6TpmMdvSPM.

p. 252 The era of privacy: Of which the most recent is Lori Andrews, *I Know Who You are and I Saw What You Did* (New York, 2012). Zuckerberg's interview with Arrington (see note above) is frequently misquoted to this effect.

p. 253 the propriety of publishing: Ackerley to David Higham, 19 February 1964, in Neville Braybrooke, ed., *The Letters of J. R. Ackerley* (London, 1975), 246.

p. 253 Of my father': J. R. Ackerley, *My Father and Myself* (New York, 1999 [1968]), 268.

Select Bibliography

Archives

Beinecke Rare Book and Manuscript Library, Yale University
British Library (BL) (Department of Manuscripts; Asia, Pacific and
    Africa Collections (APAC); and Sound Archive)
Croydon Local Studies Library and Archives Service (CAS)
Croydon Council – Fostering and Adoption Service (CC)
ESDS Qualidata, UK Data Archive, University of Essex
Glasgow University Archive Services
Harry Ransom Center, University of Texas
King's College Archive Centre, Cambridge University
Langdon Down Museum of Learning Disability
London Metropolitan Archives (LMA)
London School of Economics Archives
Mass Observation Archive, University of Sussex (MOA)
National Archives of Scotland (NAS)
National Archives of the United Kingdom (TNA)
National Library of Scotland
Open University Archive
Rare and Manuscript Collections, Carl A . Kroch Library, Cornell University
Special Collections, Bristol University Library
Tavistock Centre for Couple Relationships Archive (TCCR)
Washington State University Libraries
Wellcome Library
The Women's Library

Official publications

Child Adoption Committee – First Report, 1924–5. Cmd 2401

Child Adoption Committee – Second Report, 1924–5. Cmd 2469

Child Adoption Committee – Third and Final Report (Tomlin Committee), 1926. Cmd 2711

Final Report of the Committee on Procedure in Matrimonial Causes, 1947. Cmd 7024

Law Commission. *The Reform of the Grounds of Divorce*, 1966. Cmnd 3123

Marriage Matters: Consultative Document by the Working Party on Marriage Guidance Set Up by the Home Office in Consultation with the DHSS. London, HMSO, 1979

Mental Deficiency Act 1913: Suggestions and Plans Relating to the Arrangements of Institutions for Defectives. London: Board of Control, 1919

Minutes of Evidence Taken before the Royal Commission on Divorce and Matrimonial Causes, 1912, I (Cd 6479), II (Cd 6480), III (Cd 6481)

Report of the Committee of Inquiry into Normansfield Hospital, Presented to Parliament by the Secretary of State for Social Services by Command of Her Majesty. London: HMSO, 1978. Cmnd 7357

Report of the Committee on Child Adoption (Hopkinson Committee), 1921. Cmd 1254

Report of the Committee on Homosexual Offences and Prostitution (Wolfenden Committee), 1957. Cmnd 247

Report of the Committee on One-Parent Families (Finer Committee), 1974. Cmnd 5629

Report of the Committee on Privacy (Younger Committee), 1972. Cmnd 5012

Report of the Departmental Committee on Adoption Societies and Agencies (Horsbrugh Committee), 1936–7. Cmd 5499

Report of the Departmental Committee on Grants for the Development of Marriage Guidance, 1948. Cmd 7566

Report of the Departmental Committee on the Adoption of Children (Houghton Report), 1971–2. Cmnd 5107

Report of the Interdepartmental Committee on Mental Deficiency (Wood Report), 1925–9. Cmnd 3545

Report of the Royal Commission on Divorce and Matrimonial Causes, 1912. Cmnd 6478

*Report of the Royal Commission on the Law Relating to Mental Illness and Mental
          Deficiency*, 1954–7. Cmnd 169

Report of the Royal Commission on Marriage and Divorce, 1956. Cmd 9678

Royal Commission on the Care and Control of the Feeble-minded (Cd 4215–4221,
          i–vii; *Report*, Cd 4202, viii, 1908)

                            Primary sources

Abse, Leo, *Private Member*, London: Macdonald, 1973

Ackerley, J. R., *My Father and Myself*, New York: New York Review of
          Books, 1999 [1968]

Addis, Robina S., Francesca Salzberger and Elizabeth Rabl, *A Survey Based
          on Adoption Case Records*, London: National Association for Mental
          Health, 1955

Anderson, Digby, and Graham Dawson, eds., *Family Portraits*, London:
          Social Affairs Unit, 1986

Annan, Noel, *Our Age: Portrait of a Generation*, London: Weidenfeld and
          Nicolson, 1990

Askham, Janet, *Identity and Stability in Marriage*, Cambridge: Cambridge
          University Press, 1984

Auden, W. H., *Juvenilia: Poems, 1922–1928*, ed. Katherine Bucknell, London:
          Faber and Faber, 1994

Babuscio, Jack, *We Speak for Ourselves: Experiences in Homosexual Counselling*,
          London: SPCK, 1976

Baird, Julia, *Imagine This: Growing Up with My Brother, John Lennon*, London:
          Hodder and Stoughton, 2007

Bannister, Kathleen, and Lily Pincus, *Shared Phantasy in Marital Problems:
          Therapy in a Four-Person Relationship*, London: Institute of Marital
          Studies, 1971

Barrett, Michèle, and Mary McIntosh, *The Anti-Social Family*, London:
          NLB, 1982

Bayley, Michael, *Mental Handicap and Community Care*, London: Routledge
          and Kegan Paul, 1973

Bell, Colin, *Middle Class Families: Social and Geographical Mobility*, London:
          Routledge and Kegan Paul, 1968

Benson, E. F., *Final Edition: Informal Autobiography*, London: Hogarth Press, 1987

Berg, Charles, and Clifford Allen, *The Problem of Homosexuality*, New York: Citadel Press, 1958

Bion, W. R., *Experiences in Groups and Other Papers*, New York: Tavistock Publications, 1961

Blacker, C. P., ed., *Problem Families: Five Inquiries*, London: Eugenics Society, 1952

Blunt, Wilfrid, *Married to a Single Life*, London: Russell, 1983

Bone, Margaret, Bernie Spain and F. M. Martin, *Plans and Provisions for the Mentally Handicapped*, London: Allen and Unwin, 1972

Bott, Elizabeth, *Family and Social Network: Roles, Norms, and External Relationships in Ordinary Urban Families*, 2nd edn, New York: Tavistock Publications, 1971 [1957]

Bowlby, John, *Child Care and the Growth of Love*, London: Penguin Books, 1955

Bowlby, John, et al., *Rediscovery of the Family and Other Lectures: Sister Marie Hilda Memorial Lectures, 1954–73*, Aberdeen: Aberdeen University Press, 1981

Braddon, Mary Eliza, *Aurora Floyd,* London: Tinsley Bros.,1863

Brown, Richard Blake, *The Apology of a Young Ex-Parson: Extracts from His Private Diary of Three Years in Anglican Orders*, London: Duckworth, 1932

Burke, Bernard, *A Visitation of the Seats and Arms of the Noblemen and Gentlemen of Great Britain and Ireland*, London: Hurst and Blackett, 1855

Chesser, Eustace, *Live and Let Live: The Moral of the Wolfenden Report*, London: Heinemann, 1958

—, *Love and Marriage*, rev. edn, London: Pan Books, 1963 [1957]

Clare, Anthony, *In the Psychiatrist's Chair*, London: Chatto and Windus, 1992

—, *In the Psychiatrist's Chair II*, London: William Heinemann, 1995

Coates, Doris, *Tunes on a Penny Whistle: A Derbyshire Childhood*, Stroud: Alan Sutton, 1993

Cockburn, Alexander, and Robin Blackburn, eds., *Student Power: Problems, Diagnosis, Action*, London: Penguin Books and New Left Review, 1969

Collins, Wilkie, *The Woman in White*, eds. Maria K. Bachman and Don Richard Cox, Peterborough, Ont.: Broadview Press, 2004 [1860]

Conan Doyle, Arthur, *Adventures of Sherlock Holmes*, London: G. Newnes, 1892

Cooper, David, *The Death of the Family*, Harmondsworth: Penguin Books, 1974 [1971]

Coote, Anna, and Beatrix Campbell, *Sweet Freedom: The Struggle for Women's Liberation*, London: Picador, 1987 [1982]

Cranston, Maurice, ed., *The New Left*, London: Bodley Head, 1970

Crisp, Quentin, *The Naked Civil Servant*, London: Duckworth, 1977 [1968]

Croft-Cooke, Rupert, *The Altar in the Loft*, London: Putnam, 1960

—, *The Verdict of You All*, London: Secker and Warburg, 1955

—, *The Wild Hills*, London: W. H. Allen, 1966

Cudlipp, Hugh, *Publish and be Damned! The Astonishing Story of the Daily Mirror*, London: Andrew Dakers, 1953

—, *Walking on the Water*, London: Bodley Head, 1976

Cuffe, H. J. A., and Lady Sybil Lubbock, *A Page from the Past: Memories of the Earl of Desart,* London: Jonathan Cape, 1936

Daley, Harry, *This Small Cloud*, London: Weidenfeld and Nicolson, 1986

Davidson, Michael, *The World, the Flesh and Myself*, London: Quartet, 1977 [Arthur Barker, 1962]

De Montmorency, J. E. G., *John Gorell Barnes, First Lord Gorell (1848–1913)*, London: John Murray, 1920

Devlin, Patrick Arthur, *The Enforcement of Morals*, London: Oxford University Press, 1959

Dicks, H. V., *Marital Tensions: Clinical Studies towards a Psychological Theory of Interaction*, London: Routledge and Kegan Paul, 1967

Drawbell, James, *A Gallery of Women*, London: Ports, 1933

Duncan, P. Martin, and William Millard, *A Manual for the Classification, Training and Education of the Feeble-Minded, Imbecile, and Idiotic*, London: Longmans, Green and Co., 1866

Egan, Charles, *A Handy Book on the New Law of Divorce and Matrimonial Causes*, London: Davis and Son, 1860

Ellis, Sarah Stickney, *The Daughters of England: Their Position in Society, Character and Responsibilities*, New York: Appleton, 1842

Elwin, Malcolm, *Thackeray: A Personality*, London: Jonathan Cape, 1932

Ernst, Morris L., and Alan U. Schwartz, *Privacy: The Right to be Let Alone*, New York: Macgibbon and Kee, 1962

Esterson, Aaron, *The Leaves of Spring: Schizophrenia, Family and Sacrifice*, London: Penguin Books, 1972 [1970]

Eyles, Leonora, *Is Your Problem Here?*, London: Sampson Low, Marston and Co., 1947

—, *The Ram Escapes: The Story of a Victorian Childhood*, London: Peter Nevill, 1953

Fenn, Henry Edwin, *Thirty-Five Years in the Divorce Court,* London: T. Werner Laurie, 1911

Firth, Raymond, Jane Hubert and Anthony Forge, *Families and Their Relatives: Kinship in a Middle-Class Sector of London*, London: Routledge and Kegan Paul, 1969

Fletcher, Ronald, *The Abolitionists: The Family and Marriage under Attack*, London: Routledge, 1988

Freud, Sigmund, *Psychopathology of Everyday Life*, London: Pelican Books, 1939

—, *Two Short Accounts of Psycho-Analysis*, London: Penguin Books, 1963

Gavron, Hannah, *The Captive Wife: Conflicts of Housebound Mothers*, London: Routledge and Kegan Paul, 1966

Goldberg, E. M., *Family Influences and Psychosomatic Illness*, London: Tavistock Publications, 1958

Grey, Eleanor, in collaboration with Ronald M. Blunden, *A Survey of Adoption in Great Britain: Home Office Research Studies*, London: HMSO, 1971

Grosskurth, Phyllis, *The Memoirs of John Addington Symonds: The Secret Homosexual Life of a Leading Nineteenth-Century Man of Letters*, London: Hutchinson, 1984

Hales, Ann, *The Children of Skylark Ward: Teaching Severely Handicapped Children*, Cambridge: Cambridge University Press, 1978

Hall-Carpenter Archives Gay Men's Oral History Group, *Walking After Midnight: Gay Men's Life Stories*, London: Routledge, 1989

Halmos, Paul, *The Faith of the Counsellors*, London: Constable, 1965

—, *Solitude and Privacy: A Study of Social Isolation, Its Causes and Therapy*, New York: Routledge and Kegan Paul, 1969 [1953]

Hare, Augustus, *The Story of My Life*, London: George Allen, 1900

Hart, H. L. A., *Law, Liberty and Morality*, London and Oxford: Oxford University Press, 1968

Hauser, Richard, *The Homosexual Society*, London: Mayflower, 1962

Hendrick, Harry, *Child Welfare: England, 1872–1989*, London: Routledge, 1994

—, *Children, Childhood and English Society, 1880–1990*, Cambridge: Cambridge University Press, 1997

Herbert, W. L., and F. V. Jarvis, *A Modern Approach to Marriage Counselling*, London: Methuen and Co., 1969 [1959]

Hewett, Sheila, with John and Elizabeth Newson, *The Family and the Handicapped Child,* London: Allen and Unwin, 1970

Hoggart, Richard, et al., *The Permissive Society: The Guardian Enquiry*, London: Panther, 1969

Hunter, Sir W. W., *The Thackerays in India*, London: H. Frowde, 1897

Institute for Marital Studies, *The Marital Relationship as a Focus for Casework*, London: Institute for Marital Studies, 1962

Ireland, William, *The Mental Affections of Children*, London: J. and A. Churchill, 1900

Isaacs, Susan, *The Nursery Years*, London: Routledge and Kegan Paul, 1935 [1929]

Jarman, Derek, *At Your Own Risk: A Saint's Testament*, ed. Michael Christie, Woodstock, NY: Vintage, 1993

King, Roy D., Norma V. Raynes and Jack Tizard, *Patterns of Residential Care: Sociological Studies in Institutions for Handicapped Children*, London: Routledge and Kegan Paul, 1971

Klein, Josephine, *Samples from English Cultures*, vol. 1., London: Routledge and Kegan Paul, 1965

Kornitzer, Margaret, *Adoption and Family Life*, London: Putnam, 1968

Laing, R. D., *The Divided Self: An Existential Study in Sanity and Madness*, London: Tavistock Publications, 1960

—, *The Politics of the Family, and Other Essays*, London: Tavistock Publications, 1971

—, *Wisdom, Madness and Folly: The Making of a Psychiatrist*, New York: Macmillan, 1985

Laing, R. D., and Aaron Esterson, *Sanity, Madness and the Family: Families of Schizophrenics*, 2nd edn, London: Routledge, 1970 [1964]

Lanchester, John, *Family Romance: A Memoir,* London: Faber, 2007

Lang, John, *Will He Marry Her?*, London: Routledge, 1858

Langdon Down, John, *On Some of the Mental Affections of Childhood and Youth: Being the Lettsomian Lectures Delivered before the Medical Society of London in 1887 Together with Other Papers*, London: Mac Keith, 1887

Langdon-Down, Reginald, 'The Feeble-Minded', in T. N. Kelynack, ed., *Human Derelicts: Medico-Sociological Studies for Teachers of Religion and Social Workers*, London: C. H. Kelly, 1914

Lapage, C. Paget, *Feeblemindedness in Children of School-Age*, Manchester: Manchester University Press, 1911

Leach, Edmund, *A Runaway World? The Reith Lectures 1967*, London: BBC, 1968

Lidbetter, E. J., *Heredity and the Social Problem Group*, London: E. Arnold and Co., 1933

Lomas, Peter, ed., *The Predicament of the Family: A Psycho-Analytical Symposium*, London: Hogarth Press, 1967

Low, Ursula, *Fifty Years with John Company: From the Letters of General Sir John Low of Clatto, Fife, 1822–1858*, London: John Murray, 1936

Lubbock, Percy, ed., *The Diary of Arthur Christopher Benson*, London: Hutchinson and Co., 1926

Mace, David, *Coming Home: A Series of Five Broadcast Talks*, London: Staples Press, 1946

—, *Marriage Counselling: The First Full Account of the Remedial Work of the Marriage Guidance Councils*, London: Churchill, 1948

MacNeice, Louis, *The Strings are False*, London: Faber and Faber, 1982

Magee, Bryan, *One in Twenty: A Study of Homosexuality in Men and Women*, London: Secker and Warburg, 1966

Maguire, Toni, *Don't Tell Mummy*, London: Harper Element, 2006

Makins, Peggy, *The Evelyn Home Story*, London: Collins, 1975

Malcolm, Derek, *Family Secrets*, London: Arrow Books, 2004

Maschler, Tom, ed., *Declaration*, New York: E. P. Dutton, 1958

McCormack, Mary, *A Mentally Handicapped Child in the Family*, London: Constable, 1978

McMichael, Joan K., *Handicap: A Study of Physically Handicapped Children and Their Families*, London: Staples Press, 1971

Melville, Lewis, *William Makepeace Thackeray*, London: Hutchinson and Co., 1889

Mill, John Stuart, *On Liberty*, London: Routledge, 1859

Ministry of Education, *The Youth Service in England and Wales*, London: HMSO, 1960

Mitchell, Juliet, *Psychoanalysis and Feminism*, London: Allen Lane, 1974

—, *Woman's Estate*, Harmondsworth: Penguin Books, 1971

—, *Women: The Longest Revolution. Essays in Feminism, Literature and Psychoanalysis*, London: Virago, 1984

Mogey, J. M., *Family and Neighbourhood: Two Studies in Oxford*, Oxford: Oxford University Press, 1956

Morris, Pauline, *Put Away: A Sociological Study of Institutions for the Mentally Retarded*, New York: Routledge and Kegan Paul, 1969

Morrison, Blake, *Things My Mother Never Told Me*, London: Chatto & Windus, 2002

Mullan, Bob, *Mad to be Normal: Conversations with R. D. Laing*, London: Free Association Books, 1995

Munro, Innes, *Narrative of Military Operations on the Coromandel Coast in 1780*, London: 1789

Musgrove, Frank, *Ecstasy and Holiness: Counter Culture and the Open Society*, London: Methuen, 1974

—, *Youth and the Social Services*, London: Routledge and Kegan Paul, 1964

Neate, Bobbie, *Conspiracy of Secrets*, London: Metro Books, 2012

Newsome, D., ed., *Edwardian Excursions: From the Diaries of A. C. Benson, 1898–1904*, London: Murray, 1981

Newson, John and Elizabeth, *Infant Care in an Urban Community*, London: George Allen and Unwin, 1963

Nichols, Beverley, *All I Could Never Be*, London: Jonathan Cape, 1949

—, *Father Figure*, London: Heinemann, 1972

—, *Twenty-Five*, London: John Lane, 1935

—, *The Unforgiving Minute*, London: W. H. Allen, 1978

North, Maurice, *The Secular Priests*, London: Allen and Unwin, 1972

Oswin, Maureen, *Children in Long-Stay Hospitals*, Lavenham: Heinemann Medical [etc. for] Spastics International Medical Publications, 1978

—, *The Empty Hours: A Study of the Weekend Life of Handicapped Children in Institutions*, London: Allen Lane, 1971

Patmore, Angela, *Marje: The Guilt and the Gingerbread*, London: Little, Brown, 1993

Petre, Diana, *The Secret Orchard of Roger Ackerley*, London: Hamish Hamilton, 1975

Phillimore, John George, *The Divorce Court: Its Evils and the Remedy*, London: W. H. Bond, 1859

Philp, A. F., and Noel Timms, *The Problem of 'The Problem Family'*, London: Family Service Units, 1962

Philp, A. F., and Douglas Woodhouse, *Family Failure: A Study of 129 Families with Multiple Problems*, London: Faber and Faber, 1963

Pincus, Lily, ed., *Marriage: Studies in Emotional Conflict and Growth*, London: Methuen and Co., 1960

Pincus, Lily, *Verloren-gewonnen: Mein Weg von Berlin nach London*, Stuttgart: Deutsche Verlags-Anstalt, 1980

Pincus, Lily, and Christopher Dare, *Secrets in the Family*, London: Faber, 1978

Pritchard, David G., *Education and the Handicapped, 1760–1960*, London: Routledge and Kegan Paul, 1963

Raynor, Lois, *The Adopted Child Comes of Age*, London: George Allen and Unwin, 1980

Rees, J. Tudor, and Harley V. Usill, eds., *They Stand Apart*, New York: William Heinemann, 1955

Rix, Brian, *My Farce from My Elbow: An Autobiography*, London: Secker and Warburg, 1975

Robb, Barbara, *Sans Everything*, London: Nelson, 1967

Rosser, Colin, and Christopher Harris, *The Family and Social Change: A Study of Family and Kinship in a South Wales Town*, London: Routledge and Kegan Paul, 1965

Rowbotham, Sheila, *Promise of a Dream: Remembering the Sixties*, London: Allen Lane, 2000

Rowe, Jane, *Parents, Children and Adoption: A Handbook for Adoption Workers*, London: Routledge and Kegan Paul, 1966

Seymour, Miranda, *Thrumpton Hall: A Memoir of Life in My Father's House*, London: HarperCollins, 2008

Sharp, Dave, *Complete Surrender*, London: John Blake, 2008

Slater, Eliot, and Moya Woodside, *Patterns of Marriage: A Study of Marriage Relationships in the Urban Working Classes*, London: Cassell and Co., 1951

Stark, Herbert Alick, *Hostages to India, or The Life Story of the Anglo-Indian Race*, Calcutta: Calcutta Fine Art Cottage, 1936

Stephens, Tom, ed., *Problem Families: An Experiment in Social Rehabilitation*, Liverpool and Manchester: Pacifist Service Units, 1947

Study Commission on the Family, *Happy Families? A Discussion Paper on Families in Britain*, London: Study Commission on the Family, 1980

Sudley, Paul [Sir Arthur Gore], *William, Or More Loved Than Loving*, London: Collins, 1933

Symonds, J. A., *The Memoirs of John Addington Symonds*, ed. and intro. Phyllis Grosskurth, London: Hutchinson, 1984

Symons, A. J. A., *The Quest for Corvo*, London: Cassell and Co., 1934

Taylor, Colonel Meadows, *The Story of My Life, edited by his daughter*, Edinburgh and London: W. Blackwood and Sons, 1877

Taylor, Theodore, *Thackeray: The Humourist and the Man of Letters*, London: J. C. Hotten, 1864

Thackeray, W. M., *The History of Pendennis*, Leipzig: Tauchnitz, 1849

Tizard, Jack, 'Quality of Residential Care for Retarded Children', in Jack Tizard, Ian Sinclair and R. V. G. Clarke, eds., *Varieties of Residential Experience*, London: Routledge and Kegan Paul, 1975

Tizard, Jack, and Jacqueline C. Grad, *The Mentally Handicapped and Their Families: A Social Survey*, London and Oxford: Oxford University Press, 1961

Wallis, Adeline, *These Three: The Story of the Mission of Hope*, London: Marshall, Morgan and Scott, 1937

Wallis, J. H., *Marriage Guidance: A New Introduction*, London: Routledge and Kegan Paul, 1968

—, *Someone to Turn To: A Description of the Remedial Work of the National*

Marriage Guidance Council, London: Routledge and Kegan Paul, 1964 [1961]

Wallis, J. H., and H. S. Booker, *Marriage Counselling: A Description and Analysis of the Remedial Work of the National Marriage Guidance Council*, London: Routledge and Kegan Paul, 1958

Wandor, Michelene, ed., *The Body Politic: Writings from the Women's Liberation Movement in Britain, 1969–1972*, London: Stage 1, 1972

—, ed., *Once a Feminist: Stories of a Generation*, London: Virago, 1990

Waugh, Alexander, *Fathers and Sons: The Autobiography of a Family*, London: Headline Books, 2004

Webb, Beatrice, *My Apprenticeship*, Cambridge: Cambridge University Press, 1979 [1926]

West, D. J., *Homosexuality*, London: Duckworth, 1955

Westwood, Gordon [Michael Schofield], *A Minority: A Report on the Life of the Male Homosexual in Great Britain*, London: Longmans, 1960

Wildeblood, Peter, *Against the Law*, London: Weidenfeld and Nicolson, 1955

Wilkins, Margaret, with Sue Freeman, *A Family Affair*, London: Michael Joseph, 1975

Willmott, Peter, and Michael Young, *Family and Class in a London Suburb*, London: New English Library, 1960

Wimperis, Virginia, *The Unmarried Mother and Her Child*, London: George Allen and Unwin, 1960

Winnicott, D. W., *The Child and His Family: First Relationships*, London: Tavistock Publications, 1957

—, *The Child, the Family, and the Outside World*, London: Penguin Books, 1964

Wolfenden, John, *Turning Points: The Memoirs of Lord Wolfenden*, London: Bodley Head, 1976

Worsley, T. C., *Flannelled Fool: A Slice of Life in the Thirties*, London: Ross, 1967

Young, Michael, and Peter Willmott, *Family and Kinship in East London*, London: Routledge and Kegan Paul, 1957

—, *The Symmetrical Family: A Study of Work and Leisure in the London Region*, London: Routledge and Kegan Paul, 1973

Younghusband, Eileen, *Social Work with Families*, London: Allen and Unwin, 1965

Secondary literature

Anderson, Michael, 'Social Implications of Demographic Change', in F. M. L. Thompson, ed., *The Cambridge Social History of Britain, 1750–1950*, vol. 2, Cambridge: Cambridge University Press, 1990

Andrews, Jonathan, 'Begging the Question of Idiocy: The Definition and Socio-Cultural Meaning of Idiocy in Early Modern Britain', pts 1 and 2, *History of Psychiatry* 9, nos. 33 and 34 (1998), 65–95, 179–200

—, 'R. D. Laing in Scotland: Facts and Fictions of the "Rumpus Room" and Interpersonal Psychiatry', in Marijke Gijswijt-Hofstra and Roy Porter, eds., *Cultures of Psychiatry and Mental Health Care in Postwar Britain and the Netherlands*, Amsterdam: Rodopi, 1998

Annan, Noel, *Leslie Stephen: The Godless Victorian*, London: Weidenfeld and Nicolson, 1984

Ariès, Philippe and Georges Duby, eds., *A History of Private Life*, 5 vols., Cambridge, Mass.: Belknap Press of Harvard University Press, 1987–91

Arnold, David, 'European Orphans and Vagrants in India in the Nineteenth Century', *Journal of Imperial and Commonwealth History* 7, no. 2 (1979), 104–27

Atkinson, Dorothy, Mark Jackson and Jan Walmsley, *Forgotten Lives: Exploring the History of Learning Disability*, Kidderminster: BILD Publications, 1997

Atkinson, Dorothy, et al., *Good Times, Bad Times: Women with Learning Difficulties Telling Their Stories,* Kidderminster: BILD Publications, 2000

Bailkin, Jordanna, 'The Postcolonial Family? West African Children, Private Fostering, and the British State', *Journal of Modern History* 81, no. 1 (2009), 87–121

Ballhatchet, Kenneth, *Race, Sex and Class under the Raj: Imperial Attitudes and Policies and Their Critics, 1793–1905*, New York: Weidenfeld and Nicolson, 1980

Barrell, John, *Spirit of Despotism: Invasions of Privacy in the 1790s*, Oxford: Oxford University Press, 2006

Bartlett, Peter, and David Wright, eds., *Outside the Walls of the Asylum: The History of Care in the Community 1750–2000*, London: Athlone Press, 1999

Bayly, C. A., *Indian Society and the Making of the British Empire*, Cambridge: Cambridge University Press, 1988

Behlmer, George, *Child Abuse and Moral Reform in England, 1870–1908*, Stanford: Stanford University Press, 1982

—, *Friends of the Family: The English Home and Its Guardians, 1850–1940*, Stanford: Stanford University Press, 1998

Beier, Lucinda McCray, '"We were Green as Grass": Learning about Sex and Reproduction in Three Working-Class Lancashire Communities, 1900–1970', *Social History of Medicine* 16, no. 33 (2003), 461–80

Bernstein, Susan David, *Confessional Subjects: Revelations of Gender and Power in Victorian Literature and Culture*, Chapel Hill: University of North Carolina Press, 1997

Beverley-Smith, Huw, Ansgar Ohly and Agnes Lucas-Schloetter, *Privacy, Property and Personality: Civil Law Perspectives on Commercial Appropriation*, Cambridge: Cambridge University Press, 2005

Bingham, Adrian, *Family Newspapers? Sex, Private Life and the British Popular Press, 1918–1978*, Oxford: Oxford University Press, 2009

Black, Lawrence, 'The Lost World of Young Conservatism', *Historical Journal* 51, no. 4 (2008), 991–1024

Bok, Sissela, *Secrets: On the Ethics of Concealment and Revelation*, New York: Pantheon Books, 1983

Borsay, Anne, *Disability and Social Policy in Britain since 1750*, Basingstoke: Palgrave Macmillan, 2005

Bourne Taylor, Jenny, *In the Secret Theatre of Home: Wilkie Collins, Sensation Narrative, and Nineteenth-Century Psychology*, London and New York: Routledge, 1988

Brantlinger, Patrick, *Rule of Darkness: British Literature and Imperialism, 1830–1914*, Ithaca: Cornell University Press, 1988

—, 'What is "Sensational" about the "Sensation Novel"?', *Nineteenth-Century Fiction* 37, no. 1 (1982), 1–28

Brewer, John, 'This, That and the Other: Public, Social and Private in the Seventeenth and Eighteenth Centuries', in Dario Castiglione and Lesley Sharpe, eds., *Shifting the Boundaries: Transformation of the Languages of Public and Private in the Eighteenth Century*, Exeter: University of Exeter Press, 1995

Brigham, Lindsay, et al., eds., *Crossing Boundaries: Change and Continuity in the History of Learning Disability*, Kidderminster: BILD Publications, 2000

Buckton, Oliver, *Secret Selves: Confession and Same-Sex Desire in Victorian Autobiography*, Chapel Hill: University of North Carolina Press, 1998

Buettner, Elizabeth, *Empire Families: Britons and Late Imperial India*, Oxford: Oxford University Press, 2004

Burston, Daniel, *The Wing of Madness: The Life and Work of R. D. Laing*, Cambridge, Mass.: Harvard University Press, 1996

Burton, Antoinette, 'Conjugality on Trial: The Rukhmabai Case and the Debate on Indian Child-Marriage in Late-Victorian Britain', in George Robb and Nancy Erber, eds., *Disorder in the Court: Trials and Sexual Conflict at the Turn of the Century*, London: Macmillan, 1999

Caine, Barbara, *Bombay to Bloomsbury*, Oxford: Oxford University Press, 2005

Central Statistical Office, *Social Trends 1994*, London: Central Statistical Office, 1994

Chase, Karen, and Michael Levenson, *The Spectacle of Intimacy: A Public Life for the Victorian Family*, Princeton: Princeton University Press, 2000

Chatterjee, Indrani, 'Colouring Subalternity: Slaves, Concubines and Social Orphans in Early Colonial India', *Subaltern Studies X* (1999), 49–97

—, *Gender, Slavery and Law in Colonial India*, Delhi: Oxford University Press, 1999

Chettiar, Teri, 'Deprived Children, Unstable Marriages, and Neglectful Mothers: On the Rise of the Psychiatric Family and the "Psychopolitics" of Emotion in Britain, 1945–c.1975', unpub. PhD diss., Northwestern University, 2012

Chinn, Carl, *They Worked All Their Lives: Women of the Urban Poor in England, 1850–1939*, Manchester: Manchester University Press, 1988

Clark, Anna, *Scandal: The Sexual Politics of the British Constitution*, Princeton: Princeton University Press, 2004

—, 'Twilight Moments', *Journal of the History of Sexuality* 14, no. 1/2 (2005), 139–60

Clark, David, ed., *Marriage, Domestic Life and Social Change: Writings for Jacqueline Burgoyne (1944–88)*, London and New York: Routledge, 1991

Clarke, William M., *The Secret Life of Wilkie Collins*, London: Alan Sutton, 1988

Clulow, Christopher, ed., *Marriage: Disillusion and Hope: Papers Celebrating Forty Years of the Tavistock Institute of Marital Studies*, London: Karnac/ Tavistock Institute of Marital Studies, 1990

Cocks, H. G., *Nameless Offences: Homosexual Desire in the 19th Century*, London: I. B. Tauris, 2010 [2003]

Cody, Lisa, 'The Politics of Illegitimacy in an Age of Reform: Women, Reproduction and Political Economy in England's New Poor Law of 1834', *Journal of Women's History* 11, no. 4 (2000), 131–56

Cohen, William, *Sex Scandal: The Private Parts of Victorian Fiction*, Durham, NC: Duke University Press, 1996

Coleman, David, 'Population and Family', in A. H. Halsey with Josephine Webb, eds., *Twentieth-Century British Social Trends*, Basingstoke: Macmillan, 2000

Collingham, E. M., *Imperial Bodies: The Physical Experience of the Raj, c.1800– 1947*, Cambridge: Cambridge Polity Press, 2001

Collins, Marcus, *Modern Love: An Intimate History of Men and Women in Twentieth-Century Britain*, London: Atlantic, 2003

—, ed., *The Permissive Society and Its Enemies: Sixties British Culture*, London: Rivers Oram, 2006

Connon, Bryan, *Beverley Nichols: A Life*, London: Constable, 1991

Cook, Matt, 'Families of Choice? George Ives, Queer Lives and the Family in Early Twentieth-Century Britain', *Gender and History* 22, no. 1 (2010), 1–20

—, *London and the Culture of Homosexuality, 1885–1914*, Cambridge: Cambridge University Press, 2008

Corbett, Mary Jean, *Family Likeness: Sex, Marriage and Incest from Jane Austen to Virginia Woolf*, Ithaca: Cornell University Press, 2008

Cretney, Stephen, *Family Law in the Twentieth Century: A History*, Oxford: Oxford University Press, 2003

Dabhoiwala, Faramerz, *The Origins of Sex: A History of the First Sexual Revolution*, New York: Oxford University Press, 2012

Dale, Pamela, 'Assistance and Resistance: Making Sense of Inter-War Caring Strategies', in Duncan Mitchell et al., eds., *Exploring Experiences of Advocacy*, London: Jessica Kingsley, 2006

Dalrymple, William, *White Mughals: Love and Betrayal in Eighteenth-Century India*, London: HarperCollins, 2002

D'Arch Smith, Timothy, *Love in Earnest: Some Notes on the Lives and Writings of English Uranian Poets from 1889 to 1930*, London: Routledge, 1970

—, *R. A. Caton and the Fortune Press*, London: Rota, 1983

Davenport-Hines, Richard, *Auden*, New York: Heinemann, 1995

Davidoff, Leonore, *Thicker Than Water: Siblings and Their Relations*, Oxford: Oxford University Press, 2011

—, 'The Family in Britain', in F. M. L. Thompson, ed., *The Cambridge Social History of Britain, 1750–1950*, vol. II, Cambridge: Cambridge University Press, 1990

Davidoff, Leonore, Megan Doolittle, Janet Fink and Katherine Holden, *The Family Story: Blood, Contract and Intimacy, 1830–1960,* London: Longman, 1999

Davidoff, Leonore, and Catherine Hall, *Family Fortunes: Men and Women of the English Middle Class, 1780–1850*, Chicago: University of Chicago Press, 1987

Davis, Angela, 'A Critical Perspective on British Social Surveys and Community Studies and Their Accounts of Married Life c.1945–70', *Cultural and Social History* 6, no. 1 (2009), 47–64

Delap, Lucy, Ben Griffin and Abigail Wills, eds., *The Politics of Domestic Authority in Britain since 1800*, Basingstoke: Palgrave Macmillan, 2009

Derrick, Deborah, ed., *Illegitimate: The Experience of People Born outside Marriage*, London: National Council for One Parent Families, 1986

Dickinson, Hilary, 'Idiocy in Nineteenth-Century Fiction Compared with Medical Perspectives of the Time', *History of Psychiatry* 11, no. 43 (2000), 291–309

Dicks, H. V., *Fifty Years of the Tavistock Clinic*, London: Routledge and Kegan Paul, 1970

Digby, Anne, *Pauper Palaces*, London: Routledge and Kegan Paul, 1978

Dirks, Nicholas, *The Scandal of Empire: India and the Creation of Imperial Britain*, Cambridge: Cambridge University Press, 2006

Doan, Laura, *Fashioning Sapphism: The Origins of a Modern English Lesbian Culture*, New York: Columbia University Press, 2001

Donnelly, Mark, *Sixties Britain*, Harlow: Longman, 2005

Dudley Edwards, Ruth, *Newspapermen: Hugh Cudlipp, Cecil Harmsworth King and the Glory Days of Fleet Street*, London: Secker and Warburg, 2003

Ellis, Catherine, 'The Younger Generation: The Labour Party and the 1959 Youth Commission', *Journal of British Studies* 41, no. 2 (2002), 199–231

Faulks, Sebastian, *The Fatal Englishman: Three Short Lives*, London: Vintage, 1997 [Hutchinson, 1996]

Fink, Janet, 'Natural Mothers, Putative Fathers, and Innocent Children: The Definition and Regulation of Parental Relationships outside Marriage, in England, 1945–1959', *Journal of Family History* 25, no. 2 (2000), 141–57

—, 'Private Lives, Public Issues: Moral Panics and "The Family" in 20th c. Britain', *Journal for the Study of British Cultures* 9, no. 2 (2002), 135–48

Finn, Margot, 'Family Formations: Anglo India and the Familial Proto-State', in David Feldman and Jon Lawrence, eds., *Structures and Transformations in Modern British History*, Cambridge: Cambridge University Press, 2011

Finn, Margot, Michael Lobban and Jenny Bourne Taylor, eds., *Legitimacy and Illegitimacy in Nineteenth-Century Law, Literature and History*, Basingstoke: Palgrave Macmillan, 2010

Fisher, Kate, *Birth Control, Sex, and Marriage in Britain, 1918–1960*, Oxford: Oxford University Press, 2006

Fisher, Kate, and Simon Szreter, *Sex before the Sexual Revolution: Intimate Life in England, 1918–1963*, Cambridge: Cambridge University Press, 2010

Fisher, Michael, *Counterflows to Colonialism: Indian Travellers and Settlers in Britain 1600–1857*, Delhi: Permanent Black, 2004

Fletcher, Anthony, *Growing Up in England: The Experience of Childhood, 1600–1914*, New Haven and London, 2008

Forrester, John, 'Freud in Cambridge', *Critical Quarterly* 46, no. 2 (2004), 1–26

—, '1919: Psychology and Psychoanalysis, London and Cambridge', *Psychoanalysis and History* 10, no. 1 (2008), 37–94

Foucault, Michel, *The History of Sexuality: An Introduction*, vol. 1, trans. Robert Hurley, Harmondsworth: Penguin Books, 1990 [1978]

Fowler, David, *Youth Culture in Modern Britain, c.1920–c.1970*, Basingstoke: Palgrave Macmillan, 2008

Fraser, Ronald, ed., *1968: A Student Generation in Revolt: An International Oral History*, London: Chatto and Windus, 1988

Frost, Ginger, '"The Black Lamb of the Black Sheep": Illegitimacy in the English Working Class, 1850–1939', *Journal of Social History* 37, no. 2 (2003), 293–322

—, *Living in Sin: Cohabiting as Husband and Wife in Nineteenth-Century England*, Manchester: Manchester University Press, 2008

—, '"Revolting to Humanity": Oversights, Limitations and Complications of the English Legitimacy Act of 1926', *Women's History Review* 20, no. 1 (2011), 31–46

Furedi, Frank, *Therapy Culture: Cultivating Vulnerability in an Uncertain Age*, London and New York: Routledge, 2004

Gabb, Jacqui, *Researching Intimacy in Families*, Basingstoke: Palgrave Macmillan, 2010 [2008]

Gardiner, Juliet, *The Thirties: An Intimate History*, London: HarperPress, 2010

Gatrell, Vic, *City of Laughter: Sex and Satire in Eighteenth-Century London*, London: Atlantic, 2006

Ghosh, Durba, *Sex and the Family in Colonial India: The Making of Empire*, Cambridge: Cambridge University Press, 2006

Giddens, Anthony, *Modernity and Self-Identity: Self and Society in the Late Modern Age*, Cambridge: Cambridge University Press, 1991

Gillis, John, *For Better, for Worse: British Marriages, 1600 to the Present*, Oxford: Oxford University Press, 1985

—, *A World of Their Own Making: Myth, Ritual, and the Quest for Family Values*, Cambridge, Mass.: Harvard University Press, 1996

Goffman, Erving, *Stigma: Notes on the Management of Spoiled Identity,* Englewood Cliffs: Simon and Schuster, 1963

Goldring, Patrick, *Friend of the Family: The Work of Family Service Units,* Newton Abbot: David and Charles, 1973

Green, Eileen and Harry, *The Fowkes of Boughrood Castle: A Study in Social Mobility,* Tenby: Eileen and Harry Green, 1973

Green, Jonathon, *All Dressed Up: The Sixties and the Counterculture,* London: Pimlico Books, 1999

Hague, Gill, *The Silenced Pain: Domestic Violence, 1945–1970,* Bristol: Policy Press, 1996

Hall, Stuart, 'Reformism and the Legislation of Consent', in National Deviancy Conference, ed., *Permissiveness and Control: The Fate of the Sixties Legislation,* London: Macmillan, 1980

Hammerton, A. James, *Cruelty and Companionship: Conflict in Nineteenth-Century Married Life,* London: Routledge, 1992

Harris, Chris, 'The Family in Post-War Britain', in James Obelkevich and Peter Catterall, eds., *Understanding Post-War British Society,* London: Routledge, 1994

Harrison, Brian, 'The Public and the Private in Modern Britain', in Peter Burke, Brian Harrison and Paul Slack, eds., *Civil Histories: Essays Presented to Sir Keith Thomas,* Oxford: Oxford University Press, 2000

Harvey, Karen, *Reading Sex in the Eighteenth Century: Bodies and Gender in English Erotic Culture,* Cambridge: Cambridge University Press, 2004

Hawes, C. J., *Poor Relations: The Making of a Eurasian Community in British India 1773–1833,* Richmond: Curzon, 1996

Hayes, Sarah, 'Rabbits and Rebels: The Medicalisation of Maladjusted Children in Mid-Twentieth-Century Britain', in Mark Jackson, ed., *Health and the Modern Home,* London and New York: Routledge, 2007

Hennessy, Peter, *Whitehall,* London: Secker and Warburg, 1989

Henriques, U. R. Q., 'Bastardy and the New Poor Law', *Past and Present* 37, no. 1 (1967), 103–29

Herzog, Dagmar, *Sexuality in Europe: A Twentieth-Century History,* Cambridge: Cambridge University Press, 2011

Higginbotham, Ann Rowell, '"Sin of the Age": Infanticide and Illegitimacy in Victorian London', *Victorian Studies* 32, no. 3 (1989), 319–37

Higgins, Patrick, *Heterosexual Dictatorship: Male Homosexuality in Postwar Britain*, London: Fourth Estate, 1996

Hilliard, Christopher, *To Exercise Our Talents: The Democratization of Writing in Britain*, Cambridge, Mass.: Harvard University Press, 2006

Holmes, Su, '*The Family* and Reality TV', in Julie Anne Taddeo and Ken Dvorak, eds., *The Tube Has Spoken: Reality TV and History*, Lexington: University Press of Kentucky, 2010

Holroyd, Michael, *A Book of Secrets: Illegitimate Daughters, Absent Fathers*, London: Vintage, 2011

Holzman, James Mayer, *The Nabobs in England: A Study of the Returned Anglo-Indian*, New York: Columbia University Press, 1926

Homer, Marjorie, Anne Leonard and Pat Taylor, *Private Violence, Public Shame: A Report on the Circumstances of Women Leaving Domestic Violence in Cleveland*, Middlesbrough: Cleveland Refuge and Aid for Women and Children, 1984

Hopkirk, Mary, *Nobody Wanted Sam: The Story of the Unwelcomed Child, 1530–1948*, London: John Murray, 1949

Hornsey, Richard, *The Spiv and the Architect: Unruly Life in Postwar London*, Minneapolis: University of Minnesota Press, 2010

Horrie, Chris, *Tabloid Nation: The Birth of the Daily Mirror to the Death of the Tabloid*, London: André Deutsch, 2003

Horstman, Allen, *Victorian Divorce*, New York: Croom Helm, 1985

Houlbrook, Matt, *Queer London: Perils and Pleasures in the Sexual Metropolis, 1918–1957*, Chicago: University of Chicago Press, 2005

Houlbrook, Matt, and Chris Waters, 'The Heart in Exile: Detachment and Desire in 1950s London', *History Workshop Journal* 62 (2006), 142–63

Hugh-Jones, Stephen, *Edmund Leach, 1910–1989: Memoir Prepared by Direction of the Council of King's College, Cambridge*, Cambridge: Cambridge University Press, 1989

Humphreys, Anne, 'Coming Apart: The British Newspaper Press and the Divorce Court', in Laurel Brake, Bill Bell and David Finkelstein, eds., *Nineteenth-Century Media and the Construction of Identities*, Basingstoke: Macmillan, 2000

Humphries, Steve, and Pamela Gordon, *Out of Sight: The Experience of Disability 1900–1950*, Plymouth: Northcote House, 1992

Hyam, Ronald, *Empire and Sexuality: The British Experience*, Manchester: Manchester University Press, 1990

Hyde, H. Montgomery, *The Other Love: An Historical and Contemporary Survey of Homosexuality in Britain*, London: Mayflower, 1970

Jackson, Louise, *Child Sexual Abuse in Victorian England*, London: Routledge, 2000

Jackson, Mark, *The Borderland of Imbecility: Medicine, Society, and the Fabrication of the Feeble Mind in Late Victorian and Edwardian England*, Manchester and New York: Manchester University Press, 2000

Jalland, Pat, *Death in War and Peace: A History of Loss and Grief in England, 1914–1970*, Oxford: Oxford University Press, 2010

Jarvis, Mark, *Conservative Governments, Morality and Social Change in Affluent Britain, 1957–64*, Manchester: Manchester University Press, 2005

Jasanoff, Maya, *Liberty's Exiles: American Loyalists in the Revolutionary World*, New York: Knopf, 2011

Jeffery-Poulter, Stephen, *Peers, Queers and Commons: The Struggle for Gay Law Reform from 1950 to the Present*, London and New York: Routledge, 1991

Jones, Mervyn, ed., *Privacy*, Newton Abbott: David and Charles, 1974

Juxon, John, *Lewis and Lewis*, London: Collins, 1983

Kaplan, Morris, *Sodom on the Thames*, Ithaca: Cornell University Press, 2005

Keating, Jennifer, *A Child for Keeps: The History of Adoption in England, 1918–45*, London: Palgrave Macmillan, 2009

—, 'Chosen Children? The Legalisation of Adoption in England and Its Aftermath, 1918–1939, unpublished Ph.D. thesis, University of Sussex, 2004

Kevles, Daniel, *In the Name of Eugenics: Genetics and the Uses of Human Heredity*, New York: Knopf, 1985

Kiernan, Kathleen, Hilary Land and Jane Lewis, *Lone Motherhood in Twentieth-Century Britain: From Footnote to Front Page*, Oxford: Oxford University Press, 1998

Kohon, Gregorio, ed., *The British School of Psychoanalysis: The Independent Tradition*, New Haven and London: Free Association Books, 1986

Kramer, Anne-Marie, 'Mediatizing Memory: History, Affect and Identity in *Who Do You Think You Are?*', *European Journal of Cultural Studies* 14: 4 (2011), 428–45

Kucich, John, *The Power of Lies: Transgression in Victorian Fiction*, Ithaca: Cornell University Press, 1994

Kuper, Adam, *Incest and Influence: The Private Life of Bourgeois England*, Cambridge, Mass. and London: Harvard University Press, 2009

Laing, Adrian, *R. D. Laing: A Life*, London: HarperCollins, 1997

Langhamer, Claire, 'Adultery in Post-War England', *History Workshop Journal* 62 (2006), 86–115

—, 'Love and Courtship in Mid-Twentieth-Century England', *Historical Journal* 50, no. 1 (2007), 173–96

—, 'Love, Selfhood and Authenticity in Post-War Britain', *Cultural and Social History* 9, no. 2 (2012), 277–97

Lawson, Annette, *Adultery: An Analysis of Love and Betrayal*, Oxford and New York: Basil Blackwell, 1988

Leckie, Barbara, *Culture and Adultery: The Novel, the Newspaper and the Law, 1857–1914*, Philadelphia: University of Pennsylvania Press, 1999

Levene, Alysa, Thomas Nutt and Samantha Williams, eds., *Illegitimacy in Britain, 1700–1920*, Basingstoke: Palgrave Macmillan, 2005

Lewis, Jane, 'Adoption: The Nature of Policy Shifts in England and Wales, 1972–2002', *International Journal of Law, Policy and the Family* 18, no. 2 (2004), 235–55

—, *The End of Marriage? Individualism and Intimate Relations*, Northampton, Mass.: Elgar, 2001

—, 'Public Institution and Private Relationship: Marriage and Marriage Guidance, 1920–1968', *Twentieth-Century British History* 1, no. 3 (1990), 233–63

Lewis, Jane, David Clark and David H. J. Morgan, *'Whom God Hath Joined Together': The Work of Marriage Guidance*, London: Tavistock Publications, 1992

Light, Alison, *Forever England: Femininity, Literature and Conservatism between the Wars*, London: Routledge, 1991

Lockley, Paul, *Counselling Women in Violent Relationships*, London: Free Association Press, 1999

Lubenow, W. C., *The Cambridge Apostles, 1810–1914*, Cambridge: Cambridge University Press, 1998

MacKenzie, Charlotte, *Psychiatry for the Rich: A History of Ticehurst Private Asylum, 1792–1917*, London: Routledge, 1992

Mandler, Peter, *The English National Character: The History of an Idea from Edmund Burke to Tony Blair*, New Haven and London: Yale University Press, 2006

Marcus, Sharon, *Between Women: Friendship, Desire and Marriage in Victorian England*, Princeton: Princeton University Press, 2007

Marcus, Stephen, *The Other Victorians: A Study of Sexuality and Pornography in Mid-Nineteenth-Century England*, London: Weidenfeld and Nicolson, 1966

Marshall, P. J., 'British Immigration into India in the Nineteenth Century', in P. C. Emmer and Magnus Mörner, eds., *European Expansion and Migration: Essays on the Intercontinental Migration from Africa, Asia and Europe*, New York: Berg, 1992

—, *East Indian Fortunes: The British in Bengal in the Eighteenth Century*, Oxford: Oxford University Press, 1976

—, *The Impeachment of Warren Hastings*, London: Oxford University Press, 1965

Marwick, Arthur, *British Society since 1945*, London: Penguin Books, 2003 [1982]

Mason, Michael, *The Making of Victorian Sexual Attitudes*, Oxford: Oxford University Press, 1994

—, *The Making of Victorian Sexuality*, Oxford: Oxford University Press, 2003 [1994]

McKibbin, Ross, *Classes and Cultures: England 1918–1951*, Oxford: Oxford University Press, 1998

McKnight, Gerald, *The Scandal of Syrie Maugham*, London: W. H. Allen, 1980

McLaren, Angus, *Sexual Blackmail: A Modern History*, Cambridge, Mass. and London: Harvard University Press, 2002

Merriman, Andy, *Tales of Normansfield: The Langdon Down Legacy*, Teddington: Down's Syndrome Association, 2007

Michael, James, *The Politics of Secrecy*, London: Penguin Books, 1982

Miller, D. A., *The Novel and the Police,* Berkeley: University of California Press, 1988

Mintz, Steven, *Prison of Expectations: The Family in Victorian Culture*, New York: New York University Press, 1983

Mort, Frank, *Capital Affairs: London and the Making of the Permissive Society*, New Haven and London: Yale University Press, 2010

Murray, Heather, *Not in This Family: Gays and the Meaning of Kinship in Postwar America*, Philadelphia: University of Pennsylvania Press, 2010

Nechtman, Tillman, *Nabobs: Empire and Identity in Eighteenth-Century Britain*, Cambridge: Cambridge University Press, 2010

Nelson, Claudia, *Family Ties in Victorian England*, Westport, Conn.: Praeger, 2007

—, *Little Strangers: Portrayals of Adoption and Foster Care in America, 1850–1929*, Bloomington: Indiana University Press, 2003

Newsome, David, *On the Edge of Paradise: A. C. Benson, the Diarist*, London: John Murray, 1980

Paley, Ruth, and Simon Fowler, *Family Skeletons: Exploring the Lives of Our Disreputable Ancestors*, Kew: National Archives, 2005

Park, Alison, et al., *British Social Attitudes: Public Policy, Social Ties: The 18th Report*, Aldershot: SAGE, 2002

Pearsall, Sarah, *Atlantic Families: Lives and Letters in the Later Eighteenth Century*, Oxford: Oxford University Press, 2008

Peplar, Michael, *Family Matters: A History of Ideas About Family since 1945*, London: Longman, 2002

Perry, Ruth, *Novel Relations: The Transformation of Kinship in English Literature and Culture*, Cambridge: Cambridge University Press, 2004

Phillips, Roderick, *Putting Asunder: A History of Divorce in Western Society*, Cambridge: Cambridge University Press, 1988

Pionke, Albert D., and Denise Tischler Millstein, *Victorian Secrecy: Economies of Knowledge and Concealment*, Farnham: Ashgate, 2010

Pollock, Linda, 'Living on the Stage of the World: The Concept of Privacy among the Elite of Early Modern England', in Adrian Wilson, ed., *Rethinking Social History: English Society, 1570–1920*, Manchester: Manchester University Press, 1993

Ponting, Clive, *Secrecy in Britain*, Oxford: Basil Blackwell, 1990

Porter, Roger J., *Bureau of Missing Persons: Writing the Secret Lives of Fathers*, Ithaca: Cornell University Press, 2011

Potts, Maggie, and Rebecca Fido, *A Fit Person to be Removed*, Plymouth: Northbridge House, 1991

Pratt, Walter F., *Privacy in Britain*, Lewisburg: Bucknell University Press, 1979

Rapp, Dean, 'The Early Discovery of Freud by the British General Educated Reading Public, 1912–1919', *Social History of Medicine* 3: 2 (1990), 217–43

—, 'The Reception of Freud by the British Press: General Interest and Literary Magazines, 1920–1925', *Journal of the History of the Behavioural Sciences* 24: 2 (1988), 191–201

Richards, Graham, 'Britain on the Couch: The Popularization of Psychoanalysis in Britain, 1918–1940', *Science in Context* 13: 2 (2000), 183–230

Riley, Denise, *War in the Nursery: Theories of the Child and Mother*, London: Virago, 1983

Robb, Peter, 'Children, Emotion, Identity and Empire: Views from the Blechyndens' Calcutta Diaries (1790–1822)', *Modern Asian Studies* 40, no. 1 (2006), 175–201

—, *'Clash of Cultures? An Englishman in Calcutta in the 1790s*, London: University of London, 1998

—, 'Credit, Work and Race in 1790s Calcutta: Early Colonialism through a Contemporary European View', *Indian Economic Social History Review* 37, no. 1 (2000), 1–25

Rolph, Sheena, and Dorothy Atkinson, 'Maureen Oswin and the "Forgotten Children" of the Long-Stay Wards: Research as Resistance', in Duncan Mitchell et al., eds., *Exploring Experiences of Advocacy by People with Learning Disabilities*, London: Jessica Kingsley, 2006

Rolph, Sheena, et al., *Witnesses to Change: Families, Learning Difficulties and History*, Kidderminster: BILD Publications, 2005

Rose, Lionel, *Massacre of the Innocents: Infanticide in Great Britain, 1800–1939*, London: Routledge and Kegan Paul, 1986

Rose, Nikolas, *Governing the Soul: The Shaping of the Private Self*, London: Routledge, 1989

—, *The Psychological Complex: Psychology, Politics and Society in England, 1869–1939*, London: Routledge and Kegan Paul, 1985

Ross, Ellen, *Love and Toil: Motherhood in Outcast London, 1870–1918*, Oxford: Oxford University Press, 1993

Rothschild, Emma, *The Inner Life of Empires: An Eighteenth-Century History*, Princeton: Princeton University Press, 2011

Rowbowtham, Sheila, *The Past is before Us: Feminism in Action since the 1960s*, London: Penguin Books, 1989

Rubinstein, William, *Who were the Rich? A Biographical Directory of British Wealth-Holders*, vol. 1, 1809–1839, London: Social Affairs Unit, 2009

Rushton, Peter, 'Lunatics and Idiots: Mental Disability, the Community and the Poor Law in North-East England', *Medical History* 32, no. 1 (1988), 34–50

Rustin, Margaret, 'John Bowlby at the Tavistock', *Attachment and Human Development* 9, no. 4 (2007), 355–9

Sandbrook, Dominic, *Never Had It So Good: A History of Britain from Suez to the Beatles*, London: Little, Brown, 2005

—, *State of Emergency: The Way We Were: Britain, 1970–1974*, London: Allen Lane, 2010

—, *White Heat: A History of Britain in the Swinging Sixties, 1964–1970*, London: Abacus, 2006

Sanders, Valerie, *The Tragi-Comedy of Victorian Fatherhood*, Cambridge: Cambridge University Press, 2009

Savage, Gail, 'The Divorce Court and the Queen's/King's Proctor: Legal Patriarchy and the Sanctity of Marriage in England, 1861–1937', in Dana Johnson and Andrée Désilets, eds., *Historical Papers: A Selection from the Papers Presented at the Annual Meeting of the Canadian Historical Association*, Ottawa: Canadian Historical Association, 1989

—, 'Erotic Stories and Public Decency: Newspaper Reporting of Divorce Proceedings in England', *Historical Journal* 41, no. 2 (1998), 511–28

—, '"They Would If They Could": Class, Gender and Popular Representation of English Divorce Litigation, 1858–1908', *Journal of Family History* 36, no. 1 (2011), 173–90

Savage, Mike, *Identities and Social Change in Britain since 1940*, Oxford: Oxford University Press, 2010

Schneider, Wendie Ellen, 'Secrets and Lies: The Queen's Proctor and Judicial

Investigation of Party-Controlled Narratives', *Law & Social Inquiry* 27, no. 3 (2002), 449–88

Schoeman, Ferdinand David, *Privacy and Social Freedom,* Cambridge: Cambridge University Press, 1992

Searle, G. R., *The Quest for National Efficiency: A Study in British Politics and Political Thought, 1899–1914,* Berkeley: University of California Press, 1971

Sen, Sudipta, 'Colonial Aversions and Domestic Desires: Blood, Race, Sex and the Decline of Intimacy in Early British India', *South Asia* 24 (2001), 24–45

Setch, Eve, 'The Face of Metropolitan Feminism: The London Women's Liberation Workshop, 1969–79', *Twentieth-Century British History* 13, no. 2 (2002), 171–90

Shapira, Michal, *The War Inside: Child Psychoanalysis and the Democratic Self in Britain, 1930–1960,* Cambridge: Cambridge University Press, forthcoming

Simmel, Georg, 'Secrecy', in Kurt H. Wolff, trans. and ed., *The Sociology of Georg Simmel,* New York: Collier-Macmillan, 1950

Smart, Carol, *Personal Life: New Directions in Sociological Thinking,* Cambridge: Cambridge University Press, 2007

Spacks, Patricia Meyer, *Privacy: Concealing the Eighteenth-Century Self,* Chicago: University of Chicago Press, 2003

Spear, T. G. P., *The Nabobs: English Social Life in 18th Century India,* London and New York: Oxford University Press, 1963

Stanley, Liz, *Sex Surveyed, 1949–1994: From Mass-Observation's 'Little Kinsey' to the National Survey and the Hite Reports,* London: Taylor and Francis, 1995

Steedman, Carolyn, *Master and Servant: Love and Labour in the English Industrial Age,* Cambridge: Cambridge University Press, 2007

Stewart, John, '"I Thought You Would Want to Come and See His Home": Child Guidance and Psychiatric Social Work in Inter-War Britain', in Mark Jackson, ed., *Health and the Modern Home,* London and New York: Routledge, 2007

Stoler, Ann Laura, *Carnal Knowledge and Imperial Power: Race and the Intimate in Colonial Rule,* Berkeley: University of California Press, 2002

—, ed., *Haunted by Empire: Geographies of Intimacy in North American History*, Durham, NC: Duke University Press, 2006

Stone, Lawrence, *The Family, Sex, and Marriage in England, 1500–1800*, New York: Harper and Row, 1977

Strathern, Marilyn, *After Nature: English Kinship in the Late Twentieth Century*, Cambridge: Cambridge University Press, 1992

Summerscale, Kate, *Mrs. Robinson's Disgrace: The Private Diary of a Victorian Lady*, London: Bloomsbury, 2012

—, *The Suspicions of Mr. Whicher: Or the Murder at Road-Hill House*, London: Bloomsbury, 2008

Sutherland, Gillian, *Ability, Merit and Measurement: Mental Testing and English Education*, Oxford: Oxford University Press, 1984

Suzuki, Akihito, *Madness at Home: The Psychiatrist, the Patient and the Family in England, 1820–1860*, Berkeley: University of California Press, 2006

Tadmor, Naomi, *Family and Friends in Eighteenth-Century England: Household, Kinship and Patronage*, Cambridge: Cambridge University Press, 2001

Taylor, Chloë, *The Culture of Confession from Augustine to Foucault: A Genealogy of the 'Confessing Animal'*, New York and London: Routledge, 2008

Tefft, Stanton K., ed., *Secrecy: A Cross-Cultural Perspective*, New York: Human Sciences Press, 1980

Teltscher, Kate, 'Writing Home and Crossing Boundaries', in Kathleen Wilson, ed., *A New Imperial History: Culture and Identity in Britain and the Empire 1660–1840*, Cambridge: Cambridge University Press, 2004

Thane, Pat, 'Family Life and "Normality" in Postwar British Culture', in Richard Bessel and Dirk Schumann, eds., *Life After Death: Approaches to a Cultural and Social History of Europe during the 1940s and 1950s*, Cambridge: Cambridge University Press, 2003

—, 'Unmarried Motherhood in Twentieth-Century England', *Women's History Review* 20, no. 1 (2011), 11–29

Thane, Pat, and Tanya Evans, *Sinners? Scroungers? Saints: Unmarried Motherhood in Twentieth-Century England*, Oxford: Oxford University Press, 2012

Thomas, Nick, 'Challenging Myths of the 1960s: The Case of Student

Protest in Britain', *Twentieth-Century British History* 13, no. 3 (2002), 277–97

—, 'Will the Real 1950s Please Stand Up: Views of a Contradictory Decade', *Cultural and Social History* 5, no. 2 (2008), 227–36

Thomson, Mathew, *The Problem of Mental Deficiency: Eugenics, Democracy, and Social Policy in Britain, c. 1870–1959*, Oxford: Oxford University Press, 1998

—, *Psychological Subjects: Identity, Culture, and Health in Twentieth-Century Britain*, Oxford: Oxford University Press, 2006

Tóibín, Colm, *Love in a Dark Time: Gay Lives from Wilde to Almodóvar*, London: Picador, 2002

Tosh, John, *A Man's Place: Masculinity and the Middle-Class Home in Victorian England*, New Haven and London: Yale University Press, 1999

Tromp, Marlene, *The Private Rod: Marital Violence, Sensation and the Law in Victorian Britain*, Charlottesville: University Press of Virginia, 2000

Upchurch, Charles, *Before Wilde: Sex between Men in Britain's Age of Reform*, Berkeley: University of California Press, 2009

Van der Horst, Frank C. P., *John Bowlby – From Psychoanalysis to Ethology: Unravelling the Roots of Attachment Theory*, Oxford: Oxford University Press, 2011

Vicinus, Martha, *Intimate Friends: Women Who Loved Women, 1778–1928*, Chicago: University of Chicago Press, 2004

Vickery, Amanda, *Behind Closed Doors: At Home in Georgian England*, New Haven and London: Yale University Press, 2009

Vincent, David, *The Culture of Secrecy: Britain, 1832–1998*, Oxford: Oxford University Press, 1998

Visram, Rozina, *Ayahs, Lascars and Princes: Indians in Britain, 1700–1947*, London: Pluto, 1986

Wahrman, Dror, *Imagining the Middle Class: The Political Representation of Class in Britain, 1780–1840*, Cambridge: Cambridge University Press, 1995

Ward, O Conor, *John Langdon Down: A Caring Pioneer*, London: Royal Society of Medicine Press, 1998

Waters, Chris, 'Disorders of the Mind, Disorders of the Body Social: Peter Wildeblood and the Making of the Modern Homosexual', in Becky

Conekin, Frank Mort and Chris Waters, eds., *Moments of Modernity: Reconstructing Britain, 1945–64*, London: Rivers Oram, 1998

——, 'Havelock Ellis, Sigmund Freud and the State: Discourses of Homosexual Identity in Interwar Britain', in Lucy Bland and Laura Doan, eds., *Sexology in Culture: Labelling Bodies and Desires*, Chicago: University of Chicago Press, 1998

——, 'The Homosexual as a Social Being in Britain, 1945–1968', *Journal of British Studies* 51, no. 3 (2012), 685–710

Weeks, Jeffrey, *Coming Out: Homosexual Politics in Britain from the Nineteenth Century to the Present*, London: Quartet Books, 1983 [1977]

——, *Sex, Politics and Society: The Regulation of Sexuality since 1800*, London: Longman, 1996

Welsh, Alexander, *George Eliot and Blackmail*, Cambridge, Mass.: Harvard University Press, 1985

Wheeler, Roxann, *The Complexion of Race: Categories of Difference in Eighteenth-Century British Culture*, Philadelphia: University of Pennsylvania Press, 2000

White, Luise, 'Telling More: Lies, Secrets and History', *History and Theory* 39, no. 4 (2000), 11–22

Wilson, Kathleen, *Island Race: Englishness, Empire, and Gender*, London and New York: Routledge, 2003

Wohl, Anthony S., 'Sex and the Single Room: Incest among the Victorian Working Class', in Anthony S. Wohl, ed., *The Victorian Family*, London: Croom Helm, 1978

Woodhouse, Douglas, 'The Tavistock Institute of Marital Studies: Evolution of a Marital Agency', in *Marriage: Disillusion and Hope. Papers Celebrating Forty Years of the Tavistock Institute of Marital Studies*, London: Karnac/Tavistock Institute of Marital Studies, 1990

Wooldridge, Adrian, *Measuring the Mind: Education and Psychology in England, c.1860–c.1990*, Cambridge: Cambridge University Press, 1994

Wright, David, *Mental Disability in Victorian England,* Oxford: Oxford University Press, 2001

——, *Downs: The History of a Disability*, Oxford: Oxford University Press, 2011

Wright, David, and Anne Digby, eds., *From Idiocy to Mental Deficiency:*

Historical Perspectives on People with Learning Difficulties, London: Routledge, 1996

Zhao, Zhongwei, 'The Demographic Transition in Victorian England and Changes in English Kinship Networks', *Continuity and Change* 11, no. 2 (1996), 243–72

Acknowledgements

Thank you to the institutions that made this book possible: the American Council of Learned Societies' Fredrick Burkhardt Residential Fellowship for Recently Tenured Scholars, Brown University, the Dorothy and Lewis B. Cullman Center for Scholars & Writers at the New York Public Library, the John Simon Guggenheim Memorial Foundation, the Newberry Library and Northwestern University. Warm thanks to Jean Strouse at the Cullman Center and to Jim Grossman at the Newberry Library, who created perfect sanctuaries at their marble libraries.

This book was started when I was a faculty member at Brown and finished at Northwestern, and I heartily thank friends and colleagues at both institutions, especially Maud Mandel and Tom Gleason, who once again sharpened my work with his ironic red pen. Students in my Spring 2008 Brown seminar on the family will see the mark of our discussions. Thanks to the UTRA programme at Brown and to the Leopold Fellowship and URAP initiative at Northwestern, I had the opportunity to work closely with students whose smarts and industry improved this book: Zoe Brennan-Krohn, Ayelet Brinn, Mike da Cruz, Chris Garcia, Lauren Sirota and Lela Spielberg. Thank you to Ivan Polancec, who applied his medievalist acumen to twentieth-century women's magazines.

Audiences at the Columbia Seminar in British History, the Columbia Society of Fellows, the Harvard Center for European Studies British Study Group, the Institute of Historical Research, the Indiana University Victorian Studies Colloquium, the Johns Hopkins University History Department Seminar, the Northeast Conference on British Studies, the University of Pennsylvania History Department, the Rutgers University British Studies Center, the Social History of Learning Disability Conference at the Open University, the Yale British History Colloquium and the Yale History of Science

Colloquium heard early versions of these chapters, and their comments and critiques helped me to hone my thoughts and to see evidence anew. For invitations to seminars and stimulating conversations during my visits, thank you to Sally Alexander, Dorothy Atkinson, Chris Brown, Kathy Brown, Arianne Chernock, Jim Cronin, Sara Damiano, Eileen Gillooly, Katie Hindmarch-Watson, Maya Jasanoff, Seth Koven, Ivan Kreilkamp, Lynn Lees, Kimberly Lowe, Helen McCarthy, Andrew Miller, Benjamin Nathans, Susan Pedersen, George Robb, Sheena Rolph, Dror Wahrman, Jay Winter – and above and beyond, Chris Waters. To my fellow fellows, especially Deborah Baker, Anna Bikont, Dan Kevles, Hari Kunzru, Julie Orringer, Lauren Redniss, Martha Saxton, Laura Secor and Ezra Tawil at the Cullman, and Jen Hill, Craig Koslofsky, Liesl Olson, Dana Rabin and Jill Rappoport at the Newberry, many thanks and fond memories.

I'm deeply indebted to Margot Finn, Durba Ghosh, Tom Laqueur, Ryan Linkof, Mo Moulton, Martin Packman, Susan Pedersen and Julia Stephens, who read chapters in progress and whose insights spurred on revisions. At various points in my research, Tim Alborn, Timothy d'Arch Smith, Teri Chettiar, Joseph Cohen, Matt Cook, Ellen Feder, Ginger Frost, Juliet Gardiner, John Gillis, Eileen Gillooly, Matt Houlbrook, Brian Lewis, Daniel Loss, Heather Love, Andrew MacKillop, Andy Merriman, Mara Mills, Sarah Pearsall, Gail Savage, Vanessa Schwartz, Robert Self, Michal Shapira, Peter Stansky, Mathew Thomson and Rick Valicenti stepped in with citations, documents, insights, introductions to other people, and objections – all very gratefully received. Sharon Marcus has been the model interlocutor, ever rigorous and encouraging. Jordanna Bailkin and Peter Mandler read the entire manuscript and their exacting questions (and blessedly specific suggestions) helped me to refine its arguments, both overarching and particular. Peter has stood by this project from its earliest days, and I thank him once again for his camaraderie and example.

The research for this book hinged on extraordinary assistance from archivists, librarians, booksellers and collectors, who answered queries, petitioned rights holders and arranged access, especially Chris Bennett, Heather Cadbury, Alison Harvey, Bridget Howlett, Ian Jones-Healey, George Locke and Alison Rosie. A very special thank you to John Cave.

Practitioners in various fields explained their work to me and intervened to smooth my path: Susanna Abse, Christopher Clulow, Henrietta Delalu, Frank Hancock, Ros Hume, Ellie Kavner, Dr Anton Obholzer, Pauline Palmer, Dr Matthew Patrick and Jane Symon. Dr John Byng-Hall, Andy Merriman, David Towle and the late Douglas Woodhouse very kindly spent afternoons with me. Else Churchill, Peter Hawkins, Daniel Jones, Helen Tovey, Claire Vaughan, Sarah Williams and especially Alex Graham helped me to understand the genealogy boom.

At Viking, this book's been shepherded with the ideal combination of tenderness and no nonsense by the incomparable Eleo Gordon, adeptly assisted by Jillian Taylor and Gesche Ipsen. Thank you to Mark Handsley for meticulous copy-editing, Emma Ewbank for the book's design, Dave Cradduck for its index and for spotting errors, and Keith Taylor for keeping the trains running. Clare Alexander made shrewd matches for the book and relished its personae.

And finally, to my relations, who have greeted the prospect of a book about family secrets without too much hand-wringing. To the memory of my father, uncle and grandparents, and with great gratitude to the Cohens, Kasdans and Packmans, especially Helen Cohen, Jennifer Cohen, Joseph Cohen, Martin and Erma Packman, and Julia Stephens. This book is for Tom Silfen, who alone knows how much it (and its author) owe him, and for our dear Alice.

Index

For data protection purposes many names in this book are pseudonyms, and appear in the same form in the index to help the reader locate them.

findmypast™.co.uk

search with the experts

Win a day with a genealogist

Now that you've read Family Secrets, do you feel inspired to find out about your own family's secrets with the help of an expert? Enter our competition at **www.findmypast.co.uk/cohen** for a chance to win a day with a professional genealogist, who will help you learn about your ancestors' lives, and an annual World subscription to leading family history website **findmypast.co.uk**. Three runners-up will each receive a 6 month Britain Full subscription to **findmypast. co.uk**.

The competition

Terms and conditions apply, please see www.findmypast.co.uk/cohen for details and to enter.

Competition runs from 6 February 2014 – 9 May 2014.

Entries must be received by 23:59 GMT on 9 May 2014.

First prize consists of one day's family history consultancy with a qualified professional genealogist, helping you to research your family tree and one annual World subscription to findmypast.co.uk. Three runner-up prizes each consist of a 6 month Britain Full subscription to findmypast.co.uk.

Prize has no cash alternative, is non-transferable and non-refundable. No purchase necessary.

Promoter: findmypast.co.uk, The Glebe, 6 Chapel Place, Rivington Street, London EC2A 3DQ

Free reader offer

Ever wondered what your ancestors' lives were like? Were there any skeletons hiding in their cupboards? Here's your chance to find out with **£5 worth of free credits** to findmypast.co.uk.

Find your ancestors in millions of records dating right back to Tudor times, including local newspapers, birth, marriage and death indexes, census, military, migration, parish and crime records. There are over 1.5 billion family history records at **findmypast.co.uk** covering the UK, Ireland, the United States, Australia and New Zealand. It's free to search these records, and with your free credits you'll be able to view, save and print high-quality scans of original historical documents featuring your own ancestors!

To claim your 40 free credits worth £5 and for advice on getting started, visit **www.findmypast.co.uk/penguin** and enter the promotional voucher code **SECRETS** before **31 March 2014**.

Free credit offer

Offer expires at midnight on 31 March 2014. See www.findmypast.co.uk/penguin for terms & conditions.